THE ULYSSEAN ADULT

CREATIVITY IN THE MIDDLE & LATER YEARS

JOHN A.B. McLEISH

McGraw-Hill Ryerson Limited

Toronto   Montreal   New York   London
Sydney   Mexico   Panama   São Paulo
Johannesburg   Düsseldorf   New Delhi
Singapore   Kuala Lumpur   Auckland

ISBN 0-07-082243-3

1 2 3 4 5 6 7 8 9 10 D 5 4 3 2 1 0 9 8 7 6

Printed and bound in Canada

ACKNOWLEDGMENTS

Pages 11, 12: THE DIVINE COMEDY, by Dante Alighieri, trans. by Charles S. Singleton, Ballingen Series LXXX, vol. 1, *Inferno* (copyright © 1970 by Princeton University Press): pp. 277-279. Reprinted by permission of Princeton University Press; page 17: JOURNALS: VENTURESOME YEARS by David E. Lilienthal. Copyright 1966 by Harper and Row Publishers, Inc.; page 31: PASSPORTS AT SEVENTY by Ethel Sabin Smith. Copyright 1961 by W. W. Norton and Company; pages 35-40, 90-1: From CREATIVITY AND ITS CULTIVATION by H. H. Anderson. Copyright 1959 by Harper and Row Publishers, Inc.; pages 39-40, 87-8: From TOWARD A PSYCHOLOGY OF BEING by Abraham H. Maslow. Published by D. Van Nostrand Reinhold © 1968 Litton Educational Publications, Inc.; pages 45-6, 52-4: Stanley Rosner and Lawrence E. Abt, THE CREATIVE EXPERIENCE, The Viking Press © 1970 by The Viking Press; pages 49-51: Reprinted with permission of Macmillan Publishing Company, Inc. from THE GHOST IN THE MACHINE, Arthur Koestler. Copyright © 1968 by Arthur Koestler.page 59: From THE NEW YEARS, A NEW MIDDLE AGE by Anne W. Simon. Copyright © 1967, 1968 by Anne W. Simon. Reprinted by permission of Alfred A. Knopf, Inc.; pages 67, 68: From IDENTITY AND ANXIETY by M. Stein, A. J. Vidich and D. M. White. Copyright © 1960 by The Free Press, a corporation; pages 76-7, 78: CHILDHOOD AND SOCIETY by E. H. Erickson. Copyright 1950 by W. W. Norton and Company, Inc.; pages 79-80: © by The New York Times Company. Reprinted by permission; pages 94-6: Headings with text abridged and adapted from pp. 153-170 in MOTIVATION AND PERSONALITY, 2nd Edition, by Abraham H. Maslow. Copyright 1954 by Harper and Row, Publishers, Inc. Copyright © 1970 by Abraham H. Maslow. By permission of the publishers; page 98: Reprinted by permission from TIME, The Weekly Newsmagazine; Copyright Time Inc.; pages 123-4: Reprinted by permission of Routledge and Kegan Paul Ltd. from SOCIOLOGY OF MENTAL DISORDER by Roger Bastide, translated by Jean McNeil; page 124: Taken from DON'T GIVE UP ON AN AGING PARENT by Lawrence Galton. © 1975 by Lawrence Galton. Used by permission of Crown Publishers, Inc.; pages 129-35: E. L. Thorndike, ADULT LEARNING, published by Adult Education Association of U.S.A., 1928; page 137; From review of ALFRED BINET by R. D. Tuddenham, *Science*, March 15, 1974, p. 183; page 142: Irving Lorge, PSYCHOLOGY OF ADULTS, published by Adult Education Association of U.S.A., 1964; pages 179, 181-4: SEA QUEST: GLOBAL BLUE-WATER ADVENTURING IN SMALL CRAFT by Charles A. Borden, published by Macrae Smith Company, 1967; pages 194-5: Maurice Goudeket, THE DELIGHTS OF GROWING OLD, published by Farrar, Straus and Giroux, 1966; pages 192-3: Alexander Liberman, THE ARTIST IN HIS STUDIO, The Viking Press, © 1960 by The Viking Press; pages 205-6: From an interview with Clementine Hunter by Mary Gibson in *Family Circle*, August 1973; pages 206-7: Edited by Walter W. Cobbett, CYCLOPEDIC SURVEY OF CHAMBER MUSIC, © Oxford University Press 1963 by permission of the Oxford University Press, Oxford; pages 221-2: From HARRY S. TRUMAN by Margaret Truman, published by William Morrow and Company Inc. © 1973; page 241: From TWO STORIES AND A MEMORY by Guiseppe Di Lampedusa translated by Archibald Colqu-

houn © 1962 by William Collins, Sons and Company, Limited and Pantheon
Books, Inc. Reprinted by permission of Pantheon Books, Inc.; pages 279-80,
283-4: From APPLIED IMAGINATION by Alex Osborn, published by Charles
Scribner's Sons, 1953.

The author also expresses appreciation for the encouragement of a number
of friends and former students in the extended task of writing the book,
especially Eve Carpentier, Vera Rosburg, Eileen Ellis, Ajmal Ali Khan, Arm-
ando Mizzoli, Manuel S. Jan, Donald E. Williams, Dennis Dunlop, Michael
Brykert, Andrew and June Wozny, C. J. Eustace, Erwin Waschnig, and Hugh
Oliver. He is especially indebted to his sister, Margaret McLeish Very, for
her interest and encouragement.

CONTENTS

To
J. Roby Kidd
world citizen, and world leader
in adult education
and
to those Ulyssean men and women,
known to the reader of this book,
whose lives have helped to light
the windows of the world

FOREWORD

The Ulyssean Adult grew out of plans originally made for an article on the same subject intended to appear in a major magazine. The projected article was abandoned because I felt that I was pouring a cup of wine into a thimble. The original idea for an article on the theme of creativity in the later years, taken to be the years from about 55 on, arose from two groups of people. The first was those who attended seminars given by me at three universities over a span of seven years, on *The Modern Adult and Adult Learning*—a preliminary study of the adult life drama, looked at from sociological and psychological points of view, and discussed among circles of graduate students mostly in their 30s and early 40s, but with some in the 20s and some in the 50s. Although few, therefore, were personally facing the issue of how to handle the later years, I was struck by the absorbed interest which my students showed in the question of the successful negotiation of the *complete* life journey. Especially fascinating to them was the question of the meaning and the durability of creative powers. Most of them were emotionally opposed to Harvey Lehman's thesis in *Age and Achievement* that the peak of creative production occurs during the 30s. Without substantial evidence to contradict this, the seminar groups felt in their bones that this thesis was wrong. To them, Lehman had not sufficiently taken into account the whole domain of what one anthropologist calls, "the beautiful creature, Man."

The other source was people I met outside the academic environment. Some I met at social gatherings, at private suppers, at bars, and on the club cars of trains; some in the diagnostic rooms of hospitals, or during the long pauses where men talk after exercise in an athletic club. Most of these conversations arose from one or two clues provided, usually unintentionally, by me: one, a question, the other a statement.

The question, which often followed what Eric Berne has called the "four-stroke" exchange of greetings, was something like this, "Are you having a good year?" or "Have you had a good week?"—a "you" query that, unlike the indifferent and fatuous, "How are things?" at least indicates some mild personal concern. Often the reply was banal enough, but in a surprisingly large number of cases among men and women in their 50s and 60s, the prompt and unsolicited reply was, "I can't seem to get through the work I used to," followed by some further comments on the problem of "failing powers." To my astonishment, a number of men distinguished in their professions, including a physician, a priest, a publisher, and an economist, referred directly to "withering of the brain cells" or "daily loss of neurons." The priest, a particularly delightful and life-loving human being, spoke pessimistically of the potential burdens of the later years, and considered it a consolation that he had been able in his 50s to learn a foreign language rapidly on demand.

The statement, couched in varying language but always expressing the same thought, was in response to my admission that I was a university teacher by profession, and that my major field of interest was the adult life drama and the roles played in it by adult learning. This subject invariably aroused immediate interest among the adults *of all ages* with whom I spoke; when I raised the matter of creativity in adulthood, the interest quickened; and when I went on to explain that I was especially devoted to the question of how creative adults can be in their later years, from the mid-50s on, the response was striking from people over 40. The issue of later creativity was clearly of high concern to many older adults— concern so strong as to suggest that much of the happiness of the later years depended upon it.

The title of the article, had there been an article, was to have been "The Ulyssean Concept," which was abandoned as being less suitable for the book. Nonetheless, the book which has emerged is essentially a confrontation between two concepts of the later years. One, to which the thesis of *The Ulyssean Adult* is opposed, conceives of later adulthood as a time of inevitable decline: not only can you not teach old dogs new tricks, but they do not perform even the tricks they know nearly so well as in younger adulthood. This is also, when all is said and done, a passive or at the best a reactive philosophy of the later years. Life is conceived as happening to oneself as a *reactor*, rather than of oneself acting influentially and decisively upon life.

The second, the opposing point of view, which is the central motive and motor of this book, is that many regenerative and creative powers which are unused form part of the equipment of man throughout his life; that life in the later years, when one's confidence is often perhaps most threatened, can be lived actively and creatively, rather than reactively and listlessly; and—as the absolute axis of this concept—that great numbers of adults in the later years are inhibited from accomplishments which would glorify those years because they have succumbed to modern myths and negative social conventions about the decline and fall of creativity. The counter-response to this philosophy of doom and decay is seen in *The Ulyssean Adult*.

Thus the book has a mission, and whether it succeeds in communicating it will depend upon each reader's response. For all its adult readers, whether in their 50s or beyond, or younger, will find themselves constantly testing the arguments of *The Ulyssean Adult* against their own life experience, good or bad. The thoughtful reader will find himself constantly engaged in a tough and reflective self-examination as he studies the arena of later adulthood in the light—one dares to say, the glowing light—of the Ulyssean Concept.

JMcL.
Toronto, September, 1975

1. THE UNLOVED COUNTRY OF THE AGING

To live in the closing third of the twentieth century in Western society is to live at a time of unparalleled potentiality for human development—notably the potentiality of our "later years," the years from about the mid-50s on. Yet great numbers of men and women in later adulthood are not fulfilling this potentiality and, in fact, few believe that such resources of personal power and satisfaction exist in the later decades.

The medical and sanitary sciences have prolonged adult life expectancy over the past hundred years by about 20 years—the gift of almost another life of mature activity. Government legislation has finally delivered substantial medical support programmes and inadequate late pension benefits. These are well supplemented for a good many adults by incomes from private industry and professional life. Modern technology and concomitant social readjustments have liberated the weekends for most adults, speeded earlier retirement, and developed a mobile society through which there are many opportunities for personal travel and discovery.

A popular low-cost culture abounds. The paperback book, the stereo set, and the cheap, good long-playing record, the mass-distributed, "do-it-yourself" hobby kit, the low-priced transistor radio set, and the ubiquitous television all seem to symbolize a society of potentiality for adults. All the more at first does this seem true of those adults, say 55-plus, who appear to be in the ideal situation of having survived the storms of earlier years to enter harbours of free time and creative opportunity.

Life and history, however, are filled with paradox, and the most tragic paradox of modern Western society is the contrast between the creative potentiality of older adults and the immobilizing effect upon them of social attitudes which stigmatize the later years as years of decline and fall, of accumulating decay, desuetude, and defeat. These attitudes, which in varying forms are dominant among most younger adults, deeply and harmfully affect the older people in our society—doubly so because the self-image of the old is largely derived from the thousands of messages they see and hear in the eyes and actions and from the lips of the young—the young who are adored in a society terrified of age.

The younger adults in turn derive their points of view mostly from the society in which they are reared: a society dominated by mobility, by machines, by incessant change which seems to make experience irrelevant; by the media, especially the electronic media which create a largely plastic world; by the drumming monotones and idiot repetitions of the advertisers, whose attention is obsessively centred upon the health, vivacity, and activities of the young. The "young" of the TV hucksters are not even representative of these fascinating human beings, with their infinite variety of deeper needs and sorrows, but depict instead a succession of mindless, ever-grinning, synthetic mannequins ignorant of life's realities: the so-called Pepsi generation. Yet the propaganda is potent —only the young have joy.

The youth and young adults of Western society have also absorbed the concept of the so-called "nuclear" family created by the crowding processes of mammoth urbanization. This is the family which has no room for its old people, and which, in the process of depositing them in sunset lodges, nursing homes, "rest" homes, and impoverished urban warrens, has multiplied and reinforced the concept of the aged in modern life as an alienated class, and far worse—as prisoners of a time of life to be dreaded and feared. Small wonder that as many as 25 per cent of the youthful respondents in Robert Kastenbaum's recent surveys of "attitudes toward old age" were willing to say that they wanted to die before their time.

Government legislation, that blundering Cyclops, has managed in numerous places to declare employment discrimination on grounds of age illegal and subject to prosecution. (It is perhaps a coincidence that this sign of political compassion appears at just the time when the older adults have developed into a significant voting sector.) But the legislation is virtually unenforceable, and is substantially nullified by the long-standing mandates of government and private industry that identify age 65 or in some cases 60, or even earlier, as the end of the adult's formal period of productivity. Where these formal definitions of the profitable years of adulthood leave off, the folk fantasies of late twentieth-century North American life take over. We have "senior citizens" (what is a junior citizen?), "oldsters" (with presumably about the same significance as youngsters, and with less relevance), golden age clubs, eventide homes, and dozens of other titles and terms carrying their own stamp of condescension. Older adults who retire (the *Concise Oxford Dictionary* suggests that this is a voluntary act, as in "withdraw," "seek seclusion or shelter," which in this sense is usually not the case) are "on the shelf," "put out to pasture," or "over the hill." If bearers of the sardonic title, "golden agers," make errors whether in world politics or personal and domestic affairs, it's a sign of their "senility." *Old age is the ultimate stigma.*

Meanwhile the media, which are programmed into the unusual and the sensational, make very plain (and quite justly) the extreme rarity of any 60 or 70-year-old's attaining a university degree or diploma (photograph of beaming grandmother, surrounded by astonished family); and make properly repulsive the antics of aged persons at jolly-jump-up events where the programmes organized by young volunteers present the old in farcical games or performing the dances and gestures of chorus girls. The put-down is relentless with the very old and immobilized: "I am not a child," says one splendid old woman, indignantly; "why then do they treat me like one?" And a society which refuses to believe that many Germans were unaware of what went on in the concentration camps of the 1930s and 40s is able to conduct its affairs without a glance or a tremor of concern for the inmates of low-standard nursing homes which become the terrible cages of impoverished and hopelessly alienated older human beings.

It is true that both adult life and the media present examples of older people seemingly accepted on their own terms in dignity and colleagueship: for example, members of certain church congregations, certain clubs, boards, and associations, certain family circles, and certain rather old-fashioned communities. In the case of the media, although the dreams, conditions, and accomplishments of older adults are almost wholly ignored, the drama series, situation comedies, and soap operas frequently present older, sometimes very old, adults to whom it is more difficult to condescend. They tend to be stereotyped into a few affluent professions: the inevitable physician and lawyer, usually sadly wise rather than vigorously creative, and the successful tycoon and aging general. (The media always see something of the best in the worst of generals.) There is, in addition, a fairly large and recurring group of shrewd and homespun grandfathers, old but heroic sheriffs, beaten-up but still gutsy leaders of covered wagons, and aging but benevolent and resourceful women actively engaged in putting right everyone's affairs. The actress, Spring Byington, in her later years was a case in point. Occasionally, too, the cinema has the wit to lure a Margaret Rutherford or a Helen Hayes in her 70s from the stage, as it turns out, to steal the show.

However, these complimentary instances and images of elderly and aged adults in our era are hardly more than cheerful lights gleaming in the extensive darkness of the prevailing folk attitudes of a throwaway society—attitudes which become pervasive, so that finally they are held by adults of all ages. The very young and the old have at least in common the fact that both are downgraded by the priests and acolytes of the Gross National Product. The young, however, are redeemed somewhat in the eyes of these people by a virtue which they deny the old—potentiality. The very young are the most innocent of observers; they see what they have been conditioned to see—great numbers of older human beings caught in a chilling sequence of poverties: poverty of financial means, poverty of energy and achievement, poverty of motivation, and saddest of all, poverty of hope and love. For a time the young feel a certain indignation and compassion at the obscene neglect by the modern state of the bodies, minds, and spirits, the *creative potentiality* of older adults. But this passes. One has to enjoy one's own life somehow in the computerized society, and try to build defences as one goes along against becoming someday like *them*.

Still, younger adults do not cease to observe. Consciously or unconsciously, they are always monitoring the scene, recording what older people are like. Because most of us someday must play the role of aging and aged, younger men and women are silently trying on certain identities which they see among older adults. It is not precisely that, when young, we see ourselves as old, but that we look with a certain fascinated curiosity at those envoys from a forbidding land who move in and out of our own world—people quite diverse in backgrounds and in the varieties of success or failure with which they seem to handle their exacting roles on the stage of later life.

Some of these "ambassadors" from the "growing old" country are, in fact, prestigious and affluent. One would expect prestige and wealth to be two sure ramparts against the hardships and sorrows of age. Yet "the man who has everything" may in fact have missed the greatest gift of all—the ability to live creatively, lovingly, and serenely through the later years. Frustrated and embittered millionaires, hardened and rigid, are well known to priests and journalists; while everyone knows penniless old men and women, racked with illness, whose timeless and cheerful spirits and productivity within their own small worlds astonish and reinvigorate the younger people around them.

At all events, wherever these people go, they are observed. When aging and old, you may be neglected and patronized, but you will nonetheless be observed—you can count on this. People who are growing old and who are in their late years have to remember that they are envoys under observation. The country they represent is a territory privately dreaded by much of society, not for its strength but for its weakness, and not for its potential but for its supposedly interminable decline into exhaustion and death. It is the country largely assumed to be one of non-roles and non-creativity—the country of Non.

If you are young, sensitive, and observant, and secretly curious about how adults negotiate the process of aging, as has been the case with dozens of students reporting in my seminars, you are certain to meet frequently at least these three envoys:

(1) The older adult to whom life always seems to have happened, rather than he happening to it, to paraphrase Erik Erikson. His lifestyle might be described as consisting of Total Expectedness. He has indeed nearly run the race and nearly finished the course; but the race has been run undeviatingly on the safe and well-pounded track of routine, without the runner's even taking an occasional sortie into the enchanting but possibly dangerous countryside that stretched out from the track. When the chips were down, and the chips were down periodically across his early and prime years, he did what was expected of him. This type of later adult is very often a "good" person, both with and without the quotation marks, but his or her life has consisted of negatives: don't rock the boat, don't step outside the limit, don't get involved, don't explore yourself too much, don't disturb your years with dreams because someday from unfulfilled dreams may come "disgust and despair."

Great numbers of these older adults may live lives of what Thoreau called "quiet desperation"—but as many do not. Some of these are the unknown citizens of whom W. H. Auden wrote: "Was he free? Was he happy? The question is absurd. Had anything been wrong, we should certainly have heard." In fact, in the late years, as they have done all their lives, they preserve a passive spectator role. Often warmly attached to the domestic scene, they are especially desolate in the later years if death or the mandates of the holy "nuclear" family leave them bereft and lonely.

Privately, the appraising observer may decide that such a role is not for him, and least of all in the later years, made more drab and bleak for many people by a dearth of money, of friends, and of meaningful days. Besides, his concept of the passive and uncreative later years has been strengthened. He may believe that in our society there is nothing much worse than getting old.

(2) The second envoy to come under the young adult's scrutiny may at first sight seem more heartening. Here is a person who at least seems to have gone through some attempts at the identification of self. Here, too, is some one who is not afraid to speak of early abortive efforts at creativity outside the expected lifestyle and career, and to talk of unrealized dreams or of untried opportunities. Besides, this is an individual who is at least conscious that in his or her life certain vistas have been missed, certain experiences that might have brought him or her closer to fulfilment.

Thus, this older adult could well appreciate a forgotten story told by Albert Edward Wiggam in his *Marks of an Educated Man*. One summer night, to the home of a bored and disappointed man in his later middle years comes a visitor who enchants him with tales of travel, adventures, remarkable friends, books read and written, and lovely deeds performed for and encountered from others; and also with his wisdom, wit, and loving-kindness. When at length the disappointed man emerges from the spell long enough to ask the visitor who he is, he replies, "I am the man you might have been."

This second envoy is also much more aware of his own identity than the first. Across the years he has made sorties into the domains of unorthodox ideas, magical concepts, human interactions across class and ethnic barriers marked "Out of Bounds"; short-lived expeditions to try out, even if timidly, his highly personal creativity. All of this has given him a certain aura which attracts younger adults.

Still, the astute young observer notes, there is an air of pathos and defeat to this representative of the multitudes of the later years. When all is said and done, he does not feel himself to be the man "he might have been," which is to his credit. But the disaster is that he clearly feels that the whole game is over. What can you do, he thinks, with the later years of adulthood, with the zest of youth faded, the neuron system closing down, and creativity a hill city left behind with the lights receding?

(3) The third representative seems at first glance to be the kind of older adult with whom one can at least join in a joyful expedition in the often forbidding country of the later years. This is the adult who has been consummately successful in his or her chosen field. The sight of such success in a world filled with half-successes and outright failures is often stimulating and reassuring to the success-oriented young. There is a certain magnetism and excitement about an older man or woman whose lament is, not that they chose the wrong field—because they chose well and found both high achievement and a measure of self-development in their choice—but rather that what they need is other worlds to conquer.

Then, with a chill of recognition, the younger observer and would-be disciple notes that many of these individuals have opted out of "the creativity game." These are sophisticated people, the smart ones, the people with the answers. Some have read Harvey Lehman's book, *Age and Achievement*, in which the peak of creative powers is placed in the 30s; or they have heard dozens of similar comments over the past twenty years. Besides, they too are infected by "the manifest condition": Isn't it *manifest* that most later adults, notably from the mid-60s on, have ceased to be creative individuals? Thus, for even these debonair performers of yesterday, there are no new worlds to conquer, because life itself and the old wives' tales of the folk culture have conquered them.

The form of "disgust and despair" that fills the lives of many of these older adults, though less corrosive and heartbreaking than that of the non-achievers, is real and poignant enough. At the same time it arises from admirable sources in the life and personality. If you are a life-lover and something of a Faust who wishes to play many parts on the stage of what Kim's lama called, "this great and terrible world", the objective is noble, and there is never enough time to realize it. A dozen lifetimes are not enough.

But in any case, this particular kind of disgust and despair does not derive its most debilitating form from the brevity of life, but rather from the tenaciously-held conviction that even with the precious time that is left little or nothing can be done of any creative significance. "It is dreadful and depressing," said a distinguished retired publisher, looking intently at me, "to think that every day of my life many more productive brain cells have been turned off."

If one can believe this—millions do—and make a way of life out of it in later adulthood, then indeed there is no place to go but down. The sadness of this descent can be seen even in apparently exuberant figures among this third group of older adults whose inner pessimism seeps into and sours their late-life style.

An interesting victim of this poisoning was Maurice Chevalier, a superbly successful achiever in his career. The late chronicle of his farewell tours, *I Remember It Well*, is an astonishing *volte-face* from the Chevalier who appeared serenely in public in his very late years. In the intimate notes of his book, hurriedly made in dozens of stop-over locations in American and European towns (and thus quite spontaneous), Chevalier oscillates between phrenetic self-applause and a morbid melancholy in which he refers repeatedly to "going below" to the Black Place. Chevalier did, in fact, attempt some fresh creative ventures when old—film reviewing, for example—so that he presents a blurred image. Still, his inner despair and preoccupation with the downward path typifies the attitude which normally immobilizes this kind of splendid achiever and life-lover in his late years.

Thus, often unwittingly, the enormous numbers of men and women who make up these three varieties of later-life adults become symbols of what the problems and challenges of aging are all about. To live, at the best, with cheerful resignation and passivity, and at the worst with despair and frustration is to choose the two terrible options which make later life menacing and dreadful for those who observe or approach it: the Option of the Hand-Falling-Idle and the Option of the Mind-Turning-Aversively-from-Challenge (light years removed from Edward Dyer's noble concept: "My mind to me a kingdom is").

Thus our society slopes downward in the great human life "cycle", as it is brutally named, to a dark valley in some ways more fearful than the Psalmist's valley of the shadow of death. And this fact is known to the young, at least as a "gut feeling"; and as a depressingly imminent state to those adults who are themselves already on the brink of old age.

It is at this point, however, that a remarkable fourth protagonist appears upon the stage. He brings light with him, the light of creativity retained or regained, and the surging joy of human powers confidently held and used.

This is the exciting later adult personality whom I have chosen to call *"the Ulyssean Adult."*

The title comes, of course, from Ulysses, the adventurer and hero of the early Greek classical world who would have been about 50 when the great series of adventures described in *The Odyssey* was coming to an end, and perhaps close to 70 when he began his last adventures. Nonetheless, so open and resilient was his mind to experience, and so dauntless and questing his spirit, that Tennyson chose Ulysses as the subject of his poem dedicated to the thesis that only death can end the creative searching of such a man—and possibly not even death.

Tennyson had been an absorbed student of *The Odyssey* for years, and the portrait he paints of the classic hero is a projection of the authentic traits of Ulysses with which he had long been familiar. However, his portrait also owes a heavy debt to Dante's conception of Ulysses in late life in the wonderful Twenty-sixth Canto of his *Inferno*. In Dante's version, Ulysses, already a man in full maturity when he had returned from ten years of adventures after the fall of Troy, makes the decision in late life to yet again

> "put forth on the deep open sea with one vessel only, and with that small company which had not deserted me. The one shore and the other I saw as far as Spain, as far as Morocco, and Sardinia, and the other islands which that sea bathes round. I and my companions were old and slow when we came to that narrow outlet where Hercules set up his markers, that men should not pass beyond. On the right hand I left Seville, on the other I had already left Ceuta. 'O brothers,' I said, 'who through a hundred thousand dangers have reached the west, choose not to deny experience, following the sun, of the world that has no people. Consider your origin: you were not made to live as brutes, but to pursue virtue and knowledge.' With this little speech I made my companions so keen for the voyage that then I could hardly have held them back. And turning our stern to the morning, we made of our oars wings for the mad flight, always gaining on the left . . ."

Tennyson's poem shows Ulysses a number of years after his

return from his Mediterranean wanderings, during which time he has ruled his little kingdom of Ithaca. But he is dissatisfied with routines of kingship which could be done as well or better by his son, Telemachus. Ulysses has, in fact, been living for some years the life of Total Expectedness. This does not satisfy his restless, searching mind and spirit.

He is grateful for his past experiences:

"I am a part of all that I have met"

but they have all been preparations for yet more adventures and discoveries:

"Yet all experience is an arch wherethro'
Gleams that untravell'd world, whose margin fades
For ever and for ever when I move . . ."

The quest of adventure, mystery, and beauty has been the compelling motive of his entire life. But for all his joy and love of life, Ulysses is too much a realist not to know that although the years have given much, they have also taken their inescapable toll. He can no longer swim as far, race as swiftly, or fight as magnificently as he did "on the ringing plains of windy Troy." Still, he calls his comrades around him, and summons them to join him in continuing adventures in which the *will* is the critical element—the will to search, to discover, to accomplish dreams—in the continuing creativity of their later years:

"Come, my friends,
'Tis not too late to seek a newer world.
Push off, and sitting well in order smite
The sounding furrows; for my purpose holds
To sail beyond the sunset, and the baths
Of all the western stars, until I die.
It may be that the gulfs will wash us down:
It may be we shall touch the Happy Isles,
And see the great Achilles, whom we knew.
Tho' much is taken, much abides; and tho'
We are not now that strength which in old days
Moved earth and heaven; that which we are, we are;
One equal temper of heroic hearts,
Made weak by time and fate, but strong in will
To strive, to seek, to find, and not to yield."

About 2,600 years separates the two great poems in which Ulysses appears as the central figure. Yet both remain among the deathless poetry of the human race, not merely because of their craftsmanship but because Ulysses himself is of enduring fascination to people of all centuries.

Ulysses has become, through this immense span of human time, an heroic, semi-mythical figure, but he is not a god. He is not a freak or a mutation, but intensely human: a man who symbolizes the aspirations of men—notably, of course, in his confrontation of time and fate. Yet this confrontation is without bravado. Ulysses turns it into a quest, and makes it a part of the human condition.

Ulysses thought and behaved as he did because of the kind of man that he was, and not because he was a king in Ithaca living among gods and heroes. The time in which he played out his intrepid and beautiful life was seemingly very different from our own—light-years seem to separate the world of the barque on the wine-dark sea from our society. But the human players, for instance, the different adults who serve as symbolic envoys from the later years, are eternal. And the fourth of these, the Ulyssean Adult, can still be found in every stratum and ethnic group in our world of the late twentieth century.

What qualities especially identify the Ulyssean person in later life?

Perhaps the most remarkable is the governing sense of quest. Ulysses has for centuries been synonymous with the restless search for travel and adventure—even to those millions who may know little of the classic but who have inherited certain widely-renowned facts of the human classical tradition. The odds are that this identification with Ulysses still exists in spite of the homogenized modern education to which younger adults have been exposed. Otherwise the story of Ulysses would not have been chosen as the subject of a hugely successful Hollywood film.

Courage is the most striking quality evinced by Ulysses in his search for new experience. He is famous, it is true, for other characteristics—shrewdness and cunning, resourcefulness, loyalty to comrades, and an all-too-human capacity for cruel revenge upon those who have hurt him or his family or who have endangered his honour. But his courage is so strong a feature of his nature that when it is combined with his unremitting sense of quest and his frequent loneliness and hardships, the result is a person not only heroic but movingly human—perhaps throughout history and legend the most human and heartwarming of all heroes.

When, therefore, in our own time we see a man or woman in the later years who maintains the questing spirit, and who does so with courage and resourcefulness in a wide variety of circumstances, many of them terribly, even tragically adverse, such a man or woman may well be described as Ulyssean. The quest, the courage, and the resourcefulness may be exhibited on a human stage of immense proportions or in total solitariness and obscurity. It is not the time or the location but the quality of the life being lived that creates the Ulyssean Adult.

The essential quality of that life is creative, and it appears in two major sorts of late-life creators. One, which for the sake of convenience might be termed *Ulyssean One*, is the man or woman who begins new creative enterprises, small or large, in later life. The other, which might be called *Ulyssean Two*, is the older adult who does not strike out on new paths and creative territories but who remains creatively productive within his or her own familiar arena of life and work from later middle age into the very late years.

The working designations, Ulysseans One and Two, are not to be taken as indicating respective grades of quality or merit. Both are equally fine in their enactment of the drama of continuing creativity in the later years; and both also supply many examples of those Ulysseans who will later be described as having been one time or many times "naked on the shore."

However, although both kinds of Ulyssean adults are equal in merit and in beauty, there is a special excitement to Ulysseans One because of their quality of *unexpectedness*. These are best illustrated by a few actual profiles of people, in this case obviously impressive and attractive to me, but whose number could be supplemented by hundreds of others suggested by the readers of this book—examples of Ulysseans One who in many cases would be unknown to "the world" but lovingly remembered as adventurers in later creativity.

Edith Hamilton, whose paperback books, *The Greek Way, The Roman Way, Mythology* and a half-dozen other titles are found everywhere in North American and British bookstores, and throughout Europe and the world in translation, had no thought of developing a career as a popular writer when she retired as headmistress of the Bryn Mawr School for Girls when nearly 60. She went back to the old family home on the New England coast and began a life of charming domestic retirement. She played expertly the roles of good sister, good aunt, delightful friend, preparer of meals, member of the community, and watcher of tides and seasons. She also told and retold stories and legends from the classical period so vividly that her friends urged her to start writing them down. For some years she resisted, refusing to believe that a wider audience existed, and insisting she was not a writer. Finally, under persuasion, she sat down and began the book which was to become *The Greek Way*, and a bestseller. Other publications followed. Yet all through her long later life, and in spite of this dramatic new venture, she maintained her other roles. She never lost her love of life. At the age of 90, having decided to visit Europe again after twenty-five years, she was amused to hear that her sister had remarked to a friend how glad she was that Edith would have a last chance to make that tour. Edith Hamilton then revisited Europe on *four* annual tours, accompanied by her close (and much younger) friend and later biographer, Doris Read. At 91, Hamilton received the freedom of the city of Athens in a moving ceremony in one of the great theatres. She described this as the proudest moment of her life. Hers was the unusual case of the Ulyssean One adult who actually touched the borders of the heroic legend itself.

Ulyssean One adults, in fact, turn up with remarkable frequency in the writing world, especially as novelists, performing a totally new role after most of a lifetime spent in other pursuits. Thomas Costain had been a prominent editor and a dedicated reader of history for years before he began at 55 writing a series of immensely successful novels. Costain had had at least an association with writing, but Cervantes, who began to write *Don Quixote* when he was almost 60, had been a professional soldier. Lloyd C. Douglas was 50 before he began *Magnificent Obsession* when he was already a noted preacher in Montreal; the story was peddled around among a dozen editors before becoming one of the most successful bestsellers of the century. Wilder Penfield was world-famous as a brain surgeon when, in his 60s, he picked up an old story which his mother had always hoped to write and never had, and transformed her notes and ideas into the radically different plot and milieu of the fine novel, *No Other Gods*. Penfield followed it six years later with another novel, *The Torch*.

In all these cases, the factor of unexpectedness is constant. No one expected the preacher, the soldier, the editor, the brain surgeon to break out into the new adventure of writing a novel, which even as a physical exercise is strenuous and demanding—and to do so in their later years.

The reverse process is found in the late life of the French novelist, Lou Andréas-Salomé, which is recorded in a few pages by Simone de Beauvoir. Andréas-Salomé entered the world and the thought of Sigmund Freud at age 50; was in her 60s when she became a practising professional psychotherapist; awakened late to physical participation in sex and carried it on for years, transferring this to loving platonic friendships with men in her very late years. Harassed by terrible physical illnesses and by the terrors of the Nazi occupation of France, she nevertheless sought to open up new channels of thought and action for herself not only in psychoanalysis but in philosophy, in the improvement of the human condition, and through tender friendships with a wide circle of all sorts of people. She experienced the full assault of the world on her body, mind, and spirit; yet her life was lovely at the close, still seeking enrichment in new interests, still unembittered. The life of this Ulyssean One, in fact, demonstrates that in spite of everything, life is always conquered by the unembittered.

Benjamin Spock, in his late 60s, was an internationally famous pediatrician—wealthy, medically orthodox, the foster father, in

effect, of millions of American and Canadian "Spock babies."
There was no apparent evidence of Ulysseanism in his late life,
except perhaps in his devotion to intelligent play and recreation.
Then the terrible Vietnam War escalated—no more terrible, in
fact, than a hundred wars before it, and far surpassed by the
obscene tragedy of World War One. But television delivered the
conflict daily into the kitchens and living-rooms of the American
people, and the tens of thousands of young Americans who enlisted
and died seemed uselessly sucked in by a quagmire. Public revulsion grew, but American patriotic sentiment was still strong, and
Benjamin Spock's totally unexpected appearance as leader of the
anti-war forces took courage and imagination. A widespread outcry
arose against him; the federal government pursued him into the
courts; the father of the "Spock babies" found himself often cold-
shouldered and scowled at in airports and streets. But the Ulyssean
adventure was a success: Spock's courage was matched by his
shrewdness, and he knew that he spoke for the forces of life and
sanity. Furthermore, his leadership on Vietnam was simply the
beginning of a second unexpected Ulyssean career in civil rights.

The same quality of surprise turns up in the career of the industrialist, Cyrus Eaton, who, however creative he may have been in
achieving the status of tycoon, showed his Ulyssean colours when
already over 70, in the creation of the Pugwash Conference. Eaton
conceived this annual meeting of significant leaders of thought and
action from both sides of the Iron Curtain as an effort to thaw the
cold war. From the vantage point of the 1970s this seems a far-
sighted concept—it has been followed, after all, by rapprochements
between the Americans and the Russians and between the
Americans and the Chinese, and by conversations and agreements
between West and East Germany. But in 1953 Eaton was, naturally,
violently criticised for attempting to open up dealings with dangerous and despotic powers who might simply exploit every sentimental overture to their own ends. Eaton was personally very
wealthy—a cynic might say that he had his wealth to keep him
warm—yet many of the attacks must have been chill winds blowing
in the comfort of his hitherto orthodox life. It was the *unexpectedness* of this Ulyssean plunge into a venture abhorrent to the
American Establishment that added to the shock of the beholders
and to the gutiness and creativity of the doer.

The Ulyssean sorties of both Spock and Eaton were in fields
other than their life careers, but obviously the Ulyssean One adult
is found many times in the exciting world of the Second (and
Third) Career. In his fine book, *Starting Over*, Damon Stetson
describes the thoughts and actions of just such a mid-life adult at
the point where he turns from one secure and successful career and
seeks another. The case in point is that of David E. Lilienthal, who

by the time he was 50 had become successively chairman of the
Tennessee Valley Authority and the United States Atomic Energy
Commission. At this point he sought "a newer world". In Volume 3
of his *Journals*, called significantly *Venturesome Years*, Lilienthal
writes:

> "At this time I was neither young nor old . . . I had to make a
> choice. . . . I could choose to play it safe. I could choose to
> live on my past accomplishments, doing what I knew I could
> do. That would have been easy—but personally disastrous.
> That course I rejected. . . . I chose instead to take on ventures
> new and untried, to do things I did not know I could do, to
> try once again to find that venturesome and affirmative life
> that I had always lived before, the kind of life in which in
> earlier years I found myself truly functioning."

The words could almost be a paraphrase of those of Dante's
Ulysses. Lilienthal travelled for a time, rested, thought much, then
entered a new world of action as a managerial and industrial consultant privately dedicated to helping improve the life of ordinary
people of all races across the globe. In doing so, he obviously made
great use of past expertise—but so did Ulysses, and so do all who
venture on new enterprises in their middle and later years, even if
it is only to use the resources from the bank of faith, hope, and
courage which they have accumulated.

Sometimes adversity, not success, is the force that drives the
Ulysseans One into wholly unexpected ventures. Misfortune also
presents one with choices: either to accept defeat quiescently or to
launch out into new creative planning and action, hoping for the
best. Ralph Knode's case, also cited by Stetson, is a vivid illustration
of this. Knode was born into an affluent Philadelphia family and,
following college and service in the air force, married, and became
a successful salesman with a cement company. He had an expensive home, and a portfolio of stocks started for him in his youth by
his family, and seemed set in the pattern of that fortunate minority
who are "comfortably fixed" for life.

Ralph Knode, however, had a severe drinking problem, to some
extent the result of work for which he was emotionally unsuited.
As is often the case, the two problems, the alcoholism and the work,
interacted upon one another. The company placed him in office
work, which he found boring. He had reached a kind of moment of
truth; fortunately he had the support of an understanding wife.
He made a radical decision, a Ulyssean One decision—with recollections from boyhood of a trip to Wyoming, Knode decided to test the
waters of a wholly new world. For a year he accepted the work of a
ranch-hand, a gruelling year of hard physical work. Then he and
his wife bought a small ranch, then a much larger one. Six years
later, in 1970, although still with heavy debts incurred by purchas-

ing the ranches, Knode's problem with alcohol had gone, he had over two thousand acres, and a very large herd of Black Angus cattle. The Knode family with its three children was united in a life which offered more isolation than eastern city routines, but had the compensations of being home on the range. For *unexpectedness*, it would be hard to imagine a more dramatic change of career. Perhaps those who seek the path of Ulyssean One would do well to remember Charles Luckman's dictum when he abandoned the presidency of Lever Brothers to return to his profession of twenty years back (architecture): you don't have to prove anything to your friends, and you shouldn't disturb yourself about your enemies.

Sometimes Ulyssean changes in middle and later life lead to not only second and third, but even fourth, careers. The Canadian educator and facilitator of cultural growth, John Everett Robbins, was 50 and had been a prominent civil servant at Ottawa for twenty years when he had the opportunity to help launch the *Encyclopedia Canadiana* as its editor-in-chief. The challenge was exciting, but the venture involved giving up the usual securities of civil service life, not least the pension arrangements. Robbins took the plunge, however, producing over five years the ten-volume publication which was hailed as a major contribution to Canada's sense of identity. What next? Robbins could have stayed on with the encyclopedia but for so innovative a person the zest was gone. Had he not had another challenge offered to him, he would undoubtedly have made his own, like Lilienthal or Knode. As it happened, he received an invitation to become executive officer of the Canadian research councils on humanities and the social sciences, an offer he accepted (he had for twenty years been the voluntary coordinator of their activities). Two years later, Robbins took on the presidency of a small college in Western Canada, which during the ensuing decade he transformed into a university. When the brief era of student confrontations arrived in 1969, Robbins resigned the presidency in disgust (not at the concept of student participation but at the Yahoo-like stupidity of the student organizers on the campus). It was a gutsy decision, because Robbins' term had three years to run, and he had no immediate prospects. In fact, he was soon considering a post as coordinator of campus contacts for the programme of external aid. But before he could begin work he was offered, in midsummer of 1969, the job of first Canadian ambassador to the Holy See. After his three-year tour, which Robbins and his wife described as "beautiful," he came home to Ottawa, where at 71 he deeply involved himself in the work of Amnesty International.

A child of fortune? Perhaps, to a degree. But Robbins was always ready to take the Ulyssean decision: to seek a newer world where the creativity which he felt to be an integral part of his life could have free play, even at the risk of occasionally astonishing friends and baffling enemies with unexpectedness.

Men who retire, and women who embark on enterprises outside the home in middle and later adulthood, are often glowing examples of Ulysseans One. One example is the New York State Commissioner of Education who, on retiring at 65 in the 1950s, announced to his startled friends that he had always wanted to be a lawyer. He thereupon enrolled at the Albany Law School, graduating at 69, and arguing cases for years, including situations where he appeared before his successors as Commissioners of Education! A recent Canadian counterpart is the Ontario medical executive, Glenn Sawyer, who at 65, in the fall of 1974, enrolled in law studies at the University of Western Ontario.

Still another Ulyssean undergraduate is Harry Craimer of Montreal, who gave up the active management of his accountancy firm in 1974 to enroll at McGill University in the East Asian Studies programme, taking courses in Chinese language and history, Japanese literature, and comparative economic systems. In studying Chinese language, he is a regular user, with undergraduates 45 years younger, of the language laboratory and its tapes and microphones. Craimer took a Commerce degree in 1933 and finds university life transformed—now often huge and impersonal. Still, he finds enormous new interest in today's campus. A profile describing him in the McGill graduate journal notes that Craimer "continues to rethink old ideas and to relish new ones."

An even more striking case of the Ulyssean at work in late studies is E. Lyall Nelson of Montreal, a former banker who retired after forty-four years and commenced B.A. studies (at Concordia University) which he had intended to pursue long before. Nelson entered in 1971, graduated in 1974 after taking twenty courses in three years, and then enrolled in M.A. studies.

Yet Craimer, Sawyer, and Nelson are mere youths compared to Mal Wickham, age 90, described in April, 1975, as "the oldest student at the University of Wisconsin." Wickham, we are told, returned to college studies after a career that included 40 years of farming. He *jogs* to his classes.

In our time enormous numbers of women now return to a former vocation after fifteen or twenty years of married life. (Increasingly, of course, they combine both work and marriage from the honeymoon on.) But the Ulyssean element enters with the re-entry of women of quite advanced years to career or educational ventures, or with those of middle years who, feeling themselves no longer growing as persons, no longer "shining in use," strike out on new paths with the inevitable hazards of possible failure. Barbara Powell O'Neill in her stimulating book, *Careers for Women after Marriage and Children*, "for the woman who wants individual self-fulfillment as well as marriage", cites Ruth K. Caress of East Meadow, Long Island, as an example of this.

Ruth Caress had reached the age of about 40 with an early college education, an able and understanding husband, a family of three children, a number of worthwhile community voluntary activities, and an attractive home. Her expression, however, of certain personal problems which she was experiencing as an individual could serve as the classic stereotype of the unrealized woman in her middle years. In her interviews with O'Neill these phrases occur: "Despite all this . . . a deep sense of personal frustration . . . a sense of being without any personal identification. . . . Deriving little or no gratification from the shape of my life. . . ." (This syndrome could, of course, be matched by many thousands of men also, about whom L. E. Sissman writes, "Men past forty/Get up nights, And look out/at City Lights. . . .")

Caress tells us that her early academic record had been mediocre; she had been long away from studies; she would have to accept teachers, if she went back, who were younger than herself. Nonetheless, she decided to take the plunge and enroll in a school of social work. In spite of the hard work and anxieties of this late studentship, it was a success; there were also pleasant surprises. For example: "The kudos from teachers and supervisors were rebuilding a self-esteem badly battered by years of intellectual stagnation." She became a caseworker for a family service organization, thus pursuing a creative Ulyssean search for a richer personal identity.

Often with women as with men, the Ulyssean One adventure is something that astonishes not only one's friends but oneself. The Canadian columnist True Davidson entered upon the extraordinary odyssey in 1968, at age 66, of becoming mayor of one of Ontario's large suburban cities, East York. When she retired from the post in 1972, it was not because she felt herself too old, but because she felt the urge for other ventures—writing a column for a Toronto daily paper was one. A characteristic of many Ulysseans is that they do not plan their unexpected moves as though these were chessboard strategies; they seek experience as "an arch wherethro'/Gleams that untravell'd world, whose margin fades/For ever and for ever" as they move. The mayoralty of a large city was not part of Davidson's long-range calculations at, say, age 60, but her Ulyssean spirit made her ready for it.

An outstanding case of how the Ulyssean One experience can be thrust upon somebody essentially ready for it is seen in the later life of the French writer and mystic, Gabrielle Bossis. This remarkable woman was born in Nantes in 1874 and died on June 9, 1950. She was the daughter of wealthy parents, a charming, loving, high-spirited girl whose mystical nature was long concealed by her participation in all the social and artistic activities of her class. She rejected the chance to become a nun, thus seeming in the church's eyes to choose the world, yet she refused offers of marriage which might have separated her from her hidden vocation. Bossis undertook "quite late in life", according to her translator, Evelyn Brown, the writing of religious plays which she also often acted in and produced. She travelled extensively, not only because of her plays but seemingly because of her *joie de vivre* and deep interest in people and their situations.

The Ulyssean adventure which marked an extraordinary development of her life occurred at age 62, when Bossis began to keep an intimate personal journal of a type which she could not possibly have anticipated in earlier years, and which is wholly original. It began with her trip to Canada on the *Ile de France*, continued through her cross-Canada tour, and ended shortly before her death. It was almost wholly devoted to a series of dialogues with a mysterious inner voice which, Evelyn Brown remarks, Gabrielle Bossis "felt with awe, though sometimes with anxious questionings, to be the voice of Christ." The journal was written through incessant travels at airports, at sea, at dozens of stops throughout France, Europe, and North Africa. Bossis was not a recluse. She had inherited money and was intensely life-loving; she had many friends, and she had made for herself in her later years a successful career in her own sphere of play-acting, writing, and producing. Still, the journal, which she kept for thirteen years, was an intensely private thing. She never attempted to exploit the experience of the Dialogue for personal gain or power. It was published very late in her life in total anonymity, and then finally, some years after her death, Bossis was revealed as the writer in the edition produced by Daniel-Rops as *Lui et Moi* (*He and I*). The news of its authorship astounded her friends.

The secret journal was the Ulyssean adventure of Bossis' later years: to read it is to encounter a loving, creative, and Ulyssean spirit.

As we have said, the man or woman in later adulthood who does not suddenly convert to new careers and enterprises but who remains richly productive within the sphere of creativity where he or she has long performed is Ulyssean Two. Interestingly enough, Ulysses himself was really a Ulyssean Two. His essential role, imposed upon him in *The Odyssey* by apprenticeship to the gods, was that of skilled captain-adventurer—his obligations as a king were both essential and incidental to his great role. The excitement of his epic voyage in late life through the Gates of Hercules was not that he had embarked upon a wholly new career, but that he had resumed the life of quest, risk and discovery when he found himself drying up and losing his sense of self-significance. Ulysses was still, at a late stage in his life, employing the arts of mariner, leader, and seeker, much as he had used them all through his odyssey.

The word "still," which can be deadly when applied to men and women caught in the nets of dull, unliberating routines ("Do you mean to say that Thorold is *still* in that job at Gray and Company?") glows with life and energy when it describes the continuation of creative achievement into the later and often very late years. Verdi was still writing successful operas into his early 80s; Thomas Mann was still producing first-rate novels throughout his seventies; Alfred North Whitehead was still so filled with the fires of thought that he published his four major works after the age of 65; Balanchine is still choreographing brilliant ballets as he crosses his 70th birthday; Ralph Vaughan Williams was still producing great symphonies and other major works throughout his 70s and 80s; William Butler Yeats took what runners call his "second wind" after a stormy and troubled middle age, and still produced nobly and beautifully until his death at 75; Buckminster Fuller's mind and hand still teem with innovation at 80 as they did at 60.

The world of painting seems to swarm with these Ulysseans Two. To take up, for example, Alexander Liberman's book, *The Artist in His Studio*, which consists of Liberman's interviews with nearly forty noted European artists of our time, is an invigorating experience. "Our time" begins with Cézanne, Renoir, Monet, and Bonnard, and concludes with a group of artists now elderly in years but in many cases still alive and fully generative: for example, Dubuffet, Ernst Richier, Bazaine, Giacometti, Hartung, and Manessier. From Liberman's pages, the first astounding fact to emerge about these Ulysseans is their longevity; the next is their vitality. All but six reached age 70, and three of the six are still living and close to the mark. Eighteen lived to age 80, and half of those to beyond 85. Liberman began his odyssey among these painters and sculptors just after World War Two, and longevity was the least of his interests. In fact, to the absorbed reader it plays a secondary role to the *élan*, the joy in the wonder of the world and its beauty which continues to characterize what are, after all, very elderly men.

At a great age, and ill, the Roumanian sculptor, Constantin Brancusi, tells Liberman that he is still working on the concept of the bird—that in fact what he seeks is the meaning of flight. Georges Rouault remarks that one must be humble and not think that one knows; that everything must be begun again; that, after all, he has waited until age 70 before going to Italy! And Alberto Giacometti, whose passionate creativity finally exhausted him at

65, says that he has been fifty thousand times to the Louvre, copying everything in drawing, "trying to understand."

Unlike Pablo Picasso, whose torrential genius continued to produce lavishly into his 90s, and who felt compelled to strip himself of any possessive hand, even the hand of love, few of these Ulyssean Two artists kept burning their bridges behind them. Nevertheless, they have found "that untravell'd world" in the inexhaustible continuity of their creative lives. Thus Georges Braque, who began in the 1930s his hundreds of paintings of noble and exquisite birds, is able to tell Liberman that the mystery of his great painting, *Grand Oiseau*, is beyond words—a symbol of an ever more mysterious cosmos. And this magnificent old Ulyssean at 78 remarks wistfully to Liberman that he needs another storey for his house to shelter his accumulating canvases!

Perhaps there is both a physical and an emotional release in painting and sculpting which promotes the Ulyssean adventure, much as with other arts, especially the so-called executant arts. Conductors of orchestras are often Ulyssean figures: Arturo Toscanini, who continued to conduct with power until close to his death at age 90, was not only emotionally intensely alive, but according to his masseur had much of the skin texture and the suppleness of an athletic young man. On the other hand, Otto Klemperer, who was still on full course as a conductor when he died at 85, conducted from a chair, having survived in the course of twenty-five years a terrible accident, a brain tumor, and severe burns. Stravinsky, who was still conducting and composing in his 80s, was a frail, pixie-like man whose varied facial expressions so distracted his youthful biographer, Robert Craft, at their first meeting, that Craft could hardly concentrate on the maestro's words. Stravinsky was in his late 60s before Craft even met him, yet his book throbs with life. The fascinating portrait Craft draws is Ulyssean from the first page: the composer's fragile body was driven along by a group of motors: a hunger for fame; a love of life; a sense of quest, the undying curiosity and wonder of the Ulysseans; and a wonderful, often corrosive, sense of humour. His humour was, in fact, the verification of David Raff's definition: "humour is a form of courage."

To be a Ulyssean Two, one must obviously be more than a repeater of the routine, regardless of the fact that James Birren, an authority on adulthood, remarks that to live long is itself a kind of achievement. There must be creative action, not merely continued motion. Ulysses could have maintained his royal routines until he was a patriarch but he would not have been Ulysses. While the dramatic and unexpected change in lifestyle and/or career which marks Ulysseans One makes the adventure and creativity of their later lives stand out unmistakably, the picture is less clear with the other Ulysseans. Here the whole question of what is *creative* living and doing arises much more urgently.

The word "routine", says the *Concise Oxford Dictionary*, means "the unvarying performance of certain acts." It has, interestingly enough, nothing whatever to do with the quality of the "unvarying performance" itself. A successful and aging comedian on national television may continue to delight viewers with comedy styles and laugh-inducers which he shrewdly repeats for the fortieth year; a preacher may continue to console or inspire congregations with repeated or revamped sermons which guarantee his acceptability; a homemaker may make the same marvellous pies and present the same appetizing menu on the supper table through years of family life; and a politician may continue to be re-elected election after election by uttering the same clichés. Routine performances carried on often into the very late years are frequently admirable in themselves, but they are not Ulyssean.

In all lifestyles, including those of the Ulysseans, a certain amount of routine is indispensable: it provides the settled minimum order of daily living which frees mind and body for higher activities. But when the routine *becomes* the lifestyle, when the lives of men and women from early middle age on become operational only within a circular track of unexamined attitudes, unimproved skills, and numbing rituals—then the creative spirit enters into a long catalepsy. This is the situation that led Whitehead to compare much of middle age to a highway clogged with cars each moving at the sluggish pace dictated by the stupefying conformity of all. At its worst, as for example in a long life surrendered to unexamined ideas and conditioned actions, the years may have erected a personality insensitive or hostile to even promising change, rigid with the drying-out of laughter and hope, and warming hands over the pale fires of old achievements and the redundant honours piled on for old deeds and offices. There are elderly prominent men (women gain few honours by the nature of the contest, but have the greater prize of longer life) who cannot seem to gain applause enough for distinctions of the past: so that their later life becomes an accumulation of citations, titles, and honorary degrees through which they walk like the bereft tycoons of Adolphus Myers' history of nineteenth-century capitalism, walking up and down like captive tigers around and through the jungle of their trophies.

This also is the world of the "if only" and the "might have been" —those terrifying ghostly arenas within which potentially still creative people fight uselessly over and over again the lost battles and chances of the past.

Much of these fates is spared the practitioners of the lively arts, and the ranks of Ulysseans Two are thick not only with painters and sculptors, but with actors, musicians, composers, poets, writers, dancers, choreographers, architects, and craftsmen. "Much" is spared, not all, because of course disappointed career people abound in these fields, too, and older performers who, deciding that they have exhausted their creativity, live in or brood upon the past. Many, too, have become prisoners of seemingly successful routines.

Yet by their nature the arts persistently present their practitioners with opportunities to be creative—if only to be individualized beings. As actors grow older, fresh roles are available to them which demand that they think out new concepts, that they look into themselves and test themselves against the parts—in a word, that they exert themselves in the direction of creativity. Dancers and singers, the two categories who typically find themselves ultimately sidelined by the physical handicaps of aging, often become choreographers, directors, and teachers of young rising artists, where again they meet successions of creative challenges which help to renew them. An astonishing late Ulyssean Two like Martha Graham should be studied by all interested in the survival of creative power into the late years. In both musical composition and poetry, the lion's share of popular attention has been reserved for youthful genius: the Mozarts, Mendelssohns, Schuberts, and other somewhat older composers like Berg, Mahler, Tchaikovsky, Schumann, and Weil, all of whom died before reaching age 50 or much beyond it. Yet an impressive number of composers have turned their later years into Ulyssean journeys; to name only ten: Haydn, Handel, Liszt, Bruckner, Wagner, César Franck, Vaughan Williams, Holst, Kodaly, and Milhaud. The remarkable case of Ralph Vaughan Williams has been cited. Perhaps there is significance in the fact that Vaughan Williams' special creed throughout his musical life was that the composer must keep himself open to and involved in the life and experience of his community.

In the lives of all these Ulysseans, the sense of quest and wonder was strong, undiminished by age. This persisted in spite of enormous handicaps: Handel's crushing debts, Wagner's neuroses, César Franck's almost constant neglect by the musical public, Holst's loss of most of the public which he had temporarily gained with *The Planets*. The quality of intense humanness was also characteristic of them all; whatever they were, they were real, not plastic, people. This human reality ranged all the way from Haydn's great sweetness of nature and affection to Richard Wagner's assortment of hatreds, the most repulsive of which was his macabre anti-Semitism. No one can pretend that all the Ulysseans are "nice" people; Chou En-lai's nature is clearly both tough and cruel, yet he would certainly qualify as a Ulyssean Two. Naturally, it is inspiring to study Verdi, Victor Hugo, and Goethe, all of whom seem projections of what the human spirit might be, but the Ulyssean path is not confined to the bearers of sweetness and light.

Just as in music a great deal of attention has been given to the phenomenon of the young genius, so in poetry a persistent myth exists that poetry is a young person's game—that the poetic fires die down as the poet enters middle age, and disappear as he or she crosses into the late years. If this were so, there would be no Ulyssean poets, but the domain of poetry is filled with them. It is well known that Thomas Hardy turned away forever from the novel at about age 50 and steadily produced poetry of the first order until his death at 85, and Yeats's wonderful late years have been mentioned. What is one to do with the astounding productivity, undimmed in quality, of Robert Frost? And the wonderful later poems of Saint-John Perse, Edith Sitwell, Paul Valéry, Boris Pasternak, Giuseppe Ungaretti, Wallace Stevens, and Eugenio Montale?

The Ulysseans are mould-breakers of conventional folk myths and pieties. Thus, Pablo Casals, Zoltan Kodaly, Justice William O. Douglas, John R. Mott, and Avery Brundage all at an advanced age marry young women, and these unions turn out to be loving and enduring. Men and women supposed to be ready chronologically for retirement homes or at the very least to settle into the safe routines of later middle age, encircle the globe in small craft or set off on humanitarian missions among people of other cultures and tongues half a world away. And older adults who tenaciously love such sports as running, skiing, and fencing (among many others) prove in their Ulyssean way that "athlete" is not, as popular usage mistakenly supposes, a word always linked with young performers, but that in fact the *Concise Oxford Dictionary* is perfectly correct in defining it as a "competitor in physical exercises; robust, vigorous man" (to which, of course, we add "woman"). It is the Ulysseans who remind us that we must refer to so-and-so as "a fine athlete" without raising in our minds the eternal concept of youth.

Much the same liberation is available in the seemingly totally different sphere of the concert pianists, and for that matter, other solo instrument performers. When I was a boy the story was widespread that Paderewski had to stop playing in his early 60s because of stiffened fingers, and it fortified the legend that this was the natural fate of pianists, violinists, cellists, and guitarists. But with Artur Rubinstein playing in creative style at 88 and Horowitz's triumphant return at 72, a new world opens—the world of the Ulysseans. The list of fine public performers in their later years is long, and includes, of course, such names as Segovia, Montoya, Casadesus, Francescatti, Malcuzinski, and Isaac Stern. To these can be added the remarkable jazz virtuosi: for example, Ellington, Count Basie, Eubie Blake, and Louis Armstrong. It was Armstrong's heart that did him in at age 70—there was nothing wrong with his fingers and his spirit; his death following a brilliant all-night private performance during convalescence was classically Ulyssean.

Likewise, Ulyssean people in great arenas of politics and state-craft break the mould that stamps elderly arrivals to positions of power as being typically "caretaker" figures. John XXIII was 78 by the time he reached the papacy of the Roman Catholic Church, an institution which until recently had the courage and wisdom to ignore artificial retirement thresholds. (Even now the defined or implicit limit is placed at a generous age 75, which nonetheless means that Angelo Roncalli would never have become pope at all.) Roncalli was a short, obese, unhandsome, people-loving prelate who remarked wryly on his election that he could not be called "a television pope." Except to the informed, who were few, he seemed to be a typical career churchman whose slow rise to the Curia after an early election as bishop had been marked by years spent on the half-forgotten peripheries of power: at 78, a useful "care-taker pope." Yet when this jolly, seeming nonentity found himself at the controls of a remarkable instrument called Papal Infallibility, he set in motion one of the most extraordinary enterprises in the church's history: Vatican Council II—a Ulyssean adventure. When he died at 83 his death was felt to be premature! A light, visible to men and women of every race and faith, had gone out.

Similarly, in another great office, the American presidency, Harry Truman arrived at the seat of power in 1945, by the earnest wish and arrangement of practically nobody— a party wheelhorse selected for the nothing office of vice president to replace the erratic and left-oriented Henry Wallace. He was, virtually every-body agreed, a "caretaker president"—even worse, he had suc-ceeded a legend, so that, after a fumbling start ("I feel," he said, "as though the sky and the stars have fallen upon me."), a national magazine scouring around for views of the man on the street, reported a truck driver's comment, "We've sure got a dumbo for a president." Worst of all, he was already 61: "too old to change." Yet in successive opinion polls thirty years later, Truman ranks over and over again as probably the best president of the century. So you never can tell with the "caretaker" people: they may be Ulysseans Two who are at last ready for the great voyage.

Most Ulysseans are not involved, however, in enterprises that catch the eye and the ear of the world. For many men and women in middle and later adulthood who feel a certain stirring or poten-tiality for the Ulyssean life but who still hesitate, there may seem as much discouragement as impetus in reviewing a cavalcade of famous Ulyssean people. "These are, after all, geniuses or indivi-duals of some kind of spectacular talent," they will say. "The life arenas they work or have worked in are in themselves of heroic dimensions, with all too little reference to the equipment and potentialities of those (like us) who don't happen to move on those Olympian heights."

There is some truth in this, but fortunately not much. There are, of course, creators among the Ulysseans who are almost demi-gods, who seem to illustrate vividly Karl Barth's definition of man as "the being who dwells on the border between heaven and earth." Michelangelo is an example who leaps to mind. Yet when one studies the many-sided portrait of Michelangelo which is presented in, for instance, Professor Robert J. Clements' biography in which the artist and poet describes himself, his genius is seen to be only an element in his Ulysseanism. Although it may seem incredible at first sight, the *dimension* of his talent is clearly irrelevant to the splendour of his later Ulyssean life.

On the other hand, there are two qualities in Michelangelo's late years which are most moving and which most fire one's imagination: his strength of will and his summoning-up of what Kipling calls, "heart and bone and sinew" for herculean tasks in spite of all kinds of fears and sorrows—these are qualities perfectly or imperfectly accessible to every adult human being who turns his or her face toward the Ulyssean trails.

Without them, the trails cannot be entered or the journeys completed. For many older adults in modern Western society with a great deal of free time, perhaps not affluent but not impoverished, probably not radiantly healthy but not in bad health, either, it is a fact that even the writing and mailing of letters seems a major undertaking. All the more so, the labour of writing a lengthy appeal to an editor, keeping a journal, organizing easel and paints and a painting trip, sitting down to study the first elements of a foreign language, even just the physical chore of writing out a short story or a small play, let alone bringing them to birth, or composing some poems, good or bad; or writing up or sketching out designs for new programmes or buildings or enterprises—in a word, all the price tags of physical and mental effort in any of the dozens of creative exercises. Any and all of these seem too much. "We are past all that."

For all of us who have been in that state, the performances of certain "great" Ulysseans are instructive. True, they have or have had unusually powerful motivations or have long conditioned themselves to methods of work which they can continue into even very late adulthood. Still, they too have the same physical equipment as other men and women (some, like Prescott, Pasteur, and Parkman worked under crippling, almost immobilizing disabilities), and in their later years are just as subject to the hazards of fatigue and debility.

Considering this, some of their applications of will and physical effort make one want to take stock of one's own days, schedules, and habits. A photograph exists of the 81-year-old Leo Tolstoy writing, bent over his desk; and it gives one pause to realize that ten years earlier he had just completed *Resurrection*, writing all of its two hundred thousand words by hand. Victor Hugo, too, who had carted the mammoth growing manuscript of *Les Misérables* in and out of France for twenty years on his various escapes and hurried journeys, and had written it all by hand, also wrote out the huge *Toilers of the Sea* when he produced it at age 63. Voltaire's marvellous satire, *Candide*, which he wrote at 64, was far shorter; nonetheless, it required a major expenditure of concentrated will and sheer physical effort. Thomas Mann, a remarkable creator of novels produced in the later years, had the consolation, if one can call it that, of the typewriter. Still, the three major novels which he published after age 70 (*Dr. Faustus*, *The Holy Sinner*, and the largely rewritten *The Confessions of Felix Krull, Confidence Man*) comprise in all about a half-million words. Much the same nerving of will and physical effort is seen in productivity after age 60 of such women writers as Colette, Pearl S. Buck, and Katherine Anne Porter.

The labour of writing these books, wholly aside from the output of creative imagination required, suggests that another characteristic of Ulyssean people is that they do not brood in advance about the physical demands of their various enterprises but simply move ahead. They so absorb themselves in the adventure at hand that, so far as possible, they put out of their minds preconceptions of the arduous chores of writing, planning, typing, shutting themselves off from social pleasures, and so on. Least of all do they fret about whether they will live to complete their task.

Companion adventures illustrate the same point. Will Durant's monumental *History of Civilization* comprises, in all, ten volumes of about 300,000 words each: three of these (*The Age of Faith, The Renaissance*, and *The Reformation*) were composed and written out or typed by Durant after age 58, the third at 65; Durant followed these with five more volumes written in collaboration with his wife Ariel, from age 69 to 89. William L. Shirer was in his mid-50s, and long removed from the success of his *Berlin Diary* when he produced the huge *Rise and Fall of the Third Reich*, evidently written over three years in the privacy of a hotel suite. Shirer then followed this with a work of equal size and importance in his mid-60s, *The Decline and Fall of the Third Republic*. Jacques Maritain was 70 when he involved himself in the labour of committing about 120,000 words to paper in *Creative Intuition in Art and Poetry*, and André Maurois was 78 when he prepared his 200,000-word biography of Balzac.

In an utterly different world—a world very close to that of the original Ulysses—the same qualities of exertion of will and of physical energy further illustrate the Ulyssean life. Francis Chichester's name became a household word in the 1960s. What everyone neglected to mention about him was the point superbly made by J. R. L. Anderson in his book, *The Ulyssean Factor*: that in 1960, at age 59, in his first transatlantic race, Chichester changed sail 118 times in forty days, in addition to endlessly trimming the sails of his *Gipsy Moth III*. He did this, moreover, under the handicaps of poor eyesight, of sometimes wretched health, and often in pitching seas. When he was 70 Chichester set out on still another transatlantic race, again alone, knowing that the illness which had pursued him for years was at last to bring him down. In fact, he had to turn back, but this took nothing from the bright fires of his spirit and will, and the nobility of the effort. Chichester was sailing, Anderson suggests, not to discover and explore anything *except himself*. And in fact, in our time, when nearly all the physical world is known, the search for the self constitutes the greatest Ulyssean adventure.

Most Ulyssean achievements are highly personal affairs and often they occur in settings which seem quite comfortable and almost effete. In 1959 Ethel Sabin Smith, an American prose poet and philosopher, when nearly 70, took a round-the-world journey by freighter, and not merely described the trip in a subsequent book but analysed what this strange Ulyssean act meant to her and could mean to others. Since the cargo ships she chose usually had good cabins, good food, good service, and pleasant crews—in what ways was the adventure Ulyssean? For one thing, because in spite of the comparative comforts of travel, the voyage itself had certain hazards for what is usually called an "elderly" person, hazards both psychological and physical. Obviously, as she was steaming from Hong Kong to Singapore on a slow cargo boat without a doctor, the only woman passenger aboard—and aged 70 at that—physical crises could occur. But more real was the emotional wrench in leaving familiar scenes and friends, and the comfortable routines of predictable days for months of unknown experiences, however compensated one might feel by new experiences and personal growth.

For another thing, the adventure was Ulyssean because of Ethel Sabin Smith's own attitude. She found, not surprisingly, that not all older adults who set out on voyages are Ulysseans, and she makes the point, without any thought of Ulysses or reference to him, that the traveller must have, or must develop, attitudes of quest and receptivity to change. Thus, writing of her own circumnavigation of the globe, cargo-ship style, (*Passports at Seventy*) she says:

"One may take a world cruise to escape from confining demands of established habits, to broaden one's physical horizon; but it takes more than steamship tickets and baggage labels, landing passes and inoculations, to release one's mind and spirit from custom. One must be able to brace oneself against mighty winds and let them sweep through one's mind; be able to face contrary opinions and beliefs when they crest and come hissing toward one; exult when, like driving rain, unexpected facts drench one. The traveler unable to endure buffeting remains below, so to speak, in the cabin of his mind, untouched, unchanged."

Openness of mind, sensitivity to the need for new ways and new experiences; resourcefulness; courage; curiosity and a continuing sense of wonder at the kaleidoscopic beauty and mystery of the world and the cosmos; acceptance of the fact of aging but not being intimidated by it; and consciousness of the quest for the self throughout the life drama—these are clearly some of the significant traits identifiable in the personalities of Ulyssean adults of widely differing eras and places. But equally clearly, the title "Ulyssean"— which is potentially available to *all* older adults—is inseparably linked with the word, "creativity."

It is not a question of the magnitude of the creativity involved as part of the Ulyssean life—the point has been made as regards Michelangelo. But it is a question of responding to one of the invitations to creative thought and action which life seems to extend at certain times throughout later life; and of making oneself so far as possible the kind of person who, arriving at those inter-sections where creative new adventures, small or large, are possible, is able to make something of the Ulyssean response.

How *special*, however, is creativity? Are some adult people wholly creative and others not? Is creativity a matter only of high domains of human thought and the lively arts or, as one observer who has studied the mysterious phenomenon for years insists, is it at the least a spark which exists in every human being unless it has been extinguished by time and disuse? Is the spark ever really extinguished? And if not, can older people assemble their learning skills and growth so that they can make abundant use of whatever creativity they have?

It is the argument of this book that the Ulyssean life is on some terms, in small or large arenas, potentially accessible to all men and women—and in that argument the concept of creativity as a universal resource plays a central role.

2. THE THEORY AND THE PRACTICE OF CREATIVITY

All authors engaged on new projects find that they are asked from time to time by friends and strangers the inevitable question, "And what are you writing about?" When in the case of this book I gave out the sub-title as "Creativity in the Middle and Later Years", I found at once an expression of heightened interest. This reaction occurred whether the inquirer was 18 or 80, a lawyer or a house-cleaner, man or woman. The phrase "later years" intrigued a good many; the word "creativity" intrigued everyone. The desire to create seems to be inherent in every human being. Even those who have no belief whatever that they can create, still yearn to do so.

The act of creation is sufficiently mysterious that Arthur Koestler could write a thousand-page tome about about it—a brilliant and beautiful book (*The Act of Creation*, 1964)—without solving the enigma. He shed light upon the subject, however, and at least largely demolished the conception of creativity as something celestial, supernatural, or at all events the domain of supermen. There was a long period of time, as Henry Murray points out, when creation could be applied only to the works of God, who made the world literally out of nothing (which, as Koestler indicates, is exactly what creation among men can never be). Even when the word was transferred to the creative works of the human race, it still had divine overtones: Murray quotes as an example Coleridge's self-image in *Kubla Khan*: "His flashing eyes, his floating hair! / . . . Close your eyes with holy dread,/For he on honey-dew hath fed, /And drunk the milk of Paradise."

The modern age supplies the other extreme. "Creation" in the world of the more vulgar hucksters comes equipped with the article "a". We are invited to admire and to lose no time in buying "a creation" from the design worlds of fashion, commercial bakeries, or automobile showrooms. Nor does it help very much that the word "create" has meanings: "give rise to," and "make a fuss" (*Oxford*), as in "he created a disturbance" or "why do you try to create that impression?"

In spite of these banalities of custom and language, the word still retains much of its intrinsic mystique for men and women. When Henry Murray goes on to argue of creativity that "many of us acknowledge that it is manifested in some way and to some extent by almost everybody", he is not debasing the currency of the creative process, but perhaps describing its special tragedy. The potentiality is there; the human individual knows that somehow in some measure it is there; he also knows that he has not fulfilled it. His reverence for the creative act, however he may disguise or conceal this feeling, comes from his deep sense that his uniqueness as a person is especially affirmed by it—perhaps even his immortality among men. The poem, the painting, the journal, the story, the discovery, the invention, the action which changes the life of another or the face of the world he knows—each reveals to him potentialities which others have realized in themselves, but not he (or she). None are so poignantly conscious of this as the young who think they have no future (for example many soldiers in wartime, or Keats, standing as it seemed at the gates of life and considering that he might never fulfil the promise of his "teeming pen"), and the old, who feel that they must simply live with a past beyond resurrection.

There is a working definition for the creative act with which many would agree: "bringing something new into the world"— but this raises a host of new questions. For example: "bringing" by what means? "new" in what sense? what or whose "world" are we talking about? The birth of a baby, an act which undeniably brings something, in this case someone, unique into the world is obviously not of the same order as the birth of Shelley's *Ode to the West Wind* or Scriabin's Piano Concerto in F Sharp Minor. Should "creativity" be reserved for the higher ranges of human performance, where the creators are, if not geniuses, at least brilliant and "exceptional" people performing in fields long ago made prestigious in human culture? Is creativity a power that declines, so that people are notably less creative in the later years? And need this be so?

In trying to answer these questions one can assemble an enormous array of facts seeming to bear upon the creative process from biology, psychology, philosophy, and the arts, as Koestler attempted to do in his *Act of Creation*. Or one can go to the creators themselves: who else should know more about creativity and its processes? This was the exciting stratagem of seekers like Brewster Ghiselin, Jacques Hadamard, Stanley Burnshaw, Stanley Rosner and Laurence Abt, as we will see later and as already briefly referred to in examples cited from Alexander Liberman.

Or one can go to wise students of the subject, scholars or practitioners whose interest in creativity as a process has been aroused in the course of their work and travels, and try to convene them in a symposium. This was the approach of Harold H. Anderson of

Michigan State University in organizing the Interdisciplinary Symposia on Creativity at that university from April, 1957 to July, 1958.

Having assembled the views of his fourteen well-known participants (some of them almost too well-known, e.g., Erich Fromm, Carl Rogers, Rollo May, Margaret Mead, and Abraham Maslow) in symposia extending over fifteen months, Anderson then attempted a summing-up: what then is creativity?

The result was something valuable but curious. The contributors scarcely referred to creativity as such, preferring to devote their attention to the "creative process," as though describing the care, feeding, and expected habits of the elephant would produce a description of the whole animal. When creativity was defined, it was the bringing to birth of something new (May); the capacity of creating useful or beautiful products (Hilgard: to which he added, however, finding ways of resolving perplexity); the urge to inquire, to invent, to perform (George Stoddard). Carl Rogers abandoned the word in favour of "creative process" and then decided that this was "the emergence in action of a novel relational product, growing out of the uniqueness of the individual on the one hand, and the materials, events, people, or circumstances of his life on the other."

Erich Fromm met the issue with the surprising answer: "creativity is the ability *to see* (or to be *aware*) and *to respond*." This then launched him upon an absorbing and typical discussion of the failure of the average person to *see* in the first place.

So involved did the symposia members become with the characteristics of creative people that no fewer than forty of these characteristics were culled from various papers in the summing-up. A partial list, omitting those which throw little or no light on creativity itself, has a certain stimulus: capacity to be puzzled; awareness; spontaneity; spontaneous flexibility; adaptive flexibility; divergent thinking; openness to new experience; disregard of boundaries; abandoning; letting go; being born every day; ability to toy with the elements; gust (that is, relish) for temporary chaos; tolerance of ambiguity.

The numerous insights of the commentators into what might be described as a circular progress into the heart of the mystery have a distinct value in themselves. For example, to Carl Rogers creativity is not restricted to some particular content, so that we are always rating one activity as nobler than another. The creative process at work does not differ, as he sees it, in such disparate activities as painting a picture, composing a symphony, developing new procedures in human relationships, or creating new formings of one's own personality, as in psychotherapy. In fact, it is the last of these to which Rogers attributes his own special interest in creativity. Watching the process of the individual person "remolding" himself in therapy, "with originality and effective skill," says Rogers, *"gives one confidence in the creative potential of all individuals."*

It is Rogers also who raises and rejects the notion that creative acts can be either "good" or "bad" except in a social and cultural reference. Thus the torturer who devises exquisite new tortures and the physician who creates new healings are both creative.

Must creativity deliver an observable product? It must, to Rogers; but here he differs with Erich Fromm, to whom the creative attitude in itself can be a creative act:

"To be creative means to consider the whole process of life as a process of birth, and not to take any stage of life as a final stage. Most people die before they are fully born. Creativeness means to be born before one dies."

And to Fromm's wonderful (and Ulyssean) statement one might add Dorothy Sayers' idea from her discussion of the nature of the Trinity: that one can be a poet without writing a poem—that is, without presenting Rogers' "observable product."

Rogers, however, fills in his conception of what creativity is by citing the conditions *within the individual* which are most closely associated with a potentially creative act:

a. openness to experience, which Rogers calls *extensionality*. "Instead of perceiving in predetermined categories (trees are green; college education is good; modern art is silly), the individual is aware of this existential moment as it is, thus being alive to many experiences which fall outside the usual categories (*this* tree is lavender; *this* college education is damaging; *this* modern sculpture has a powerful effect on me)."

b. an internal locus of evaluation. . . . Have I created something satisfying to *me*? Does it express a part of me—my feeling or my thought, my pain or my ecstasy? One is not oblivious to the judgements of others, but the basis of evaluation lies within oneself.

c. ability to toy with elements and concepts. To play spontaneously with ideas, colours, shapes, relationships—to juggle, to juxtapose, to shape wild hypotheses (here Rogers approaches the "brain-storming" of Osborne, or the "excursions" of Gordon's Synectics process), to express the ridiculous, to translate from one form to another. Hence arises the *hunch*, the creative seeing of life in a new and significant way.

"To bring something new into the world"—the phrase has an exciting ring to it, but it is intimidating too and may have inhibited innumerable adults from embarking on creative adventures. They also will have thought: 'What or whose world are we talking about? And how likely is it that we can possibly bring anything original into it?' "

Erich Fromm pierces the centre of the problem by citing what he calls "the experience of self," of "I", as one of the indispensable conditions of the creative attitude. For example, the automatic use of "I" which one learns from early childhood, the use which one hears thousands of times from adults and from one's own lips, "I think this", contributes to an illusion. Am I thinking this, or are these alleged I-thoughts actually those of everyone else except me: the media, other people, thoughts never thought through since placed in my mind in childhood?

To quote specifically from Fromm:

> "[This adult] is under the illusion that it is he who thinks of this, when actually it would be more correct if he said, 'It thinks in me.' He has about the same illusion a record player would have which, provided it could think, would say, "I am now playing a Mozart symphony," when we all know that we put the record on the record player and that it is only reproducing what is fed into it." Likewise with feeling: the man *says* at the cocktail party: I feel very happy—what he *feels* may only be what is put into him for the occasion."

Then Fromm reaches his destination:

> "The sense of *I*, or the sense of self, means that I experience myself as the true centre of my world, as the true originator of my acts. This is what it means to be original. *Not primarily to discover something new, but to experience in such a way that the experience originates in me.*" (My italics.)

And to his analysis of the glib speeches and attitudes which inhibit and destroy true creativity, Fromm adds his concern that we are losing "the ability to concentrate", another necessary condition as he sees it of the creative attitude. "It is rare in our Western culture; we do five things at the same time, and we do nothing." And what is nothing? Nothing, in the sense that *we* do it as a manifestation of our real powers, of which *we* are the masters. If one is truly concentrated, the very thing one is doing at this moment is the most important thing in life. . . . There is only the here and now."

Moreover, the real sense of self and the development of the ability to actually concentrate should be aided by another transforming agent in the quest of creativity: the ability to *accept* conflict and tension resulting from the polarity of opposite forces in one's life, rather than to avoid them.

"Conflicts are the source of wondering, of the development of strength, "Erich Fromm remarks, "of what one used to call 'character' . . . . I refer here to the conflict between the fact that at the same time that we are tied to the animal kingdom by our body, its needs, and its final destruction, we transcend the animal kingdom

and nature through our self-awareness, imagination, and creativeness."

How far is creativity a property of childhood which is usually
lost by adulthood? This point of view, much beloved by the more
sentimental critics of the formal school systems, is warmly
espoused by Judith Groch (*The Right to Create*, 1969), mildly ridiculed by E. L. Thorndike in his classic book on adult learning, and
supported with qualifications by Erich Fromm. Perhaps it is not so
much creativity that every one is talking about as the freshness of
vision which is seemingly one of the vestibules to the creative act.
   Thus Groch laments the effects of social upbringing upon the
child's creative impulses: "His vision is frozen. His heart has been
dismissed. The two-way elephants, dilapidated dinosaurs, and
rakish kings are gone, and the marvellous blue one-eyed people
appear no more—except in the works of a Picasso. What is it, we
wonder forlornly, that the adult has lost? He has lost the ability to
react to his own experiences. His world, seen through a glass
darkly, is two-dimensioned and flat, and he is too." Groch's point
is made again in the delightful modern song by Lipton and Yarrow
about Puff, the Magic Dragon: "A dragon lives forever/but not so
little boys./Dragon wings and painted swings/make way for other
toys."
   Thorndike supplies something of a corrective to all this by
noting the undoubted magic and excitement caused by the sight of
one's first cow, but asking after hundreds and even thousands of
cows, can the magic hold? It is a shrewd point, but to Erich Fromm
it is the wrong point:

> "It is striking to see the difference between this kind of adult
> behaviour [he has been referring to adult boredom with
> common events, often repeated] and the attitude of a two-
> year-old child toward a rolling ball. The child can throw this
> ball on the floor again and again and again, seeing it roll a
> hundred times, and never be bored. Why? If seeing a ball
> roll is merely a mental act confirming the knowledge that
> balls roll, one experience is enough. There is nothing new in
> the second and third and fiftieth experience. In other words,
> one gets bored in seeing it again and again; but for the child
> this is primarily not a mental experience but a delight in
> really *seeing* the ball rolling, a delight which many of us still
> feel when we watch a tennis game and see the ball bouncing
> back and forth."

And Fromm transfers his image: "If we are fully aware of a
tree at which we look—not at the fact that this is correctly called a

tree, but of *this* tree, in its full reality, in its suchness—and if we respond to the suchness of this tree with our whole person, then we have the kind of experience which is the premise for painting the tree." Normally in adulthood we see the tree, as it were, only with our brains, as part of the *genus* "tree". It is, Fromm concludes, "only the representative of an abstraction. In full awareness there is no abstraction; the tree retains its full concreteness, and that means also its uniqueness. There is only one tree in the world, and to this tree I relate myself, I see it, I respond to it. The tree becomes my own creation."

The architect, Alden Dow, quotes a friend who told him how as a boy he was setting out to take a trip across the United States. Before he left his father had some advice for him: "No matter what you see, look at it with this point of view in mind: I'll never see it again." Much the same attitude emerges from the remarkable letters exchanged between John Ruskin and his father when the youthful Ruskin was making his first tour of Italy, from which were later to come *The Stones of Venice* and other creative criticism.

The humanistic psychologist Abraham Maslow, who popularized the concept of "self-actualization", always made much of the contribution of the quality of childlikeness to creativity in the adult years. Maslow, like Rogers, sees what he calls "creativeness" emerging not only in the special talents of people in the arts and sciences, but in transformations within the individual personality. One of these transforming agents, if one can call it that, upon which Maslow dwells a great deal is the attribute of childlikeness. In his study of a group of "self-actualized" adults (1954), all of whom were in their 50s or 60s, Maslow was struck by their openness to experience—his word is "*non*rubricizing" (from rubric, the rigid direction for conduct of a divine service, printed in red!).

These childlike characteristics, however, were different in quality from those found in children. Maslow thus describes it: "If children are naive, then my subjects had attained a 'second naiveté', as Santayana called it. Their innocence of perception and expressiveness was combined with sophisticated minds."

Maslow also included in his analysis of this attribute of the creative person the possibility that it could be lost and regained: that, to suggest a familiar metaphor, one can go home again. Maslow's own phrase from his symposium paper is as follows: "Let us say that my subjects had either retained *or regained* at least two main aspects of childlikeness." (My italics). Exciting as the thought is, and important as one avenue to the Ulyssean life in late adulthood, it of course requires more evidence than Maslow's observation provides.

Among all the commentators on creativity, Maslow is the most articulate and insistent in maintaining that the creative moment and creative products are universal in every avenue of life. For example: developing a business enterprise could be a creative "activity", and a perfect tackle in football as aesthetic a product as a sonnet and could be approached in the same "creative spirit". As we have seen, Carl Rogers transferred the act of creation to such an arena as the reconstruction of one's own personality; and Harold Anderson, alone among the Western Michigan symposia panelists, insistently urged the role of the creative process in high moments of social interaction. The noted botanist Edmund Sinnott eloquently urged the claims of creativity for the whole of the life process; and to the architect Alden Dow, it is "a way of life."

Erich Fromm's testament, that "to *see* and to *respond*" is to be creative, opens great windows on limitless domains. Still, it is Maslow who hazards the peril of becoming lost in the bogs of banality and triviality which were recognized at the beginning of this chapter, by citing people, situations, and areas of action which seem light-years removed from the worlds of the writer, the scientist, and the artist.

Maslow had always in his earlier studies thought of creativeness in terms of products, and had confined it in his mind to the areas made famous by tradition. His "self-actualizing" people broke him of this attitude:

> ". . . these expectations were broken up by various persons among my subjects. For instance, one woman, uneducated, poor, a full-time housewife and mother, did none of these conventionally creative things and yet was a marvellous cook, mother, wife, and homemaker. With little money, her home was somehow always beautiful. She was a perfect hostess. Her meals were banquets. Her taste in linens, silver, glass, crockery, and furniture was impeccable. She was in all these areas original, novel, ingenious, unexpected, inventive. I just *had* to call her creative. I learned from her and others like her to think that a first-rate soup is more creative than a second-rate painting, and that generally, cooking or parenthood or making a home could be creative whereas poetry need not be; it could be uncreative.
>
> Another of my subjects devoted herself to what had best be called social service in the broadest sense, bandaging up wounds, helping the downtrodden, not only in a personal way but in an organizational way as well. One of her 'creations' is an organization which helps many more people than she could individually.
>
> Another was a psychiatrist, a 'pure' clinician who never wrote anything or created any theories or researches but who delighted in his everyday job of helping people to create themselves. This man approached each patient as if he were the only one in the world, without jargon, expectations, or

presuppositions, with innocence and naiveté and yet with great wisdom, in a Taoistic fashion. Each patient was a unique human being and therefore a completely new problem to be understood and solved in a completely novel way. His great success even with very difficult cases validated his 'creative' (rather than stereotyped or orthodox) way of doing things."

From his new conception of the meaning of creativity, Maslow felt compelled to distinguish between two types of creative people: those with "special talent creativeness" (the scientific discoverers, inventors, poets, novelists and other writers, painters, sculptors, great creators in statecraft, and so on), and those with "self-actualizing creativeness", which Maslow defined as showing itself much more in creative changes in the personality, and which as it were lived creatively: showing itself in a tendency to do *anything* creatively.

Maslow's conception of the nature and range of creativity is as far away as one can get from the mystical awe of which Henry Murray wrote, or the mysterious high process which fascinated Wordsworth, Shelley, and Coleridge in the nineteenth century, without descending into the junk which the twentieth-century world at times calls "creativity".

As a professional scholar, Maslow was not, of course, in the same tradition as the poet or the artist. And important though his contribution is to the debate on the nature of the creative phenomenon, one still has little choice but to turn also to the more celebrated practitioners in the arts and in scientific discovery to probe the meaning of the creative act as seen by a creative human being. Maslow's great other constituency of the self-actualized creators seldom seems to analyse its creativity, or else is seldom or never asked to do so.

Does it follow, however, that the great creators whom we turn to simply because we all know them are the soundest guides to the meaning of creativity? Some, who had nothing formal to say about the creative process, have at least contributed to the opinion that eminent artists and scientists are at any rate extremely eccentric people. Beethoven, who could appear almost a maniac when interrupted in the midst of composition, also caused astonishment and consternation in the countryside by singing loudly and gesticulating violently as he walked. Elizabeth Barrett Browning is widely supposed to have composed most of her work in a dimly-lit Italian bedroom; and Proust, all his work in a mausoleum-like Paris bedroom from which he shut out the light of day and never stirred. Balzac prodded inspiration by dressing in the robes of a monk;

Schiller by keeping a drawerful of rotten apples because that particular aroma increased his productivity; Liszt, who composed far into his late years, did so while conducting a strange bicameral life in which he spent his mornings as the devout *abbé* lost in prayer, and his evenings as the dazzling pianist in the salons of Rome.

C. G. Jung was convinced that creators in the arts usually paid a high price for their heaven-sent gifts. He condoned and explained the frequent moral aberrations of artists on the grounds that they could not afford to have what he called their "spark of life" extinguished. Poets to him were unusual and semi-divine creatures who had presentiments and perceptions of a strange spiritual and demonic world which lies on the misty boundaries of consciousness —the collective unconscious of man. Jung's views, although complimentary to creative artists, did little to lessen the sense of mystery and of the exotic which popular fancy still attributes to these particularly gifted human beings.

In fact, the few compilers who have had the imagination and the industry to assemble the views of celebrated creative people on creativity have not pierced the riddle, but they have turned up a remarkable consensus on one major item. Writers, artists, and musicians are overwhelmingly aware of a process taking place in the unconscious which seems to assemble and present whole ideas, configurations, and even complete works to the conscious, so-called rational mind of the creator. Brewster Ghiselin, himself a biographer and a poet, put together an anthology of these experiences as reported by celebrated creative people themselves in various papers, journals, or reported interviews.

Thus Mozart, whose fecundity as a composer remains one of the marvels of the world, was as much astonished by it as were any of his admirers. The music of his symphonies, concertos, and hundreds of other compositions poured in upon him while he was travelling, walking, or restlessly seeking sleep—to try to force inspiration only blocked or damaged it. The technical transference of this flood of creation to paper and instrument is, of course, another process; as is the inevitable editing which the rational intelligence performs.

Van Gogh, in a letter to a friend, described exactly how such a forcing of the creative process failed. He attempted a number of drawings of what was to be a famous painting: they all failed. Then a mysterious spring opened: the next drawings, unforced, appeared with the feeling which he wanted and which made them live. The modern French dramatist Jean Cocteau described how he was "sick and tired of writing"; he fell asleep, slept poorly, woke with a start, and as though in a trance saw played out before him three acts of the play *The Knights of the Round Table*, which he transcribed long afterwards. Cocteau describes this as "a visitation"; he talks

about "unknown forces" working deep within us, in ultimate collaboration with events in daily life.

The abortion of all but the first eighty or so lines of Coleridge's
marvellous fragment, *Kubla Khan*, as the result of an interruption
by "a person on business from Porlock" is almost too well known
to bear repetition. Coleridge talked with his innocent enemy for
over an hour, and when he went back to resume writing down his
vision found that it had dispersed. (Ghiselin wittily and charmingly
dedicates his anthology to "the man from Porlock".)

These were all cases where the precise words, musical themes,
stage actions and dialogue, and artistic drawings appeared before
the creative artist almost, to use Cocteau's phrase again, like visitations. A. E. Housman, whose youthful and poignant lyrics seemed
to belie his later deliberately assumed role of the conventional and
committee-bound Oxbridge don, remained nonetheless in himself
a sensitive and beautiful spirit. He described how two stanzas of
one of his best-known poems came into his head "just as they are
printed while I was crossing the corner of Hampstead Heath—a
third with a little coaxing after tea." The fourth he had to "turn
to and compose it myself, and that was a laborious business. I
wrote it thirteen times, and it was more than a twelve-month
before I got it right." Nietzsche reported in *Ecce Homo* that while
in Italy, walking near Genoa, all of his famous work *Thus Spake
Zarathustra* came to him: to use his words, "perhaps I should
rather say—*invaded me.*"

The American poet Amy Lowell had this experience so often
that she ultimately supported the bromide: poets are born, not
made. She joined the English poet Robert Graves, however, in the
view that whoever aspired to be a writing poet must "have knowledge and talent enough to 'putty up' his holes." Lowell cites Keats's
The Eve of St. Agnes as a notable case of a heavily puttied poem.

In this process of the delivery of whole thoughts, ideas, poems,
theories, almost whole books from the unconscious, is the creative
person listening as though to dictation? Or, what is the nature of
the experience?

Lowell herself speaks of hearing not a voice, but the words
pronounced, and pronounced without tone. "The words seem to be
pronounced in my head, but with nobody speaking them." Stephen
Spender, who also speaks of lines "flashing into my head", and
who was able to bring only six poems out of over a hundred pages
of writing through the cerebral process for many months, writes
that "sometimes, when I lie in a state of half-waking, half-sleeping,
I am conscious of a stream of words which seem to pass through
my mind without their having a meaning, but they have a sound,
a sound of passion, or a sound recalling poetry that I know." Einstein, replying to a circular letter sent out by Jacques Hademard

to distinguished mathematicians, inquiring about their involvement in the creative process, clearly had an experience similar to but much more remote from the articulateness of language of Lowell and Spender: "The words or the language, as they are written or spoken, do not seem to play any role in my mechanism of thought." Einstein speaks fruitfully of the "combinatory play" between psychical entities and relevant logical concepts. But, he goes on: "Conventional words or other signs have to be sought for laboriously *only in a secondary stage* [my italics], when the mentioned associative play is sufficiently established and can be reproduced at will."

Surely this powerful role of the unconscious and the preconscious in the creative process is one of the most fascinating aspects of creativity, and of man. The testimony comes from every creative sphere, and across a time span stretching from Wordsworth to the contemporary fashion designer Bonnie Cashin. "When your Daemon is in charge," wrote Kipling in *Something of Myself*, "do not try to think consciously. Drift, wait, and obey."

The modern novelist Isaac Bashevis Singer, replying as one of the twenty-four respondents in the remarkable series of interviews arranged by Stanley Rosner and Lawrence Abt, remarks: "You just cannot prepare to write a story. In some cases, you have a feeling as if some little imp or devil is standing behind you and dictating to you, but he gives it to you slowly, drop by drop. How our subsconscious works we never really know. No man can ever describe how an idea comes to him." The architect Ulrich Franzen describes how he builds big cardboard models, pulls them apart, puts them back, plays endlessly with the preconception; then, "things begin to emerge." And he adds laconically, "Somehow it's unconscious." Franzen notes the wonderful role of accidents: "I just wish I could design as if my pen had just been slipping all the time." For him, "my ideas just assert themselves, though they may not be fully thought out." The brain surgeon Wilder Penfield, a famous explorer of the physical brain, uses the expression, "the back of the mind". He also is fascinated by the unexpectedness of the appearance of creative ideas, the sudden breakthroughs. A fine example of the Ulyssean adult in the virtuosity of his late years, Penfield describes how, during the writing of his first novel, *No Other Gods*, "while operating . . . when things were quiet and I was closing up, these characters would come to the back of my mind and we'd talk and plan." And Bonnie Cashin says, "I'm constantly re-designing subconsciously."

Some of the theories of how the various states of the unconscious, the preconscious, and the conscious seem to operate and to interrelate in the process of creativeness are intensely interesting in themselves, and a brief discussion will be reserved for them. But an immediate practical question arises here from the stream of comments by creative people about the role of a kind of jinn, daemon, or creative spirit (or whatever) operating from the unconscious.

If the unconscious contributes so impressively to the creative process, can it possibly matter to whom or in whom these creative acts take place, and is not this the same as saying that every human being has some creative ability? Yes, it does matter, and no, it is not the same thing.

The word central to the individual person involved in these creative dramas is *preparation*: preparation of mood, of attack with one's resources upon a fascinating problem, and along with that, preparation of skills and competence to handle the "visitation" when it occurs. Thus, the tides of invention which constantly flooded Mozart with seemingly effortless music on travels and on walks and at meals were part of the process of a human being whose *whole* life was one of readiness and attunement to musical composition. Cocteau's three acts which he awoke to see played out before him as though in a trance followed a long period of writing which had made him "sick and tired". Housman's two stanzas leapt into a conscious mind already filled with the receptivity of a poet. One of the most familiar cases of the unannounced arrival, that of the mathematician Henri Poincaré, concerns the wholly casual way in which he solved two original and intricate theorems, or so to say, they solved themselves, ideas arising in clouds after he had drunk black coffee and lain restlessly awake. And again, when some time later he was putting his foot on the step of a bus, apparently out of nowhere an idea came to him which was a revelation. But in both cases, and in many other instances with Poincaré, the mysterious arrival came to a conscious mind already stretched to create, or exhausted or quiescent after days of striving.

Thus, whoever inhabits the strange country of creativity, two human types ordinarily do not: the hard-working no-nonsense individual who is going to force the locks of his numerous problems by sheer commonsense; and the dilettante or smatterer (defined by the *Concise Oxford Dictionary* as "one who toys with a subject or concentrates on nothing"). The creative process indeed calls for the toying with ideas, the rolling of them about in Einstein's "combinatory play", but this is another exercise. There is much to be said for dilettantism, but its only apparent role in promoting the creative act is in providing temporary relief for the already creative person: a change of mood from which may emerge almost fully born, it appears, original or transforming ideas which have their generative power and completion within the creative person.

Aside from their mental and emotional openness to the "visitations" delivered from the unconscious, the highly identified creative people are notable for two qualities: patience and tenacity. They may talk impatiently or suffer bouts of irritation arising from staleness and frustration, but in fact patience is one of their virtues. Poets may have to "putty up" the gaps in poems which first arrived in so many glorious fragments, but they will certainly do so if the quest means enough to them. It is typical of this category of creators that the bones of unfinished creations lie all over the place, but equally typical is their tenacity. Allen Tate added an exquisite refrain to one of his major poems nearly five years after writing the first draft; Hart Crane is said to have worked for months and years on a poem before the high moment when he could announce to his friends what seemed to be a sudden inspiration—and, in fact, was a creative integration not unlike Poincaré's mathematical configurations or divine summations. Ghiselin himself spent nearly a year on the composition of a poem of which some of the earliest lines, he remarks, "flew into my mind as casually and effortlessly as the shore birds of the coast fly across one's vision out of the light and foam mist." And Housman took his "twelve-month" to find the fourth stanza of his beloved poem.

The great breakthroughs in industrial and pure science and in medicine are made from ground prepared with incredible patience and tenacity. The appearance in the twentieth century of such transformers of society as the automobile and the typewriter was not a total celestial event like the rare appearances of the Virgin Mary, but an evolutionary process usually begun and intermittently advanced by the wonderful interventions of the creative unconscious. Gutenberg's patient tenacity in searching for the key to the riddle of a printing-press (he found it, unexpectedly, years later while watching some wine presses at work) is an example of the wedding of the almost cosmic illumination, which is brief, with the lifestyle of the creative adult in search of new shapes of truth and beauty—a process which is long.

To say that there is potentiality for creativity in every human being, including all adults in their later years, is obviously not to ignore the existence of an aristocracy of creative people. It is an aristocracy unique of its kind, since it has no barriers of race, class, age, sex, or even intellect—although as one writer on creativity remarks, brightness is no handicap.

Age is not a barrier to it. This is precisely the explanation of the phenomenon I have termed, "the Ulyssean adult". Such an individual teaches us that creativity, in Maslow's phrase, can be "retained and regained" regardless of age—although the governing verb, of course, is "can".

"Although I'm not at all sure creativity can be taught," says Bonnie Cashin, "at least a young mind can be stimulated by proper exposure, and perhaps some degree of creative excitement will find its own way out."

This is also the thesis of this book except—and the exception is of overwhelming importance—that the same fully applies to adults in their later years. Readers who agree with this, or wish that they could agree with it, or disagree with it, are invited to join in a brief examination of two concepts of the creative process which relate closely to the question of its availability to a constituency of adults.

The first concept is: that the mysterious process by which the unconscious seems to deliver creative visions and configurative solutions to the conscious mind is a general attribute—it is not something confined to a handful of creative geniuses.

The second concept is: that creative achievements, although very obviously distributed in a hierarchy of social and cultural significance, (so that it is manifestly absurd to equate a new recipe in the family kitchen with Goethe's *Faust* or the discovery of penicillin) nonetheless are authentically found in an enormous number of spheres of human activity. As such, they often transform the creator's *own world*, and the excitement which generates this transformation can be stimulated and can (not necessarily "will") find its own way out.

Whatever creativity is, it is not just productivity. A 68-year-old executive or a 78-year-old gardener may continue to be productive in doing the things which each has done for forty years, and of course late productivity is admirable. But unless they are not only responding to change but inaugurating it—testing out and developing new ideas and practices—what they are involved in is not the creative process. Even less so, of course, is the activity of those older adults who hold jobs and functions without producing very much—perhaps one could describe this style of life as "stayativity". This is the kind of career ultimately honoured with the conventional gold watch for "fifty years of faithful and loyal service".

If one stays at it long enough even "stayativity" is an achievement—but it is not creativity. To say, as Isaac Bashevis Singer says, that "All human beings are creative," to which he then adds, "We all have this creative desire to do something," is not the same as saying that human beings are productive, but that they are capable of engaging in performances which in however small a degree transform the world about them, or change the unique world of their own individuality.

It means that in addition to one's brain and hands, each human being has the potentiality of experiencing, whether many or few times in his or her life, the triple process which so fascinated the mathematician Jacques Hademard: *preparation, incubation,* and *illumination* in the performance of some creative act. This can be immensely visible to the world, or wholly hidden from the world but of transforming importance to one's own mind and soul.

Possibly adults lack confidence in their own creativity, or worse, suppose that they lose it as they enter the later decades of the life cycle, or that children have it and adults have not, because so little attention has been devoted to obtaining the reactions of non-celebrities to their creative experiences. The inquirers typically engage in a circular exercise which begins by identifying famous people from history or celebrated performers from our own times as creators and investigates how they experience the creative process. Then, drawing what conclusions they can, they re-apply or fortify their results by fresh applications to well-known creators. Of course it is a valuable exercise—but it is conducted, one could say, on a kind of mountainside or summit remote from the thronging plateaus and streets where hundreds of types of people in thousands of situations and vocations live out their lives.

Thus we learn a great deal about how the creative process takes place—at least in what Maslow termed "special talent creativeness" —and not much about how all this applies in so-called everyday existence. Yet when all is said and done, there is value in the exercise: it is a reasonable assumption that what operates success-fully in these highly visible performers operates also throughout the human species, although on a kind of creative rheostat from dim to full power.

Can this power be tested?

The American psychologist E. Paul Torrance thinks so. In 1966 he issued a Research Edition of the *Torrance Tests of Creative Thinking*, commenting that "knowledge and understanding about creative thinking are yet in a relatively underdeveloped state"— which is putting it mildly. Torrance of course had to come to terms himself with the question, "What is creativity?" and he developed the following definition:

"Creativity is a process of becoming sensitive to problems, deficiencies, gaps in knowledge, missing elements, disharmonies, and so on; identifying the difficulty; searching for solutions, mak-ing guesses, or formulating hypotheses and possibly modifying and retesting them; and finally communicating the results." Torrance contends that this definition describes "a natural human process." And he goes on: "Strong human needs are involved at each stage" —implying that life presents situations to us as problems, which call for resolution, setting up the kind of tension out of which creative solutions typically come.

To Torrance there are probably two kinds of imagination: reproductive, and productive or creative; as Torrance himself notes, this concept was developed by W. H. Burnham over eighty years ago out of Kant's *Critique of Pure Reason*.

For our purpose, it is sufficient to note at least two contributions which these tests, put together and evaluated with enormous care over ten or more years, seem to make to the discussion of creativity in adult life:

1. Torrance's tests, some of which are built from the work of earlier psychologists and adapted for the testing of "creative thinking", were given to people of an enormous range of occupations, from professional to unskilled, and of a wide variety of ages, underscoring the conception that creative potential does exist as a universal phenomenon among human beings.

2. The tests invite the person taking them to engage in what are in effect games of the imagination: for example, in the improvement of a given product or object (Torrance makes the point that for adults at all age levels it is an interesting task, permitting them to "regress in the service of the ego", playing with ideas they would not dare express in a more serious task); unusual uses of objects— a tin can, for example; "just suppose" activity; incomplete figures activities, and so on. The problem that will not let the testers rest is how to establish valid criteria for the results. Unlike the murderously definite, computer-graded marking of many psychological tests, the creativity tests are inevitably open-ended. What do you do with the aesthetic problem in drawing? Or, if you ask a college freshman, "What would be your most desired summer vacation?" and he replies, "Carrying rugs to Astrakhan"—is he a prankster, a poet, or just a bright boy? (This illustration is mine.)

Besides, an important weakness exists in using short tests to try to estimate creativity in individuals, as Myron A. Coler, director of the Creative Science Program at New York University pointed out in a 1966 paper:

> The problem [of testing creativity] has also been compounded by the necessity of spending a relatively short time in testing individuals. Creative people are often unimpressive in short tests *which do not allow adequate time for playing with the problem*. Such people are more apt to come up with extraordinary solutions given their own good time.

Nonetheless, investigators like Torrance help free one's mind of the error that there are creative and non-creative persons, rather than human beings each possessing what his fellow psychologist D. P. Ausubel calls "a generalized constellation of intellectual abilities, personality variables, and problem-solving traits"—abilities which may or may not carry the individual into and through creative activities, depending upon circumstances, motivation, interests, and the development of the productive imagination as a lifestyle. However, Ausubel denies that this constellation of general abilities can be said to be the "essence of creativity."

What *is* the essence of creativity? No one knows. But many of the readers of this book will feel that at different points of their life they have many times experienced the three reactions to human society, the world, and the cosmos which Arthur Koestler describes as the AHA reaction (after gestalt psychology), the HAHA reaction (after Dr. Brennig James), and the AH reaction—responses which illuminate the creative process at work in what Koestler calls the action of *bisociation*. In fact, in Koestler's own language, bisociation *is* "the essence of creativity."

For Koestler, "all creative activity is a kind of do-it-yourself therapy, an attempt to come to terms with traumatizing challenges." Life at certain points in their careers presents scientists and artists with certain problems which, one might say, overload the circuits, and force the human personality and organism to find new routes, devices, strategies, inventions. (Koestler is preoccupied, as almost all distinguished writers on creativity are, with the famous creators; but what he has to say about these practitioners of creative art is perfectly transferable to tens of thousands of other human adults living and working in a thousand different arenas.)

Part of the individual trauma in the face of challenge to customary ways of thought is that people often have a good deal of *un*learning to do before they can carry through the creative act which must be done if they are to solve the problem, create, or achieve some other breakthrough. This unlearning or repudiation of things learned long ago may be intensely difficult because of the rigidity and conventionality with which we all get locked into habits, patterns, and rubrics of thought. If this is so—and for Koestler it is typical of the truly creative challenge—then the individual who seeks the creative breakthrough will temporarily abandon the conscious world, including sometimes its preoccupation with words, which Koestler, unlike Peter Abelard, thinks are often the barriers to creative thought. (For Abelard, intellect created words, and words intellect.)

What the individual does is to retreat into the unconscious— not simply Freud's unconscious, which may be immobilizing in its emotional obsessiveness, but several levels of mental activity which Koestler insists are "cognitive systems in their own right": among them, the paranoid delusion, the dream, the daydream, and free association of ideas. For Koestler all these alternative forms of mental action, although each has its own set of rules, are less rigid, more tolerant, ready to "perceive hidden analogies between cabbages and kings. They are games of the underground, games that must have the disciplined rules of games, or the result will be waste and loss, not creativity."

"But under exceptional conditions, when disciplined thinking is at the end of its tether, a temporary indulgence in these underground games may suddenly produce a solution—some far-fetched, reckless combination of ideas, which would be beyond the reach of, or seem to be unacceptable to, the sober, rational mind."

Most of the time, according to this theory, adult people employ *associative* thinking—which is to say, the logic of ideas rationally following one another on a single plane. But the *bisociative* act involves living on several planes at once. It is close to Einstein's "combinatory play"; to Jacques Hadamard's "preparation, incubation, illumination"; to Jean Cocteau's "visitation"; or to Poincaré's experience, as described earlier.

Koestler's whole proposition is summed up in his use of the phrase, *"reculer pour mieux sauter"*: the temporary regression followed by a forward leap.

Commentators on creativity as diverse in interests as the poet Robert Frost and the neurosurgeon Wilder Penfield have commented upon the special moment when, as Frost suggests, the box clicks shut, or, as Penfield observes, some missing piece suddenly fits in, resolving the whole puzzle. Koestler's expression is "the flash of illumination", when, he asserts, the bits of the puzzle suddenly click into place. Only God, he suggests, created something out of nothing. For human beings, the process of creation is a cross-fertilization of ideas, percepts, concepts, and items of information within the brain of the individual seeking to achieve the creative act.

This is *bisociation*, and one of its remarkable fruits is the marvellous moment when the inventor, the researcher, the poet, the mathematician, the planner is electrified by the sudden knowledge that *this* is the missing piece. This is the moment of the AHA experience, as the gestalt psychologists call it.

But then Koestler adds the HAHA reaction, a term which he attributes to his friend Dr. Brennig James. The sudden explosive laughter which greets a truly comic episode or story is testimony to another turn of the bisociative faculty in creativity. The incongruous, the intersection of two normally separate processes or situations produces the same kind of openness to the bizarre, to the unconventional, which is the milieu of creativity. Koestler makes the point about the HAHA reaction by the following story about an eighteenth-century marquis finding his wife in the arms of a bishop.

After a moment's hesitation, the Marquis walked calmly to the window of the boudoir, leaned out and began going through the motions of blessing the people in the street.
"What are you doing?" cried the anguished wife.

"Monseigneur is performing my functions," replied the nobleman, "so I am performing his."

And Koestler insists that in humour the story builds a creative tension which is not completed or resolved as in the AHA situation, but is rather exploded by the laughter, since the tension in any case is denied by reason.

"All original comic invention," Koestler remarks, "is a creative act, a malicious discovery." Koestler's process is also seen at work in the following two stories which might be considered further examples of the HAHA potential. One is the famous and venerable North American story which from its first line shows the intersection of opposites to create absurdity: "A gorilla walked into a bar and ordered a drink." (This first line is almost a creative comic experience in itself.) "He noticed the bartender staring at him, and remarked crossly, 'Well, what are you staring at?' 'Well,' said the bartender, timidly, 'we don't often see a gorilla in this bar.' 'I would think not,' snorted the gorilla, 'at $2.00 for a whisky sour.' "

The other is the Myron Cohen story about two Jewish gentlemen at a newstand. One says to the other, "Why have you got your hand in my pocket?" Says the other: "I'm looking for a match." The first: "Why didn't you ask?" The second: "I don't talk to strangers."

This dialogue displays all the creative counterplay of opposites. It opens with a ludicrous situation produced by the multiple intersection of folk mores, mellow tolerance, conventionality; carries its tension on through its short life, each line heightening the bisociative and hence creative tension; and finally explodes the tension, although not really resolving the situation, with an hilarious misapplication. Thus emerges the HAHA reaction, probably experienced far more frequently than the AHA reaction by most adults, although regrettably not often analysed with the joyous originality with which Koestler probes it.

Equally common is the third of Koestler's trio: the AH reaction. For Koestler this is the moment of *self-transcendence*, a form of the creative process. The bisociative process here is one in which the tendencies of the human individual to fulfil himself are transferred beyond the personal self, and beyond society, to another plane—the plane of God, nature, or art—to some extrapersonal being or force. Koestler usefully borrows from Freud and Piaget to make his point. Freud's expression was the "oceanic" feeling (a concept which Maslow also borrows, as will be seen), and Koestler compares the experience to being "in an empty cathedral when eternity is looking through the window of time, and in which the self seems to dissolve like a grain of salt in water." This is the AH reaction.

Koestler employs Piaget's well-known theory of "symbiotic consciousness" in children to consolidate his point. From the very earliest years, when self and universe are symbiotically fused, the human child gradually grows into the experience of objective reality. The former interfusion does not entirely disappear, however. From it comes the "symbiotic communion", which is the source of the "oceanic" feeling and from time to time in certain situations the AH reaction.

For Koestler this source feeds both artist and scientist and is best exemplified by the actor who presents us with two worlds at once, which we observe simultaneously in the theatre. This is bisociation at its height. Furthermore, the AHA, the HAHA, and the AH reactions are all fed from the same springs and sources.

This theory, in spite of its inevitable inconclusiveness, bears the ring of truth. But there are some footnotes that one wants to add at once. A comment about the unconscious from the noted investigator of psychic phenomena F. W. H. Myers is worth keeping in mind: "It is a rubbish-heap as well as a treasure house." Human creativity owes immense and continuing debts to what Henry James called in his famous preface to *The Spoils of Poynton*, "the deep well of unconscious cerebration"; but in addition, one cannot discount the role of the intellect and the disciplined art, craft, or lifestyle.

Some of the most remarkable people in the Rosner and Abt interviews never appear "on stage" at all, but like so many millions of human beings remain in the wings. These off-stage people turn up almost incidentally in the interviews—a mother, a father, an editor, a psychoanalyst's patient, a group of cowboys gathered together on a ranch: the list could be considerably extended. Bonnie Cashin's vivid creativity emerges even in the charm and unself-conscious love of life of her interview, but filling in her analysis of herself as a creative person are her references to her mother: "a really great dressmaker . . . she could do anything with her hands and much of this rubbed off on me. I remember her building a brick wall beautifully. I remember her upholstering a wild pink-striped chair, and most vividly I remember her miracle hands in a garden. I grew up with living colour. . . . She was the one who cleared the way for me to grow creatively."

Cashin remarks that her practical-minded father urged her to take up typing! And yet:

> "My father with whom I did not feel at ease was a brilliant and erratic man. . . . He had a very inventive mind, always concocting something or other, often to the family's sad

fortune. I remember, when I was a small child, that he drew
a lot. I remember a large charcoal drawing of Christ that held
me in wide-eyed awe. I wish it hadn't been lost. He also had
a photographic studio. He loved the mechanics of cars . . ."

Wilder Penfield's mother

"had an excellent mind. It was she who started me off on my
writing my first novel. In 1935, I went out to see Mother for
the last time. She'd been trying to write a novel for fifteen
years, and as she grew older, her plot got more and more
confused, and so, on this trip, I suggested, 'Let me take your
manuscript, and maybe I can make something out of it.'
She was so distressed because she couldn't get on with it.
She was the kind of woman who, having set herself this
problem, would not give it up, you see. I thought it would
relieve her if I promised to look it over. I returned here with
all her manuscripts and her books, and then word came that
she had died. And I couldn't use her manuscript. It was quite
impossible to do anything with it. It was the story of Sarah
and Abraham . . ."

Penfield put the manuscript away, and *eight years later* in
Teheran picked up Leonard Woolley's *Excavations at Ur*. Ur was
Abraham's birthplace—and for Penfield the bisociative mechanism
clicked into place: his promise to his mother, his keeping of the
thought of her book in the back of his mind, his unanticipated
presence in the Middle East. The result was Penfield's fine novel,
No Other Gods.

Readers of Agnes de Mille's autobiography, *Dance to the Piper*,
will recall the beautiful off-stage presence of de Mille's mother, a
warm creative woman whose devotion to her daughter's long-
frustrated dream of becoming a star in the ballet world is one of
the many pleasures of reading the book. Ulrich Franzen's mother
made "quite lovely little watercolours". However, it is his brief
vignette of his father that has a special interest: "My father was
an essayist. I think he had a lot of potential but he never fully
realized it. I think he was probably quite a frustrated man in many
ways. But I think he was a very bright person."

The molecular chemist Paul Saltman, whose interview might
perhaps be described as tough in tone—but not unfeeling—refers
rather movingly to his immigrant father who brought up his family
in the strict expectation that they were to excel. "My father was
really a nut about education, and he was largely self-educated."
Saltman speaks of his own fierce, unrelenting ambition to achieve:
"This had to do with my father. My old man said that he wanted to
learn how to ride horses. His knowledge of horses was that of the
Cossacks coming through the Russian village. And yet when he got
enough money so that he could afford horses, he went out and he

bought a five-gaited horse and a jumper and he used to ride the five-gaited horse in shows, and I had to learn to ride the hunter like it or not. . . . He could go in and use any machine in his factory as well as any of his mechanics. He was not a furniture maker and previously had sold shoes, but that was the way he did things. In a sense I'm sure that I was affected by those attitudes."

The open-mindedness and curiosity which contribute largely to the creative process are no respecters of class barriers. The anthropologist Froelich G. Rainey reports:

"In front of psychologists, I don't know if I should say this, but you know, I was really brought up by a bunch of cowboys in a bunkhouse. . . . You'd be surprised at the discussions that go on in a bunkhouse. You wouldn't call it intellectual, but they're certainly curious. They're interested in what the world's all about and why things happen, what this all means, and so on. There are long sessions among these rather uneducated boys who are herding cows. They have a lot of time to think. No question about it. I suppose that's the way it is with rather isolated people who are spending a lot of time with themselves. They may develop more curiosity about the world around them than somebody who's deeply involved in urban civilization, and who is going at a high pace all the time, and who is distracted by other things, whereas these boys are not. Not educated, but intellectually curious. Intelligent, a lot of them. It could be. I couldn't put my finger on it, but it certainly may have been" [Rainey means that the young bunkhouse men might have stimulated his own intellectual curiosity].

Rainey's remarks find an echo in the traditional cowboy lyric, "Home on the Range":

How often at night, when the heavens are bright
With the light of a million stars,
Have I stood there amazed, and asked as I gazed
If their beauty exceeds that of ours.

None of the experiences which creative people cite as typical of the creative process is alien to the general potentiality of human beings, although there is a marked variation in intensity of such occurrences. Among many men and women they are commonplace.

The AH and the HAHA reactions are familiar experiences in human life. The AHA reaction is surely rarer, but even here it may be of interest to readers of this book to test frequent episodes in their own life against still further reports from the articulate creators. Through our dreams and daydreams we have intimations of that mysterious process which Jung called "a strange something that derives its existence from the hinterland of man's mind." Ideas arrive aberrationally: the linguist Noah Chomsky speaks of the "sudden appearance of possibly interesting ideas at some odd moment", for example, while reading. Bonnie Cashin refers to ideas that sometimes "tumble upon each other". Like Chomsky, ideas of potential creativity come to her while reading that are wholly irrelevant to what she is reading.

The mathematician Morris Kline, finding himself locked into a problem that seems intractable, leaves it, and comes back later. Paul Saltman, in a similar situation, "walks away" from unyielding data, tucks them away, and comes back to find fresh insights at work. The psychologist David Krech comes by accident across a paper in a journal that normally he never picks up—and it sets in motion a fresh and sometimes productive train of thought. D. H. Lawrence had seen camellias hundreds of times, but once saw a cluster of them "like a vision", and could paint them. Like the Canadian painter Arthur Lismer, Lawrence had been given models to draw and paint at school without experiencing the slightest inspiration. The same haphazard poetry of the unconscious at work of course affects responses to music and its creative process. Hundreds of readers will have had my own experience of buying a long-playing record for the stereo after having heard it once and being enchanted; finding that Lawrence's "vision" had unaccountably ceased to operate; neglecting the record; and then almost with a shrug picking it up one more time on a certain winter evening, to find that all the enchantment had returned. The sculptor Henry Moore speaks of "universal shapes to which everybody is subconsciously conditioned and to which they can respond if their conscious control does not shut them off."

Arthur Koestler describes how a sudden idea, which he insists is not daydreaming or dreaming but an idea in process in the preconscious breaking through, comes to him while he is in a shower; Wilder Penfield talks of how at a movie, or in a hot bath, or while reading aloud with his wife, interesting anomalous ideas arrive. A friend of mine, a teacher and a poet, was showering at his health club after badminton and swimming, when a poem came to him so compellingly that he hurriedly left the shower, wrapped himself in a towel, took a pen, and sat down on the bare bench of the athletic club to write the first stanzas of what turned out to be an exquisite love poem. He had to finish the rest of it later "by himself"! Is such an experience unique? The psychoanalyst Morton Prince recounted years ago how a woman unknown to the world of letters wrote a poem automatically under hypnosis which, although not great poetry, was acceptable.

The novelist Dorothy Canfield, describing how a new story seems to be born, writes of "a generally intensified emotional sensibility, such as every human being experiences with more or less frequency."

So fascinated was Jacques Hadamard with the mysterious process contributing to what he called "preparation, incubation, and illumination", that he raised—without really answering it—the question of whether imagery can be educated. Hadamard was impressed with the experiments in this sphere by the psychologist James L. Titchener, who especially feared the rigidifying effects of language in confining the powers of creative thinking. Titchener attempted to develop the faculty of substituting visual and auditory images for the verbal material which he read and which he felt became too inhibiting to imaginative thought. Whether this can be done or not by deliberate acts of volition, Einstein's creative process was in non-verbal images, as already mentioned, and Spender's creativity also escaped the deep freeze of over-articulated first thoughts.

Bonnie Cashin, as has been seen, suggests that creativity can be stimulated; Ross Parmenter, that any one can contribute to self-creativity by training the eye to see imaginatively; and E. Paul Torrance, that creativity is a component of human life which can be identified and measured, and in time perhaps predicted.

For me, creativity is the process by which an individual introduces his original ideas, products, or performances into the environment around him or into the environment of the inner self so that a degree of transformation, large or small, takes place in these environments.

What brings the whole discussion into the glorious sphere of the Ulyssean adult is the emphasis which seems to come from every sector of the creative world on openness of mind as the nurturing ground of creative thought and acts, on flexibility, on opening or relaxing one's emotional and spiritual being (entirely different from slackness), and on a deliberate surrendering to or immersion in forms of the oceanic feeling. This argument, with a more extended discussion of how to improve one's potentiality for the more creative, in this context, Ulyssean life is developed later in this book.

The astonishing omission in all the discussions of whether older adults can live valuable creative lives is the absence of any reference to the powerful role of the unconscious in the later years of adulthood. You will find much attention devoted to the question of whether mental powers do or do not decline, to the issue of physical debility (and its delay), to the influences upon older adults of social, economic, and family conditions. When an individual reaches the period of the mid-fifties and later, and reflects upon his status as a member of a throwaway society, he is likely to add up for better or for worse his resources in mental powers (declining, he usually thinks), physical capacity (declining), friendship circle (typically declining), income (declining), and seeming influence in worlds as diverse as politics, business, and the family—usually declining. Others may also estimate his potentiality in productive and creative resources in the same crude terms, and when someone mentions the value of "experience", this is often typically shrugged off as out-of-date, contributing to rigidity, or irrelevant—although twenty years earlier he could not have got a job without it. A process of social brainwashing goes on, so that great numbers of older adults have been conditioned to believe in the poverty and continuous depletion of their resources.

No one seems to recall that in terms of creativity, which is almost a synonym for the life-giving spirit, the older adult is more than just a brain, a physical body, an economic or social unit (or cipher?), or even perhaps a soul, in the religious sense. He also carries with him (or her) that remarkable hidden self, the unconscious, about which we know little except that it contributes heavily to the creative process. Of course, it must vary in the degree of its mysterious beauty and richness from one human adult to another, but so far from being crippled or corroded by time, it is possible that for many people late life is exactly the period when this marvellous resource bank of creativity is best equipped. At least, the Ulyssean adults conduct their lives as though this was so.

However, it is a fact that the Ulysseans have often prepared for creative late years by living self-actualized lives; and that they have usually achieved the extent of understanding of self-identity which Erikson suggests is one of the ways of avoiding ultimate "disgust and despair".

It will be suggested later that it is always possible to begin on some terms to enter the Ulyssean world, however late. But the Ulyssean attitudes are typically the product of the life drama, and the Ulyssean of the later years is typically the product of the earlier —even when this process is long hidden from the outer world.

3. SELF IDENTITY, CREATIVITY, AND THE ADULT LIFE DRAMA

"We brought nothing into this world, and it is certain we can carry nothing out"—so says the Book of Common Prayer, quoting from Paul in one of those enormous half-truths that have done so much to promote and destroy the Christian faith. In fact, we bring a great deal into this world: our genetic equipment, which is crucial, the famous "nature" of the nature-and-nurture duality out of which our lives are fashioned (the mysterious "I" completes the trinity); and our shares in the folk unconscious, from which Jung evolved most of his concepts of creativity.

And we do carry something out of the world; certainly not material possessions which, when the chips are down, matter least, but our personal "self", the great work of art upon which we have been engaged all the years of our life.

Sooner or later in the adult life cycle—one school of observers arbitrarily places the beginning in the age period 50-plus—men and women become critical assessors of the validity and relevance of their lives. At first glance such a proposition seems absurd: are not many people all their lives self-critical, almost morbidly so? Yes, but the difficult and beautiful country of middle age throws an especially probing, poignant light upon our perspectives of ourselves. Disguise it as we will—we are "no longer young", we are in "our prime", then our "later prime"—use what euphemisms we will, the first cool winds of the evening that is at hand begin to blow, even although the summer sun is still burning vividly in the afternoon sky.

The fact that we have in the late twentieth century what Anne Simon calls "the new years," a "new" middle age—a period of potential life-productivity denied to most people in previous generations—does not alter the centrality and poignancy of middle-life self-assessment for great numbers of adults. It is part of the human condition.

Anne Simon's new middle age is a kind of superb central span connecting two lesser spans, young adulthood and aged adulthood, in the great arch of the human life journey. The people of this central span are not only heavily engaged in many productive activities of their own, but usually assume the burdens of those on the earlier span, and try to grapple with the problems created by the sorrows and debilities of the later. Simon's book, *The New Years*, has a happy ending:

> "For the first time in history and for the first time in his life, the man of middle age can comprehend the great sweep of the life span as it now stands revealed. He can order his life to suit the new facts about getting older which it has brought to light, seize its options, pioneer. . . . The pioneer can afford to be independent, to search out ways to be contemporary with his times on his own terms. Independence is his passport to loving, to being loved, to being useful and needed. It is his extraordinary option."

The governing word throughout is "can": the real euphoria is for the future. Simon's book is splendid because of its belief in the potentiality of adult human beings; she labels the twentieth century "this savage century," and she sees the *present* multitudes of middle-agers in North America as being victims in many ways of a universal cult of youth: "all are drawn into the whirlpool with youth at its spiralling core." In short, the adult in his middle years becomes the secret watcher of the implacable clock of the life drama which measures and demythologizes his younger dreams, and carries him onward to the dark outlands of a youth-dominated society.

In an article in *Time* in July, 1966, almost simultaneous with *The New Years*, the happy ending is at the beginning. America, we are told, has a ruling class, a "command generation": one-fifth of the whole population of the United States or nearly 43 million people between the ages of 40 and 60: the middle-aged Americans. The first half of the article glitters with dozens of names of middle-aged celebrities; the actress, Lauren Bacall, then 41, adorns the cover of *Time*, and supplies the glamorous central theme of the discussion. A compelling case is made for the undoubted power and glory of the middle years, and for the colourful and fascinating maturity which separates adult men and women from adolescents and early adults. As happens once in a while with national magazines, and as was to happen again with *Time* in another presentation on a major life-cycle problem (*The Old in the Country of the Young*), the pulse of society is taken authentically on a critical issue.

This euphoric presentation of middle age in our era may have contributed a new zest and confidence to many North Americans passing through the period which one British psychologist describes as that of "menopausal man."

Yet the article gives almost as much attention to the panic and melancholy which descend on great numbers of middle-agers—victims of what T. S. Eliot called the "hoo-ha's" that invade them when they are alone in the middle of the night, in the middle of the bed. It is Eric Berne's "balance sheet" time, a period of agonizing reappraisal, and not only for the individual. Many marriages which were once flooded with youthful passion, or which were anchored in family cares and joys, suddenly seem drab and empty; it is the age of the second affair; the peak period of alcoholism, of pre-geriatrical drugs, of escalating cardiovascular attacks, often the result of being strait-jacketed by fate.

This conception of the middle-age crisis crosses cultural frontiers in the Western world. Thus, Dr. Martin Herbert, writing in 1972 about middle-aged men in Great Britain, describes the purposeless-ness and greyness of much of the period through which many mid-dle-agers pass during their so-called "prime" years. Some feel suffo-cated, like one man who felt his life comparable to that of a dying fish lunging about at the bottom of his rowboat; his possessions and commitments had stifled him—the *real* him. Others feel that they have become old fogies prematurely. Others, still, that life somehow has passed them by. "For a large part of life, we are looking ahead, looking forward to various new experiences, fresh and exciting goals. And then, one day, the individual realizes that he has com-pleted most of his tasks . . . there is nothing really new to look forward to, no particularly exciting goal to attain."

The malaise of middle-age is a favourite topic of the literatures of Western society. The critic Frederick Losey identifies the fas-cination of *Antony and Cleopatra*, a drama of Shakespeare's mature years, with the theme of "the tragedy of middle life": "Idealism and inexperience will ever protect youth from a similar tragedy, and age is exempted by coldness of blood; but middle life, with the dimming of its idealism, its awakening sense of the worthlessness of earthly honour, and its consciousness of abundant physical powers, will always be peculiarly susceptible to mistaking a new and strong sexual appeal for the 'nobility of life.' " A different aspect of passion is portrayed in Thomas Mann's *Death in Venice*: the novelist, Gustave Aschenbach, in late middle age enmeshes himself in a strange silent infatuation for a handsome boy, and forsakes the dignity and discipline of thirty years to assume the dyes and other tricks for disguising age.

Simone de Beauvoir was barely 60 when she wrote her massive study *La Vieillesse* for which she herself hardly qualified as a subject. Besides, since her youth she had had a brilliant, productive life. Still, she writes with melancholy of the "vast miscomprehen-sion" that exists between what people conceive a successful man to be and what he experiences himself to be. And she refers to an earlier judgment of hers in *La Force des Choses*, with which she still concurs: "The promises of my youth have been kept—nevertheless, I have been swindled." In Arthur Miller's play, *Death of a Salesman*, on the other hand, the promises have not been kept, and the sense of time running out on a life unable to identify with its dreams produces a tragedy of middle age of epic and unbearable poignancy.

In the film, *Sunday Bloody Sunday*, Peter Finch plays the role of a middle-aged physician, an admirable doctor and human being, himself engaged in a dual love affair with a girl and a youth that he is unable to resolve. At the same time, he sees among his patients an executive in his 50s who has developed into a hypochondriac, and who can no longer compete with the youth cult which has at last penetrated his sphere of business. In fact, the executive explains bitterly to the young personnel officer who is going to try to get him a job: "They gave me the golden handshake." And he adds, "How can I tell my wife?"

These situations are the stuff of excellent drama, but the middle-age malaise for most men and women is closer to the experience of Herman Hesse's character, Harry Haller, in *Steppenwolf* and Louis Bromfield's *Mr. Smith*.

Haller in middle age lives on a plateau of mediocre and toneless existence: the lukewarm days of discontented middle life pass, unchallenged, purposeless, unswept by great devotions or emotions, beyond dreams. There is safety in this "normal and sterile" life, and a kind of contentment, but "it is just this contentment that I cannot endure. After a short time it fills me with irrepressible loathing and nausea. Then, in desperation, I have to escape into other regions, if possible on the road to pleasure, or if that cannot be, on the road to pain."

The same was true of Haller's contemporary in North America, in Bromfield's novel, written when Bromfield himself was in middle age. Mr. Smith is a successful middle-aged American executive, a charming man who finds that he is drowning in business and social roles, commitments, committees, engagements, obligations to his wife and his wife's friends—he has lost his *self*. His wife is obsessed with "togetherness," a favourite cliché of the 1950s, and delights in the thought that she and her husband are always together. If Smith goes to the bottom of the garden to read a book by himself, she comes flying down to be with him so that they will be "together." He is a man of peace who has no peace. Among his business circle is an older executive in his early 60s whose special form of the malaise is to indulge in a bacchanal once a year when away from home at a convention—a fact well-known to and lovingly accepted by his wife, who actually understands his needs. When, however, he dies in the excess of emotion of one of these escapades, and when Smith's wife refers caustically to "that dirty old man," this is the breaking point for Smith, who deeply respected his associate. Smith seeks escape to one of the war fronts of the Far East, and achieves freedom—and death.

Mr. Smith may have felt himself drowning in his business and social roles and obligations, but this was a later phenomenon of middle age. One can be sure that at an earlier period, during perhaps the vigorous decade of his 30s, when he built up this array of roles and activities, he was content to assume that *they* were *himself*. In modern North American society as well as many other Western cultures where failure in vocational achievement and material ownership is the unforgivable sin, in an unremitting war from which there is no discharge, men and women of the middle and later years condition themselves to believe that their personal self can be identified by the labels, titles, functions, and participations which present them to others in various social and business roles. Consider, for example, the aged academic who still permits his seventeen honorary degrees to be printed with the attributed universities. Likewise, how far is the *Who's Who* account a version of the real person?

In addition, there can be so extreme a misidentification of self with a vocational or social role that one can literally die within a few weeks or months after the severance of one's job or of the death of a spouse. However, all this does not mean that one should assume that there is some kind of pure and idealistic "I" wholly divorceable from the self's many different social roles. We are—to return to Chapter One and Tennyson—"a part of all that we have met," and usually we are the richer for it.

Human adults in early and later middle age are likely to experience a malaise which for many will intensify as they move into the late years of the life drama, but it is important to note, as many negative commentators on the scene do not, that maturity usually brings its own repertoire of compensating skills and resources. Bernice Neugarten writes about what she calls "the executive processes of personality in middle age: self-awareness, selectivity, manipulation and control of the environment, mastery, competence, the wide array of cognitive strategies." This is good academese, and translated it still makes sense. As one British authority of motivation notes, people in middle and late adulthood usually have some conception of how to cope with failure and frustration: after all, they have met these conditions many times. Mostly, adults in the age range 40–60 have learned such simple strategies as when to postpone decisions; how to be patient and wait out a personal dispute; and how to relate things seen and read to the experience of one's life—like the man of 50 who understands *Antony and Cleopatra* with a depth his adolescent children cannot.

Life for many adult men and women in the age periods after 50 is undoubtedly filled with good harvests and serene pleasures, justified feelings of pride, continuing and deepened connubial and filial love, and cherished friendships—all of this in addition to varying degrees of participation in the so-called "command generation." It is a fact that most writing in praise of the pleasures of the middle and later years is based upon the affluent middle or upper class groups of North America. When Neugarten speaks, in *Middle Age and Aging*, of "the executive processes of personality in middle age" her adjective "executive" is almost transposed. She sought her data for this particular study from a special constituency of college graduates and *Who's Who* individuals. The pleasures of middle and later life are not usually inhibited by money, prestige, and power.

Still, anyone who has seen enough of life to have met many older adults of limited or little means from small towns, farming areas, and working-class areas in great cities can testify that many of them have acquired across the years mature resources with which to confront the almost inalienable stresses of middle and later adulthood: courage, wisdom, and love deepened by time, and ways and means to handle the recurrent threats and challenges of on-going life.

It is certainly true, as Charlotte Buhler, the psychologist of the life-cycle maintains, that there is a large group of adults in late maturity who feel that they have successfully completed their life's work and are content to rest and relax. Some may have set their own life-goals, and felt—or at least declared—that they had met them; some may have accepted goals directed by others, and have acquiesced also in their termination and the approval of this action by others. Amongst these seemingly contented finishers are the people who declaim somewhere in full course that "I have found my niche"—a chilling phrase to the Ulysseans within earshot.

It is significant that Buhler and others, from their many studies of middle and late adulthood, find that there are at least three other major categories of people reacting to their life performances: those who feel that there is no point at which one sits back, but that one continues seeking and creating to the end of physical life (these, of course, are what this book calls the Ulysseans); those who are dissatisfied with their life's work, but for a variety of reasons feel they must resign themselves to the situation; and those who have conspicuously misused their lives, and are now tortured by what Erikson calls, "disgust and despair."

Verification of this comes from what is coming to be the ample investigation and report from a critical field of adult human opinion: the retrospective views of the dying. Here the attitudes vary according to the role and place one occupies in the life journey: from the extreme anguish of a young adult struck down unexpectedly by some illness or mortal accident to the calm memories of some very old woman whose only apparent regret is that she must leave the children, grandchildren, and great-grandchildren who have been the fruit of her life. But there is a characteristic that runs like a threnody through the closing weeks and months of life of many middle and later adults whose lives here are ending: it is a note of not so much despair as of poignant regret, and regret not just for leaving "the beautiful and terrible world", but for unfinished business, for the personal might-have-been, for promise and self-promise still unfulfilled.

The motor of our lives is the self-image, and it is the self-image which essentially differentiates the Ulyssean adult from those adults who, at the opposite extreme, are immobilized by disgust and despair.

In the wonderful phrase, "Yes, I can", which Sammy Davis Jr. uses as the title of his autobiography, is contained a response to life which is not just a jolly-jump-up attempt to meet its often formidable problems with a momentary show of spurious self-confidence, but rather grows out of a self-concept which unbinds and liberates the self that must do business with the world, and generates creativity. The reverse is perhaps summarized in the short and moving memoir of an anonymous British writer describing the deluge of misfortunes which he feels he cannot handle: *The Answer to Life is No*. Indeed, for some adult people the answer to life may indeed be No: we are not engaged here in making judgments about the morality or validity of the choices people make in their response to life—nor are we capable of doing so—but, both in the memoir and in living, the role of the self-image in arriving at these Yes, I Can's and No's is clearly a powerful one. Consider the symbolic suicide of a young man who shot himself on top of a garbage dump. The deed described and underlined the self-concept.

Of all the two million or more species moving upon the earth, according to philosophical geneticists, man is unique in possessing the self-awareness wherein, as Martin Herbert remarks, the individual becomes an object to himself. Since we cannot tell with certainty what occurs in the mind of the ibis, the panther, the dog, the lark, or the octopus, such a claim might simply seem human arrogance, except that in the case of man we are dealing with a being more than animal. Soaked in crimes and stupidity though he undoubtedly is, as Stephen Spender says, man is still the "beautiful creature" with his extraordinary brain, hands, and language systems. These, and the domains of thought and creativity which they make possible, give the human species an unmatched magnitude of self-awareness: a Promethean gift which carries its own torments with it.

Popular speech uses the word "self" millions of times daily without defining it, in compounds which are like signs pointing the way but never really going there: "self-inflicted", "self-satisfied", "self-imposed", "self-organized", "self-centred", "self-pitying", and so on. In fact, the "self" as part of the human being has never yielded its ultimate mystery, although enough light has been shed on it by contemporary and earlier seekers to make discussion of one's own self possible. The most striking thing about it is its personal uniqueness: it appears in the individual vocabulary as "I," and as such enjoys a designation which cannot be confused—as terms like "star", "king", or even "you" can be confused.

Yet the self is also the product of human interaction. If a solitary child were born into a dead atomic world from the womb of the last mother and by some miracle survived and grew physically, it would have or be a kind of self but one so different from the selfhoods we think we know as to be grotesque. The emerging self of the child in a so-called normal world, which is to say a world filled to the brim with human transactions both good and evil, achieves much of its identity by innumerable relationships with other human beings—parents, peers, strangers—and from many seemingly less important human interactions and events. He or she "encodes and decodes," as the communications theory people say, among multiple patterns of moral systems, social roles, folklores, political and legal habitats, and other influences of the organized society and what might be called, the "hidden" society (the living but officially rejected sub-cultures). He or she is also the inheritor of the historical memory of the world.

Thus, it is possible to speak of the self under different cognomens: the environmental self, the psychological self, the mythological self, the physical self, the mysterious quintessential self, which a friend of mine calls the "core self" and which has connotations with Kant's "pure self".

Perhaps the reverse of the solitary child born into a dead world is that of the individual fully equipped by the world and the many contributions of social and psychological interaction who finds himself in the position of having these brutally and systematically stripped from him. The writings of Viktor Frankl and others indicate how under sadistic treatment or the rigorous determination of hostile authority to break and re-make the captive personality, men and women who have had almost every level of existence taken from them short of death still maintained their selfhood. These cases help illustrate how far or not there is a quintessential self and how it is formed or appears. Gordon Allport, at least for the purposes of the analysis of the self from the standpoint of psychological insights, rejected the concept of what he called a "trans-psychological" self, acting, as it were, as a control agency. Yet nothing removes the strange enchantment for many thoughtful adults of the venerable phrase: "I know that I know."

In very late adulthood there sometimes occurs the terrible phenomenon of open self-hatred—that revulsion against the self which has wasted or destroyed many lives.. Chilling reports exist of an old man or woman found standing before a door-length mirror in a nursing home bitterly cursing their own image. This is one dramatic and pathetic form of the rejection of the self-as-seen, which can assume psychoneurotic forms of either personal immobilization or the alienated building, so to say, of a second self. Of the elderly self-hater one can remark in parenthesis that not only does he or she represent the extreme example of Erikson's "disgust and despair," but it is curious and sad that in such cases the sense of loss and alienation is so overpowering that the individual wholly rejects or ignores the credit side of the despised life: the astonishing number of good choices and actions made and good knowledges and skills acquired: the attempts also to love and be loved which *in themselves* form part of the art of the self-in-growth.

In advanced years, in hostile environments like bad nursing homes, this same terrifying rejection or alienation of self may, of course, derive from conditions all too close to Viktor Frankl's experience, if old men and women find themselves stripped of all possessions, all friends, all contacts, all respect, all authority, all love.

Karen Horney underlined the importance of the self-image as a dynamic force by noting the presence in therapy of two forms of the image: the way each of her patients regarded his *present* roles, status, and abilities; and the way he regarded his (or her) potentialities—specifically, his aspirations for himself—the *idealized* self-image, as Horney called it. The idealized self-image provides much of the generating power of human adult life. At its best it supplies what Allport has called "an insightful cognitive map"; at its worst it can be both so unrealistic and so obsessive that it maims and destroys much of the life action. One need hardly point out that the very old who curse, not God—as Job's wife advised—but themselves, clearly realize that time has run out, and that there is no arena left in which the idealized self-image can function. Their plight is perhaps not unlike that of a Scrooge for whom the fresh chance of a Christmas Day with its "piping cold air" will never come.

Erik Erikson is loath to let go the Freudian term "ego" in discussions of the self. In fact, he ultimately abandons what seems to him to be the seemingly irresolvable debate on the roles and relevance of the "ego" and the "self," but before he does so he makes a pronouncement which shows the dynamism which he clearly conceives to be part of any individual's existence: "The ego, then, as a central organizing agency, is during the course of life faced with a changing self which, in turn, demands to be synthesized with abandoned and anticipated selves." And this leads him to the concepts of *self-identity* and *self-diffusion* as powerful generators and inhibitors of wholeness and creative action among, at first and notably, late adolescents who are just passing through the fateful gates of adulthood.

Erikson is speaking of young pre-adult patients who break down because of latent weaknesses in self-identity which are exposed under real or supposed rejections by others, whether peers or older adults:

> "Where [the interaction] fails . . . the young individual recoils to a position of strenuous introspection and self-testing which, given particularly aggravating circumstances or a history of relatively strong autistic trends, can lead him into a paralyzing borderline state. Symptomatically, this state consists of a painfully heightened sense of isolation; a disintegration of the sense of inner continuity and sameness; a sense of over-all ashamedness; an inability to derive a sense of accomplishment from any kind of activity; a feeling that life is happening to the individual rather than being lived by his initiative; a radically shortened time perspective; and finally, a basic mistrust, which leaves it to the world, to society, and indeed, psychiatry to prove that the patient does exist in a psychosocial sense, i.e., can count on an invitation to become himself."

This description, although it is specifically of a young pre-adult soon to cross into adulthood, is clearly applicable to great numbers of adults across the lifespan who, in varying degrees, exhibit the deficits of unsureness of identity. Many of us, in moments of seemingly unbearable stress, at all ages, have felt a temporary slackening of or dimming of our ordinarily strong feeling of self-identity, like the swift blurring of a photograph projected on a slide-machine. In Franz Werfel's novel, *The Forty Days of Musa Dagh*, the hero-leader of the beseiged city, although he successfully brings his people through their long trial, is occasionally overcome by the experience of what Werfel describes as a "whirling" of the little world about him. This occurs at periods of extreme stress, and may perhaps be the novelist's shorthand for a form of identity crisis.

At times the anxiety of the self to escape from the unbearable challenges to its identity results in a marked dimming of the photographic plate; or even an attempt at self-diffusion: to project oneself onto other identities, which in extreme cases may lead to the attempt to assume other roles and backgrounds altogether. The late adult male executive who seeks relief from the stresses of menopausal man (and later) by becoming an older hippie among younger people or engaging in bizarre sexual adventures is an example. At all events, the anthology in which Erikson's paper appears bears the significant title, *Identity and Anxiety*. And Frieda Fromm-Reichmann, writing in the same anthology, speaks of anxiety as "the most unpleasant and at the same time the most universal experience, except loneliness. We observe both healthy and mentally disturbed people doing everything possible to ward off anxiety or to keep it from awareness." She quotes Poulson, Berdyaev, Riesman, and other social psychologists as finding "the source of man's anxiety in his psychological isolation, *his alienation from his own self* and from his fellow men." (My italics.) And she notes Rollo May's definition of anxiety as "the apprehension set off by a threat to some value which the individual holds essential to his existence as a personality."

Clearly, anxiety—which obviously has a constructive as well as a destructive role—can become a turbulent and damaging force in the adult life where an unrealistic gap and unbearable demands are postulated between the self-image-as-now and the idealized self-image. Or where, as in Erikson's hypothesis, the ego, the central organizing agency, faced with a "changing self which, in turn, demands to be synthesized with abandoned and anticipated selves", finds itself successively unable to complete the synthesis.

All adults are need-bearers, including the hilariously-titled "man who has everything" (everything except the consciousness of his enormous need to become a fully-actualized human being?) and the often grotesquely misnamed "beautiful people." The supreme need for each individual adult is surely to achieve identification and fulfilment of self, not to be the echo or carbon copy of others, or to merge oneself with giant thought systems whether political, economic, or religious, so that one can never be exposed as a divergent being or scrutinized as an agent of change. The paradox, of course, is that our selfhood grows from interaction—interrelationships with other beings and with the very systems which would absorb and crush us if they can. Furthermore, selfhood grows from love of oneself and love for others: this is not a paradox at all, but a creative union of immense potentiality.

In Franz Kafka's terrifying story *Metamorphosis*, the central character is a young salesman who in the course of his routine and empty life has lost any love for himself and any real love for others. His life has become so much a matter of routine and his rejection of the claims of growing self-identity so complete that he awakens one morning to find himself, a cockroach. The story is a parable:

to be a human being is to develop a unique and growing individuality. To be a cockroach is to exist by living from the refuse of others.

"The essence of neurosis," remarks Rollo May, "[is] the person's unusual potentialities, blocked by hostile conditions in the environment (past or present) and by his own internalized conflicts turning inward and causing morbidity." And May aptly quotes from William Blake, whose own life demonstrated his constant nourishment of his selfhood and the fertility of his self-concept: "Energy is Eternal Delight: he who desires but acts not, breeds pestilence."

We are the product of the days of our years, of 20,000 days by the time we are age 55. The adult in his later years has lived a very long time with himself, with his *self*. Is it possible over so long a period to live, as it were, aversively: that is, avoiding in all possible ways confrontations with the inner voices of the self, or fugitively, fleeing from the invitations to more vivid and fertile selfhood which the small mobile cosmos of our personal life successively opens to us?

It is indeed possible, and very common, just as it is possible to actualize the experiences of the life drama to help bring into being a self open to all the potentialities, at least, of creativity. Those who do so will become the Ulyssean adults. Yet so complex is the life journey, and so varied the network of experiences and interactions which occur even in the apparently most commonplace lives, that one cannot arbitrarily separate Ulysseans and non-Ulysseans at a gateway of the mid-50s. This is not an affair of the lighted banquet hall with its doors irrevocably closed to the virgins without the lamps.

If the human adult is subject to a high degree of rigidity and passivity in the course of life experiences, he is also a being who is never wholly programmed. Far more, he is capable of some degree of virtuosity, however small, to the end of his life. Thus, it is wiser not to speak in absolute terms of Ulyssean and non-Ulyssean adults whenever one is speaking of *potentiality*. In this sphere of discussion, it is better to speak of comparative degrees of the Ulyssean life, spirit, and performance.

There is an important package of good news about the human life drama which, if one could only get it distributed widely enough and listened to carefully enough, might surprise by joy a great number of adults in their later years.

The good news is that the human adult can continue to grow, to learn, and to create through his or her life to the very late years, and *through them*. Traditional folklore, which likes to believe that it can reduce life to certain huge sentimental generalities, likes to conceive of the life drama as a simple curve, the arc of a semi-circle, rising from childhood to the full prime of manhood and womanhood and descending to second childhood. Jaques's familiar description of "the seven ages of man," in which the sixth age is that of the "lean and slipper'd pantaloon" and the last age of all that of the individual "sans teeth, sans eyes, sans taste, sans everything" are widely quoted as the epitome of folk wisdom, but in fact they are murderously naive and misleading.

The human life journey cannot be intelligently charted by a single curving line. Such a line is perhaps a fair approximation of an adult's physical progress, since there is a certain decline in the power of the various physical senses. Even here, however, there are instances galore of men and women who survived a sickly childhood and early adulthood or who emerged vigorously from a period of flabbiness in their 30s and 40s to enter and maintain glowing health and strength in their later and even very late years. Single-line curves ignore the incredible complexity of the life drama, the varying domains in which adults live out their lives and the kaleidoscope of individualities, as numerous as the sands of the seas, that have to be taken into account.

Adult individuals do indeed play many parts, but of a complexity far surpassing Shakespeare's wildwood philosopher. The University of Chicago sociologist Robert Havighurst, who has devoted much of his career to the study of adults in the modern life journey, has reminded us of at least ten vocational and avocational roles played by most North American adults: worker or employer, parent, spouse, child of an aging parent, homemaker (whether male or female), church member, club (and/or union) member, citizen, friend and user of leisure. Although Havighurst does not say this, it is a fact that when an adult dies there are, as it were, ten chairs vacant—at least ten chairs—among the thronging circles of life which, infinitely multiplied, make society run. Havighurst's tendency is to identify much of his comment with American middle-class society (a common trait of scholars and philosophers about the nature and future of our twentieth-century world). But in fact there are important adaptations of the ten roles according to class membership. One recalls here Lloyd Warner's too broad but exhilarating and helpful analysis of the 1950s in *Yankee City*, of society divided into upper-upper, lower-upper, upper-middle, lower-middle, upper-lower, and lower-lower. It is intriguing that Warner found close affinities between much in the life attitudes of the upper-upper and the lower-lower. However, the essential point here is that even these social roles of the individual adult in the life drama have important modifications of style according to class.

The word "role" is a much more sophisticated word than it

appears in Havighurst's useful listing. We all—except the most brainwashed of our generation—have hidden roles and hidden agendas. We often live actual sub-lives or other-lives which usually escape the inquiring mind and the eager pen of the sociologist. And some of us live fantasy lives that, in some cases, have a power and a hidden governing force which appear, disappear, and reappear at different stages of the life drama.

To the individuality of each person, and to the multiple social roles and the modifications of class patterns, one still has to add the tasks and expectations mandated by one's being a member of a seemingly well-defined age group. Havighurst has his own version of the "seven ages of man", infinitely more complex and sophisticated than Jaques's, but with something of the same rise, decline, and fall. Havighurst divides the adult life-cycle neatly into decades which he calls "cohorts", and then attributes certain roles, functions, psychological concerns, and major life-cycle problems to each cohort. For the reader of Havighurst's stages there is a certain fascination in seeing how well one fits (or otherwise) into a cohort at age, say 35, 55, or 75. The older adult, age 55-plus, may especially ask, "Was this true of me?"

For example: in Havighurst's cycle, age 20–30 is the period of Focussing One's Life: one achieves psychological, then social, identity; chooses a job, a marriage partner (usually), a community; tries to develop a consistent ideology. Chief concern is with oneself and one's personal life. It is a decade of trials and trying out, and much taking of schooling, largely with an eye to upward social mobility in the job and class structure.

Age 30–40 is the period of Collecting One's Energies: one steadily organizes and grows: it is the time of early production as worker, homemaker, scientist, teacher, parent. It is the period of least introspection: Havighurst makes the extraordinary statement that "doubts about oneself have been put to rest." Older women, he says, look back nostalgically to this cohort. Educational activity continues, again chiefly with upward mobility in view.

Age 40–50 is the period of Exerting and Asserting Oneself. This decade is for many people the peak of the life-cycle. There is a great investment of energy by the ego in the "outer world" of affairs: in a man's career, in a woman's clubs and community work or in her return to the job market; and in homemaking. Some deficiency begins in the physical process: it is notably the decade of retirement from competitive sports requiring abundant energy and aggressiveness. In all, however, it is a decade of expanding activities and powers: if not in careers, at least in civic and cultural study and activity. More leisure is available; more interest in art and theatre, in travel, and in homemaking and gardening skills. It may be a cohort among which are found more "self-initiating," or autonomous learners than the previous ones, since there is a marked falling-off in enrolment in learning groups.

Age 50–60 is the period of Maintaining Position and Changing Roles: of increasing physical inefficiency; in addition, "the libidinal fires die down, producing a threat to the ego. Many adults reach the plateau of their world of work." The self sees the world as complex in ways not perceived before, and doubts its ability to master it. As thought takes pre-eminence over action as a lifestyle, people of this cohort engage in increased introversion. The process which Elaine Cumming and W. E. Henry especially made celebrated: "disengagement" from affairs and attachments as age comes on, begins, often as a hidden self-determination. This is a decade of re-arrangement of one's working, sexual, family lives and of many other relationships. The parent becomes the grandparent, and the sense of the constriction of time leads to an urgent feeling of priorities. Havighurst is unsure about education's role in all this— perhaps to stress learning "for perspective," for greater depth.

Age 60–70 is the period when, says Havighurst, most men lose their jobs, most women their husbands. Thus major reorganizations are thrust forward for many people. "Disengagement" continues as an important process: from many activities, most of which are turned into shorter-run exercises; from many emotional attachments to people and objects. This also is the cohort of the "oldster" who will not give up some long-held responsibility. Thus, Havighurst baptizes this decade with the title: Deciding to Disengage, and How.

Age 70–90, not surprisingly, is named Making the Most of Disengagement, a designation which is, to say the least, non-Ulyssean. Havighurst's tone, through all his writing, is in the main humane and hopeful. Still, he is a child of his people and his epoch, and he does not really know what to do with these late life-cycle people. He quotes Charlotte Buhler on "self-fulfilment" as one solution. (One is tempted to be satirical here: if, after all, this is Shakespeare's "sans" age—what else is left but the self and its fulfilment?) As though (I cannot help returning to this point), the self were the least and lowest of our possessions, and when life has stripped us of everything else—power, money, sex gratification, prestige, and most of our friends—we can almost as an after-thought turn to the fulfilment of self.

What has this particular arrangement, perhaps the most complete and celebrated of the life-journey statements, got to say to adults in the middle and later years who are thoughtful enough to look back pensively at the drama of their life?

At first reading, it seems somewhat naive. For example, can one classify adulthood into precise decades? Is not this the gaucherie of the very young in our time who think that age 30 is some kind of Berlin wall separating the just (the up-to-30s) from the unjust (the past-30s)? Even more, how can one take the infinite variety of human adult types: the young who are prematurely old in thought and life, the old who retain marvellous traits and responses of youth, and deposit them all in Procrustean beds called decadal cohorts? What do you do with the great numbers of working-class men who reach their job plateaus in the 30s? Or with those many "successful" executives who by affluent lifestyles and heavy drinking, attempt to cover up their failure at age 45 or 55 to achieve self-identity? Is it conceivable that the period 30–40 is so euphoric that "doubts about oneself have been put at rest", or that it is the period of least introspection?

At second reading, one recalls with gratitude that in taking the plunge to try to describe a whole panorama of the life drama, Havighurst has wholly demolished the naiveté of the single curving line. He reminds us that each one in his time indeed plays many parts, but they are not the monochromatic roles of Jaques and the folklore. Although his late-life subjects appear blurred and lost, he has filled his canvas with throngs of people playing many roles, with many different experiences across the life span; he has reminded us of the complexity and diversity of living which can affect even seemingly "normal" lives; and from time to time he strikes resonantly some note in the human condition which all who have reached at least the middle years instantly recognize.

Take one example: the ebullience common to many in their 30s, and the detachment and retrospection which are typical of many adults in their 60s and 70s. My own mother, then about 68 and widowed for several years, was present with me at the successful live studio production of a Home and School broadcast. The volunteer producer, a young public relations man, and two or three teacher colleagues, all in their 30s, had expended as much energy and excited concern on this show as though it were a major network programme. Watching them quietly, my mother, who was what the older North American idiom used to call a "booster," or in the British idiom, a "well-wisher," was expected as usual to add her warm and happy congratulations. Indeed she did this, but before the production ended she turned to me and said with an expression of indescribable sadness, "When I see the work that Gerald and his friends are putting into this, and all it means to them, I think of how your Dad and I used to plan and dream, how excited we used to get." Her comment astonished me. I was not insensitive—I was simply age 35, and was myself in the throes of the ebullient decade. This charming and life-loving woman, who turned out to be a Ulyssean herself, had simply a greater perspective from the further heights of the life journey.

Since Havighurst is a sociologist, he naturally stresses the influence of the human environment upon the adult's growth and development. What is admirable in his studies, and in all those of the so-called Chicago Group of which he was a member over a period of roughly thirty years, is the way they have combined insights provided from both the psychology and sociology of adulthood to present a dynamic scene in which each adult person faces a series of *developmental* tasks which respond to and act upon the various life roles already described. Thus adult life is not governed or even dominated by psychosexual functions or malfunctions running back to the mysterious world of the child, but is also a psychosocial phenomenon. The adult self—the miniature cosmos with its awesome uniqueness, in part comprising the ego and in part organized by the ego—is constantly challenged to grow by the succession of roles and tasks which confront it emerging from the surrounding cosmos: human society, time, space, and fate.

If this seems like an elaborate statement of a self-evident truth, keep in mind the power inherent in a theory of adult life which places its emphasis on challenge and growth *throughout the whole lifespan.* The human adult is not a being delivered into the first years of adulthood as a finished work of art composed from childhood and adolescence and thus to be taken as completed for better or for worse, but a growing self and an interactive agency capable of change and development *at all stages* of life. In the light of this concept, even James Birren's definition of the human individual as "a biological, psychological, and social constellation moving forward in time" is quite insufficient unless one adds another of his phrases: "and is in a dynamic transformation from his past to his future"—and then adds the still more pregnant words as an amendment to Birren, "*throughout his entire existence.*"

Carried to its positive conclusion as a personal philosophy, or simply acted out as a whole way of life throughout the life drama, this is the belief and the actuality of the Ulyssean adults. Where the Ulysseans and the Chicago Group of human development scholars seem to diverge most sharply is in their attitudes to the now celebrated "disengagement" theory.

Scholars have to report what they see, not what they might wish they could see, and Elaine Cumming and W. E. Henry, drawing from data accumulated by them on two hundred middle and older adults from age 50 to age 85 (the Kansas City Study of Adult Life), described a process beginning about the early 50s, where the individual, at first almost imperceptibly, commences a gradual process of withdrawal from the social system in which he or she lives. Meanwhile, society itself is commencing and continuing disengagement from its side, through, for example, retirement mandates; or through attitudes toward the aging so strong that virtually compulsory withdrawal or disengagement is required in many voluntary offices and activities.

Furthermore, according to this theory, the older adult cuts down on his or her emotional investment in other persons and in human "causes"—both of these dimmings of the lamps of human interaction coming simultaneously with increased preoccupation with the self. Although all this sounds negative, it need not be wholly so, since the *right kind* of preoccupation with self might well be a liberation for many adults who have gradually let the hectic investment they have placed in affairs and people usurp and impoverish the time they should have devoted to greater self-discovery and actualization.

But is disengagement necessary for older adults, and is this the route to psychological well-being in one's later years? The Ulyssean answer to both questions would be No: nor in saying No either verbally or in the more powerful language of their lifestyles is the Ulyssean position one of holding on at all costs, say, to certain offices. (One remembers the story of the old bishop of whom it was said that he had every virtue except resignation.) Few figures are more pathetic than the very elderly persons who are determined to hold on tenaciously to official or voluntary posts where they have long since ceased to make the slightest creative contribution.

Cumming and Henry develop their theory with intelligence and sophistication; but the Ulyssean counter-position seems to arise from what might be called a gut feeling that the word "disengagement," whether fostered by society or the individual, in itself generates a climate of negativism and defeat. The Ulyssean adult can understand how arrival at the middle and late adult years brings with it certain perspectives, nostalgias, feelings of detachment, sorrows: these are some of the legacies of maturity. He can see with open eyes the callousness and stupidity of a society which attempts to allot and deploy human beings by their age tags. What he cannot accept is that certain general tendencies said to be true of carefully studied small samples of older adults but subject to numerous interpretations, should be applied as a kind of decalogue: "Thou art 50-plus. Thou must expect to disengage." At all events, it is not, he thinks (when he thinks of it at all), applicable to him.

The Ulyssean would not re-order the whole life-order, say, of Havighurst; but because of the infinite variety of human experiences, he would refer the question to the final court: the individual adult life. He would dispense with rigid time boxes. And he would have a revolutionary concept about the middle and later years: that for many they are years of beginnings, not conclusions. He would quote Jung's dictum that it takes a human being about fifty years simply to assemble and truly identify the self; or the challenging assertion of Frank Underhill, the Canadian political scientist, when in his late Ulyssean 70s, that "nobody knows anything until he is 50"; or the statement of Professor (later Sir) Fred Clarke at McGill University which used to send me and my undergraduate colleagues into bewildered fury: "Really, no one is fit to begin teaching until he is 50."

Even when we accept the fact that adulthood is a lifelong developmental process, it is often difficult to translate the theory to the particular individual we happen to be contending with in some bleak hour of a routine day. Is it possible to believe that, for example, this self-promoter with the wide cold smile; this jolly non-stop trouble-maker, busy poisoning her wells; this cynical derogator of all high plans and sweet hopes; this arrogant intellectual, lost in his own petrified forest of unrevised views; this square-voiced traveller, proclaiming as loudly as ever the superiorities of his own environment over outdated cultures; this ferocious junior official, busy demonstrating her equality with the worst of masculine qualities—is it possible to believe that these individual human adults, in so many ways not adult, in too many cases seemingly unloving, unlovable, and unloved, bear any relationship to the good news that adults can grow and increase their creative powers to the very end of the very latest years?

And indeed, when Erik Erikson, who always writes with compassion, comes to the last of his "eight stages of man" he passes a kind of sorrowful judgment upon those who have sought isolation rather than love in their earlier years, and who have stagnated rather than generating what one might perhaps call epicycles of love and creativity: "Only in him who in some way has taken care of things and people and has adapted himself to the triumphs and disappointments adherent to being, the originator of others or the generator of products and ideas—only in him may gradually ripen the fruit of these seven stages."

This is what Erikson calls "ego integrity," and its bleak opposite is what he calls simply "despair"—despair in the face of the imminent end of one's lifespan, the fear of death: "The one and only life-cycle is not accepted as the ultimate of life. Despair expresses the feeling that the time is now short, too short for the attempt to start another life, and to try out alternate roads to integrity. Disgust hides despair, if only in the form of 'a thousand little disgusts' which do not add up to one big remorse: 'mille petits dégouts de soi, dont le total ne fait pas un remords, mais un gêne obscure.' (Rostand)." One could not put the case of the life-felt-to-be-lost more poignantly.

Nonetheless, Erikson's tenets are tonic and liberating in their insistence that all of us, including those whose selves and productivity may seem to us aborted and sterile, are at least at work and play in a life arena where we are not somehow permanently maimed by some purely psychosexual wound experienced in early childhood. Erikson is a neo-Freudian, who, as a recent biographer remarks, has not rejected Freud but has simply chosen as much of Freud as he deems suitable in the development of his own conception of the ego in action. To Erikson, the development of the individual human being is a highly psycho*social* encounter. It seemed evident to Erikson that Freud, whose life was itself filled with intense questionings and encounters, was a living example of the limitations of the purely psychosexual approach.

Since unfortunately great breakthroughs in thought, once popularized, often get out of control and assume fantastic shapes never envisaged when they were first developed, psychoanalysis became not merely a kind of rule of life for large sectors of the more affluent Western society but contributed largely to conceptions about the growth of the self among enormous numbers of adults who could never afford and would never have a psychiatrist.

And this carried with it a frequent and damaging image: that success in the mastery of one's life was really a psychosexual affair. "Adjustment" depended on reviews of weaning habits, toilet-training, Oedipal hatreds and obsessions, and other mysteries of the earliest childhood years, mostly shrouded from conscious memory; and of course, analysis of dreams. One went to one's psychiatrist to engage in an expert and searching return back along the trails of childhood to try to find the wound, and if possible, heal it. The process had something in common with Arthur Koestler's *"reculer pour mieux sauter"* in the search for the creative activity: regress and retreat again in order to assault the fortress: life itself.

Freud's weakness lay in his obsession with the psychosexual bias, but in one contribution (among others) certainly he was magnificent. He helped emancipate Western man from the treatment of mental and emotional illnesses almost as demonic possession, and made at least possible, through the new therapeutic relationship between psychoanalyst and patient, a new rule and role of love. However, new fetishes appeared. One in particular may be responsible for a great deal of damage to adults struggling to make headway against the complex demands of the self and society. This is the conviction, rather rarely expressed openly, that after all as adult personalities we are static and completed: whatever is deeply wrong with us somehow happened "back there". One catches overtones of this in a special kind of bitterness sometimes voiced by adults about their childhood years. It is also their scapegoat, as Viktor Frankl makes plain. "It" incidentally, is always the work, therefore, of someone else: "If my father had not been . . .", "if my mother had not had such neurotic obsessions . . .", "if my brother . . ." And my sister. And my early playmates.

The humanist psychologists and other thoughtful commentators upon the adult life journey may bring good news for modern adults, but they bring reminders of new responsibilities with them. Erik Erikson, in a passage in *Childhood and Society*, reminds us that our interaction with society plays a crucial and continuing role, highly favourable as well as inhibiting to the child growing through adolescence to adulthood and on throughout the adult life drama (my italics):

> "For psychoanalysis has consistently described the vicissitudes of instincts and of the ego only up to adolescence, at which time rational genitality was expected to absorb infantile fixations and irrational conflicts or *to admit them to repeat performances under manifold disguises.* The main recurrent theme thus concerned the shadow of frustration which falls from childhood on the individual's later life— and on his society. In this book we suggest that, to understand either childhood or society, we must expand our scope to include the study of the way in which societies lighten the inescapable conflicts of childhood with a promise of some security, identity, and integrity. *In thus reinforcing the values by which the ego exists, societies create the only condition under which human growth is possible.*"

What therefore appears upon the stage of adult life is the psychosocial encounter innumerably repeated, but with certain major stages or phases to be negotiated. Of Erikson's "eight ages of man", four are devoted to childhood, one to adolescence (identity *vs.* role confusion), one to young adulthood (intimacy *vs.* isolation), one to middle adulthood (generativity *vs.* stagnation), and the eighth to later adulthood (ego integrity *vs.* despair.) Each of these is a developmental stage, that is, a bridge to continuing growth; each presents a kind of critical issue or crisis for the ego, but the issue is not encountered on a once-and-for-all basis. As an example, ego identity is so critical at the period of adolescence that it gives its name to the fifth "age", but as indicated earlier it is also found throughout the life-cycle as a continuing issue, notably in periods of great crisis.

Psychosexual conflict and deficits remain important for many lives, but they do not become the obsessive point of reference, as was (or is) the case with the classic Freudian approach. Adult life, therefore, is a continuing thrust forward, with the surrounding society adding numerous instances to the individual's problems in negotiating life issues, but in many ways strengthening and supporting him or her. One's life is successful and productive to the degree that one negotiates each of what might be called the toll-gates of adulthood. The good news which emerges from all of this is that the adult is provided with a wide repertoire of skills and social and psychological resources in a major game in which only death blows the whistle.*

To put the matter succinctly: not merely youth, but the whole of life, is potentiality.

Psychiatrists, long preoccupied with the study of traumas and disfunctions of the personality arising out of episodes of infancy and childhood, and their healing, are beginning to turn their attention to the turbulent periods of adulthood that arise from largely psychosocial stresses. One of the most articulate and discerning of these is Herbert L. Klemme, head of the Industrial Mental Health Division of the Menninger Foundation at Topeka, Kansas. Klemme, in a lengthy interview for the *New York Times* in July, 1971, was particularly struck by the high rates of alcoholism, depression, suicide, and divorce that occur at the point, or bridge, of transition between young adulthood and middle age. Klemme called this point of migration between young and mature adulthood, the "mid-life crisis", and found that it seems to arise at approximately the end of the period roughly from ages 21 to 35—the period which David L. Gutmann of the University of Michigan has named the phase of "alloplastic mastery": in which young adults try to achieve mastery over the external world, seeking material gain and the approval of others. (Gutmann's interesting version of the life drama includes two other major phases: "autoplastic mastery", the period from about 35 to 60, and "omniplastic mastery", the period from age 60 on, when the person who has successfully met the tests of earlier periods often turns his or her attention to broader concerns.)

What Klemme found absorbing and often tragic was the number of times that people could not successfully negotiate a major period of transition, and the effect this had on them. He describes how adult people "may spend the rest of their lives making futile attempts to work through" an unsuccessful negotiation, and how others who after early success are suddenly overwhelmed by disenchantment:

> "Those who have difficulty making such transitions, regardless of age, often resort to similar behavioral patterns. Such a person may retreat temporarily to struggles of an earlier

*In the course of a series on re-incarnation and conceptions of the after-life on the Canadian Broadcasting Corporation outlets in the late winter of 1975, it was stated that Robert Munroe, a California businessman who is also a serious student of psychic phenomena affecting himself, and author of *Journeys Out of the Body*, had helped prepare a number of dying people for the *next* stage of their cosmic journey. Indeed, why not?

phase, which by comparison are now more comfortable. . . .
A man in his late 30s may resume extramarital dating
behavior more characteristic of his earlier 20s, and enjoy the
relative comfort of behavior already learned, *perhaps to
avoid the pain of advancing to another development level."*
(My italics.)

So great, in Klemme's view, could be the mid-life crisis, that

"failure to make the transition smoothly can begin a long
process of personal frustration and failure. A woman whose
children have grown to where they no longer seem to need
her may become depressed or decide to have another baby.
To restore a sense of excitement, a man may resort to risk-
taking behavior, indulging in rigorous physical activities or
investing in risky stock ventures—a common symptom of
middle-aged physicians and dentists. And alcohol often becomes an escape route leading nowhere."

Those who weather the crisis, according to Dr. Klemme, often
do it by finding new meaning in their work or by switching to a
more satisfying career. On the other hand, persons who have
endured the financially unrewarding aspects of such a job through
young adulthood may suddenly find meaning in their work and a
sense of newfound purpose in life.

As a footnote to the concluding comments of the interview, it
is surely more than a coincidence that Dale Hiestand, in his
fascinating study on why and how middle and older adults switch
careers in mid- and later-stream, entitles his book, *Changing
Careers after 35.*

Although Erikson has made important contributions to the
conception of the adult life drama as an arena of continuing
potentiality of development arising out of major psychosocial encounters, his references to late adult life are like an artist's rough
sketches of a proposed design, compared with his great canvas of
psychosexual and psychosocial development in infancy, childhood,
and adolescence. Besides, his alternatives of ego integrity or "disgust and despair" would seem for many adults to close the amphitheatre of late adulthood to the possibility of Ulyssean adventures.
In fact, it is hard to see how Erikson's disappointed and despairing
people would ever find their way to a Ulyssean beach. They may,
however.

There are two powerful factors at work which make it probable
that for many people Ulyssean options remain, in spite of perhaps
a former anti-Ulyssean lifestyle. One of these factors is that most
people are not totally classifiable in absolute categories; few adults,

for example, can be described as totally adventureless. With every-one in life one has to ask the questions: "At what place and time?" "In what circumstances and conditions?" Surely the mature phrase in all adult assessments and controversies is, "It all depends."

The second powerful factor mitigating seemingly irreversible life processes is the succession of psychosocial intersections—of life-giving and life-corroding alternatives. Consider in this con-nexion the stimulating and liberating conception of the life journey by the American psychologist, Robert C. Peck. Here is a distin-guished writer on adult development, little known to the general public, whose theories—which I will call a psychology of dynamic alternatives—break the ground, more than any other, for the possibility of the Ulyssean concept. An admirer of Erikson, Robert Peck takes up where Erikson leaves off. Peck's career had involved him in the psychological analysis of the personalities and life processes of several thousand people in business, mostly men. From these studies, he became convinced that to try to sum people up in various time capsules (the 30s, the 40s, the 50s, and so on), or even in defined types or type-situations (for example, Erikson's integrated as against despairing people: or the Kansas City Studies' Mastery Typology; or the Berkley references to the Mature, the Rocking Chair, and the Armored Types) was too categorical and fixating.

Peck asks the sensible question: Is there not a great variability in adult life in the years of arrival at situations of psychic crisis? For example: young fathers and old fathers—how can one possibly compare the lifestyles in which they are operating, or the effects upon them, therefore, of children growing up and moving out? We do not grow across adult life in horizontal time-lines, as students move from one grade or form to another in the older-fashioned curriculum; but rather, we progress vertically in different masteries and skills. Therefore, Peck would discard much of the chronological and imprisoning classification. He accepts two giant classifications by age: Middle Age and Old Age—but he is driven to this by the sheer semantics of the whole life-cycle controversy. The tacks which he uses to build his concepts of adult people-in-process are not ages but stages: the female climacteric, for ex-ample, regardless of age; or the retirement point for men, which now is beginning to vary enormously.

To adopt Peck's position is to introduce a fluidity and resilience to the processes of adulthood *at all ages* which is in itself exciting and liberating. However, it is his discussion of what I call "dynamic alternatives" that lights up the board depicting our progress and the destiny of our self across the second half of life.

I was sufficiently fascinated by the potentialities inherent in Peck's schema of alternatives to attempt to illustrate what they

THE MAJOR GAME ADULTS PLAY:
A CHART ILLUSTRATIVE OF THE CONCEPTS OF ROBERT C. PECK

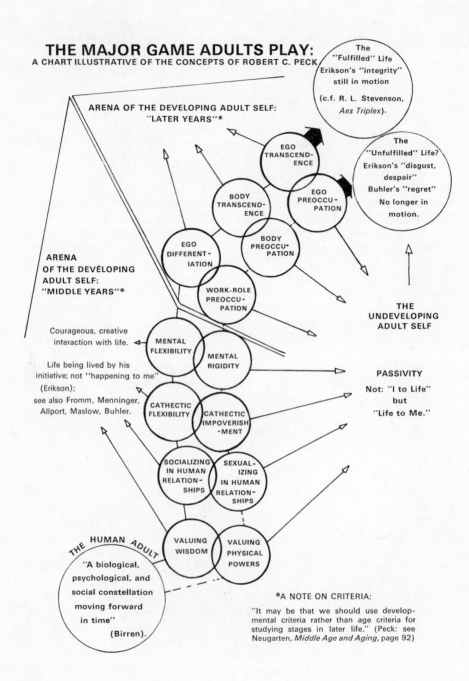

The "Fulfilled" Life Erikson's "integrity" still in motion (c.f. R. L. Stevenson, *Aes Triplex*).

ARENA OF THE DEVELOPING ADULT SELF: "LATER YEARS"*

EGO TRANSCEND-ENCE

BODY TRANSCEND-ENCE

EGO PREOCCU-PATION

The "Unfulfilled" Life? Erikson's "disgust, despair" Buhler's "regret" No longer in motion.

EGO DIFFERENT-IATION

BODY PREOCCU-PATION

ARENA OF THE DEVELOPING ADULT SELF: "MIDDLE YEARS"*

WORK-ROLE PREOCCU-PATION

THE UNDEVELOPING ADULT SELF

Courageous, creative interaction with life.

Life being lived by his initiative; not "happening to me" (Erikson); see also Fromm, Menninger, Allport, Maslow, Buhler.

MENTAL FLEXIBILITY

MENTAL RIGIDITY

PASSIVITY

Not: "I to Life" but "Life to Me."

CATHECTIC FLEXIBILITY

CATHECTIC IMPOVERISH-MENT

SOCIALIZING IN HUMAN RELATION-SHIPS

SEXUAL-IZING IN HUMAN RELATION-SHIPS

THE HUMAN ADULT

VALUING WISDOM

VALUING PHYSICAL POWERS

"A biological, psychological, and social constellation moving forward in time" (Birren).

*A NOTE ON CRITERIA:

"It may be that we should use developmental criteria rather than age criteria for studying stages in later life." (Peck: see Neugarten, *Middle Age and Aging*, page 92) might mean in a simple pictorial chart (Chart I). In designing this "major game adults play", I have tried to convey the movement and flow of alternatives which present themselves innumerable times in continuing daily life. The circles representing arenas of behaviour I have shown as intersecting, because which of us is ever totally and at all times in one circle or the other? In the chart, I have had to draw the circles equal, but in fact—complex and interesting creatures that we are—each of us has a larger circle in which we participate more than in the smaller. Readers may, in fact, find it an interesting exercise to consider what their own life graph from the "system of alternatives" would look like if projected on a screen.

What does it mean to age successfully?

Peck found from his spectator's role in the reported life experiences of several thousand men (his observations transfer easily to women also) that a critical point seems to be reached in middle age somewhere between the late 30s and the late 40s. This is a turbulent period for many middle-agers because it confronts them with the waning of certain physical powers, either of strength and sports prowess, in the case of men, or of physical beauty if defined as "young-looking" in the case of women. Many adults have invested themselves heavily in these powers, and the confrontation with loss forces upon them a major traumatic alternative of choice: *valuing wisdom or valuing physical powers.* Peck naturally distinguishes "wisdom" from "intellectual capacity": wisdom is the ability to make the most effective choices among the alternatives which the wide repertoire of middle-aged adulthood provides in compensation. Some people cling to physical powers as their chief tool for coping with life; as the powers decline, so does the individual's competence to take on successfully life's inevitable frustrations and disappointments. They become more and more depressed, disillusioned, and bitter: and this affects and infects their reactions and relationships. On the other hand, in Peck's words, the successful "agers calmly invert their previous value hierarchy, now putting the use of their 'heads' above the use of their 'hands', both as their standard for self-evaluation and as their chief resource for solving life's problems."

The second of four major alternatives which Peck sees as confronting adults in the middle years is a choice between *socializing vs. sexualizing in human relationships.* When I first introduced Peck's concepts into my own seminars on the adult life drama, I found some students very hostile to what they felt to be his moralistic antagonism to sexual activity and play, perhaps because Peck uses terms such as "egocentric sex-drive" and "sex-objects" in describing the negative "sexualizing" alternative. In fact, it seemed to me that in leaping to this conclusion they were listening to voices within themselves, rather than to Peck. Peck is simply

saying that in negotiating the turbulence of middle life "climacteric" and anxiety, adults must try to view other men and women
as companions and friends in increasing depth, and less and less
as objects of mere sexual play. He might have usefully developed
the point that to be egocentric is not the same as to have love of
self, and that obsessive sexual play can leave the beautiful search
for both one's own self and the real selves of others, neglected or
empty.

Middle life also brings the periodic loss of the nearness of
people, young or old, who were or are beloved: elderly parents
die; children grow up and leave home; long-cherished friends die.
At the same time, the bridge position of middle age, stretching
between young adulthood and late adulthood, carries with it access
to a wide traffic of human types and relationships. Thus a new
and major alternative arises: the middle adult who is drawing
steadily from whatever capital he has left in the bank (these analogies are all mine, not Peck's) can allow the passing years to become
increasingly impoverished; or he can reinvest his emotional sym-
pathies in new relationships. In addition, he can redefine and
imaginatively deepen or extend or adapt his "cathexes" or emotional investments within family and friendship circles. (Consider,
for example, how successfully or not, many parents in middle and
late middle age adapt their cathectic relationships to sons and
daughters now grown-up and married to persons new to the circle;
or to single grown-up children, themselves struggling to adapt to
the assets and deficits of not being married.) This third major
alternative of middle age, Peck calls choosing between *cathectic
flexibility and cathectic impoverishment.*

Finally, and crucially, people in the great middle span of the
life journey can, again by countless choices at branch alternatives
on the autoroute, choose *mental flexibility vs. mental rigidity.* Here
Peck deals trenchantly with one of the most seductive temptations
of the middle-agers: to seek continuous warmth and security in
reflecting comfortably upon the value of one's experience after 40
or 50 years of life, or more. Experience is indeed one of the best
advertisements for middle age—but only if well-used. *It must be
reinvested, retested, used to build new perspectives.* Peck is dealing
here with a phenomenon supposedly most typical of old age: the
rigid mental set, harping upon experience, testing (and rejecting)
liberating ideas by measuring them wholly against one's own unswerving attitudes drawn from "life." But this condition begins, at
least, in mid-adulthood, when one may often be rather exuberant
at having seemed to reach a kind of peak where many problems
appear to have been solved.

Three great alternatives confront adult people in what Peck
calls, laconically, "old age." Presumably on a time scale these are

folk who have reached 65 or 70 but, as already mentioned, Peck distrusts horizontal time boxes. To him, people are "old" in certain ways and traits and "young" in others; still, he has to apply his alternatives concepts to people of, say, 75 or 80 or more. Even if they feel like people in mid-life, and most Ulysseans do, life and society are going to categorize them otherwise.

When the later years are at hand in a society where too many men have identified their "self" with their career or work-role; where it has set their clocks, governed their style of life, produced whatever prestige they have—can they accept the shock of loss when this all-absorbing working self disappears? With most women the problem is different and has perhaps chiefly occurred at the menopause (except that increasing numbers of women with careers will know the men's experience). Peck calls the problem presented here that of *ego differentiation vs. work-role preoccupation.* Simply and briefly, he is saying this: in the later years we have to have learned or learn how to differentiate ourselves among different roles—to find *self-worth* in varying ways of love, service, and creativity. One invests one's self in various fields where the harvests continue on through later and later seasons.

A second life-giving or life-dimming choice opens before us in the late years, and on into the very late years where by the clock of life we are indeed old. This is the period when one is often beset by physical decline, feelings of debility, loss of recuperative powers, bodily aches and pains. How is one to meet this more-common-than-not human experience? We can, Peck suggests, become pre-occupied with our physical deficits: became querulously self-centred, full of complaints, a late sad state of egocentricity. Or we have an alternative: we can transcend the physical unease of the body, finding continuing joy in human relationships, in the wonder of the world, in mental activities. The late years present us with this choice: *body transcendence vs. body preoccupation.*

Inevitably for the old and very old, death is a presence which becomes a reality, not a philosophical question. As previously mentioned, R. L. Stevenson writes in *Aes Triplex* of the high courage it must take for some ancient gentlemen to put their old bones into bed at night, not knowing what the morrow may bring. To Robert Peck, this raises the alternative which concludes his schema: *ego transcendence vs. ego preoccupation.* The imminence of death may immobilize many late adults as bringing into view the terminating of the "one and only life" (in Erikson's phrase), the night of the ego. Others, however, will transcend their fear of extinction, which is the natural human tendency, by investing their emotions and their energies, however weakened, in people around them. They might also, as Simone de Beauvoir suggests, conclude their life with an attachment to great social or cultural causes which will somehow better the condition of mankind. Thus they transcend themselves, their *self*; or rather: they extend the arena of creative activity beyond egocentric fear and despair so that the self, in investing itself in other people and causes, affirms or re-affirms its own healing *self-worth*.

The conclusion of the matter, of conscious and active choices through innumerable acts of the seven major alternatives which continue to fulfil one's "best" self, is that I need not live at any age as though life were simply "happening to me," but rather that *I am happening to life*.

To reflect upon the nature of "the self," and of one's own self; and to relate these reflections to the panorama and the dynamics of the life drama—this is the beginning of wisdom. Who else on the time scale of life is as well-equipped to do this as the older adult?

So far from moving "over the hill" and steadily down into an arid valley, the proper comparison for the progress of older adults should be that of moving up the sides of a splendid mountain with the perspectives and strategies of the wise and experienced mountaineer. Like him, the older adult should have acquired dynamic wisdom—wisdom which is not simply dormant but which is used and constantly reinvested. And, like the mountaineer, the man or woman in later adulthood should have become equipped with enough self-knowledge and self-reliance to negotiate the difficult, often dangerous, critical places on the route not merely with fortitude (which is admirable though passive) but with creative thought and imaginative action—which are active and potential, and in the course of time, Ulyssean.

The operative verb forms, however, are "should be" and "should have," and in them lie both the opportunity and the tragedy of later adulthood. George Laughton, a noted British-born preacher, once built a famous sermon upon the slogan of the Watchtower sect (now Jehovah's Witnesses) which was, "Millions Now Living Will Never Die!" Laughton's sermon title was, "Millions Now Living Are Already Dead!"—that is, seemingly dead in full adulthood to higher opportunity, to greater (or any) creativity, to the full sweet tides of human love and compassion. He was talking about death-in-life, the condition wherein men and women never risk looking fully into the eyes of life.

This situation is not usually improved by sermons, even great sermons. We have learned, as indicated earlier, that in middle and later adulthood we are not simply the hopeless prisoners of psychosexual neuroses dating from infancy and early childhood; likewise, we have learned that the anxieties and inferiorities generated from psychosocial encounters can also find healing in the comradeships and assuagements of society. Institutional society, which many of us have criticized with burning anger, provides multitudes of supports, guides, healings, and stimuli for psychosocial man. "Do you realize," asks the old alcoholic Church of England priest, in John Masefield's *The Everlasting Mercy*, of the wild naked youth running down the road, half-mad with the world's injustice, "do you realize how much effort it takes just to get the world up and moving every morning?" Much of the apparatus of routine life is a valuable safeguard for healthy living, or even for creative activity.

Yet the chief end of man is not to be found in safeguards, survival kits, and guaranteed highways—least of all Ulyssean man, that seeker to the end of life of the full state of what Abraham Maslow, using Kurt Goldstein's term, called "self-actualization." For Maslow there was something saddening about "the ease with which human potentiality can be destroyed or repressed" by what he called the lack of "good preconditions": in the family, in the physical body, in the chemistry of life, in the ecology, the culture, the interactions of people. Why should a "fully-human person," he asked, seem like a miracle—"so improbable a happening as to be awe-inspiring?" Yet Maslow, who might then have gone on to be as pessimistic as Schopenhauer, become one of the most optimistic of modern observers of the human scene. His optimism, which bears directly upon Ulyssean adulthood, arose from a view of man as need-bearer—Maslow called him "the wanting animal"—and from the plain evidence before all our eyes that remarkable human beings exist who have apparently somehow managed to "actualize" all or nearly all of their potential.

Maslow is the author of one of the most *un*quoted and most remarkable statements ever made about the superiority of the older years of adulthood over those of youth (precisely the reverse of most of the propaganda of our age.) By Maslow's criteria:

> "Self-actualization does not occur in young people. In our culture, at least, youngsters have not yet achieved identity, or autonomy, nor have they had time enough to experience an enduring, loyal, post-romantic love relationship, nor have they generally found their calling, the altar upon which to offer themselves. Nor have they worked out their *own* system of values; nor have they had experience enough (responsibility for others, tragedy, failure, achievement, success) to shed perfectionistic illusions and become realistic; nor have they generally made their peace with death; nor have they learned how to be patient; nor have they learned enough about evil in themselves and others to be compassionate; nor have they had time to become post-ambivalent about parents and elders, power and authority; nor have they

generally become knowledgeable and educated enough to
open the possibility of becoming wise; nor have they generally acquired enough courage to be unpopular, to be un-
ashamed about being openly virtuous, etc."

What Maslow is saying in extreme terms is what Jung has
already said in his: that it takes much of a lifetime to assemble and
integrate a personal self which is capable, not simply of many-
sided self-activity, but of rich self-*actualization*, which is a very
different thing. And what Maslow is, of course, emphatically *not*
saying is that the steady addition of years and of "experience"
bring self-actualization in and of themselves. Otherwise we would
not have the phenomenon that the "fully human" person seems
"like a miracle." You typically look for self-actualized individuals
among people well or long past youth, but even in these supposedly
maturer phases of the life drama, too few are embarked upon
what Maslow calls "good-growth-toward-self-actualization", a process which is already found among a certain proportion of the
young. (Maslow's term reminds one of John Dewey's lovely definition: "A good man is someone trying to be better.")

How far, indeed, is it possible for the self, contending with the
multiplicity of influences, incentives, and frustrations produced in
an unceasing flood within the private cosmos and its interaction
with the great cosmoses of society and eternity, to continue the
process of "becoming"? Is man, when the chips are down, simply
a behavioural animal as perceived by a Pavlov or a Skinner? Does
he merely react to powerful drives when stimulated so as to remove
the feeling of tension, in order that the whole organism can then
achieve a sense of homeostasis, or return to the normal state?

For anyone who believes in what I call "the Ulyssean concept"
this point of view is untenable. It derives from a century of what
critics have recently and unkindly called "rat-oriented psychology"
—the conviction that there are overpowering analogies between
rats and man. "If only," Maslow once asked innocently, "we could
really know what is going on in the rat's mind." The being, Man,
soaked in cruelty and ignorance though he is, is much too versatile
and elusive a creature to be trapped in the box of the Stimulus-
Response mechanism.

Researchers have, of course, learned much about functioning
by experimenting with rats, monkeys, and pigeons. Still, human
being are not simply classifiable as animals, and experiments
seeking analogies fall ludicrously short of the mark. Maya Pines
puts the matter trenchantly when she writes:

"People have allowed themselves to be burned at the stake
and have murdered other human beings for purely ideological
reasons. We are governed by a whole world of abstractions

that never affect other animals. Our large cortex produces a complex interplay of associations, memories, and learned programs. Our forebrain, with its planning areas, allows us to see the possible consequences of our acts. What we will do in any circumstance is never simply the result of an electrical stimulus or a drop of chemical. . . ."

Maslow turns a flood of light not only upon what motivates human adults—but also specifically on what motivates the Ulyssean adults of the later years.

The title—even the order of the words—of Maslow's chief work on the subject is itself significant: *Motivation and Personality*. In it, Maslow introduces his conception of a "hierarchy of basic needs." So far as man is an animal, he is a wanting animal: no one satisfied desire keeps him satisfied for very long. He is not so much governed by drives, (although of course they have a role) as pulled by fundamental goals or needs—and these needs arrange themselves in what Maslow calls "a sort of hierarchy of prepotency." Thus the needs at the base of the hierarchy or ladder are physiological, and although while he is satisfying them the human being already has the potential for higher needs, these physiological wants must usually be satisfied before the man or woman can get on to less body-centred desires. For example, intense hunger normally monopolizes the whole attention of the "wanting animal", who otherwise with his restless, never-satisfied desire system would be moving on to yet new domains of needs and goals.

Next are the safety needs (for example, security, protection, freedom from fear, good order, and so on). Maslow, concerned as he is with adults, notes parenthetically how crucial, however, safety needs must be in childhood. Consider the case of the child threatened by parental break-up, by assault, by the name-calling of his fellows, by a hundred seemingly uncontrollable threats. Some of the roots of adult neuroses are here. For Maslow, a neurotic adult is "a grown-up person who retains his childhood attitudes toward the world . . . it is as if childish attitudes of fear and threat reaction to a dangerous world have gone underground, and untouched by the growing-up and learning processes, were now ready to be called out by any stimulus that could make a child feel endangered and threatened." Hence arises the "basic anxiety" of many adult people which Karen Horney wrote about in *The Neurotic Personality of Our Time*. (Compare "the whole complicated structure of neurosis" which Andras Angyal described as being "founded on the secret feeling of worthlessness, that is, on the belief that one is inadequate to master the situations that confront him and that he is undeserving of love.") Maslow's self-actualized adult, and just as much so, the Ulyssean adult, are human individuals who have either found healthy surety in the safety needs, so that they can go on to the higher desires and challenges of the hierarchy, or have by various means surmounted the feelings of insatiable craving for safety which otherwise would make them cocoon-dwellers and milquetoasts.

And indeed, apropos of Angyal's comment, in the next rank in Maslow's hierarchy of human needs are what he calls, *the belongingness and love needs*. Here is a new hunger—the hunger for affection, for inclusion: the longing not to be left lonely, ostracized, rejected, friendless, rootless. The phenomenon of sex, with all its facets, is physiological; love, on the other hand, is a generator of deeper and more subtle motivations toward the final two major levels of the hierarchy. Maslow is at pains to stress that the love needs incorporate both the giving and receiving of love: and here one turns usefully again to the wisdom of Andras Angyal.

To Angyal, who sees the human personality in this case as two-dimensional: "self-determination on the one hand, self-surrender on the other," it is destructive to the individual personality to lose "the freedom to love." For this freedom "presupposes that instead of anxiously standing watch over one's safety, one dares to go out of oneself, to abandon oneself, to participate in the life of others." And this participation of love implies the "recognition and accept-ance of the *otherness* of the other person" (my italics): "in order to love, it is essential that a man come out of his shell, that he transcend his individuality, that he 'lose himself'." Thus: "one is enriched through a vital participation in another life without want-ing, however, to possess the other person."

Close to the summit of Maslow's hierarchy are the *esteem* needs: the need of the esteem of others, and far more, of self-esteem. At this point Maslow approaches the great sphere of the self-image. He rapidly diverts attention from needs for reputation and prestige, for fame, glory, dominance and importance, to needs for strength, for adequacy, for mastery and competence, for inde-pendence, freedom, and "confidence in the face of the world." Thus he returns to some of the themes of Alfred Adler who developed the concept of the inferiority complex as the deep basis of neurosis.

To feel that one is useful, to feel that one's life has worth! Off-stage one hears again the voice of Andras Angyal, deeply moved: "Often one wonders why the child accepts the verdict that he is worthless, instead of blaming the parent for being so obviously lacking in understanding, so wrong and selfish. The answer sug-gests itself that the child needs so much to feel that he has 'good parents' that he tenaciously adheres to this belief, and would rather assume himself to be evil or worthless than give up the idea that he has good parents." Perhaps in the long process of "becoming," the child, grown to adulthood, and among certain good healings and companionships of the world, recovers his self-esteem; perhaps as a young adult he shoots himself on a garbage dump; or as an old adult obscenely curses his image before a mirror in the antiseptic climate of a nursing home. Perhaps he is one of the great armies of emotionally healthy people who Maslow insists exist, who carry self-esteem with them to such a degree that it actively promotes feelings of capability and self-confidence.

At all events (according to Maslow), here is another powerful and highly-governing growth need which can pull adult men and women upward in the long process of "becoming." It is one which, if it is to be actualized and in turn promote the continuing growth of the wanting animal, Man, must be based on deserved respect from self-recognized real accomplishment, rather than simply the opinions of others.

Thus we approach the summit territory of Maslow's hierarchy: *the need for "self-actualization":* that is the restlessness which develops in someone in whom the other great hierarchical needs have been wholly or chiefly met, and who is typically looking for the individual creativity which he must actualize and fulfil.

In fact, at this summit level of the basic needs, it is perhaps tiresome but necessary to point out that no one is expected to interpret the passage of a human being through the various levels of needs or goals as a total exercise of completion at and for each level. Life is rarely lived that way. On this Maslow himself remarks:

> "In actual fact, most members of our society who are normal are partially satisfied in all their basic needs and partially unsatisfied in all their basic needs at the same time. A more realistic description of the hierarchy would be in terms of decreasing percentages of satisfaction as we go up the hierarchy of prepotency."

And Maslow suggests that new needs may appear when the current or "prepotent" need is largely, not wholly, satisfied.

It is important also to point out that Abraham Maslow did not construct his hierarchy simply sitting at a desk, pen in hand, but rather from years of clinical and semi-clinical observations, and from several thousand personal contacts.

Like the man confronted on the midsummer evening by "the man he might have been", all of us have unrealized potentialities that would astonish and sadden us if we knew. For many people there is a kind of general malaise, a soul sickness, which overtakes them when they are frustrated (or frustrate themselves) from developing "the kingdom of the mind." An all too common phenomenon to practising psychiatrists and priests is the man or woman who is blocked from the satisfaction of intellectual curiosity, the constant exercise of perhaps a once supple and lovely mind: to such an extent that their condition is beyond malaise, it is neurotic, even pathological. Maslow writes angrily about the general depression of the body and the steady deterioration of the intellectual life of "intelligent people leading stupid lives in stupid jobs"; and tells of seeing "many women, intelligent, prosperous, and unoccupied, slowly develop these same symptoms of intellectual inanition."

I recall a number of years ago mournfully watching the slow slide into wholly unnecessary senility of an elderly former school teacher in a London, Ontario nursing home—the kind of nursing home where everything was clean, warm, safe, full of official smiles. This resident had, however, no visitors, no money, no books: the thought of books had never penetrated the acquisitive mind of the absentee owners. Here was a bright, normally curious woman only in her mid-70s, bravely trying to draw me or other visitors into conversation, in the room filled with bed-ridden (sometimes senile) old ladies. Her laughter, in this well-disposed prison, was nervous and uncertain even in the first days. Months later, in the terrible desert of her loneliness and the damming-up of her intelligence, she had become a taunting, increasingly senile shadow not merely of the woman she might have been, but the woman she had been for years previously.

The powerful thrust which adult human beings ordinarily have toward some kind of self-actualization is borne out in many ways. The studies of the Canadian adult educator, Allen Tough, dealing with why adults learn and the manifold ways in which they try to learn, have lighted up a much neglected fact: that a great number of adult people throughout much of their adult lives are engaged on one or more learning projects, often virtually unaware that they could be described in these terms, and with their activities unknown to most or all of their friends. Tough's formal writing has little to say about adults in their later years, but one of my students, who was captivated by the idea of this unseen learning, went through her apartment building in Toronto interviewing a number of people of all ages, and found fascinating verification of Tough's theme. The fact, incidentally, that many of these learning exercises are so-called "temporary systems"—that is, experiences and decision-making exercises that "have their day and cease to be" (a jury at a murder trial, or an abortive attempt of six weeks' duration of a 40-year-old man to teach himself the guitar)—does not destroy their interest or validity.

Further evidence of the self-actualization surge and flow in adult life is seen in the widespread phenomenon of mature people of all classes and racial groups who are fascinated by the possibility of somehow recording their life stories, either in a printed memoir or a tape recording or through handwritten notes for those who "come after." This common feeling and tendency of later adult life is not always, as cynics would claim, mere egotism and vanity: a useless expiring attempt to salvage the identity of the individual self against the indifference of the world and the final coming of the night. It is also an authentic impulse toward self-actualization: a creative design, however small or obscure, containing within it the dynamism of continuing growth. (It may, of course, be sometimes a wholly self-adulatory exercise, sealing off the life from its remaining potentiality.)

One can find still further evidence of the universal thrust toward some form of self-actualization not only in Abraham Maslow's whole "hierarchy" theory, but by taking issue with him on one of his famous theses. Maslow, as already noted, suggests that if safety needs are heavily threatened, the human being will tend not to get on to the higher needs and goals—and Maslow specifically cites the people and situations involved as being neurotic or near-neurotic individuals, economic and social underdogs, or "social chaos, revolution, or breakdown of authority." But in fact one could build an enormous catalogue of adult people who have engaged in self-actualizing creativity even in the midst of seemingly terrifying threats to their safety worlds. In the case of neurosis alone (which Maslow largely abandons in his discussion of motivation and personality on behalf of what he rightly suggests are the neglected "healthy" members of society) one could make a substantial case for the possible contribution of neurosis to personal creativity, in spite of the vehement denial of this thesis on the part of observers like Arthur Koestler and L. S. Kubie.

To be *self*-actualized: once again, as in so many of the compounds involving "self," the strength of the noun is lost in the verb. Likewise, an enormous problem of adult human life is lost among the innumerable conventionalities and clichés about the life journey. The problem can be put as a sombre question: why do so few of us develop so faint an outline of what could be the full richness of our achieved potentialities? When all our undoubted deterrents and legitimate excuses have been put into the assessment—could we not have been, and still be, far more self-actualized human beings? And our omissions—those deadliest of sins—could they not have been, and still be, converted into commissions with their own splendour, secret or public, small or large?

Although Maslow and his associates conducted an extensive survey on young, developing people, the centre of their attention and analysis was adults mature in years and experience, and they turned both to living individuals and to "historical personages." Maslow's study, which in any event was largely unorthodox in its inevitable by-passing of conventional reliability, validity, and sampling, had serious difficulties in assembling, sorting, and evaluating the data from the lives of living people. Probably just because of the kind of self-actualized adults they were, the "subjects" tended to laugh off the exercise, become self-conscious about so formal an analysis of their qualities, or simply break off their participation in the study.

Maslow and associates obviously did not have the same problem with the "historical personages", except that as with all selective lists, some of the names included and omitted will strike the reader as curious. Where is Freud, for example? In addition to about fifteen contemporaries who took part but whose names could not be divulged, Maslow's definite list of public and historical figures included Thomas Jefferson and Lincoln in his last years, Einstein, Eleanor Roosevelt, Jane Addams, William James, Albert Schweitzer, Aldous Huxley, and Spinoza. His less definite list comprised G. W. Carver, Eugene V. Debs, Thomas Eakins, Fritz Kreisler, Goethe, Pablo Casals, Martin Buber, Danilo Dolci, Arthur E. Morgan, Keats, David Hilbert, Arthur Waley, D. T. Suzuki, Adlai Stevenson, Sholom Aleichem, Robert Browning, Ralph Waldo Emerson, Frederick Douglass, Joseph Schumpeter, Robert Benchley, Ida Tarbell, Harriet Tubman, George Washington, Karl Muenzinger, Haydn, Pissarro, Edward Bibring, George William Russell (A.E.), Renoir, Longfellow, Peter Kropotkin, John Altgeld, Thomas More, Edward Bellamy, Benjamin Franklin, John Muir, Walt Whitman.

What were the criteria upon which the selection was based, and which arose, of course, from the personalities of those selected? I have provided below as a kind of code my own lean summary of Maslow's "characteristics" of self-actualizing people. Readers will undoubtedly find themselves reacting to the list very much as we all do to a group photograph in which we have a place —our reactions concentrating intensely on how we appear in the photo. Needless to say, this abbreviated version can only suggest the richness with which Maslow treated the subject in *Motivation and Personality*.

> *Characteristics of Self-actualizing People: a Study of Psychological Health:*
> 1. *More efficient perception of reality and more comfortable relations with it.*
>   Unusual ability to detect the fake and the dishonest in personality. In all spheres could see concealed or confused realities more swiftly and more correctly than others. Good perception, much less tinged by wish, desire, prejudice, fear. They are comfortable with the unknown; actually seem to take a certain pleasure from difficult decisions.
> 2. *Acceptance (Self, Others, Nature).*
>   Not self-satisfied—but they accept their frailties without undue concern. "Water is wet, rocks are hard, etc." They

see human nature as it *is;* not as they would prefer it to be. They accept themselves and others at the healthy animal level; at higher levels also; they are the *un*disgusted; they're without pose and don't like pose in others (but accept it). They don't feel unnecessary guilt and shame. They feel badly about the discrepancies between what is and what may be.

3. *Spontaneity.*
   Keep up most of the conventions out of consideration for others; but are actually internally unconventional, spontaneous, natural. They make their issues over large matters, not the trivia of custom. They often feel like spies in a foreign land. Often they show their inner spontaneity; they're more truly "aware" than the weighed-down "adjusted." To them motivation is just "self-actualization."

4. *Problem-Centring.*
   They are problem-centred rather than ego-centred. They like compelling tasks which are not for small or petty and selfish ends. They seem to impart to colleagues a certain sense of larger horizons, *sub specie aeternitatis,* more serene, less fraught with worry.

5. *The Quality of Detachment; the Need of Privacy.*
   They can be solitary, without discomfort or damage to themselves. They like solitude and privacy more than the average do. They know the quality of "detachment." They have a certain intrinsic dignity in the midst of misfortune. Their "detachment" is often interpreted by others as "coldness." Actually, even in misfortune they see the problem of the *situation* beyond or above that of ego or people. They can concentrate to an unusual degree (seemingly absent-minded).

6. *Autonomy, Independence of Culture and Environment.*
   These people are *growth*-motivated, not deficiency-motivated. Hence they are more independent of environment, more self-contained. Real self-development and real inner growth are more important to them than honours and status. (They must have had a lot of love and respect in childhood.)

7. *Continued Freshness of Appreciation.*
   They have over and over again the same euphoria or ecstasy from beautiful things, people, scenes, relationships.

8. *Mystic Experience; Oceanic Feeling.*
   Experiences are frequent, including during the sexual encounter, in which "horizons open"; feelings of awe; feelings of disorientation with time and space—the person then being transformed and strengthened in his daily life.

9. *Gemeinschaftsgefuhl.*
   They have feelings for mankind of identification, sym-

pathy, affection—desire to help the human race: "they are my brothers." The self-actualizing person is different from others in thought, impulse, behaviour, emotion. This gives him great advantages, but potentially great frustration and exasperation. Still, he maintains what Adler called "the older-brotherly" attitude.

10. *Interpersonal Relations of the Self-Actualized.*
They are less ego-bound, have deeper interpersonal relations than others. More fusion, more love (but often among themselves!). Kind or patient to almost everyone, they have few close friends—close friendship takes and demands time. They understand pomp and pettiness and meanness; don't condone them, don't like them, but understand them. When hostile, their hostility is not character-based, but is reactive or situational (compare Erich Fromm's views). They attract disciples but try to discourage them.

11. *Democratic Character Structure.*
They are friendly with anyone of suitable character regardless of class, education, political belief, race, or colour. These individuals, themselves élite, select élite people for their friends—but an élite of character, capacity, and talent, rather than of birth, race, fame, power.

12. *Means and Ends.*
They put their stress on ends; have moral standards; they do right, not wrong, but their "right" may not be conventional.

13. *Philosophical. Unhostile Sense of Humour.*
Not addicted to slapstick, hostile humour, superiority humour, authority-rebellion humour but, rather, humour which is spontaneous and which helps produce perspectives.

14. *Creativeness.*
The creativeness of the self-actualized is different from the "special talent" creativeness of the genius. Rather it is a special way of looking at life all their life: a fresh, even naive way, similar to that of children. It is a creative attitude not killed by acculturation, and promoting creativity as a life style. Thus they often become trailbreakers for all others.

As with any catalogue of virtues or virtuous people, Maslow's list of the notable qualities possessed by the self-actualized adults is certainly overpowering. Small wonder (thinks the reader) that a "fully-human person seems like a miracle." Besides, despite the enormous attention which Maslow gave to attempting in as scholarly a manner as possible (considering his impressionistic approach) to refract the many-splendoured colours coming from these human supernovas and other more obscure but splendid stars, one cannot wholly dispel the feeling that a hortative element is present.

What has all this to do with creativity and its cultivation? In a study of over 300 pages, Maslow devotes only five or six to a discussion of what he prefers to call "creativeness"—but the discussion is worth it. "Creativeness" is an attitude toward all of life: to possess it is to touch everything one meets, works with, and experiences with a kind of magic—the magic of the freshness of the child.

It is a beautiful concept: as I have already indicated, it democratizes and universalizes creativity and opens up potentialities for self-esteem and a sense of investment and reinvestment in growth as no other concept can do. If it also seems to vulgarize creativity, no doubt Maslow's defenders would cite his development of the "other" concept of creativity—special talent creativeness—as satisfying all the requirements of high originality and exclusiveness.

What has it all got to do with the Ulyssean adult—the adventurer of the later adult years? Both much and not much, depending upon one's view from the bridge. "Much", because to be self-actualized, Maslow-style, is also to realize certain Ulyssean attributes: for example, openness to experience, realistic appraisal and acceptance of others, ability to be solitary without being unsocial, capacity to generate one's own growth, and to rely on one's own self-evaluation, rather than the imposed values of the world. The more one becomes self-actualized during the first five decades of one's life journey, the more potentiality one has, surely, to become Ulyssean in the later years.

"Not much," perhaps, to the extent that the pure equability of attitude, style, and seeming performance of the Maslovian self-actualized adult presents an idealized state very different from the chaotic, sin-soaked, guilt-ridden, and fear-bedevilled personal arena in which great numbers of adult people live out their lives and still, by personal heroisms, become Ulysseans. Even on a less dramatic scale, the experience of middle and later adulthood is often composed of periods of consecutive or sustained turbulence: often, in the late twentieth century, the turbulence of change.

For example, in January, 1971, Thomas Holmes, professor of psychiatry at the University of Washington in Seattle, reported a study on the hazards of change to the American Association for the Advancement of Science. Holmes was fascinated by what might be described as the negotiable levels or thresholds up to which adult people could efficiently handle the stresses of change without breaking down. Over a period of two years he and his associates carefully observed and recorded the many events causing change in the lives of eighty Seattle adults, and then attempted to correlate their personal-change histories with whatever physical and mental illnesses had occurred. There was a certain level of accumulation of changes and stress in individual lives, Holmes found, beyond which the human adult self could not go without danger to physical or mental health.

In what looks like an all-too-simple technique, but which at least had the advantage of vividly illustrating the essence of his argument, Holmes allotted a score of 50 points to the act of getting married, and then established various allotments for thirty-eight other stress-creating life changes. He took advice on his list of scores from people in several countries who rated the change-event against the basic 50-point event of marriage. (See Chart II) What

Chart II
RATING LIFE CHANGES

Life Event	Value	Life Event	Value
Death of spouse	100	Change in responsibilities at work	29
Divorce	73		
Marital separation	65	Son or daughter leaving home	29
Jail term	63	Trouble with in-laws	29
Death of close family member	63	Outstanding personal achievement	28
Personal injury or illness	53		
Marriage	50	Wife beginning or stopping work	26
Fired at work	47		
Marital reconciliation	45	Beginning or ending school	26
Retirement	45	Revision of personal habits	24
Change in health of family member	44	Trouble with boss	23
Pregnancy	40	Change in work hours or conditions	20
Sex difficulties	39		
Gain of new family member	39	Change in residence	20
		Change in schools	20
Change in financial state	38	Change in recreation	19
Death of close friend	37	Change in social activities	18
Change to different line of work	36	Mortgage or loan less than $10,000	17
		Change in sleeping habits	16
Change in number of arguments with spouse	35	Change in number of family get-togethers	15
Mortgage over $10,000	31	Change in eating habits	15
Foreclosure of mortgage or loan	30	Vacation	13
		Minor violations of the law	11

Time, March 1, 1971

is least impressive in the rating of the life changes is the assignment of the scores. But what is most impressive, and very relevant to discussions of fully self-actualized and of Ulyssean adults is the often overlooked panorama of stress-in-change which Holmes's approach provides. One can conceive Maslow's fully-actualized adult moving with nobility through these many hazards and crises, but at least a continuously-running motion picture should appear as a background against which the human actors play out their various roles.

Neither has Maslow's portrait of the fully self-actualized adult, for all its value, much to do with the late Ulyssean life in one important sense. Ulysseanism implies, not only that you may indeed have prepared for it through the fifty or more preceding years of your life drama, but that you may have to begin *where you are* in your anxiety-filled, guilt-ridden arena of the self to start the Ulyssean process—*and that such a start is possible.* Maslow has an infuriating habit of separating the population radically into healthy or "intact" people, on the one hand, and "sick, neurotic people" on the other: "sick neurotic people make the wrong choices; they do not know what they want, and even when they do, have not courage enough to choose correctly", and so on. Enormously human and liberating as he is, Maslow does not pay sufficient attention to the unbelievable complexity of people's open and hidden existences; their struggles with Holmes's thirty-nine life-change stresses; confused and mysterious potentialities; and half-aborted neurotic tendencies which make up many of the lives of middle-aged and older adults who *may yet* choose the Ulyssean way. In this respect, at least, Robert Peck's system of choices-still-remaining between "I happening to life" and "life happening to me" remains a strong and moving complement to Maslow's growth-inducing but perhaps too formidable image of the fully self-actualized.

In fact, what holds back great numbers of later adults from Ulyssean adventures has little to do with neurotic fear. It is rather a fundamental lack of confidence, based on a gigantic misconception: that one's powers must steadily decline and increasingly lose the ability to cope with the challenge of creativity in the later years. To choose between the Good Life and the Dark Life—yes, that is different. In North American society where institutional religion is largely passé among the young, those of us in our 40s and older who were schooled in it and (whatever our faith) in the Puritan ethic, still have the feeling in our bones that ethical recoveries and "better lives" late in the day are always possible. We understand the situation of the large, middle-aged, mild-spoken Montreal taxi-driver who said to me in the course of a long ride in the summer twilight: "When I was a child of darkness, before I became a child of light. . . ." He astonished and intrigued me with his appearance and style, but I had no problem accepting his premise and his situation—nor would many readers of this book.

But to actualize and continue the *creativity* of the self, to maintain its productivity of mind and hand—this for many is quite a different matter. As the self enters the later stages of its long journey through life, it often loses heart. Where once it may have identified itself with achievement and strength, it begins now to identify itself with deficits and weakness. As its image of itself as effective human learner blurs (that self-image which is the governor of all our lives), its confidence falters.

We live at a time and in a society where two powerful influences converge to undermine and often sweep away the confidence which is indispensable to human adults in their later years. One is the almost universal practice of retiring to the sidelines of the great vocational game everyone except entrepreneurial professionals, small business proprietors, people in the arts and, of course, our indispensable politicians. The other is society's morbid obsession with the cerebral or cognitive process isolated from the whole personality or self, and then conceived of as being in steady decline.

The second influence is especially pernicious: all the more for being founded upon an illusion. Human history, of course, is filled with the records of mass delusions, usually fostered by powerful minority or authority groups for their own benefit, or springing from the dark folklore of the past. But it has been reserved for late twentieth century North American society—the society *par excellence* of the "voice of science" and the mass media—to retain and embellish an ancient myth, and then to propagate it on an unprecedented scale: the myth that adults in their later years must steadily lose their powers to learn, to create, and to produce—and that therefore they must become the bystanders and the onlookers in the amphitheatre of active life.

4. THE PERILS AND POTENTIALS OF THE LATER YEARS

Two formidable antagonists stand on the great highway which leads to the late creative years, menacing those adults who still seek to be Ulyssean. Their names are Lack of Time and Failure of Powers, and not even the monsters met by John Bunyan's Pilgrim on his heroic journey were as fearful—although they are blood relations of Giant Despair.

Late middle age, for those who are reasonably fortunate, has both a real and a deceptive beauty. The tired analogy which compares the life journey and the seasons was never truer here. For just as in early fall there is a period when nature seems to remain poised between summer and winter, so the later years also have their halcyon period.

Certain excitements, dreams, and pleasures are past. For those who married, the children are grown and away, and at last there is the chance to live for oneself and rediscover oneself. For those who are unmarried, elderly parents and other relatives, lovingly protected while they were here, are gone, and along with the sadness of their absence comes the understanding of releases to be more oneself and to re-awaken certain subdued aspects of the self. Certain feverish ambitions are past: either older adults have attained much of what they wanted, or else they have become mostly reconciled to whatever state their talents, their deficits, and especially the element of sheer luck, have delivered them to.

For those later adults who seem fortunate, there are the satisfactions of a pleasant house or apartment, secure for many years; a circle of friends for encouragement and stimulation; the opportunity to continue and to enrich the reading habit acquired long ago in good schools and homes; the chance to travel as never before and funds to do so; and the possibility of taking up any of dozens of interests which may lead to further self-discovery and creativity in the later years. In any "good" neighbourhood there is an abundance of houses of youngish grandparents where the lights go on later on Christmas morning than they used to, and where the convivial lights of late afternoons on week-ends welcome in circles of people like themselves, as well as younger people for whom such people often represent the good life.

Millions, literally millions, of older adults are not so fortunate. They are pursued into the later 50s and 60s of their lives by all or some of the same conditions which have harassed them during most or all of their adulthood. They are without financial security, without good and secure housing, without good health, saddled with debt, and bedevilled by the anxieties that come from family disruptions and misfortunes—especially by Anxiety itself, the great Fearmaker.

For such older travellers on the Ways it is possible to stand in a kind of autumn paradise, sun, air, and earth calling to one from every sector within view, and to have one's pleasure senses so eclipsed by fear, worry, and grief that much or all of the paradise is lost. These are the multitudes of people in later life for whom no glib rhetoric or frenetic strategies can meet the complex needs of their dilemmas.

For only a proportion, it is true, is the loss of joy in the halcyon years total. For many, in spite of continued misfortune and deprivation, some of the components of the enchanted early autumn of the life journey emerge, on their own terms, and in these personal arenas which are so radically different from those of the "fortunate" people—arenas which nonetheless offer opportunities for continuing growth and creativity.

"Nonetheless", because personal growth of the self, which should be the great continuing adventure of the whole adult life journey, may be aborted among the so-called "fortunate", and may, on the other hand, be stimulated by defeat and adversity—in some cases, even by despair. Blandness and comfort may be, and often are, the embalmers of the creative spirit.

Too often, however, the accumulation of negative forces—consecutive sorrows, impoverishment, wretched health, loneliness, remorse, disgust at chances lost, gnawing insecurity, fear of helpless abandonment if struck down by some crippling illness, and little or no equipment to make use in later years of the kingdom of the mind—may extinguish what is left of the self-actualizing spirit. The fate of the once buoyant priest in H.M. Robinson's novel, *The Cardinal*, is symbolic of great numbers of older adults. Joyous and confident when he first took on the pastorate of the monstrously debt-laden church which drained away his life in a struggle to bring fresh light and life to it, at the end his physical and emotional powers were as crushed as though the huge building itself had fallen upon him. The theory of Abraham Maslow's "hierarchy of human needs" finds confirmation enough in the fate of many later adults who, because they have been less successful and less fortunate, are condemned to coping with safety, and even subsistance, needs, at the point when they should be happily released into the halcyon country where their greatest life concern should be creativeness and self-actualization.

Yet many of the physically and environmentally "fortunate" cease to be active seekers. Not only are they as a group liable in any case to many of the fundamental perils of the later human condition but many of them become as locked into a constricting, spectating, and non-personally creative life style as though they were not liberated, as they technically are, to pursue the highest domains of Maslow's hierarchy.

Almost any category among the later adults who have any vulnerability and sensitivity at all—whether they are the impoverished and overwhelmed or the fortunate and seemingly liberated for self-actualization—will feel the shadow on the trail ahead of the twin monsters, Lack of Time and Failure of Powers. But it is especially the seekers, the would-be Ulysseans, those later adults who are, of course, the truly "beautiful people", for whom the menace of these sombre giants may seem most potent and most tragic.

For these people are the bearers of dreams. The dream may be very recent, born late in the day out of the mysterious processes of the unconscious self, or it may be (and very often is) a dream cherished for years but never actualized because of force of circumstances. Thus Lloyd C. Douglas and Thomas Costain kept their ambitions to be novelists in rein until far along the life-cycle; Grandma Moses did not begin to paint until past 70; Alcide de Gasperi was forced to suspend his plans and hopes for a new Italy until at the age of 64 he was finally released from the obscurity of a librarian's post, where he had waited out the interminable years of World War Two. One can also cite cases again from the noble army of the uncelebrated: the educator who deferred his dream of graduating as a lawyer until he was 69; the elderly woman who waited until her 80s to begin studying a foreign language; the two senior men in Canadian broadcasting, both in the early 60s, their wives recently dead, their children grown, who began at last the studies for the priesthood which under different life conditions they would have started years before.*

For those who are the bearers of secret dreams which must be hidden or at least deferred, Time—so often the ally and healer of men and women—is the antagonist on the Way, and his new and dark name is Lack of Time. The adult seeker often becomes intensely conscious of the ages and exploits of veritable doers who are reported in the media—including the absurd comedy of the news magazine which brackets the ages of "people in the news" in all

---

*A fascinating reverse case is seen in the career of John Tettemer, an American Passionist monk, who in 1924 at age 50 left the Order in which he had become the second highest world officer to assume secular life, marry, have children, and become a film actor in his later years. The separation from his Order was without rancour, and in fact with affection on both sides.

accounts, regardless of whether age has any relevance to the situation or not. For example: "unsmiling, balding Wendell Supercrat (48) stumbled out of the 6.30 a.m. flight from Kansas City." The news magazine clearly dislikes Supercrat, but the ultimate idiocy is its obsession with his age.

We are constantly told by one of the few hoary classical tags that still have wide currency in an era too clever for the classics, that life is short and the arts are long—but in fact there is a period when there seems all kinds of time ahead, say, during the 20s and 30s and even into the early 40s, in spite of the self-consciously tragic statements often made to the contrary by the inhabitants of those cohort periods. For example, the typical "reading adult" reads widely and carelessly during much of that stretch of the lifespan. Many people realize only at age 50 or 55 that there is only so much time left and so many books to read—books that really matter—that one must establish some kind of rigorous priority system.

As with reading, so with many other of life's delights. There are so many plays to be seen, so many countries to be visited, so many talented musicians to be heard; so many new and growth-bearing experiences to be encountered, so many people worth knowing to be known; so many creative efforts, large or small, to be made. And, in what the psychologists persist in calling the affective domain, so many loving relationships to be opened or deepened, so many ways of actualizing one's role as wayfaring companion to the companionless, that it seems that there is world enough, but no time, no time. Where has all the time gone?

Even for the most mature seekers in the best of conditions in the enchanted halcyon period there is a chill in the air. Now the temptation is to play a new numbers game—secretly to subtract one's age from the announced average lifespan of men and women in our time, and to balance the difference against the needs and goals of the older adult, opportunities lost and possibilities remaining. Since priests and clergymen seem to have remarkably little to say about all this, one can go quietly by oneself to the pages of Ecclesiastes or to Cicero's *De Senectute,* or acquire for oneself the undoubted wisdom that life is, after all, a kind of smorgasbord—we could never have everything we want. To try is certainly to encounter the tragedies of either Faust or Hamlet. *Wisdom is selection:* our rational self knows this to be true. But man is also insatiable—that is both his tragedy and his triumph. And it is also what Maslow and other humanistic observers of the human scene in our time are talking about when they speak (each in his own terms) of the unremitting thrust toward continuing and escalating goals and needs of the human species.

Nor is the longest shadow thrown on the trail ahead in the later adult years that of Lack of Time alone. If one were to play out the last quarter of the game in a state of superb health and undimmed powers of mind and concentration, there would be little enough time. But in fact, for many older adults the greater threat is Failure of Powers; many believe it is so, many can feel that it is so, and almost everything in the folklore of the human life journey reinforces their pessimism.

Clearly, the decline of physical powers is one of the rules of the game. Diminution of perfect hearing begins at an early age in adulthood, usually from about 30 on; loss of high tone perception is common among adults over 40, and increases rather markedly for many after 65, for men more so than women. The same is true of sight: visual acuity begins to decline slightly from about the mid-20s to the 50s, and then often shows a rather pronounced deterioration: the bifocal years are a stage in the process, with the late years presenting for some adults the problem of cataracts, fortunately usually solved by modern surgery. Among the aged population of a huge home in New York, 86 per cent were reported as having from good to adequate vision; in an even bigger institution in California, out of 1500 late adults, only 3 per cent were described as functionally blind. Blindness, although it occurs, is not a serious threat: for those who seek to live as fully as possible, and to create, the fatigue induced by waning powers of sight may be the greater hazard.

Power to taste is apparently slightly affected for many people by a slight decline in the number of taste buds up to age 70, with a greater decline thereafter. Still, taste is a highly individualized reaction which does not yield easily to research criteria. In any event, for some items of the modern North American diet, loss of the sense of taste would not necessarily be a catastrophe; the taste of mass-produced bread, for example (loaded, of course, with its rejuvenating vitamins)—which led the Ulyssean Henry Miller to write indignantly on returning to America after many years that "not a bloody mother in the bloody land can bake a bloody loaf of bread."

Investigators of physical decline have tested the power to respond to touch of young and old adults, and of course the power to smell. On the latter, there is little to report, in spite of the occasional complaints of loss of this sense by older adults: for some this may be one form of the pastime, which some relish, of enjoying loss of youth. On the former, the evidence of researchers is that there is no change in sensitivity to touch until about perhaps age 50 to 55. Curiously enough, such loss as occurs in the later years is in the lower body rather than in wrists, hands, and elbows, which retain nearly all of their sensitivity.

What disturbs and saddens many adults as they enter and proceed through the later years is their feeling that they are now more exposed to the great organic killer illnesses—strokes, heart diseases, cancer—than before, and this is of course true. Birren's remark, that to live to be elderly is itself a kind of achievement, is some consolation but for the Ulysseans perhaps not much. Besides, many older adults fear the approach of old age as bringing with it generalized infirmities, pains, and sorrows.

The modern writer who has most thoroughly documented what she conceives to be the almost undiluted tragedy of old age is Simone de Beauvoir, in a recent book of almost 600 pages. Other than certain mechanical and clinical accounts by researchers in geriatric medicine, in which of course the living and breathing personality is wholly missing from the factual analysis of the decaying organism, Beauvoir's description of the aging process is surely the gloomiest and most disheartening treatment of this theme available. The reader might have been warned by her handling of her mother's last days in her earlier book, A Very Easy Death, a mordant title which one does not fully appreciate until putting the book down, fingers chilled. Because Beauvoir writes like an angel; because of her compassion for the oppressed and the deserted; and because the theme is, after all, a powerful one, one reads The Coming of Age with a certain obsessed attention. The book, too, is full of wonderful cameos of notable people from the past, mostly Europeans, in the late stages of their life, and it has important things to say about the treatment of the old in modern society.

However, Beauvoir is almost wholly despondent about the effect of the late years of life on a human being. Old age clearly fills her with revulsion, and few of its lineaments reveal anything to her but dark, macabre shapes. Thus she is driven to choose incidents from late life, excerpts from journals, and recorded statements by individuals, which ultimately build an overwhelming portrait of old age as a time of bitterness, desolation, and defeat. No one escapes. The wonderful Ulyssean, Victor Hugo, at first raises one's heart with the magnificence of love of life and the creativity with which he illuminated his late years, but Beauvoir pursues him into the very late phases, when he lost much of his power after a stroke. Here, as in a hundred other cases, Beauvoir piles everything upon the evils of old age: Hugo, after all, might well have been immobilized by a massive heart attack at 48, or have died at 55! For so fine a writer and thinker, it is extraordinary that she does not see that nearly all lives end in anti-climax: the sad short finish of Eleanor Roosevelt's life takes nothing away from the splendid Ulysseanism of her last seventeen years, after the death of her husband.

Likewise, it is prejudicing the case to quote three or four sentences or brief extracts from the journals which many Europeans have kept, and which reflect their civilized sense of culture and of time. Valéry and Gide are both quoted as hating to look in the mirror when they were very old; yet each handled his late years with admirable style. Gide, especially, quoted by Beauvoir as complaining of "all the little indispositions of great age that make an old man such a wretched being" and that "my mind almost never succeeds in distracting me from my flesh", in fact emerges in the *full* journal of his last years as a still vital, intensely human being beyond age 80, still attempting to "get up" his Latin, still curious and interested in the human scene. Indeed, twenty years earlier, on his trips to North Africa, Gide had little complaints to make about his physical condition, and he once recorded the comment that because he normally sat down to write in his journal in a serious mood, the diary might seem to reflect a too continuously sombre personal attitude.

Actually, the same is true of Beauvoir's *The Coming of Age.* Only at long intervals does one get the flash of humour of which she is capable, as in her delightful comment on Victor Hugo's eager curiosity to see and to talk to God, "that is to say, another Hugo." But even when Beauvoir seems to be conceding that old age has attributes of joy, she then consolidates her case that all in the late years is vanity and sorrow. Thus, Gide's charming and inspiriting comment, "My heart has remained so young that I have the continual feeling of playing a part, the part of the seventy-year-old that I certainly am" makes her speculate, surely unreasonably, that for Gide it may have been "out of horror of old age that he looked upon his behaviour as a seventy-year-old in the light of an act."

Still, the Beauvoir book is probably indispensable for all who are weary of the frequently printed fatuities of those writers and "experts" on the late years who try to gloss over the undoubted rigours and anxieties of old age; and for all who, in any event, are entranced by the spectacle of a powerful mind grappling with a significant topic and doing so with splendid style.

Actually, the long shadow of Failure of Powers appears as early as late middle age (for some people, still earlier) in the two physical domains of beauty and of psychomotor skills.

Beauty, of course, is a "power" since it plays an important role in the building and maintenance of the self-image, which in turn affects both a person's own performance throughout the life drama and one's day-to-day relationships with other human beings. "Beauty" here means not merely the "combination of (physical) qualities . . . in human face or form . . . that delights the sight" (*Concise Oxford Dictionary*), but the whole personableness of the individual which conveys some degree of charm or magnetism. To pure physical beauty per se, the aging process is of course considered to be the supreme threat, with the exception of disfiguring illness. Chilling, semi-clinical accounts exist, taken from many novelists and other recorders of life, of the inroads of physical aging upon both male and female beauty. (It is part of the long sickness of Western—and especially North American—society, that it has for so long denied "beauty" to both sexes.)

Whatever beauty is (and many have struggled to define the aesthetics of beauty) it manifests itself in the perfection of face and form of young men and women which is always susceptible to the alterations of the aging process. A homely example of this is seen in the rather morbid but fascinating little books entitled *Where Are They Now?*, which present two illustrations in writing and in photography of once-famous stars of stage and screen. It is hard for the reader, no matter how mature in attitude, not to be saddened at the transformation that the years have made of the physical appearance of many of these once beautiful young adults. And this, of course, is precisely what they themselves, and millions of other adults who play out their own stage roles in the small circles of their lives among friends, family, and competitors, are aware of as the most conspicuous aspect of the Failure of Powers.*

There is, however, a higher maturity which makes different judgments, and sometimes, interestingly, it develops early. For example, a youthful student friend of mine from Finland once made the arresting comment that "No matter how old a woman gets, she never really loses the beauty of femininity." This was the kind of wisdom one also expected from the Canadian best-seller of the '60s, *In Praise of Older Women*, the account of a succession of love affairs, until one found that the "older women" in question were only in their 30s. Nonetheless, the higher maturity wisely notes that for both men and women what the years take away in the pure fresh loveliness of face and form they restore with a different kind of beauty. In fact, to the exponents of the higher maturity, nothing is more incongruous or disappointing than the constantly "lifted" face which in the later years shows none of the etching of sorrow, joy, anxiety, compassion, and pain.

Sometimes, also, in the case of men and women ugly in their youth in the opinion of almost everybody, aging performs a special miracle. As *The Fairfield Journal* remarks: "She was old: her ugliness had faded."

It is well for all of us who are moving through the later and the late years of the life-cycle to achieve the higher maturity, because the aging process leaves no one's physical self unscathed. Once in a long while one sees among the men who throng the pools and exercise rooms of the great YMCAs of the continent (and who may be of all ages from very young to very old) a man of age 50 or 55

---

*The eternal footnote, "for his (or her) age", becomes a kind of threnody of comment upon middle-aged and especially later adults which they have to learn to expect. "John jogs daily at the Y; he is in really excellent condition *for his age*"; or, "You remember what a show-stopper Ursula was? Well, she's still a beautiful woman, *for her age*." And so on.

or even older who has retained the form of one of the youths thirty years younger who is racing away to the handball court or the weight-lifting room—but he is not the same. In close proximity to him one usually finds him an admirable person, but he is no longer a youth: age has put its mark upon his hair, skin, and eyes, and of course (as will be treated at greater length below) upon his suppleness and his psychomotor skills. Likewise, the silly advertising which attempts to confuse the television audience as to which of the pair of women is mother or daughter ("Yes," says the brightly smiling plastic mother, once identified, with her vacuous expression, "both Kathy and I use Multi-Miracle Magic") is itself as cosmetic an exercise as the product it displays. The mother is not the daughter. The years will continue to make their transformation. Her peril lies in identifying the beauty of her self with the face and form she had as a girl; the potential lies in recognizing the new forms of beauty which arrive along with the undoubted deprivations of the years. And the higher maturity says that these forms of beauty which are swiftly discerned by sensitive artists, for example, are acquired not in spite of the sorrows and crises, and the physical losses, encountered and endured across the long passage of the years, but *because* of them.

As for the domain of psychomotor skills, the naked human eye can see the effects of aging in slowing the swift ease of movement which is at least the potential state of most young people. The picture is somewhat clouded because of the appalling deficiencies in carriage, speed, and grace of large numbers of late adolescents and people in their early 20s. The ascending lines of people going up to street level in the subways of the North American cities and often moving at tortoise pace are as likely to be slowed by some slouching and slow-footed teen-agers as by some old man or woman. Older people tend to be slowed down by the thickening and stiffening of their bodies, but many who could walk and even still run with speed and grace actually think themselves into a routine of staidness and slowness, sometimes disguised under the rationale that too great haste leads to premature heart attacks. We are not talking, however, about haste, but about the swift grace which adds cachet and zest to the life process.

Birren usefully defines a psychomotor skill as "an acquired pattern of finely coordinated voluntary movements . . . [not] merely as muscle movements, but rather as complex chains of events in the nervous system, with resulting muscle movement." Thus there is a complex interrelationship between the muscle movement function of the body and the line delivery via brain and nerve cells. For many older adults there is some physiological loss, either because of physical attrition or disuse, and there is the possibility, where mental zest is lost, of increasing slowness or awkwardness in delivery because of a certain slowing of the line communications.

Much of the evidence is concealed because older workers in industrial plants, for example, develop a system of compensations that wipes out or diminishes the losses of performance which aging might bring. Numerous studies indicate little or no change in worker performance through most of the working life of the adult up to the mid 50s. Even beyond this point, the output of many older workers excels that of younger ones. Perhaps, however, a selective process is at work here, only the most proficient of older workers surviving the route to age 65. Temporary losses clearly occur in cases where industry keeps demanding changes in techniques, and they naturally occur where the worker has been injured on the job, although not immobilized.

However, there is a true sense in which practice makes perfect: much heartening evidence exists that even into the 70s, a good many individuals continue to show marked proficiency in the psychomotor skills of occupational tasks. These are a minority of remarkable people about whom we need to know much more, if only to gain more and more evidence for the Ulyssean life. Certainly from age 40 on there is as a rule a reduction of capacity in strength and in sensory acuity; reaction times begin to be longer —a factor which surely contributes the major component to the relatively high traffic accident rate of age 65-plus, and very certainly age 70-plus. The twin peaks in North American statistics for traffic accidents are ages 16-20 and age 70-plus. A study by B. W. Marsh in 1961, on "Aging and Driving" cited speed as the major contributing factor for accidents for drivers under age 30, double that of people in the 70s, whereas exactly the reverse was true of right-of-way conflicts, where the older drivers, in spite of usually slower speeds, were also markedly slower in reaction responses.

Athletics, of course, provides the most striking illustration of loss of psychomotor power with aging. This problem of adjustment especially affects boys and men, since they are more involved in sports than are girls and women. One of the great adjustments which the human male has to make from as early a period as age 30 on is the increasing limitations which aging places on his athletic skill and prowess. For many men, coming to terms with this fact of life is quite as traumatic as a woman's having to adjust to the loss of youthful beauty. The record varies, of course, with the sport, nor do many men realistically expect to become champions. Still, one can hardly name a sport in which champions emerge at age 40 or more.

In some sports the champions are incredibly young: Olympic swimmers, for example, are "old" at 22, and slalom ski champions and figure-skating champions are sometimes in their teens. In other fields, once considered (almost derisively) the domains of middle-aged men—for example, golf and curling—younger men and women in the 20s or 30s are either dominant or are taking over. A magnificent golfer like Sam Snead has represented the older adult who rarely wins a title, but is still considered a superb performer "for his age". However, there are not many Sam Sneads.

Because the aging process slows the reaction time for many adult men and women, so-called top competition becomes impossible in numerous sports, while the nature of most of urban adult life in the late twentieth century almost guarantees that the strength required for many others (the powerful championship drive in golf, for example) will decline. It is not even primarily a question of sustained practice: practice may make perfect, but it will not put the 45-year-old boxer or tennis player back into the championship circle or even among the near contenders (wonderful exceptions like Archie Moore and Pancho Gonzales only prove the rule.) Occasionally an enterprising older adult will create his own arena for conquest, like the remarkable South African of the '60s who became world record-holder for events requiring the running of sixty, eighty, and hundred mile marathons. And some fields of very intense psychomotor activity can certainly be classified as sports—round-the-world competitive yachting, for example—in which astonishing older adults are leading figures.

Sportswriters are very familiar with the traumatic experience undergone by many team athletes, let alone individual performers, when they realize that they must, quite literally because of age, go out of high competition. It is true that much of what professional athletes miss as they move into retirement in their 40s is the fame and the excitement which participation brought them, but the shock is deeper than this. To the body-oriented man who is the athletic devotee, there is an actual beauty to the superb working of his whole physique, which has legitimate comparisons with the pleasure that a woman takes in her physical beauty; to each, the loss of this form of joy is often a problem of crisis proportions. Besides, in the case of sports, even the atmosphere of the arena, the gymnasium, the grass court or links, or the great pool, and the camaraderie of locker rooms and companions can make up a milieu and a lifestyle which becomes literally beloved. One of Franklin Delano Roosevelt's biographers reported that years after his crippling encounter with polio, and even when he had with supreme courage attained the presidency of the United States, Roosevelt would still turn his face away when his car passed a golf course.

Yet, says the higher maturity, there is no essential tragedy in the fact that human beings lose long before the middle years the capacity to be championship contenders or even high performers in many sports. This is the human condition. And even here there are many exceptions: fishing, hunting, cycling, hiking, hill-climbing, billiards (what psychologist of adulthood ever had the imagination to study Willie Hoppe?) and dancing (who has had the wit to do other than superficially interview Fred Astaire?)—there are numerous others before one begins to reach the world of parlour games. In addition, it may be that with the "new athlete" of recent years we are on the threshold of new breakthroughs in longevity of performance.

The real tragedy is the abdication which enormous numbers of men and women make from one of the most important domains of the self—the physical. The most remarkable phenomenon about the gymnasiums and arenas where sports are played in North America is the absence of adults in their middle years and older. To participate in no activity in which the body is released to feel the sheer delight of its own freedom and movement, never to enter a physical world where all creatures are at play, and to attempt to replace this loss by eternally watching professional athletes on the TV screen is a mournful and, in some cases a dangerous, choice of alternatives. Health rationales aside, the tragic loss is psychic.

To love one's self: this is where all psychic healing begins; to *love*, not to adore, not to condone, not to deceive. And an aspect of self-love almost wholly neglected by the pundits, and by people in general, is the role of love of one's body. It is a peril of all the adult years, but a special danger of later adulthood, that one will be repelled by one's physical state. This destructive self-revulsion, conscious or unconscious, and turned into a sour hatred of youth and beauty, can poison the wells of the creative and Ulyssean life. Some psychological historians have traced this state to its most dramatic climax in international and legal affairs by speculating on the role played by the hatred of old men of power for the youth and beauty of young men in the making of war and the delivery of hideous verdicts in the courts.

No doubt this tendency to transfer self-revulsion to antipathy and hatred for others is at work in thousands of less dramatic arenas every day. But the crucial intersection between Failure of Powers in the physical sense and the capacity to maintain vital and creative growth through the later adult years provides the chance for physical joy *on some terms* for almost everyone. And it has little to do with size and shape for those who are on the way to the higher maturity. Throughout nearly all of life, into and through the very late years, it is possible to tap some of the springs of joy in one's body, to keep experiencing some glow of pleasure in the marvellous human system which is one's own, and vicariously in the marvel of other human bodies, including the young.

Some older adults, on the contrary, seem to get a mournful

satisfaction out of the Failure of Powers. One once noted educator, well known to me, a man who is now as they say, "quite elderly", finds his consolations (or his kicks) in not only noting his own decline and supposed fall but observing and marking that of others including the middle-aged. For example, he is the originator of the following little hurried dialogues on elevators or on busy streets:

> *Elderly educator*: Oh, hello. Where are you going?
> *Oneself*: Back to the office, really. I managed to forget my briefcase.
> *Elderly educator*: Yes. Well, that's what happens when we get older.
> Or:
> *Elderly educator*: (with anxious pleasure): You're looking rather tired.
> *Oneself*: Well, I didn't sleep awfully well last night.
> *Elderly educator*: Well, that's what we have to expect as we get on in years.
> *Oneself* (drily): There was a four-alarm fire in the apartment house next door.
> *Elderly educator*: Oh. Oh, well, we can't take these things so well as we get older.

Thus in the only game which he still plays—the game of Mournfully Enjoying Failure of Powers and in which he must find a partner—he is at least always able to return your shot. But it is a game in which he is also the continual and disastrous loser. Once a handsome and impressive man, with an air of verve and confidence, he has shrunk not only physically (something of this often occurs in the very late years) but in the inner self and in his self-image, which are the generators and creative agents of his life. He is watching what he conceives to be his inevitable decline with fascinated regret, and he is determined to pull others into the sinking craft with him. Anything further from Ulyssean adulthood cannot be imagined.

In one of the greatest of physical joys, sexual intercourse, there is also, of course, a certain failing of powers across the adult life-span. Among the adult population a small minority might be described as natural celibates who abstain from all intercourse; a large number of others, in the Puritan idiom of North America, "indulge" in intercourse as part of the pattern of what "normal" people do, and then as the years seem to bring some waning of sexual powers, seem content to relinquish much or all of this area of their lives, in numerous cases almost with relief. A large group of men and women (much more often men than women) form a third category. They view the decline of sexual virility and fertility as a catastrophic threat to their selfhood and for them waning sexual strength becomes one of the most disorienting and disfunctionalizing influences in their disappointed later years. This is truer of men than of women. A 1975 poll of a large cross-section of North Americans found that middle-aged and older men rated sex third in their personal priorities, while women rated it eleventh. There is, of course, a fourth category: the Ulysseans—whose style, *if* they remain interested in sexual intercourse, is simply to go ahead and enjoy it, without worrying that they may not have the full sexual stamina "as in old days", but who continue to find a wholesome pleasure in the fact that "much abides."

Does much abide? Certainly it does. Nothing is more absurd than to proclaim that old men and women are not capable of rewarding sexual experiences. According to A. C. Kinsey's study of sexual behaviour among North American adults, the frequency of orgasms per week in the male declines in a steadily falling line across the lifespan. Thus, where the "median frequency" of orgasms was more than three per week at ages 16-20, and just under three at ages 21-25, the number lessens to about one per week around ages 51-55, and declines somewhat again in the next few years. These are, of course, median figures, and a considerable number of older adults would exceed the number given for age 51-plus. (Victor Hugo's doctors had to advise him in his late 70s to slow down on his sexual activity.) The frequency of marital intercourse declines on the same steadily falling line—again for the median and with numerous and notable exceptions among individual couples.*

What might be called solo sex, which is to say masturbation, with its accompanying fantasies, likewise declines (if the many respondents were reporting accurately to Kinsey)—interestingly enough, less so in women than in men, although women in general masturbate less frequently than men. In spite of the often traumatic experience of the menopause for women, sexuality remains a factor in the lives of many older women, however it may be sublimated to attempt to conform to what is "expected" and "fitting" in conventionalized society—one aspect of the life of Total Expectedness.

At one time there was an omnipotent pseudo-Christian and Puritan viewpoint which morbidly maintained that all play functions of the body in sex were channels to self-entrapment, venereal disease, and destruction of self. Dr. Alex Comfort has pointed out

*In 1972 an American study of approximately eight hundred professional men over age 65 revealed that 70 per cent of them regularly had sexual intercourse and that clergymen were the most active. For some curious reasons, medical doctors, editors, publishers, and journalists were relatively low performers. The men questioned came from *Who's Who in the United States*, people from business and the arts as well as the professions. When Dr. J. A. Silcox of the University of Western Ontario medical school commented on this study, he remarked that society wrongly looks on sex for older people as humorous or bizarre.

that the more hysterical promoters of this attitude helped to spawn terrifying books designed to frighten boys and young males out of the "damnable" practice of masturbation. As he suggests, a certain proportion of older men may be sexually crippled by having read books by sadistic physicians and quacks whose nightmare prescriptions to control an innocent practice make up an appalling memoir.

From the same sexually sick society emerged the conception of the "dirty old man" or woman—"dirty", that is, because they maintain an obvious interest in sexual life and experiences into the late years of the lifespan. The same society which so much of the time brutally ignores or neglects its older adults is nonetheless busily attentive to what it considers their "acceptable" behaviour. Both Kinsey and the now equally important reporters of *Human Sexual Response*, William J. Masters and Virginia Johnson, found a marked reluctance on the part of males over age 60 to give information about their sexual practices or non-practices. This nervous withdrawal from a mature and valuable area of inquiry is surely one sign of how afraid or shy older adults are to even admit confidentially to frankly sexual fantasies, desires, and thoughts, let alone deeds.

According to Masters and Johnson, "aging males" tend to diminish, and desist from, their earlier sexual activity for reasons having little to do with actual physical competence to continue. For example, these following factors contribute greatly to inhibition of sexual play and intercourse: boredom with a repetitious sexual relationship (often, presumably, however well beloved the partner); preoccupation with career activities; mental or physical fatigue; overindulgence in food or drink; various species of physical and mental infirmities; fear of failure (which Masters and Johnson consider of enormous importance in hindering and arresting the sexual practice and achievement of the male past, say, age 60-plus).

Surely Simone de Beauvoir is right in stressing the negative and often tragic role which unliberated public opinion still plays in constructing a widely held image of older adults as people for whom it is neither "nice" nor natural to talk about sex, to enjoy it obviously, and to have sexual desires and drives. They must be, as Beauvoir admirably says, made "ashamed of their own desires." She quotes the thorough research done by the American medical scientist, Dr. J. P. Runciman. Runciman closely studied the sexual practices and the responses of two hundred adults aged 40 to 89. He concluded that "psychological barriers" were chiefly responsible for forcing an end to the sexual activity of older adults. In his view, the taboos of the Victorian morality in which they had been brought up were too powerful for their personal needs and desires to prevail.

Western society—by no means only North American society

(as witness Beauvoir)—has long sought to make the older adult who continues to "indulge" in sexual interests and activity a figure either of shame or of comedy. Literature across the centuries has always ridiculed men whose wives are unfaithful, but none is so absurd as the old cuckold. This assiduous refusal to accept sexuality as a natural and beautiful phenomenon among older adults is seen again in the perennial jokes about May-December marriages. In spite of examples of happy marriages between young women and elderly men, or at least men over sixty, in such cases as Pablo Casals, Zoltan Kodaly, Charles Chaplin, and Pablo Picasso, or similar relationships outside marriage, people are always to be found who impute the worst of motives to one partner or the other. When Justice William O. Douglas of the United States Supreme Court at the age of 78 married a girl of 21 as his fourth wife, a group of imbeciles in Congress attempted to get legislation passed to cancel his appointment to the bench. Their real motive was Douglas's long support of liberal causes, but it is significant that they cloaked this in what they conceived to be a widely-accepted folk attitude.

Even more incomprehensible and unacceptable, especially to the species *Americanus vulgaris*, which has its equivalent in all cultures, is the sight of a young man marrying an elderly woman. Yet instances abound, in spite of the obsessive references to "gigolos and exploiters of women", of successful and deeply loving relationships between older women and young men, sexual—if not always manifested in actual intercourse—at least in the many loving physical contacts which also are expressions of sexuality. Edith Piaf was a case in point.

No doubt cases like *The Roman Spring of Mrs. Stone* abound, or something comparable. In this film a middle-aged woman is driven partly by genuine feelings of love and partly by sexual hunger into a transient affair with a young man of intense physical attractiveness, an affair which fails, and after which in despair she finally opens her hotel suite to the dangerous and handsome hustler who has long been watching and waiting in the street below her window. It is also clear that many homosexual adventures in which one partner is an older man or woman often end in bitterness and recrimination and with both partners resuming the eternal hunt. Yet, especially in the arts, there have been many successful relationships, sexual, platonic, and also what can be described as generalized non-copulative affection.

When that wonderful human being, André Gide, was far on in the life journey, he still had a deep fear of contracting venereal disease, and this presumably inhibited him from much sexual intercourse. A homosexual who had married and who loved his wife, but found it—to his later remorse—difficult to maintain a devoted relationship, Gide continued his love of adolescent boys far into his later years. This took curiously moving and innocent forms, which yet were exercises in sexuality. In the summer near the seashore, he would interrupt a game of chess or a conversation with a friend in the garden looking out on the sea, to drag his friend down close to the shore where they could see three or four adolescents bathing and shouting in the sea. Or he would feel a certain pleasure in the accidental touching of a handsome youth in the bus. Once he wrote of his delight in observing the beauty of a young Parisian standing absorbed at the side of the pool in a Turkish bath.

Unconventional though these predilections and small adventures in Gide's domain of love would seem to many North Americans, only a very sick mind could describe Gide as a "dirty old man". His "deviation from the sexual norm" (to employ one of the dreary phrases of psychology) was not a block to his creativity nor a disgrace to his old age. He was, of course, often frustrated and unhappy (are we to suppose that these are the attributes only of old age?), but his late sexual life seems to have operated under the code of love: that is, in what he did he tried not to harm others, or himself. A certain radiance filled his old age.

Sometimes elderly people, even very old people, marry each other. In the case of a very late marriage (often of two residents of a nursing or retirement home), the event is frequently treated by younger people with amused astonishment or hardly veiled contempt, as if to say, whatever the aged should be doing, they should not at least be engaging in the futility of very late marriage. Much of this attitude clearly springs from the belief that active sexuality is an exercise both impossible and undesirable for the old. Since such a marriage is not common, the media play it up, often with a tolerant schmaltziness which is almost as distasteful as hostility. To the press it is all one with the absurdities of old ladies traipsing on a platform as can-can girls, or the hymn-sings which are supposed to be the staple of the institutionalized old. Of course, if the couple are people of private means, the marriage passes in public silence, and no doubt in private peace except perhaps for the exasperated comments of frustrated heirs.

This is not always the case, nor should it be. Pope John's words, "Any day is a good day to be born, and any day is a good day to die," transpose perfectly to marrige at any age, provided it is indeed a marriage of two people who cherish one another. Besides, the sexual encounter is dispensable in a very late married life, although the partners are usually quite capable of it. The Mexican saying that each man has three loves: in his youth, in his prime, and in old age, is a fine example of discrimination between the sexes— women in their very late years have this privilege too.

There are, of course, people in their late years who bring an atmosphere of nervous comedy to anything in their life which appears to disturb the stereotypes which at heart they accept as readily as the rest of a conventional and rigid society. Due to courage or perhaps desperation, they take the plunge, but all the time they persist in seeing themselves in the mirrors of "what is expected"; their tense bravado or strained apology partly destroys the calm dignity of actions which are purely their own business. And this includes the decision to marry very late, which often may be a creative decision in the direction of a richer life.

It is important to keep in mind that if one is going to consign the sexual life to some nostalgic area unattainable to the alleged "failing powers" of the later years, one places an undue load upon the success of earlier experience and signs away the possible recompenses and joy of sex in later life. Innumerable tensions and neuroses throng the marriage and sexual relationships. Yet people persist in looking at the "senior citizens" as though they were flat photographs in a sentimental family portrait. Beauvoir insists that the very young are shocked at evidences of sexual activity in the aging: but in fact it is precisely the "new young" of modern society who are probably most sympathetic.

Just as it is beautiful to see adults in their later years making the decision to continue their sexual life and interest, taking it for granted that this is a natural and continuing function of the life drama, likewise there is another choice among "those that mourn", which is moving and beautiful. For many men and women, when death has taken a beloved companion in the late 50s, or the 60s —in our society the one lost is much more often the man than the woman—the last lines of the play have been spoken.

For these later adults, the path taken is well described by the forgotten lines of Fanny Kemble in the poem, "Absence":

> What shall I do with all the days and hours
> That must be counted ere I see thy face?
>
> I'll tell thee; for thy sake I will lay hold
> Of all good aims, and consecrate to thee
> In worthy deeds, each moment that is told
> While you, beloved one! art far from me.
>
> I will this dreary blank of absence make
> A noble task time . . . .
> So may my love and longing hallowed be,
> And thy dear thought an influence divine.

If the consecration so made does not become a kind of mortification and turning away from, for example, the glow and vitality of the lively arts, and if especially it lovingly accepts the very different lifestyles and strategies in sorrow and loneliness of others contending on their own terms with the later adult years—then it is something very beautiful indeed, and one of the loveliest trails to the Ulyssean life.

In the case of long-term marriages, where the partners pass through much of the late-life phase together, an important psychological arena exists in which each must cope with losses of confidence and pride which may result from the waning of sexual power. This requires an empathy and skill in which many men and women are inadequate or, what is more important, unwilling to exert themselves. For the male especially, this can be unfortunate. For example, Masters and Johnson quoting from their own and other studies of recent years note that "when the aging male is not stimulated over long periods of time, his responsiveness may be lost." And they qualify an optimistic statement of late-life capacity for sexual stimulation and enjoyment by the conditions of "*maintained* regularity of sexual expression coupled with adequate physical well-being and healthy mental orientation to the aging process."

Yet the field is full of light for those who will turn to see it:

> The incidence of sexual inadequacy in the human male takes a sharp upturn after 50 years of age. . . . [However], just as the secondarily impotent male over 50 years old can be reconstituted, so can the potent aging male's responsive ability, dormant for physical or social reasons, be restimulated, if the male wishes to return to active sexual practices and has a partner interested in sexual performance. If he is in adequate health, little is needed to support adequacy of sexual performance in a 70- or even 80-year old male other than some physiologic outlet or psychologic reason for a reactivated sexual interest. . . . Even if coital activity has been avoided for long periods of time, men in these age groups can be returned to effective sexual function if adequate stimulation is instituted and interested partners are available.

Nor is the picture any less full of incentive and of potential light for the aging woman:

> There is no reason why the milestone of the menopause should be expected to blunt the human female's sexual capacity, performance, or drive. The healthy aging woman normally has sex drives that demand resolution. The depths of her sexual capacity and the effectiveness of her sexual performance, as well as her personal eroticism, are influenced indirectly by all of the psycho and sociophysiologic problems of her aging process. In short, *there is no time limit* drawn by the advancing years to female sexuality. (My italics.)

5. THE UNFAILING MIND

One domain of aging in later adulthood takes precedence over every other for those who feel some commitment to keep growing—and notably for the Ulysseans. This is the kingdom of the mind, the "seat of consciousness" *(Concise Oxford Dictionary)* which arises from, but is an entity different from, the human brain, the most remarkable phenomenon in the known universe. Modern popular science has its own typical shorthand for the wonder of the individual brain: "If a computer were designed attempting to do what the brain does, it would need to be the size of the Empire State Building."

Actually the conventional descriptions of what is known about the brain are in themselves exciting. To Stanley Burnshaw, who writes brilliantly about the possible role of the brain functions in language, thinking, and creativity, the human brain is "probably the most complicated six inches on earth: the supposedly ten billion cells in the cortex, tens of thousands of nerve cells in the spinal cord, with millions of receptor fibres converging upon them—the center of the retina of each human eye, for example, [with] nearly a half-million sensitive cells, each connected with a single nerve fiber" constituting a magnificent and baffling instrument.

In the enigma of memory alone, Burnshaw goes on: "Millions of neurons are involved. Since this is the working effect of a trace, can we wonder that experts regard the profusion of interconnections among the cells as beyond human power of imagining—at least 10 billion neurons, each receiving connections from perhaps 100 others and connecting it to still 100 more? The transmission of a 'wavefront' may sweep over 100,000 neurons in a single second (it can operate not only on nearby cells but also on distant parts of the cortex); the entire wavefront can advance through as many as 1,000,000 neurons in a second."

And Burnshaw quotes the striking image of the British physiologist, Sir Charles Sherrington, who compares the human brain to "an enchanted loom where millions of flashing shuttles (the nerve impulses) weave a dissolving pattern, always a meaningful pattern,

though never an abiding one; a shifting harmony of sub-patterns."
Actually, the biochemist Robert S. De Ropp prefers to speak, on
anatomical grounds, of *four* brains, so distinctive does he consider
the four centres of "the brain" to be in their governance of instinct,
movement, emotion, and intellect.

With "intellect" we enter the sphere of discussion on the nature
of so-called "intelligence" as will be discussed fully later in this chapter. Indeed, it seems to be a fact about twentieth century Western
society that when an older adult worries about Failure of Powers,
he or she is thinking chiefly, if not wholly, about the supposed decline and fall of the cognitive or intellectual powers. If so, the
reason may be attributable in very large degree to the climate of
the age. Contemporary society is obsessed, consciously or unconsciously, with the concept of the measurable intellect, the measurement then being used to promote or inhibit the life progress of the
individual. If Will and Ariel Durant had carried their latest work on
The Story of Civilization up to our time, they might well have had
to entitle it *The Age of the IQ* or *The Cognitive Age*. The concept
of the measurable intelligence, usually taken to be the cognitive
or intellectual intelligence, has saturated our society.

The modern folk culture through its attitudes and its language
fortifies all this. Thus, in our time, everything is "stupid": in a
hundred cases where what "he" or "she" has done bears no relationship to the mind or brain, they are still "stupid." Thus, you may
do something demonstrably selfish or rude or rash—no matter: it
is such a *stupid* action. We are living in a Cognitive Age.

Little wonder that when an older adult thinks of Failure of
Powers—and he is likely to think of it privately a great deal—the
first concern that nags at his mind is the possible decline of his
cognitive capability—and this concern takes the form of three
typical questions: Will I suffer continuous brain cell loss and disfunctionalizing brain damage?. Will my mental capacity steadily
decline in comparison with younger, "more productive and creative"
adults? Will I be able to continue to learn efficiently?

In short, can older adults create and produce as they once did
in the early years and the so-called "prime years"—*and even better*?
"And even better": these are the daring words which seemingly no
one among the gerontologists and adult educators who are obviously
sensitive to the possibilities of the later years will pronounce—yet in
many cases they can be true, in many are already true. We return
to this neglected hypothesis later in this chapter in the discussion
of "intelligence" and its "testing".

On the subject of physical loss and mental performance, everyone knows that there are severe strokes, either global or selective
in their effects, which can temporarily or permanently interfere
with the full efficiency of the brain. Likewise, cerebral illnesses of

various kinds can also produce senile decay: certain of these can appear at early middle age—although they are rare. Elderly patients who have been institutionalized because of psychoses of the senium are notoriously much inferior in their capacity to perform on so-called intelligence tests than are healthy older adults, who of course form the vast majority.

No one knows how many people in the later years secretly dread the thought of senility. At any rate, the word is used not only pejoratively but often abusively as an epithet to deride or demean the old—as, of course, "young" is used to deflate youth. The commonest private analysis of politicians who in their late years make various apparent blunders or failures in policy is that they are, after all, senile. If a woman makes her third marriage at age 80 her relatives may well conclude that "she is a senile old fool." These are attributions rather than proven conditions. True senility is all too evident when one sees it: the wonderful instrument of the brain running blank with a few sounds like the TV set after the last show; body and brain ultimately comatose, to match the ever-accommodating folk language: "they say he's just a vegetable." He is *not*, as the late Bishop Austin Pardue was at pains to point out, just a vegetable; he is still a soul. Even if one does not believe *that*, he is still someone to be respected and perhaps cherished.*

No one wants to become senile even if it is the price tag of a very extended life. But the number of the truly senile is comparatively few; even the number of the immobilized aged in institutions is only something like two to four per cent of the whole population past 70.

The real concern of later adults is the effect of the aging of the brain upon continuing mental productivity and creativity. The equation of anxiety runs somewhat like this: the brain is extremely sensitive to lack of oxygen and quickly atrophies and dies without it; it is the bloodstream which supplies the oxygen and nourishes the brain; interference with the bloodstream reduces the flow of oxygen to the brain; narrowing of the passage in the blood vessels is a common phenomenon of aging. *Therefore*, the process of aging must bring impaired mental efficiency and productivity with it. Anxious older people, and naturally oftenest those who have learned to prize their mind, are likely to take this simple equation on its face value without investigating the whole context.

Medical and psychiatric scientists, indispensable though they are, suffer from the same occupational hazards as, say, psychoanalysts in that they become preoccupied with pathological or abnormal states. An enormous amount of attention has been given

---

*In Bede's *History of the Church in England*, there is a moving account of the extended loving care given to an old abbess until her death from global paralysis by the younger nuns around her.

to the psychoses and brain damages of older adults, especially the aged. When attention is turned to the great army of healthy or viably healthy individuals, some important facts emerge. James Birren in an admirable essay on the psychopathology of aging summarizes the studies done on *healthy* older men at the National Institute of Mental Health in Washington as clearly demonstrating that "reduction in cerebral flow and metabolic rate are not necessary concomitants of growing older. In general, men above the age of sixty-five who were judged to be healthy, or free from significant somatic disease, *had blood flows and cerebral metabolic rates approximately equivalent to those of young men.*" (My italics.)

The geriatric scientist Hallgrim Klove thought he discerned a significant superiority in test performance of brain-damaged young men over brain-damaged 45-year-olds and older. However, this was a cross-sectional study (comparing different populations) with obvious disadvantages as against what R. W. Kleemeier did, as reported in his presidential address to the American Psychological Association in 1961 ("Intellectual Change in the Senium *or* Death and the I.Q."). Kleemeier made an intensive study of thirteen elderly men (the youngest was 65) tested on four occasions over twelve years, using the Wechsler-Bellevue test. He found a decline in test scores over the period, but the slope of decline did not seem to be related to age. Kleemeier was struck by the effects of ill health rather than aging upon the performance of his test subjects. Since it may seem at first glance difficult to separate the two, this is how Kleemeier put it: "There is no evidence for *age change* in intelligence in the senium, and the changes which are found are better related to the physical state of health of the organism."

In fact, it is an heroic exercise trying to discern the role of cerebral physical functioning in so-called mental performance, if only because of the host of environmental factors involved. This is now becoming dramatically evident in changing attitudes to what the fearsome word "senility" really means. There are reputable scientists who contend that senility, when it occurs, comes usually not from physical/cerebral disease but from psychosociological sources. Simone de Beauvoir, who usually takes a melancholy pleasure in recording the sad decline into old age and death, finds herself able to report a French geriatric scientist, Bastide, as writing in *Sociologie des maladies mentales:* "It may be asked whether senility is a consequence of aging or whether on the contrary it is not rather an artificial product of a society that rejects the aged."

Bastide himself quotes another French medical scholar, Répond:

> "Indeed, it is reasonable to wonder whether the old concept of senile dementia, the alleged result of cerebral disorders, should not be entirely overhauled, and whether these pseudo-dementias are not the result of psycho-sociological factors—

whether they are not rapidly made worse by removal to inadequately equipped and managed institutions and by confinement in psychiatric hospitals where these patients are abandoned to themselves, deprived of the necessary psychological stimuli and cut off from all vital interests, and where they have nothing to look forward to but an end that everybody hopes will come soon. We even go so far as to claim that the clinical picture of senile dementia may be an artifact, due in the majority of cases to shortcomings in the treatment and in the attempts at prevention and rehabilitation."

One example possibly verifying Répond's hypothesis would be the elderly school teacher in the nursing home, described earlier; one can easily see further evidence in the marked difference in the degree of recovery between those later adults, laid low by a massive stroke and in effect abandoned by physicians and family, and those who from the time of the onset are given the constant therapy of communication, encirclement, encouragement, and companionship. Some extraordinary recoveries ensue: for example, this was true of my mother.

In a fine chapter in his book, *Don't Give Up on an Aging Parent,* (1975) Lawrence Galton calls senility "a wastebasket diagnosis . . . too often no diagnosis at all, but, rather, an easy disposal category." Galton lists a small catalogue of physical conditions, including hardening of the arteries, that contribute to seeming senility, which are treatable and controllable, and in many cases curable. Galton remarks: "Senility involves the whole person. It is not an isolated disease, confined to a single body compartment. Many alterations, often subtle ones, individually or collectively can conspire to create the appearance or actuality of senility . . . when these disturbances are sought for and actively treated, the diagnosis of senility may be abandoned or the hopelessness about it may vanish very quickly." And Galton discusses at length the contributions of "attitude therapy" in returning aged human beings from alleged "senility" to active, meaningful life. He describes the brilliant work of Karl A. Menninger and Howard V. Williams at Topeka in restoring to health the patients once classified as suffering "senile dementia", and he quotes a superb statement by Menninger: "I apologize for this abominable term. It is what we called the state of utter despair and demoralization some of our old people reached as they lost their faculty for readaptation and coping. We know now that the condition is not properly called a 'dementia'."

Everyone ages across the life-cycle—this is the unalterable fact of life. Everyone in the later years will be assailed by certain deficits and threats which are inalienable from the aging process. Mindless euphoria about aging does nothing to improve the situation: it worsens it, and in some cases increases its elements of pathos.

The brain ages, and Birren reminds us that the brains of some distinguished men whose competence was universally accepted through their active phases until the period just before death, have been shown to contain large amounts of senile plaques, indicators of brain disease. If so, this merely testifies further to the stamina and the mysterious virtuosity of the human brain.

Even in dramatic cases of severe cerebral injury, the marvellous brain is still able on occasion to employ, as it were, reserve circuits and operations which confound the experts. Many readers of this book will have known cases where the physicians have decreed that So-and-So "will not walk again"—but he or she *has* walked again, not merely because of the wonderful courage of the patient, but because of mysterious and unforeseen powers in the organism. The physicians were not usually inexpert; sometimes they were among the finest in the world. There simply exist in the anatomy and physiology of the brain and nervous system of the body, hidden forces and channels of recuperation still undeciphered by medical science. A close friend of mine, who had suffered terrible head injuries and undergone massive operations, heard the ultimate verdict: "We are sorry to tell you that you will not be able to walk again, and you will have to expect a considerable amount of pain during your life." He recounted this to me, a year after the verdict, at a party, limping across the broadloom of a large hotel room to give me the details; all pain has long since disappeared.

Where physical and psychological loss occurs among older adults—loss notably of some swiftness of reaction or response, the powerful factor of compensation enters in. Where some damage to brain functioning occurs through aging, the process is usually a lengthy one. There is time to make use of the wide repertory of adjustments and solutions which men and women have usually developed in their work-life and personal living. In addition, few of us—none of us?—ever deliver the full potentialities of our body and mind, of our *self*. Most of the time, when we fancy that we are highly integrated and strongly motivated, we deceive ourselves; it takes the stimulus of threat or danger to spur us to reach into the repertory of our skills and strategies to live at a new level of creativity. Koestler paints a picture of man passing aeons of time upon the earth without really knowing how to employ his magnificent possession, the human brain.

And Robert de Ropp, enlarging the discussion to include the whole of the inner self, remarks that "within the psyche of man are secret rooms, vast chambers full of treasures with windows looking out on eternity and infinity. Man does not enter these rooms, or does so only rarely. They are locked. He has lost the key. He lives habitually in the lowest, dreariest, darkest part of his inner habitation."

The arts of both compensation and creation have heavy investments in experience. Because aging is asymmetrical, people have
different degrees of deficits and sorrows, increments and hidden
joys, which are both close to and widely different from those of
others. Although many older adults do not use it well, the repertory
of experience that the years bring has been usefully defined by
Adlai Stevenson; in discussing what a man knows at 50 that he
did not know at 20: "The knowledge he has acquired with age is
not a knowledge of formulas, or forms of words, but of people,
places, actions—a knowledge gained by touch, sight, sound, vic-
tories, failures, sleeplessness, devotion, love—the human experience and emotions of this earth and of one's self and other men."
Stevenson's moving phrases are, however, those of the older states-
man-poet. Closer yet to the intensity of the adult journey which
supplies compensatory powers would be references also to neuroses
mastered, obsessive anxieties controlled or overcome, terrible sorrows transcended, the nightmare of debt survived, certain expectations and disappointments in love, marriage, and careers encountered, and the silent company of many secret fears endured. In
many of these cases, failure has been aborted or transformed,
problems unlocked, and resilient strategies acquired.

From all these experiences older adult people have acquired
much of their lifestyles, and the lifestyle is crucial in encounters
between the physically aging brain and the needs of learning and
living. Not everyone would agree with Wilma Donahue's gallant
assertion: "No toy (the brain as giving pleasure, amusement, and
satisfaction) if properly used, can improve so much with age." But
two powerful theses about the brain in later adulthood are hard to
deny.

The first is that to keep the mind active, growing, life-loving,
problem-solving, is as close to a guarantee as one can get—barring
the cosmic disasters that can befall any of us *at any age*—that a
man or woman can inhabit the kingdom of the mind with rich
pleasure and creativity to the end of the life journey. The second
is, that each older adult possesses in the human brain, even when
he thinks it has suffered some deficits, a magnificent instrument
which at any phase of his existence could serve him better than
he permits.

What Wilma Donahue also says is substantially true: "Cerebral
function is the most dependable servant that can be called upon
over a long span of years." What Robert de Ropp says is most certainly true: that man lives habitually in the lowest storey of his
inner habitation or psyche, which includes the functioning of the
mind and the brain.

But the older adult who virtually immobilizes himself at the
mere thought of Failure of Powers specifically affecting his physical

brain has not only lost the key to treasure chambers—he has thrown it away.

One may be, in fact, as most adults are, quite able physically or with compensatory skills to take on the tasks of continuing mental growth and learning, but the will to learn may be a broken spring. And what of those powerful twin motivators of learning: curiosity and the sense of wonder?

The American psychologist William James, who by 1900 had become a giant figure as the founder of the North American school of pragmatism, and who had brilliant and provocative opinions on all too many topics, was at least on home territory when he asserted categorically in his massive *Principles of Psychology* (1893) that:

> "Outside of their own business, the ideas gained by men before they are 25 are practically the only ideas they shall have in their lives. They *cannot* get anything new. Disinterested curiosity is past, the mental grooves and channels set, the power of assimilation gone. Whatever individual exceptions might be cited to these are of the sort that 'prove the rule'."

Twelve years later Sir William Osler, in the course of a farewell address at Johns Hopkins University, caused an international uproar by his half-jesting references to the unproductivity of men over 40 and the possible advantages of chloroforming men at 60. (Osler was himself age 55 and heading for yet another creative phase of his career, at Oxford.) Osler did not deny that "occasionally there is a sexagenarian whose mind, as Cicero remarks, stands out of reach of the body's decay." And, a Ulyssean himself if there ever was one, Osler went on to recommend that, at the least, all men over 60 as they felt "the silver cord loosening" should do as the Athenian philosopher Hermippus did, "who cut himself clear from all companions of his own age and betook himself to the company of young men, mingling with their games and studies, and so lived to the age of 153." And Osler deduced from this that "only those who live with the young [can] maintain a fresh outlook on the new problems of the world."

Osler was a world-famous medical figure, and his suggestion (originally Anthony Trollope's) that men over 60 might beneficially be chloroformed reverberated through Western society where a high proportion of the most prestigious and powerful posts in the worlds of politics, scholarship, business, and religion were held by sexagenarians. Missing entirely the facetiousness with which Osler had delivered his address, which as his biographer, Harvey Cushing, suggests was partly to mask his own sorrow at having to leave Johns Hopkins after many happy years, the newspapers appeared with headlines typified by "Osler Recommends Chloroform at Sixty." An enormous and hostile uproar ensued from editorials, cartoons, letters to the press, and a flood of letters to Osler. There were even some threats! Osler handled the situation with his usual high good humour and intrepidity but the notoriety followed him for years, and he suffered somewhat because of his enormous previous popularity. Mrs. Osler, who had a sense of humour, remarked shortly afterwards to a Johns Hopkins friend whom she and Osler met as they walked in Baltimore on Sunday, "I am escorting the shattered idol home from church."

Osler's few subsequent references to the speech and its aftermath showed clearly enough that he was indeed half-serious as well as half-jesting. He repeated a number of times that "the real work of life is done before the fortieth year"—a dubious and unproved thesis which H. C. Lehman was to attempt to establish systematically nearly fifty years later with his book, *Age and Achievement*. However, for all his fame and authority, Osler was not a specialist in the science of the functions of the mind as William James was. A single speech, for all its notoriety, has nothing like the effect of a massive text; nor did Osler have his disciples scattered across the United States as professors and practitioners of the relatively new field of psychology, as James did. James's typically dogmatic and well-turned phrases had a wide and accepted currency for many years among the academic centres generating psychological ideas: "They *cannot* get anything new. Disinterested curiosity is past, the grooves and channels set. . . ."

The devastating answering cannonade by Edward L. Thorndike and associates of Columbia University, published in 1928 as the now-celebrated book, *Adult Learning*, must have been one of the longest-delayed counterattacks in the history of controversy. Thorndike, as Roby Kidd relates, had arrived at Columbia with his enormous zest and vitality blowing ahead of him, children in tow, crates of chickens and other experimental animals in train, ready to address his fine mind and enormous energies to whatever major psychological issues, especially in learning, should first offer themselves. In the mid-1920s he was age 50, and his attention had been caught again and fascinated by William James's statement which, in effect, he used as the text for his attack in *Adult Learning*.

Thorndike and his colleagues examined a large number of the many small, obscure studies done on adult learning during the period from 1900 to 1926. One area of study which had attracted research attention was the ability of adults to improve in simple sensorimotor abilities. The trials were varied and curious: improved accuracy in tossing shot into a glass; learning not to blink when an empty object was struck; keeping balls going in the air; tapping a telegraph key at maximal speed. All adults participating improved steadily and at rates which were in a number of instances on a swiftly climbing curve. The data, however, were of young adults still in their 20s, nor was a competition set up between, say, adults in early mid-adulthood and late adolescents or very early adults. Other tests had measured adult ability to improve in forming simple habits, in learning more elaborate systems of habits, in memory (for example, remembering series of nonsense syllables), and in complex abilities. In all cases, practice, if it did not make perfect, at least led to marked improvement. (This partly confirms the point which Wilma Donahue makes so insistently: that we must not simply sit back and relegate adults of any age group to some category of non-learners; we must bring them into the practice field where old skills and habits which have gone rusty can be reburnished, and new ones learned.)

Some intriguing oddities turned up among these early investigations. The psychologist E. J. Swift had decided that if medical researchers could experiment on themselves, surely psychological inquirers could do the same. At age 43 he submitted himself to two self-administered exercises. He practised typewriting by the sight method for an hour a day for fifty days, steadily improving, attaining finally the not very stunning rate of 17½ words per minute. Then this intrepid pre-Ulyssean studied shorthand for sixty-eight days for an hour and a half a day, writing (was this done ironically?) William James's *Talks to Teachers* from dictation and reading back copy taken down ten or more days earlier. Within two months (Swift was during this time doing the many other things his daily work required), he had raised his speed of reception and transcription so that his score climbed by 500 per cent. Swift's curiosity about himself, his precision in trying to measure his achievements, and his gutsy self-disciplining until the exercise was completed, still could be emulated in our time by adults of all ages who want to change themselves from dilettantes to productive learners.

On the basis of what he called "a formidable array" of these early results, which included one of his own, Thorndike felt himself already able to say that the adults concerned seemed "plastic and teachable in every mental function that was examined." However, some studies used so-called "superior" adults, including graduate students. In addition, the competitive encounters between varying age groups were missing, and these were needed to supply some kind of evidence that the late teens, the 30s, the 50s, the 70s, for example, really did operate at different levels of speed and proficiency. The alternative would be to test various individuals in typing skills or tossing the shot at various times in their lives from preadolescence to senescence!

Taken all in all, the many small early studies preceding Thorndike had suggested that the differences in rates of learning between old and young were small in comparison with the differences within either group, and Thorndike was prepared to say rather gingerly that indications from early, usually isolated, experimentation was that "adult ability to learn is very close to that of the late teens." However, what Thorndike sought was a more comprehensive attack on the problem raised by James, and with his associates he devised a number of experiments which he described at length in *Adult Learning.* A number of the more interesting of these are worth reporting here.

The Thorndike group decided to test adult ability to learn a new hierarchy of habits by working with eight adult people who had always written with their right hand and getting them to agree to try writing with the left in a learning situation which tested for improvement. The ages of the volunteers were 22, 28, 28, 33, 34, 41, 42 and 52. Thorndike remarks:

> "When one changes the hand in writing, not only do none of his old habits of movement fit the new demand; they are distorted in a complicated way. Nevertheless, the mere general control given by knowledge of the desired appearance and by vision enables the adult learner to counteract tendencies to write in mirror fashion, and to establish rather quickly a new hierarchy of habits."

And he concludes that:

> "within the short period of fifteen hours of practice, plus forty minutes' allowance for the practice effect of the tests themselves, those subjects who maintained the same quality of handwriting, much more than doubled their speed. Those subjects who worked for a higher quality obtained it and still made very substantial gains in speed. . . . In general, the gain of these eight adults from less than sixteen hours of practice was greater than the gain proposed by experts as suitable to be accomplished by children using the right hand in two years of growth and schooling, including one hundred or more hours of special practice in handwriting."

How did the 52-year-old do? In quality of writing he came in eighth in the field of eight; in speed he came fifth. The quality of his first performance was also fifth—he lost ground as a result of the increase in speed. However, what was ideally sought was improvement in both quality and speed.

Thorndike was struck by the motivation displayed by his eight adults—yet, as he says, the motivation was surely less than that of some adult compelled to learn to write with the wrong hand because of accident. And is not the economic motive a powerful factor, he asks, in the case of the great numbers of adult men and women who are required by industrial changeovers to learn new skills? He speculates also on the motivation of sheer pleasure, as in learning new games.

Thorndike and his group repeated the experiment on general lines with two groups of university students, seventeen in a group aged 20–25, and sixteen in the other group, aged 35-plus. The measured gain of the older group was less than the younger; still, they made impressive gains by Thorndike's Scales for measuring children, as already indicated above.

The zest with which Thorndike and his associates attacked the question of adult capability to learn is wonderfully seen in their search for the right test content for what they cited as "learning a systematic logical subject." After all these years, one feels the gusto of an investigator who can write:

> "We considered making up for our experimental work a brief intellectual system wholly independent of any of the existing sciences, of which all learners would have little and equal knowledge at the start, and in learning which very little of the stock varieties of human knowledge would be of specific help. A system of ethics from the point of view of the domestic cat or an artificial agglutinative language using nothing of Indo-European syntax or vocabulary are samples of the sort of material contemplated. But on the whole it seemed better to use Esperanto."

Esperanto, the artificial language designed as a means of international communication, seemed to the investigators to have the virtue of presenting to the would-be learner a consistent, logical, intellectual system which could be said to be largely representative of the intellectual efforts required in the learning of various foreign languages, sciences, mathematics, and social sciences. Besides, the experimenting group felt that the would-be learners could cover and grasp the general nature of the system within fifteen to twenty hours. One other advantage was suggested: the adults taking the test of learning Esperanto would be, it was hoped, on a more even base of equality of preparation (a very moot point).

The test groups were particularly interesting because they were formed of people with almost identical scores on a standard "intelligence" test and were of *three age categories:* a group of eighteen, aged 20 to 25; a second of nine, aged 26 to 34; and a third group of twenty-one, aged 35-plus. The youngest was 20, the oldest 57. All were university students, the older ones presumably senior people from the teaching profession taking graduate degrees.

In global returns, the 20 to 25-year group gained 31.5. The 26 to 34-year group gained 26.3. The 35-plus group gained 24.7. However, Thorndike adds that "the superiority of the younger adults is due almost entirely to their greater gain in the oral directions test. In the other three tests, there was little or no difference." (The "other three" were vocabulary, printed directions, and paragraph reading.)

Thorndike raised a highly controversial point in concluding

his description of this experiment. In a separate experiment, this time using pupils 9 to 18 years of age from "a good private school" who had twice as much class study time as the adult group aged 35-plus, and theoretically with much more home study time, the school group gained scarcely more than half that of the 35-plus adults. Slower still were the children aged 9–11. Thorndike is just on the point of arguing from this that adulthood is a better time than childhood to master a foreign language. Then he draws back: after all, a natural language demands a tremendous amount of habituation because of its enormous number of irregularities. Then he goes on, anyway, to say that adults between 20 and 40 at any rate would outperform children 8 or 10 or 12, given the same time for the experiment and equal abilities.

Actually, David Ausubel of the University of Illinois, argues in a cogently-reasoned paper (1968) that "the widespread cultural belief that children learn languages more readily than adults do . . . is highly vulnerable. Ausubel states that whereas children have unequalled powers as mimics in language learning, "their cognitive immaturity and lack of certain intellectual skills preclude many approaches that are feasible for older age groups."

The Thorndike group conducted a series of other experiments in adult learning including rates of learning achievement among prison inmates of "inferior intellect"—that is, inferior according to certain current mental tests—in such concerns as learning to read, write, compute, and form certain simple habits; learning by adults of "near average" to "very high" intellectual levels of typical high school subjects in evening classes; and the learning of typewriting and stenography among adult pupils in secretarial schools, again from "average" to "very high" levels. A fascinating section of the Thorndike studies is devoted not merely to whether adults can continue to learn and learn well, but whether they can *un*learn. This involved the worlds not only of familiar skills, but of attitudes, prejudices, and antipathies. Thorndike tried to probe into such questions as when the fear of snakes, of thunder, or of blood was first aroused, and at what age if at all it was overcome; at what age certain prejudices arose regarding race, religion, and political affairs, and when these prejudices were put aside—if at all. His questionnaire on this whole area, although primitive, would be a marvellous exercise for any reader of this book who, at long last, will school himself to sit down and really analyse how his prejudices and fears were aroused, and how they were solved or healed, if they ever were. This is the learning of unlearning.

Along with this, Thorndike examined a number of more familiar things: when people learn to dance, swim, and skate, for example. ("Age is evidently not an insuperable barrier, learning to swim and dance occurring at all ages to 50.")

Thorndike's study of attitudes was based on a sample of ninety-nine people, all with a college education or its equivalent. Thirty-nine of these were age 40 or older, and if one screens out a few cultural oddities special to the 1920s, some components appear in the summation of replies which have been re-affirmed in other occasional studies across the years. Thus, there was a general confidence that one could learn many things at least to age 50; that age inhibits the learning of "things of the mind" less than it influences motor skills; and that if adults in their middle and later years find it difficult to learn or even to begin to learn something out of their usual life and routine, it is (to quote Thorndike): "in part due to a sensitiveness to ridicule, adverse comment, and undesired attention, so that if it were customary for mature and old people to learn to swim and ride bicycles and speak German, the difficulty might diminish."

The over-all effect of Thorndike's *Adult Learning* is curiously mixed. On the one hand, it is impossible to put the book down without feeling that an impressive case has been established for the continuing ability of adults to learn; that they have not lost their "plasticity"; that they can entertain and assimilate into their "self" new ideas and can unlearn old fears, prejudices, and antipathies; that they can perform well in fields seemingly more the domain of young people. Rough-hewn though some of the experimentation of the Thorndike group seems to be when one looks back at it after fifty years of research, it is still clearly a watershed study.

As such, however, it has suffered the fate which seems to come to many early watershed studies: endlessly referred to in general terms, but almost never really read; and endlessly quoted from some passage or episode which is catchy to the eye but in fact is carelessly extrapolated and is one of the least convincing parts of the study. For example, writers of self-improvement best-sellers and subsequent adult learning books have frequently cited almost without comment, as though it were some kind of mystic delivery from the gods, the following table of estimated learning capacities (100 is alloted for age 20–24 on the assumption that this is the maximum period for effective learning):

57 for age 14–16
84 for age 17–19
100 for age 20–24
86 for age 25–29
87 for age 30 or over

Shortly after Thorndike's book appeared, this table began to be presented as a summation chart of the comparative abilities of adults to learn. However, what Thorndike was offering was a suggested comparison of the ability of certain age groups to learn in *a specific study dealing with the learning of high school subjects by adults in public evening classes*. It is true that the sample was large—886 evening adult students—and the subjects covered were broad (algebra, biology, civics, English, French, German, Latin, and Spanish). Still the sample was not typical of the whole population, and Thorndike's heroic efforts to free his group of participating people from "the influences of color, school and language difficulty" and the fact that he was unable to resolve a number of other incredibly difficult control problems leaves even the sympathetic reader unconvinced. But then who needs to read the book who has already been provided with the chart?

Thorndike was convinced, when his comprehensive review of his own studies and those of others was finished, that James's assertion thirty-five years previously was grotesquely wrong, and since he himself was also a rhetorician, and a good one, he presented his view in conclusion with great strength:

> "In general, nobody under forty-five should restrain himself from trying to learn anything because of a belief or fear that he is too old to be able to learn it. Nor should he use that fear as an excuse for not learning anything which he ought to learn. If he fails in learning it, inability due directly to age will very rarely, if ever, be the reason."

Thorndike did not set his limit at age 45 because he thought learning stopped there—it was simply that most of the studies undertaken by him and his colleagues were done with conveniently handy adults or groups who were typically at work in some form of studies in university or evening high school courses. In fact, Thorndike had scarcely finished writing the above paragraph when he added, "Age, in itself, is a minor factor in either success or failure. Capacity, interest, energy, and time are the essentials."

He did, it is true, believe that there would be a decline in learning power across the lifespan. He is widely quoted as saying that the decline might be something like one per cent a year after age 25, but in fact Thorndike is insistent that there is little difference in capacity between ages 22–42; and his off-the-cuff comments about possible degrees of decline after 45 or 50 are unsubstantiated and wholly speculative. In his summation, Thorndike is obsessed with two factors he considers crucial to getting adults to learn, unlearn, relearn: first, the *will* to learn (in a splendid throwback to the James dictum, Thorndike writes: "By the age of twenty-five most persons have, within certain limitations, learned a great part of what *they wish to learn*" [my italics]); and second, the *opportunity to learn* under conditions that maximize the potentialities of the individual.

In fact, *Adult Learning* is a kind of Universal Declaration of

Adult Rights to Learn. Thorndike calls for a society in which there will be a redistribution of the formal hours of learning experience —so that these might be spread into and through adult life. He notes how usually inadequate both content and teaching strategies are for adult learners. He cites the need for the availability of counselling for adults—the mature counselling by peers for those whose hesitation on the brink of learning, or discouragement many times in the course of it, hinders their learning adventures. He urges a more sensible approach to the "dropout" from adult classes —perhaps the adult happens to know what he needs and does not need, or perhaps there is a message for the instructor and the institution. He notes compassionately the many pressures that converge on adult learners. He stresses that wonder—James's "disinterested curiosity"—is perfectly accessible and a part of adulthood. And Thorndike deplores people who apply to adults tests validated and standardized for child and school use.

In its time boundaries, *Adult Learning* was not a Ulyssean book. But in its summation of the directions and potentialities of the individual man and woman as adult learners, and its indication of the fresh productive and creative life which they might inherit if society's values were what they should be, it has its own share of Ulyssean beauty—and Thorndike's later life was Ulyssean.

In "The Age of the IQ" or "the Cognitive Age", it can be expected that performance on intelligence tests would be taken as an obvious diagnostic instrument to find out whether adult mental abilities hold up with advancing age.

The intelligence test approach is so clean and definite; it lends itself beautifully to curves on a graph; and its potential efficiency lends it an unmistakable charm for the North American system. There is, however, a slight problem—what is "intelligence"?

Is it so straightforward a thing as "the ability to solve problems"? So anatomical and baffling a thing as "a function of the cerebral cortex"? Is it a number of things—the plurality of intelligences that William Sheldon described in *The Varieties of Human Temperament*? Is it a product of nature or nurture? And how does it relate to wisdom? Where is the Wisdom Quotient?

In the early days of testing, just after 1900 when Binet devised his tests for atypical children, it was widely accepted that intelligence was a genetic factor, fixed or pre-determined at birth (so-called "innate cognitive intelligence"), relatively fixed at age 16, and readily assessable by standardized tests. From this general position, together with careless teaching and learning and slipshod communications, arose what one might call the cash-and-carry concept of the IQ (codified or indexed by dividing the subject's

Mental Age or MA by his chronological age or CA, and multiplying by a hundred).

The so-called "intelligence test" was administered either individually or as a group process; the IQ was determined, and then unfortunately extrapolated from the whole life of the person being tested, usually a child or early adolescent, attached to his records for various future directions in educational choices or for the opinions of teachers and, far too often, of others. In "good" situations it usually formed part of a cluster of judgments: for example, achievement tests, "interests" tests, school performance, or in the case of suspected neurotic students and others, such tests for abnormality as the Rorschach Inkblot tests, and the Minnesota Multiphasic Personality Inventory. But the IQ retained its aura for better and, too often, for worse. It is interesting to speculate on what effect the knowledge of a supposed "IQ" (often derived in slipshod testing and bandied about in slipshod talking) has had on educational motivations in later adult life.

Compared to the primitive conception of intelligence as a fixed inheritance from the genetic system, some much more attractive definitions of "intelligence" have been advanced within the past twenty years. R. B. Cattell and D. O. Hebb described two kinds of intelligence, not one. In Hebb's concept, Intelligence A is found in the genetic potentiality or basic qualities of the individual's central nervous system; Intelligence B, however, is mainly the result of experience, learning, and the interplay of environment with the self. Cattell's concepts are of "fluid" and "crystallized" intelligence; like Hebb's, they have had wide influence.

The psychologist H. J. Butcher suggests an interesting verification of these views of intelligence in the following comment:

> "An astonishingly large proportion of the cerebral cortex has been surgically removed from some adult patients with very little effect on their scores on standardized intelligence tests, whereas cognitive development in children is severely impaired by similar damage. It thus appears that brain cells needed for the *development* of intelligence are no longer essential to maintain a high level once it has been developed."

David Wechsler's definition of intelligence is comprehensive and illuminating: "Intelligence is the aggregate or global capacity to act purposefully, to think rationally, and to deal effectively with one's environment." However, the Wechsler definition raises a host of new problems in its adverbs: What is "purposefully"? Who judges "effectively"? and so on.

A definition which sounds complicated but assembles and integrates with considerable skill some of the many problem components in the search is Butcher's own statement:

"Intelligence is a quintessential high-level skill at the summit of a hierarchy of intellectual skills. It integrates with different hierarchies and with varying ceilings of complexity according to the *experience* of the individual."

This definition owes something to Jean Piaget, who has suggested that the nature and functioning of intelligence change quite radically from one age to another. It is impossible to place under a single convenient label such different entities or functions as the formal intelligence which adults typically use, the concrete intelligence of mid-childhood, and the sensorimotor intelligence of infants and very young children.

Is there a domain of intelligence which should be entitled "creative intelligence"? There are at all events (as indicated earlier) tests for creativity. Butcher, who has all kinds of fascinating comments to make about the enigma or semi-enigma, raises the question of whether the constant acceleration of man's knowledge of computers will pour additional light on what we mean by "human intelligence" through mimicry or simulation of human thought processes.

In reviewing Theta Wolf's life of Alfred Binet (1973), Read Tuddenham was struck with the fact that the great father of testing had, himself, some very strong reservations about what one might describe as no-nonsense definitions of intelligence. Noting the neglect and the distortions that have been Binet's lot ever since he and Simon devised their famous intelligence scale, Tuddenham remarks:

> "Those who would suppress such tests in the service of egalitarianism may be surprised to learn that Binet declined to define intelligence lest he foreclose its exploration, that he specifically believed in the power of training to increase it, that he invariably used the phrase 'mental level' (*niveau*) to avoid the connotations of 'mental age,' and would certainly have objected violently to calculating the IQ (Simon called the IQ a betrayal!)"

Two great problems were bound up with the concept of the IQ from its earliest years. The first problem was, as already indicated, that the attempt to sum up the "intelligence" of a complex human being in a single box score was too naive. The second, that it became evident as the years passed that the IQ (whatever it was) was anything but a fixed entity. The tests were saturated with the culture attitudes and knowledges of the testers. Thus, if you re-tested a young person after a period of improved environmental conditions and better training in language, the IQ increased—in some cases by as many as twenty points.

Since the IQ was essentially a label for schoolchildren, its application had little to do with adults and the life-cycle until the adoption of testing on an enormous scale for the assessment of young adults seeking to enter commercial and industrial life. For that purpose, much of the testing is invalid: the applicant may have taken heaps of tests, often the same ones, in a three-month search for work among various firms, and under very uneven conditions of administration—no matter. There must be scores in the dossier, from which the solemn sub-priests will try to construct his competence and his suitability. Sometimes the material is highly personal and is a flagrant invasion of his rights as a private person. Older adults have become involved as job mobility has become a major phenomenon and as large numbers of women, after a period of marriage, have returned to work that involves retraining or new training. Besides, the increasing vogue for "mature matriculation" at universities has increased the trend to test the mental abilities of adults especially in the age range 25–50.

There is a fearful simplicity and arbitrariness in the idea that mental capacity can be plotted on a curve and that ability to learn will follow the curve across the life journey.

Folk knowledge, which for centuries, and long before the rise of psychology, thought it could speedily recognize the "dullard" and the "wit", probably rarely pursued the classification into the late years. Dullness, if it did not precisely fade like ugliness, at least became camouflaged by the myriad disguises of old age conventions. Thorndike believed that a dull young man would certainly be a dull old man; and that a bright old man was certainly brighter than an average young man.

Reports of performance by adult people at various age levels are now normally given not simply as composite scores on tests, but rather as performances on various sectors of whatever "intelligence" test is used. Thus, typical tests examine verbal competence as seen in strength of vocabulary, skill in handling problems designed to test abstract and practical reasoning, and rote memory. Later adults hold up well in the sections of the tests requiring competence in vocabulary and in information; they typically show declines in sub-tests dealing with rote memory, digit symbol arrangement, and picture arrangement; they naturally show a decline in psychomotor skills. These are, remember, general summations. One of the most essential things to recall in reporting all adult testing is that there are numerous older adults who surpass younger in certain and in all categories; and that there are greater disparities in individual scores among a given age group, say 60 to 65, than between the ages 60 and 40.

David Wechsler, who made a brilliant effort to design a mental abilities test especially for adults, and which would be standardized for each adult age group (instead of against children and youths)

—the Wechsler Adult Intelligence Scale—is convinced that there is a progressive decline in intellectual ability as the years pass. In Chapter 9 of his interesting study, *The Measurement and Appraisal of Adult Intelligence*, Wechsler argues that on all sub-tests of the WAIS the decline is found, and he states categorically in summation: ". . . whatever it is that the tests measure, the argument advanced does not controvert the fact that the abilities involved alter with the aging process. The least one can say is that for most persons intellectual ability, after reaching a peak in early maturity, declines progressively with age. The correlation between age (after age 25) and scores on tests of intelligence is always negative."

Wechsler is a formidable scholar and debater in the fields of adult testing and learning. He assembles and presents the results of his research with much power; besides, it is surely impossible to argue that he had an axe to grind. He devised the WAIS not to prove that adult mental capacity declines in pure curves, but simply to determine what the picture is, and also to provide a far juster measurement of "intelligence" than had previously been possible with child-oriented tests inherited from Binet.

Nonetheless, there are enormous cracks running through Wechsler's rock of finality. The convolutions through which his arguments go in attempting to arrive at a clearly acceptable definition of "adult intelligence" are themselves evidence of this. In fact, he fails. *"Whatever it is that the tests measure"* is a remarkably obscure statement of the enigmatic central domain of "intellectual ability," which, however, by an easy bridge hardly noticed perhaps by either the writer or the reader becomes the centre of a summation statement of dazzling certainty: "the least one can say is that for most persons intellectual ability, after reaching a peak in early maturity, declines progressively with age."

Perhaps the most impressive evidence that could be brought forward of the continuing power of operation of the human mind would be its intimately observed ability over considerable lengths of time to make creative solutions of problems or challenges produced from within the domain of its on-going interests. And this is virtually untestable by the ingenious tests so far devised by psychologists of learning—brief, usually closely-timed tests, with, in effect, "canned" exercises which it is hoped will display the varying competences of younger and older adults. The mature mind at its best is not engaged in once-for-all enterprises, even although it is true that conventional or routine living does present its own version of closely-timed trial test situations, day by day. For example, how does the driver of a large automobile most rapidly and successfully make his way through the glut of traffic separating him from the city boundary and his downtown committee meeting? But this is a far cry from the solution of abstract problems for which one may have to assemble one's forces time and again to solve, after perhaps successive failures.

James Birren, in *The Psychology of Aging,* notes that tests of intelligence to a great extent measure achievement or stored information, and goes on to define the essential quality in the performance of intelligence which the tests fail to measure directly as "inventive concept formation" or "inventive conceptualization." Birren is referring to "the more labile [that is, fleeting] qualities displayed by individuals who are able to integrate simultaneously available, but previously disparate [that is, diverse, or essentially different], facts *into some new synthesis.*" (My italics).

This problem of testing creative conceptualization among highly individualistic human adults by means of inadequate, usually rigorously timed test exercises is only one of swarms of others which descend upon the devoted psychological seeker of pure curves of intellectual power and learning capacity in human life. The difficulty of testing and plotting wisdom on a grid has already been mentioned. One indirect approach to this is the struggle to determine whether people have become more or less rigid in their attitudes with the advancing years. Testers seeking to determine this have employed such devices as trying to find out how far different age groups agree with clichés, how far they seem to cling to settled habits as against trying out new approaches, and so on.

Although a number of studies since 1958 in Great Britain and the United States claim to have shown that rigidity, inflexibility, and dogmatism increase after, say, age 50 or 55, the control problems are overwhelming. In probing for rigidity in attitudes and opinions, the line is very thin between middle-aged stability or thoughtful conservatism, for example, and rigidity. The probing exercise may be too brief, too impersonal, and too judgmental without the real data for judgment; the subject's apparent drawing-back and drawing-in may be symptoms of deep anxieties which were as acute at 30 as at 60. Surely the best device for studying the onset and progress of rigidity in attitudes and opinions would be longitudinal case studies—biography supplies some of these, but one would need many hundreds more.

In a study at Wayne State University conducted by Paul Cameron, the investigators interviewed three generations: Wayne State University students, their parents, and their grandparents:

> "First, we discovered that the older generation actually depended on fewer persons for advice, emotional support, and general information than did the middle or younger generations, and that they made fewer demands on the persons they did depend on. *In fact, the grandparent generation seemed to give more interpersonal support than they received from others. . . .*
>
> The older generation did express more caution when they

faced decision-making situations (and) were less likely to take action under all conditions. However, it was possible to make almost all of the younger subjects as cautious as or more cautious than the elders by adjusting the amount of information and interpersonal approval. *When the young adult grandchildren saw themselves as deprived of factual information, they, too, became cautious. . . . By taking away information and social approval, we can establish conditions [among young adults] that resemble those in which many elders must function.*"

And Cameron cites the study of Clarence and Sylvia Sherwood on the supposed political conservatism of elder adults, noting that the older people studied in the survey were actually more liberal than their offspring. In any event, he goes on to point out that "many old persons develop conservative streaks because of what society has taken away from them—status, work, social opportunity, privacy. If fewer things were taken from them, they would feel less threatened, less need to cling to whatever is left." (Reported in *Psychology Today*, December, 1971.)

Within the testing domain itself, a considerable number of important studies refute Wechsler's position that a downward curve is the normal direction of adult mental abilities. Irving Lorge was also convinced that the intelligence tests given to adults were often invalidated by being originally drawn up, validated, and standardized for children. Lorge, especially, was struck by the extent to which the tests were dependent upon the level of education of the adult. (Older adults earlier in this century had had notably less schooling than the young adults they were often pitted against in intelligence testing, and this is in general still true.) Besides, Lorge disliked the rigid and (he thought) unfair controls which closely-timed testing imposed upon people in their middle years and older. What was the special virtue of the frozen time limits, other than that the tests were devised in a modern society especially obsessed with technology, so-called efficiency, and the clock?

Lorge had not been Thorndike's disciple for nothing. In his irrepressible way, Thorndike had introduced a "corrective" factor, a sort of handicap score included in the research calculations, in cases where he felt that disadvantaged adults would be rated unfairly against better educated people. In 1936 Lorge—as one example—took three adult groups, aged 20–25, 27–37, and 40–70, and tried to match the people in them as carefully as possible, person to person. In initial runs he turned up a declining curve on efficiency working under rigid time limits. He took this and computed a handicap, including corrections for slowness, for time away from school and consequent loss of learning habits, and for lack of motivation. Lorge's conclusion was that if the same individuals could be followed in *longitudinal* studies, there would be no decline in the curves of tested mental capacity.

He maintained this after many years of experiments:

> "Age as age probably does little to affect an individual's power to learn or think. His performance may be reduced because of changes in his speed, sensory acuity, or self-concept, or shifts in values, motivation, goals, and responsibilities which come with aging. Adults learn much less than they might partly because of the self-underestimations of their power and wisdom, and partly because of their own anxieties that their learning behaviour will bring unfavourable criticism. Failure to keep on learning may affect performance more than power itself."

Support for Lorge's main thesis came from a study by E. E. Ghiselli and associates in which they worked with a group of 1,400 adults aged 20 to 65. Ghiselli used only well-educated people and his testing situations, as in Lorge's case, excluded speed as a parameter. Ghiselli found that his older adults held up as well as the younger. The Fels Institute tested 72 women and 59 men over a period of about seventeen years, using the Otis Mental Ability Test as the instrument. During that period, the average level of the IQ calculated for the group remained almost unchanged. There were many *individual* changes in the scores: as many up as down.

An impressive study was undertaken in 1958 by Celia M. Friend and J. P. Zubek, reported in the *Journal of Gerontology*. Here was a study that set out from the beginning to try to ascertain the effects of aging on *critical thinking* ability. The group comprised 480 people from age 12 to age 80, and was asked to respond to the Watson and Glaser Critical Thinking Appraisal. The results were mixed. As a group, the quite elderly respondents fell well below younger groups—yet a substantial number *individually* made scores as high as young adult respondents.

The great need, of course, was for studies which followed the *same adults* across their life journey, and in testing them pitted their performance at 20 or 30 against their performance twenty or thirty years later: that is, longitudinal studies. This would remove the educational inequalities, and reduce certain control problems of trying to match personalities, an almost insuperable task. Longitudinal studies are not as impossible as they at first seem: testing of adults goes all the way back to World War I, and in addition, devoted researchers like Nancy Bayley and others reported below set up programmes deliberately planned to retest the same adults at periodic intervals. Bayley decided in 1933 to do a longitudinal study of the same seventy-four subjects from babyhood into and through adulthood; she has found after forty years that the fifty-four subjects who remain in the project are showing little change from their performances at eighteen. Bayley's study still falls short of the

Ulyssean boundaries, but the returns so far do not support the "declining curve" theories.

The most important report of recent years on adult ability to retain learning powers is that of Jarvik, Eisdorfer, and Blum, *Intellectual Functioning in Adults* (1973). In this anthology of studies, Samuel Granick and Alfred S. Friedman note how research "has, to a large extent, followed the orientation of our culture in focusing on the debilitating aspects of aging. It seems to have inadvertently helped to justify the tendency to view the aged as infirm and in constant need of support and protection. Associated with this are the powerful social, cultural, and economic pressures that lead the aged to disengage from active, dynamic involvement in society, and into a depressed, deprived, and unproductive existence."

And L. F. Jarvik, in making the summation review of dozens of *longitudinal* studies, remarks that, while psychomotor skills "relentlessly decline" beginning even between the ages of 16 and 36, *"the stability of intellectual abilities emerges once more."* (Jarvik's italics.) For example, in R. Schoenfeldt's longitudinal study of Iowa subjects, those "entering the seventh decade at the time of their last testing, had maintained their relative standings on mean total Alpha scores *for 42 years."* (My italics.) This was true even into the late years: Jarvik notes that "Eisdorfer and Wilkie, and Rhudick and Gordon, whose subjects were followed from the seventh to the eighth decades, were also impressed by their failure to find rapid declines in these later years."

It is true that the same studies found that good health and good education were powerful factors in maintenance of these abilities at the full. Jarvik is able to quote from research at the New York State Psychiatric Institute to the effect that "if illness does *not* intervene, cognitive ability is the rule and *can be maintained into the ninth decade."*

Thus, in the most persuasive of all testing approaches—longitudinal studies—strong evidence exists that adult "mental abilities" performances hold up well, and in the case of some subjects increase, even through the very late years. Yet, at the best, all the investigators have been engaged in probing into one of the most elephantine problems in human life: what adult intelligence is, how it affects adult learning, how the environment interacts with the performance of intellectual capacity, how the physical body interacts, what the role of the self is (for example, the mysterious thing called "ego strength"), and how far the whole repertoire of drives, motivations, fears, loves, greeds, needs, and the hidden creative hungers and "leaps forward" are involved.

Although many scholars would wince at the thought, it is a fact that in all matters dealing with human beings there are certain "manifest conditions" or situations which the wise naked eye of experience can see and record. For example, everyone with any knowledgeability at all knows that adults in later life can continue to learn. Whether they learn as well as before is a matter for discussion, as seen above, but who in our time would agree with Freud's incredible statement, "Old people are no longer educable"? Freud's own later years gave the standing lie to this fatuity.

Aging *in itself* seems very clearly *not* the governing factor in the decline of adult mental and learning capacities where these declines occur. There are clusters of conditions which camouflage themselves as typical of the late years and old age which can play havoc with the performances of later adults: certain types of chronic ill-health, for example, whether the subject is young or old, apparently lower the attack-set of the individual. Substantial deficits in education, and long periods of lack of practice in answering tests and going through any routines of formal learning under instruction are conditions which not only create less competence in carrying out the testing assignment with success, but may be confused (as already noted) with "older adult rigidity." The natural tendency of many older adults to try to conserve what they conceive to be their diminishing energy bank will cause many of them to seek what the investigators of adult life call "load shedding". This is a spontaneous attempt to avoid overloading situations, coming close to Holmes's thresholds of permissible anxiety.

On the other hand, every careful observer can see that great numbers of adults in their later years do little or nothing to keep alive the fires of mental alertness and learning capacity. They confront rich potentiality only with passiveness, which is indeed a form of resistance. Or they have organized their lives as a flight from the occasional discomforts and real delights of systematically breaking into new fields. It is a truism of the adult learning world that performance is transformed by an active rather than passive mind-set, and by a life filled with the thrust for learning. Passivity and a turning-away from the challenges to learn are not part of the aging process *per se*, but of self-induced or peer-induced attitudes about the roles and purposes of older adults.

Yet not wholly. Something else happens to older adults, some of whom find themselves in the corrals of the testers, which has little to do with aging but much to do with time. Many adults get beaten up by life. By the time they are age 50, or 60, not only have they often encountered immense personal sorrows and disappointments, but they have experienced social and psychological shocks simply as participants in a succession of upheavals in political and economic life, and in the sphere of customs and morals. Only unusually sensitive young adults recognize in older people the heroic achievement it has been for many of them to carry on their lives usefully and lovingly in spite of these stresses and storms.

Select from these men and women a group for testing, to see

how they respond to paper-and-pencil or laboratory episodes skilfully conceived to test strength of vocabulary, stored information, conceptualization, and such psychomotor performance areas as object assembly, digit symbol, and block design. What you will obtain is "whatever it is that the tests measure." The result is not unlike a stop-action photograph in black and white of this remarkable creature whose life runs on like a full-colour film. Remember, too, that each of these lives also is governed by what might be called an expectations threshold. Many older adults no longer expect as much of themselves as they did in their younger years. They are usually no longer as hungrily competitive, as superficial in certain inner values—nor does the folk eye of society expect them to perform as though they were younger.

By contrast, the numerous Ulysseans I have met in my life have continued to expect a great deal of themselves throughout their lives, if not in old fields, then in new. Without being obscurantist about it, one can say that they seem to have their own measure of "adult intelligence", and so far as I can discern it, a Ulyssean would put it in about such terms as these:

"Yes, I feel certain physical losses from my earlier years. *But otherwise* I feel that whatever you call my mind is burning more brightly and beautifully than it ever did before. It isn't just this or that—it's the whole of myself, everything running together, not just adding sums and repeating from rote as in school days, but a whole complex, a constellation: perceptions, understandings, judgments, selectivity—the great feeling I have that I'm free but not chasing up and down every meadow as I did when young. Insights, answers, and compassions keep pouring from all the experiences I've had in my life. Not that I have all the answers! Sometimes I feel that I know nothing—there's so much to explore. When I think of it, it's not just the mind, whatever that is—it's the self, my whole self, that makes me feel young, but a different 'young' from my youth, in many ways just as beautiful—in some, more so."

Still, it is impossible really to speak too exactly for the Ulysseans —they come in so many different conditions and personalities. Except that common to all their attitudes are the sense of quest, an active mind and spirit, a loving pursuit of life on whatever terms, and great expectations.

And if this older adult goes on to say that he cannot turn off his mind; that day after day it remains enchanted with the variety and the mystery of life, and that it searches in dozens of ways, no matter how small because of limitations sometimes imposed by circumstances, to obtain more and more sights and views of an horizon which never ceases to expand—then, of course, you have, whether rich or poor, well or wretchedly ill, the Ulyssean adult.

6. IS THERE A "PEAK OF CREATIVITY"?

Some investigators like to conceive of the power and creativity of the mind in such a simple analogy as a hill-shaped curve, which one climbs to a presumed peak of productivity and creative achievement, then tumbles down the other side. Among them are several original searchers who have sought confirmation of their ideas in the "peak years" of noted inventors and creators. The theory is intriguing, not least for its simplicity of approach. You look up the career profiles of hundreds of people, living or dead, whose work in science, the arts, politics, athletics, and business has brought them sufficient fame to be listed in the encyclopedias or in the *Who's Who* of their field. You determine at what age each created his or her masterwork; and then you do the necessary statistical runs and correlations, and produce a composite figure for the typical "peak" age at which men (in these studies it is almost invariably men) produced their best work as mathematicians, poets, statesmen, chemists, and so on.

Apparently the first modern investigator to attempt this type of study was W. A. Dorland, in a book published in 1908, *The Age of Mental Virility*. In spite of the originality of his approach, the Dorland study is forgotten, nor did it seem to arouse very much interest at the time—another of many cases, no doubt, of an idea appearing before its time. Dorland chose the lives of four hundred famous men (the four hundred may have been fortuitous, or a kind of overhang from the American fascination with the social "Four Hundred" who dominated the New York scene!) Dorland opened himself to criticism at once by choosing his own four hundred famous creative people, and he made no allowance for the age of death. His conclusions were that age 50 was a kind of over-all typical "peak" for production of the masterpiece. Dorland's efforts deserved widespread attention if only because of his originality of approach. Since he pursued the subject in later papers up to about 1930, he was in fact quoted in a number of popular psychology texts, but the main work rapidly disappeared from view, and is now a collector's item.

The irrepressible and indefatigable Thorndike decided to employ and improve the Dorland approach, in one of the main papers which make up *Adult Learning*. Thorndike's real interest was whether "great ability" declines later than average ability. In the investigation, Thorndike delegated to one of his associates the task of choosing three hundred and thirty-one names from the *Dictionary of National Biography*. These were all either "men of affairs" (that is, "statesmen, reformers, and business men") or "scientists" (physicists, naturalists, astronomers, chemists, mathematicians, and inventors). Of course it was critical that for each person the correct *magnum opus* should be chosen. Thorndike and his associates thought they had done this, and produced an "average masterpiece age" of 47.4. However, the records of the study produced in *Adult Learning* are scanty, and huge questions remained unanswered: how do you rationally lump the supposed "masterworks" of physicists, statesmen, and businessmen together and come up with a single composite age? The enigmas of all such studies thus come forward at once: "What is the nature of creativity? how is it expressed? how do you determine its *single* peak?" Thorndike tried, almost incidentally, to correct a glaring oversight in his survey: where are the writers? Just at the end of the study, his team analysed the lives of forty-six eminent English writers "from Chaucer to Matthew Arnold, who lived to be seventy or over." The selection of the masterpieces was "objectively" made from five histories of English literature; the median masterpiece age was 47.

An early contrary view (aside, of course, from William James's declamation already quoted earlier) was that of Robert S. Woodworth of Columbia University in a text on psychology published in 1921. Woodworth's comments were not a study—they simply illustrated the fascination of a topic which, after all, was a perfect theme for the dons' table, or for any group of interested men and women discussing life on a winter evening. Woodworth was almost an echo of James: he would concede only a "few" great inventions, "artistic or practical" to the old, and "comparatively few" (whatever that means) "from the middle-aged". Woodworth had decided that the period from age 20 to age 40 seemed to be "most favorable" for inventiveness.

His position was attacked seven years later in a paper published in the *American Journal of Psychology* by seemingly one of the very few women commentators on the question. The writer, who used the pseudonym "Helen Nelson" for some reason best known to herself (what was so daring about her field of comment?) made the not very sensational claim that in a considerable number of cases of famous people whom she cited, "invention of the highest order, far from being in decay at forty, seems to be at very prime or just ready to begin."

Modest though the statement was, it so roused the psychologist Harvey C. Lehman that he attributed to it much of his motivation for writing *Age and Achievement*, published in 1953. Lehman's formidable study remains the most comprehensive in the field; it reflects an enormous amount of work and planning; and although Lehman may have started with a case to prove, or at least the unfortunate "Helen Nelson's" to disprove, he certainly sought for objectivity throughout. One reads him with respect, and at times admiration. Accepting his conclusions, which are offered with an air of exhaustive finality, is quite another matter.

Age and Achievement is important not only for the massive documentation which it attempted, but for its inevitable influence as a major study, cited many times in texts on adult psychology and the life-cycle. So able and normally cautious an authority on human aging as James Birren quotes Lehman's book extensively and takes it at its face value in his chapter on productivity in *The Psychology of Aging*. The same cannot be said for Simone de Beauvoir, who refers to it in passing in *The Coming of Age*, accepting Lehman's comments on a handful of chemists, physicists, and inventors, and then abrasively dismissing him in the following footnote: "Lehman's statistical method is utterly erroneous when it is applied to art and literature. In science it is easier to evaluate the number and value of the discoveries." It is hard to know which is the worse fate: to be wholly ignored or to be dismissed in so summary a style. There is a point here, however. Although Lehman is well worth attention, Beauvoir's brilliant and penetrating mind, in a single cutting remark, goes at once to one of the central weaknesses of his whole study.

Lehman's survey is really a kind of fugue, in which the original theme is handled with a series of imaginative variations. The theme is the old one: is it possible, from the study of the lives of acknowledged human creators, dead and living, to fix upon the masterwork of each, and thus as the evidence pours in to determine the "peak" age of human creativity—or at least, the peak period, say a decade, or half-decade? In Lehman's case, he went to great pains to avoid what might have seemed to be the errors and *gaucheries* of reporters like Dorland, Thorndike, and "Helen Nelson".

For example: Lehman inevitably turns to all available major encyclopedias, dictionaries of biography, and histories of art, science, and literature as resource banks for the lives and accomplishments of famous creators. However, he does not rely on his own judgment to select these, as Dorland did; nor upon one or two close associates, as Thorndike did; but rather upon many lists of creative people and their dates of produced work compiled by previous selectors who at the time could have had no idea that a Lehman, hungry for evidence on the creative "peak" and armed with statistical techniques, was going to use their data. Or else

Lehman occasionally relies on living juries, usually his colleagues at Ohio University, to make selections in certain areas. One approach is illustrative: if you are trying to determine when the single masterwork of a scientist or inventor or of an artist or writer was issued and composed, you first determine the pre-eminence of the work by the number of citations it has received in histories of science, art, invention, and so on. The same "honourable mention" approach helps to identify the most creative period or half-decade, since Lehman divided his graphs into five-year periods.

Because Lehman was fascinated by the question of the "outstanding" work as indicating the peak, he became impaled time after time on the criteria of the masterpiece. Most of the subjects in his study are dead, and we are informed that decisions on their top performances have been taken by someone's culling histories, encyclopedias, and "best-seller book lists", a democratic but hardly convincing technique. Nonetheless, Lehman does seem to succeed in putting personal bias out of the process, or cancelling it out; and he has other merits.

He does not, for example, attempt to deliver some composite score on the age of peak of creativity, made up by sweeping together the top achievement ages of people of almost wholly disparate fields, but builds his "peak age periods" *within* each major field (chemistry, painting, athletics, and so on), and then, with an ultimately mesmeric effect, reminds us that the summit age for creativity is virtually the same across almost all fields of human activity. Still, he is cautious enough to remind his readers, presumably pounded into acceptance by the deluge of data, that his "averages" are not the whole story—that in every creative category, numerous individual exceptions exist.

For Lehman, the peak period for the production of outstanding creative work is the half-decade between 30 and 35,closely followed by the half-decade between 35 and 40. Thereafter in all fields except "leadership" (in politics, diplomacy, finance, and the church, where the peak occurs later) there is a decline, usually a sharp decline, broken in some fields under report by lower peaks in the 50s, sometimes, rarely, in the 60s. Lehman often presents additional broken-line graphs to indicate the line of production of works of lesser merit or, in fact, the best productions of people of lesser merit. These lines are often quite different from his main mountainscopes, but Lehman's interest in them is clearly minimal, although it is hard to see why, for example, the production of "510 contemporary orchestral works written by Americans between the years 1912 and 1932" is any less a barometer of age and achievement than "53 very superior orchestral works which have survived the test of time". In the case of the contemporary works, as it happens, the peak of a graph which looks like a profile of almost any range in the Rockies occurs in the 50s, and the next highest twin heights are in the 30s (Lehman's sacred period) and the *late 60s*.

Nothing escapes Lehman's Zeus-like eye and his ever-ready statistical techniques. At what half-decade did men (women hardly can get their heads in) produce their most important masterworks, not merely in physics, philosophy, and genetics, but in such heterogeneous fields of activity as hymn writing, treatises in education, money-making, movie-acting, eloquent orations, runs batted in in baseball, corn-husking championships, appointment to the American Supreme Court, and the composing of vocal solos? Throughout the whole book one dimly hears the hum of the dynamos set working to furnish this staggering accumulation of data and charts.

Throughout *Age and Achievement,* whatever the domain being analysed, there on the mountainchart of "outstanding works" is the almost inevitable peak rearing itself in the 30 to 40 period. When the dazed reader puts the book aside for a while, however, and takes a stroll or steps on a bus, or does whatever induces his or her creative analysis, some unsatisfied questions begin to rise.

For example, what does Lehman really mean by "creativity"? Incredibly, although he uses the word, and also the adjective "creative" hundreds of times throughout the book, he never defines what he means by these words. What he really does is to perform an enormous statistical count and charting of years in which certain selected masterworks or masteractions appeared or were performed, and to equate this with the creative apex of the individuals mentioned. While it is true that most people would join Carl Rogers in wanting a product as evidence of creative power, this in no way dispenses with the fact that human beings can continue to be immensely creative thinkers even though they rarely publish—what do you do with the modern philosopher Wittgenstein, as one example? Or if by attentive, almost painful investigation of a large number of musical histories, you discover that Wagner's *Die Meistersinger* is rated twelve times out of seventeen books listing "best-loved operas", you are to suppose that this opera was the creative "peak" for Wagner (if you can believe that, you can believe anything); or you find Leonardo's *The Virgin of the Rocks* listed as his one contribution to a naive list of the forty-four "possibly greatest paintings" of the world, painstakingly culled, of course, by checking lists of one thousand six hundred and eighty-four oil paintings in art books and identifying those appearing ten times or more—not only are your criteria wide open to assault, but what were Wagner and Leonardo supposed to be doing with the rest of their "creative" lives? In fact, *Age and Achievement* gives us very few glimpses of the views of the actual creators, and those we have are, to say the least, off-putting.

The very people who should perhaps know more than anyone else about the peaks and valleys, the ebbs and flows of their own creative life—the creators themselves—never get a chance to speak at all. The mathematician Poincaré turns up on page 308 stepping on the same bus, but otherwise our judgments of when the writers, scientists, inventors, painters, athletes, musicians, and statesmen achieved the "peak" of creative action are left to armies of ghostly commentators and critics or to paragraph writers in encyclopedias. Their verdicts are marshalled and counted by anonymous scrutineers in a healthy democratic exercise culminating in the placing of the masterwork in its appropriate half-decade for charting. Since many popular books dealing with the arts and with scientific discovery are highly redundant and simplistic, there is no special safeguard in collecting seventeen of them, nor is the creator's "peak" of creativity guaranteed by inviting several university colleagues in separate rooms to identify his single masterwork. There is probably one excellent approach to the whole question: to examine the life and work of a given number of noted creative people in various fields each as a total life, including both *their* views of their creative lives, and also those of their most comprehensive and discerning biographers, for example: Leslie Marchand on Byron; G. D. Painter on Proust; Aniela Jaffé on Jung. A review of the whole life is necessary, not just of the composition and production date of a single masterpiece.

In the rare instances in *Age and Achievement* where Lehman and his associates go so far as to mention human creators, one wonders where everybody has gone. For example, in Chapter 14, in a very fair effort to reinforce his point that "although man's creative achievements occur most often during the thirties, . . . any stereotyped conception of later maturity is quite untenable", Lehman provides a list of some seventy-five "older thinkers and great achievements". (He takes away the fragrance of this reluctantly-offered flower, however, by prefacing it with a catalogue of dull things—largely recapitulative—which the elderly are "more likely to do".)

The omissions from Lehman's list of older thinkers and great achievements are grotesque: one can only conclude that someone not otherwise well equipped has been busy again with one of those confounded lists of "Two Hundred People Who Contributed to World Culture." Lehman's people, diligently searching through their pre- packaged lists and popular encyclopedias, had apparently never heard of William Butler Yeats, Robert Frost, Edith Sitwell, Saint-John Perse, André Maurois, and Boris Pasternak; of Thomas Mann, Hermann Hesse, Tolstoy, and Kazantzakis; of Titian, Tintoretto, Claude Monet, and Picasso; of Henry Moore, Le Corbusier, Frank Lloyd Wright, and Inigo Jones; of Colette, Costain, Rose Macaulay, Wallace Stevens, and Rabindranath Tagore; of George

Santayana, Alfred North Whitehead, Jacques Maritain, and Fran
cois Mauriac; of Charles de Gaulle, Benedetto Croce, and Thomas
Hobbes; of Auguste Piccard, Arthur Eddington, Lise Meitner, and
Buffon; of Samuel Morse, Lee DeForest, and Gilbert Lewis; of
Hieronymous Bosch, Wanda Landowska, Claudio Monteverdi, and
Joseph Haydn; of Wyndham Lewis, Richard Burton, Ivy Compton-
Burnett, and Shaw; of Charles Doughty, Henrik Ibsen, Henry James,
and James Barrie; of Oliver Wendell Holmes, Thomas Jefferson,
William Ewart Gladstone, Winston Churchill, and Kurt Adenauer;
of Sophocles, Euripides, Claudel, and Voltaire; of Edith Wharton,
Ellen Glasgow, William Hogarth, and Kathe Kollwitz; of Freud,
Jung, William James, and Auguste Poulain; of Bruckner, Stravinsky, Schoenberg, Delacroix, Goya, Donatello, and Max Ernst. This
informal list of more than seventy Ulyssean names could be put together in an hour's reflection.

Even Lehman's very fair attempt to include more among his
"older thinkers" who are scientists falls flat, since his list omits at
least 125 of the names of noted scientists which turned up as Ulyssean in a small sub-study of mine, which is reported in the Appen-
dix. From that study, which I entered on Lehman's terms, half expecting his thesis to have special force, I emerged startled by two
undoubted facts: the continuing creativity of great numbers of
scientists and mathematicians, and their longevity!

Lehman evidently intends to console his readers for the depressing effects of his main thesis, that "man's creative achievements
occur most often during the thirties", notably in the sciences and
in mathematics—a thesis which everyone seems to accept. In fact,
no consolation is needed. The only conclusive way to determine the
creativity of scientists and mathematicians is to study their individual careers, not to back into the problem by surveying various lists
of certain noted discoveries or inventions. Lehman's whole emphasis
is on publications and products; but it is naive to suppose that these
alone measure creativity, or that ultimate break-throughs are the
only criteria. One cannot say, for example, that a scientist was
"uncreative in his later years" simply because his efforts to derive
a satisfactory generalized field theory in astrophysics did not solve
the enigma: he may have shown brilliant creative power in the
assault without taking the bastion.

Writing about "creative output versus age" in *Physics Today*
(July, 1975), Lawrence Cranberg of Austin, Texas well defines the
weakness of commentators who make easy generalizations about
age and creativity based on identifications of so-called peak achievements. He writes:

> "It is plain confusion to identify creative output, which
> may be readily defined in simple terms, with creativity, which
> is something quite different, and is at least as hard to define

and measure as intelligence, emotional maturity, integrity, and other personality traits. . . .

Creative output is almost certainly facilitated by a fund of accurate, discriminatingly collected knowledge, proven judgment, success experience in a variety of undertakings, and the corresponding increase of self-confidence, and these can only come with age. If the downward trend prevails in spite of these factors, there is an abundance of social factors to account for that trend, including the misinterpretation of output-versus-age curves, and career patterns that confine the individual to a narrow subject-matter range (the job-equals-rut syndrome) or which channel the creativity of later years into non-scientific areas."

And Cranberg concludes with the valuable comment:

"The role of reward and recognition systems may also be important in shaping the output curve. In this connection, it is interesting to compare the careers of Newton and Galileo.

Newton, showered with honors, terminated his scientific career in his early forties. But Galileo, under house arrest to the end of his years for his challenges to the "establishment", continued his remarkable scientific career into his seventies."

It is impossible to conclude this commentary without referring to one other extremely interesting approach to the intriguing game of creative "peaks" in the life-cycle—that of Wayne Dennis of Brooklyn College. In 1966 Dennis published a paper in the *Journal of Gerontology* entitled "Creative Productivity between the Ages of 20 and 80 Years". In it he used the Lehman method of consulting various bibliographies, encyclopedias, and catalogues of scientists, writers, historians, philosophers, mathematicians, and musicians (for some unknown reason, he omitted artists). Otherwise his approach differed sharply from Lehman's, because Dennis was concerned with the peak or peaks of *productivity* of seven hundred and thirty-eight persons, all of whom lived to age 79 or more. The governing factor in Dennis's study is described, oddly enough, almost at the end of the paper: "It is our view that no valid statements can be made concerning age and productivity except from longitudinal data involving no drop-outs due to death."

Using these ground rules, Dennis found that "the highest rate of output, in the case of nearly all groups, was reached in the 40s or soon thereafter." Productivity remained strong throughout the 50s in all categories except inventors, opera composers, and poets. In the case of these three groups, the inventors were on a rising curve to their production peak in the 60s; opera composers were on a drastically dropping curve which continued to fall through the 70s. Five categories reached their production peak in the 60s: historians, philosophers, botanists, inventors, and mathematicians.

Other very strong producers in the 60s were "scholars", geologists, composers of chamber music, and novelists. Poets and biologists maintained something like a sixty-five to seventy per cent production of their best decades, in each case the 40s. Sharply declining categories included architects, dramatists, and librettists. Chemists dropped in the 60s to about half their performance in the 40s, but recovered somewhat in the 70s.

In fact, in Dennis's study the 70s have a special fascination. Six categories continue as powerful producing groups: historians, philosophers, "scholars" (I quote the word, because although Dennis is quite clear what he means by this category: English historians, English philosophers, and English scholars of Biblical, classical, and oriental literature, I am at a loss to know how these persons differ from other scholars), botanists, inventors, and mathematicians. Three categories, all in science, continued through the 70s to produce half as many publications as in their best decade. Seven categories, all in the arts, fall off sharply in the 70s—the percentage of their best decade is indicated after the category: composers of chamber music (forty-three), poets (forty), novelists (twenty-four), composers of operas (sixteen), architects and librettists (twelve each), and dramatists (nine). Even in these sharply declined groups, the production of poets, novelists, and composers of chamber music *in the 70s* is surely impressive.

Although Dennis was wholly concerned simply with discernible productivity, as distinct from quality, his data have some significant references to two important sectors of the whole discussion of the relationship between age and continuing achievement. First, productivity, even if defined as undifferentiated by quality, cannot be wholly divorced from quality. For example, if poets (who, unlike historians, cannot be accused of surrounding themselves in their 60s and 70s by cadres of research assistants) are still producing at about the level of forty per cent of their "best" producing decade, the 40s, there is no reason to believe that whatever they produce is second-rate. In fact, we have ample evidence to the contrary. Second, productivity has a great deal to tell us about the energy banks of adults in their later years. Since two factors which have nothing to do with "decline of intelligence" may be powerful inhibitors to creative production in the later and very late years, namely *loss of will* and *loss or diversion of energy*, this surprisingly strong series of production performances, even in non-selective productivity, may have important messages to convey to all who, like the Ulysseans, wish to set out on new enterprises in their later years.

Meanwhile, where are the records of creative action of those remarkable people, the later adults whose names are not found in "celebrated" lists; who in their late 50s, 60s, 70s, and far older cannot turn off their minds; who remain entranced by the wonder of the world; and whose later years make a mockery of the claim that the curve of the life journey is a simple hill with a summit at age 50 and a progressive decline thereafter? Who plots the curves of the lives of these creators whose creativity extends to dozens of domains never mentioned in the conventional studies of famous performers in the arts, sciences, politics, and invention?

The answer is that nobody plots them: nobody does longitudinal studies (the only studies that can produce convincing evidence of the profile of creativity across the lifespan) of these fascinating human beings of all cultures whose immensely varied creative adventures help light the windows of the world.

These Ulyssean people have one thing in common—they are all seekers, and this is reflected in the trajectory of their lives. Some are chiefly thinkers and readers, adventurers in ideas, some chiefly doers, many are both; all are in pursuit of new enterprises for the mind, the body, or the spirit. The scale of the enterprises, whether large or small, is incidental; the symbol of the Ulyssean is the prow of the ship in which Ulysses and his comrades had so many encounters on the swift-running seas. The thrust is outward, ever inquiring, searching, dreaming, *growing*—outward, not downward.

Among these people is one category which so interested the adult educator Cyril Houle, of the University of Chicago, that he devoted a small but unforgettable study to the subject in his Knapp Lectures at the University of Wisconsin-Milwaukee in the spring of 1960. Calling his report *The Inquiring Mind*, Houle asked the central question: in a world which "sometimes seeks to stress the pleasures of ignorance", what are the men and women like whose lives seem governed by the desire to learn, so that the act of learning "pervades" their existence? Houle accepts the fact that all adults are affected at some points and to some degree by the desire to learn, that no one lives a permanently semi-vegetative existence— if only because one "must occasionally learn how to be more like everyone else". It is the self-compelled adult learners, who maintain their addictive activity throughout their whole lives, who fascinate Houle—the people I have described as being among those "unable to turn off their minds", and whose response is to seek every conceivable avenue to learning, including notably *self*-learning.

Houle decided to base his inquiry on the responses of adult learners themselves, twenty-two men and women selected in the first place because they had been identified by friends and colleagues as deeply and continuously engaged in all kinds of learning. Houle's interest was not in older adults as such—although ten of the group were over age 50, and two of these over 65, but in the phenomenon of the continuous hunger for learning. The distributions of income and education were rather curious: sixteen of the group were estimated to be from the lower income groups, yet only four had less than high school graduation. All lived within a seventy-five mile radius of a great city (Chicago), and the responses to questions were obtained in the course of relaxed interviews of an average of a little over two hours in a quiet and congenial setting. The sample of people was very small, and the limitations in variety of types are obvious—still, each of the respondents represented a small world of his or her own, and Houle took great pains to test and pre-test his interview instruments, so that the replies could be fitted into some sort of comparable setting. Perhaps nothing like this had been done before, and the first shafts of light on what Houle aptly called "the inquiring mind" among human adults are full of interest and at times a kind of beauty.

Houle found that his voracious learners could be divided into three categories: the goal-oriented (people who took courses or began self-directed study with "practical" or fairly clear-cut goals in mind: often a succession of short-term goals); the activity-oriented (people who took part in courses and other group learning experiences for other reasons than the ostensible objectives of the course); and the learning-oriented (people who pursue knowledge "for its own sake"). The categories are best thought of as intersecting circles, one of which, however, represents an individual's chief orientation.

The goal-oriented are the obvious category: it is not their motivation but their unceasing persistence in pursuing goal after goal that gives them a special interest. (The following illustration is fictional, composed from live examples cited in my seminars, but I believe it is a true portrait of Houle's "goal-directed" learner.) A woman, widowed for some time, begins to stir into new life after a passive period of sorrow; she has to make some kind of sense out of her husband's investments, and enrols in an extension course for lay people in investment management. She finds the area about her home threatened by the cruder type of city developer and joins a group to make a confrontation; in doing so, she discovers the value of public speaking, and for the first time takes part in the public speaking group of her women's club. Persuaded to accept office in the club, something she had never agreed to before, she finds as one office succeeds another, that a knowledge of parliamentary procedure is useful, and studies this. Still, she is much alone and inflation undermines her income from insurance and investments, so that she decides to return if she can to the only professional field she has had, namely nursing, and finds that a programme for older returning former nurses, Quo Vadis, is available. This involves not only one but several "refresher" areas, since much has changed in the twenty years since she left nursing. Often very tired between the demands of the programme and of her private life, her temptation is to coast and watch television night after night for weeks on end—but that is not her lifestyle. She has the inner hunger of "the inquiring mind". Thus she takes up oil painting as a side activity; in the house, still empty without her husband but with the memory of various adventures they had embarked on together, she keeps an easel always set up, not only because she finds relaxation in painting, but because she loves small oils, cannot afford to buy them, and has found an acceptable talent of her own.

There is a travel plan for nursing employees where she works, and she can go on a charter trip to Spain, a country that has long intrigued her. She could go in a sealed and packaged group without the pains of contact with a foreign language and strange people—but that is not for her. Her goal is to savour the country, to sense something of what it means to be Spanish, to try to get the feel of Spain. So she enrols in a group at the nearby university who for one winter are studying Spanish life and language. The trip, her studies of the preceding winter, and the contacts made both then and later, remind her of how little access anyone in her community and city has to the arts, music, and culture of Spain. There are, for example, no authentic shops. She thinks, "Suppose I could start a very small charming one in a good accessible location. But then I know nothing about how you import things. Where can I find out? Who would know? I *must* find out—" Thus a new goal appears, clear, practical, one of dozens in her life, and seemingly with no connection whatever with her earlier adventures in public speaking and the Quo Vadis refresher courses for nurses.

The activity-oriented people, like the goal-oriented, pursue learning activities continually throughout most or all of their adult years, but their motivations are complex and indirect by comparison. Personal loneliness may drive many of them into learning groups. One woman remarked tensely to the interviewer that she wished adult educators would start "selling cordiality or something", that she and others like her would "learn anyway", but the world was drab, and what they sought was "the real joy of participation". Or the deeper motive may be the search for a husband or wife; escape, from the frictions and unhappiness of a bad marriage, from the claustrophobic atmosphere generated by a demanding elderly parent, or from a monotonous or unpleasant regular job; or, for a more unusual reason, because family tradition dictates that one must be seen to be growth-oriented and progressive (one man interviewed remarked of his family, "We are forward-moving people" and Houle supplies the delightful illustration from John P. Marquand's *The Late George Apley* of Apley's collecting Chinese bronzes, not because he liked them, but because he felt compelled in his position to collect something).

Especially fascinating among the activity-oriented people are those who might be called credit accumulators—men and women who have been taking courses for so long and with so little coherence that the meaning of the process has been lost. One man, a salesman, had for twenty-five years "taken every course available to him, sometimes gorging himself with as many as five or six at once, in a wholly meaningless profusion, with no pattern, coherence, or apparent effect." In his case, the process seems to have assumed something of the role of a magic charm: if you took courses enough, long enough, fortune would finally smile upon you.

Houle does not make the point, but there is some peril that the so-called "activity-oriented" will be viewed judgmentally by adult educators and other watchers of the scene as being less serious or "less well motivated" (whatever that means) than the other two categories. But in fact one can almost make a homily out of exactly the opposite position: *any reason that induces people to begin and to continue learning is a good reason.* Although the current emphasis among leading writers on adult learning is to stress how natural learning is to human beings, there are innumerable cases of men and women who hold back from enrolling in learning adventures because they cannot summon up the confidence and the will to do so. Thus any motivations which serve as bridges to new learning and often new lives are "good".

The third major category, the learning-oriented people, clearly entrance Houle, as they would anyone interested in human beings as learners. Searching for a terse description of what motivates these remarkable people, Houle adapts Juvenal's famous phrase, *cacoethes scribendi* "the itch to write", changing it to *cacoethes studendi* ("the itch to learn"). Thus, a 38-year-old skilled labourer in an automobile assembly plant, the son of poorly educated parents who was himself forced by poverty to leave high school, describes how from childhood he was an avid reader. Reading was more important than any of the usual activities of boyhood. No one discouraged him at home. His father, with a grade three education, had trained himself to be a critical newspaper reader and zealous conversationalist; his mother, much less fond of reading, still indulged the boy who would "roller skate twenty blocks to the library and back". Sleeping in a bedroom just behind the elevated tracks, he would read until he fell asleep. When wakened by the screech of a passing train, "I'd read until I couldn't fight off sleep any more. Then I'd wake up at dawn and reach under the bed and get the book and read again. I always went everywhere with a book, always, my whole life." Yet this book-addicted father of four children was a participant in his union, in many courses, in the YMCA, in *active* listening to FM radio, in personal social life. He thought that he was regarded as a "character"; people seem to think you must study only for a purpose that you can "see, feel, touch", and that "a dollar must come out of it". But he, long ago pursuing his personal adventures in three fields, philosophy, history, and economics, can only describe this governing passion of his life in this way: "All I can say is, negatively, there was no one to discourage me and positively I always enjoyed it. The more I fed my appetite, the greater my appetite became."

The joy of learning: this appears over and over again among the responses of the learning-oriented. It appears in a wonderful interview in the Houle study, that of a 60-year-old woman, the only black respondent among the group. She had been abandoned at birth, had had little schooling, and a life full of hardship. Yet listen to this: "When Billy was a baby in his carriage I used to take him out. I used to go up to the University that's built up on a knoll and right in the back of this knoll there is the hall where the lectures are held. Well, I used to sit in there and listen to all those lectures. I would sit there and even when he got to be three or four years old I still went up there, but I taught him that he must be very quiet. He could take his toys or he could take a book, but he must be very quiet. We were never molested; we were never told not to come there." No wonder that Cyril Houle compares her to Jude the Obscure in Hardy's novel, the untutored handsome working youth who longed to enrol in classes at Christminster (read Oxbridge) a hundred years ago, but whose small and timid efforts to make connections with some don or official never succeeded. This extraordinary woman was endowed with the *joy* of learning, as well as the hunger.

And there is the glorious case of the 40-year-old branch librarian who cannot figure out from her avid reading and study life where learning begins and fun stops. Her quenchless love of growing into new knowledge has led her into the world of ballet, into Great Books groups, into chess, into wandering through the museums of England, into forays with bird-watchers. She is always learning—the process is continuous but, in her own words, "Is it education? Or is it fun?"

It is all too easy to suppose that when men and women set out on numerous adventures to grow by learning something, they do so with the glowing support of family, peers, and colleagues. The Scots, who are well known for their love of learning, and rather famous for their competence in taking over large sectors of everyone else's economy, have a folk figure in the little, somewhat dour Scots mother urging on her sons to learn and to conquer. The schizoid American society, with its frustrating blend of sentimental idealism and terrifying, even mordant realism, has in its folklore a similar, gentler image: the young wife bidding a fond farewell to her husband before he goes off to his evening class, consoling him when he is discouraged, typing his notes. Other benevolent figures are kindly boss, warm-hearted friends, respectful colleagues learning of his studies, and so on.

But is it so? To a degree probably yes. To update the image, the

young wife in our time may often herself take classes, and be cheer-
ed on by her husband; the boss may actually bring courses and
channels of advancement to the attention of the young man, married or not; friends and colleagues may often be the means or the
incentive to continuing learning and growth. Yet Houle's study revealed a quite different situation, at least among about two-thirds
of his respondents. These people reported that their friends and
associates showed aversion to and disapproval of their participating
in successive learning exercises, especially if the learning activity
had nothing to do with job advancement or increase in money-
making potential. This reaction has been verified many times in
discussion in my own seminars. It is not a blanket situation: thus,
an insecure manager of limited education will take a dim view of
adult learning activities of a bright younger man on his staff—for
obvious reasons. In such cases, even the rationale that so-called
"practical" courses are acceptable, breaks down.

Houle did find that in only one case was the marriage partner
opposed to his or her spouse's being out of the home for regular
learning experiences, or often absorbed and silent in reading when
back in the family circle. However, Edward Weiss, in a study of
urban middle-class couples in the United States, found strong opposition from both wife and husband to the idea of either spouse
spending time in study activities out of the home. They viewed it
as an escape, either from one's partner or from the needs and "togetherness" of the home. There are also, of course, famous instances
of family opposition in other cultures to members of the group
seeking to "improve" themselves in such a way as to cast a certain
supposed condescension upon the standards and previous accomplishment of the family—this is notably the case in working-class
England.

The question of social controls over an individual's efforts to
break into new worlds of growth and learning is one of concern to
those older adults who want to live their lives as Ulysseans. One
of the privileges of the later years which is supposed to counter-
balance one or more of its deficits is the opportunity at last to do
innovative, and if need be "unconventional", things without the
eternally disapproving eye of mother, father, aunt, autocratic boss
and corporation, and the prison compound of community mores.
Yet many older adult couples and single people find themselves still
locked into certain regimens, styles, and protocols by the social
group they have come to identify as their "circle"—more locked in,
in fact, because the hammer of the years has rivetted everyone
concerned more immovably to a structure which is accepted as
being as indestructible as the pyramids.

In his paper delivered to the Syracuse University Conference in
1962, Raymond Kuhlen describes the case of an intelligent Ameri-

can couple in their later years who have to make what turns out to be the quite unpleasant decision whether to discontinue a Saturday bridge-playing group which has come to be considered the criterion of their friendship in and for the "circle", a group unbroken for a number of years, or to take on new learning adventures which will entail living out-of-town some week-ends. They choose the new adventures of the mind, but the decision leaves a trail of wounded feelings and alienations.

Similarly, Houle mentions one of his respondents, "a financially successful 50-year-old merchant" who described in detail how he made a similar break with acquaintances of many years: "You take your drinks, you eat your hors d'oeuvres, you have a fine dinner, and just about the time you are enjoying your dessert, somebody says the card games are about to start. Well, you sit down with three people. Any conversation is taboo. You sit down and you play cards. If you hear a funny remark or if something occurs to you and you say it, well, you're squabbled at, and so forth. I know some of the leading businessmen and lawyers in this town and all I know about them is that they either bid a strong no trump or a weak no trump. And I have been putting up with that for years until this year. This year I just said to heck with them. I don't go to them anymore. It just isn't my kettle of fish. It's caused a lot of comment."

Lest anyone should think this is an American phenomenon, he might do well to spend a year or two in, say, the community hotel of a small Canadian city. Here in the Seventies he will find flourishing and seemingly indestructible the institutional dance— this Saturday the insurance executives, next Saturday the local regiment, the following Saturday one of the service clubs, and following that the Chamber of Commerce. Most of them, in some cases all of them, are attended by the same set of solid citizens; there are inevitably other people according to the purpose of the occasion, but they are incidental. The group is there, a large group, engaging in a ritual as mandatory as fire and rain dances, only far more frequent and far less poetic. One young professional man, fond of reading and not fond of dances, told me that once, going up to his room, he met a group of these people and heard the comment, "There he goes, with his book", followed by a trail of guffaws and titters.

The point is not that there is anything wrong with dancing— it can be one of the dozens of delightful channels to the Ulyssean life, especially for those who have been too shy to try it. There is a great deal wrong, however, when any social group activity acts as a powerful counter-control against new adventures of mind, body, and spirit. In the later years of adulthood one should have crossed the border into freedom: freedom to be unique, and to try individual adventures that heal the spirit and enkindle the mind.

Cyril Houle devotes a fascinating section of his study of avid adult learners to ways and means by which they can build their own environments of support for learning. They can, he says, form or join what he calls "enclaves". The choice of word is exceedingly apt, since it is defined (*Concise Oxford Dictionary*) as "territory surrounded by foreign dominion". Enclaves can be of many easily recognized types: a whole family devoted to the idea of the individual growth of each as he or she wishes; an extension seminar, held regularly throughout much of the year; a study group in a women's club; a university campus. However, Houle cites a type of enclave not easily recognized, one deliberately fashioned by a group of individuals to help sustain mutual learning under normally adverse conditions. For example, a group of young servicemen at a naval base in the South Pacific who had become bored to death with the unvarying routines and shop talk of service life, kept meeting informally to discuss questions about life in general ("the other fellows thought we were nuts. I mean, why worry about these things"). Of absorbing interest in this case is the fact that the young men themselves were curious about why they were like this. They found nothing but diversity in their backgrounds except for this strange hunger to pursue the enigmas of existence in the midst of a highly routinized and socially-mandated life. Houle also usefully cites Benjamin Franklin's famous JUNTO or club of mutual improvement, in which every member agreed to contribute topics and essays for discussion on *"any subject he pleased."*

A form of the JUNTO existed for many years in Ottawa, where a group of journalists, business and professional people, civil servants, and university teachers, weary of the rigid sectionalization of the capital, with its career cliques, formed what was charmingly known as The Mourners. Meeting every week, they formed a tiny enclave in a foreign dominion chiefly barren of interdisciplinary thought. Still another unusual enclave was assembled by an imaginative Anglican priest in downtown Montreal in the 1940s. Left almost high and dry by the loss of its parishioners, the church was used on week-days as a centre for discussion luncheons on all sorts of topics by business and professional people. When I (as a young man much devoted to social reform) was invited to attend, and did so for several sessions, I finally asked what practical social objectives the group had. The reaction of the group, most of whom were much older, was confused and apologetic: they had no special objectives or plans other than just to meet every week and talk about every topic under the sun except their business. In fact, there was no need whatever for apology—they were admirably fulfilling the mission which they had set for themselves: to give support to one another in the pursuit of questions that might enkindle the mind and liberate it from the eternal constrictions of vocational life. Although they were quite unaware of it, they "had a handle" on one of the approaches to the Ulyssean life.

Older adult men and women can enjoy in enclaves, if they only wish to, the best of a Janus-like experience with the mind—looking backward at the best of their past to draw strength and compassion from it, but also looking forward to the still marvelous potentials of the species to which they belong. Why are so few adults in their 50s and older to be found in the ranks of the Futurists, the name given in our time to the slim ranks of those people whose chief passion it is to look into the creative possibilities of tomorrow? This is excellent "enclave" territory.

Small circles of adults who otherwise will spend the time without actualization can make it a practice to gather deliberately to investigate and discuss the many shapes of tomorrow which could give the lie to the doom-sayers of mankind. Thus, Douglas Leiterman's film, *The Machine City*, is a reminder that cities of the future can be so designed as to preserve and advance the human grouping of people and their access to earth, sea, and sun, although the models look like the cities of a science fiction novel. Comparable films for sixteen-millimetre machines are available at manageable costs to groups of older adults, and nearby schools and colleges may make a film machine available to groups enterprising enough to ask. Likewise, in almost any area architects can be found who are only too glad to describe the work and significance of Futurists like Le Corbusier, Doxiatis, or Frank Lloyd Wright—but who asks them?

When an international conference on ekistics was held in Toronto in April, 1975, the programme was well announced as dealing with challenges of the future in the area of the development of great city areas or megalopolises and environments of tomorrow. The assembled cast of expert commentators was impressive: Margaret Mead, Buckminster Fuller, and Marshall McLuhan, together with Jean Gottmann, John Papaioannou, and other noted scholars and practitioners of the world of Futurism were available for a week of discussion in the superb council chamber of the new Toronto City Hall. The public were invited to attend all the sessions without charge, and to take part from time to time in the discussion. At the coffee breaks, the delegates mingled easily with those of the public who attended. Few in the age groups 60 and over took advantage of this invitation, although the final afternoon of the seminar, Mead, Fuller, McLuhan (themselves Ulysseans) and others engaged in a wide-ranging summation debate which was so exciting that one left the hall with one's pulses throbbing. Where were the enclaves from the older adults? Perhaps opportunities like this are rare outside of great cities; but hundreds of campuses throughout the continent make something comparable to them possible;

and television, for all its deadening effects, frequently redeems itself by programmes which will stir the mind and renew the spirit of "enclave" groups of adults who are perfectly capable of continuing self-actualization no matter how "advanced" their age.

The modern social climate which the Canadian historian Arthur Lower has described as worshipping "the Great God Car" is a formidable force against the free play and growth of "the inquiring mind". It is not a total force (consider the best of the media, for example) but it is very formidable, for many an overwhelming force. Cyril Houle movingly quotes the philosopher, Irwin Edman, as saying that as a long-time teacher in the modern university he has observed "the death-in-life that assails the spirits of young men who had been alive when I knew them in college," adding, "There are times when, if one thought about former students too much, one could not go on teaching." Clearly one answer for men and women who find the climate around them too stultifying or even hostile to later adult learning is to develop the stratagem of "enclaves".

To live the Ulyssean life is to live the kind of life that believes in the Second Chance, and, for that matter, the Third Chance and the Fourth Chance. Few phrases in the English language are sadder than that which runs like a threnody through the conversations of many older adults: "I always wanted to be a lawyer" (or a physician, or a teacher, or an architect, or a farmer, or a nurse, or a journalist). To the tough challenging question of the men and women who greatly pride themselves on their "realism" and practicality, "Well why didn't you?", there are usually a dozen good and authentic answers: no money at the time, no outside incentives, no certainty of one's talent, too early a marriage, older people to care for, no useful guidance, tried but the selection process was too rough, too old to apply, too many family responsibilities and problems, too eccentric an idea except when young. (Few seem to think that this long-held and unfulfilled ambition could in fact have been built on an illusion.)

Yet extraordinary people among the more than 15 per cent of the population in our time who are over 55 have every year for many years made later adulthood the arena of the Second Chance. There are few of them, but the fact that they exist is proof enough that the Second Chance is possible, and that high potentialities abound among older adults although they require nerve and stamina to exploit them. The meteorologist who becomes a priest, the retired educator who becomes a lawyer, the insurance agent who becomes a teacher, the advertising man who becomes a social worker, the editor who becomes a psychologist—all of these and many other cases of remarkable embarkations upon new career and personal lives testify to two notable qualities among these adventurers: first, they think (correctly so) that they can learn competently and richly despite their age; and second, they are prepared to take on the pleasure and possible pains of learning in a group.

A current and justified euphoria exists among adult educators about self-directed, or what I call "solo" learning—in many respects it does indeed foretell the climate of the future. However, no one, young or old, achieves graduation in a professional field or is even (as sometimes happens) permitted partial completion of it, without a great deal of participation in lectures, seminars, symposiums, group tutorials, often laboratories or clinical sessions—all involving groups at work. The same is obviously true of undergraduate study in arts and science; in large sectors of graduate work; in an enormous part of the domain of extension education offered by universities, community colleges, school boards, and private organizations. Strong trends exist in certain fields of learning to develop individual contracts and projects in the midst of group activities, to encourage the self-actualization of students and to emphasize, in place of the intimidating group tests at the end of semester or year, the use of continual tests more sensitively adjusted to the needs and growth of the individual—even self-testing to an extent. No matter: these excellent innovations in more tailor-made learning are still set in spheres of group or class instruction.

The fact that this is so has an important influence on the extent to which older adults, finding time they never had before, and at least the stirrings of hope that they can still seize the Second Chance, will in fact enroll in formal learning activities and will maintain their studies once they do so. For many would-be Ulysseans the road to continuous and happy activity must seem at times somewhat like the giant-bestridden road in *Pilgrim's Progress*.

People who take naturally to all kinds of learning, group and solo, may well have difficulty grasping the reluctance of older adults to re-enroll after they have been away from formal learning groups for many years. They may be hindered by memories of unsuccessful or unpleasant experiences in classes at school and college, like the British actress who, for all her fame, could never overcome a dread of the theatre in Manchester where as a young woman she had had a disastrous failure. They may make the fine resolution to resume or begin studies in some form only to find (or to think they find, which in effect is the same thing) a certain indifference and coldness on the part of the institution of their choice to older adult students. Dale L. Hiestand, in his excellent *Changing Careers after 35*, found that there was a variety of attitudes among American institutions toward enrolling full-time and part-time adults over the age of 35 and that admissions policies *within* the universities were very uneven. In certain faculties a substantial minority of the students were over 35, for example, library science, divinity, social work, and the graduate departments of education and public administration. In others, for example medicine, law, and engineering the number was only a tiny group in large enrolments. Where graduate and professional schools were hesitant to enroll students of, say, 50 or older, the most important reason was the feeling that the career time after graduation was too brief to justify the admissions committee in replacing a young competitor with an older one.

However, aside from such rationales Dale Hiestand and his associates discerned what they conceived to be considerable hesitancy on the part of institutions to develop a liberal policy toward registering older adults for degree work, even where the public policy of the institutions was liberal. There were a number of possible reasons: older applicants are more difficult to assess than young ones because of their distance from formal schooling and their unfamiliarity with conventional "intelligence tests"; some types of officials fear they will not adjust and settle in so well as the young; other administrators are concerned about failure—they too are often obsessed by the "downward curve" of the later years.

One perception of the nervousness of some faculty and officials of universities and colleges about older adult students was put forward at the Syracuse Conference of 1961 by the psychologist Kenneth Benne. He noted that three populations ordinarily inhabit the universities: the largely unregenerate group of undergraduates, who are viewed as being in the process of humanization or civilization; then the graduate students who are much cherished—Benne acutely compares them to the acolytes of priests. Then, says Benne, there are those strange unclassifiable carpetbaggers who come in out of the night from alien worlds outside the university, and return to work and live therein day after day. These are really disturbing intruders; not least, their adulthood and its experiences and expertise constitute standing challenges, even if largely silent, to the carefully cultivated world of the dons.

Thus, when a man or woman in the 50s or older decides to pursue the Second Chance, if it involves entering or resuming professional education, they can expect a mixed reception from those university officers whose decisions make the adventure possible or not. Entry to undergraduate degree work in arts and science is less formidable. Some remarkable universities have long been open to older adults, especially in part-time evening and summer credit work; and others are becoming increasingly so, perhaps spurred on more by dropping undergraduate enrolments than by a high-hearted confidence in the creativity of the later years. University extension *non*-credit offerings, of which there are thousands in North America, are almost by definition without prejudice to age.

Still, many adults in their 50s and older require courage and stamina, not only to break the rigid protocols of one's family or social group (as mentioned above), but to establish the beachhead in the long unfamiliar or wholly new territory of higher education. The telephone and counter staffs of extension and registrars' offices had better not be flip, irritable, or indifferent, otherwise they will lose the enrolments of some of the most delightful and valuable potential students in the land. For the kind of sensitive person who has long thought about taking some kind of evening or summer studies but is basically insecure, lack of real interest or cold routines may provide him with just the rationale for never enrolling which his inner daemon is looking for.

Once enrolled, the older adult finds himself or herself involved in forms of group process—which is where we came in some paragraphs above. The experience may be pleasant or intimidating; in extension classes the other members are likely to be mostly adults of all ages, with the majority in the 20s, 30s, and 40s. If the class is a large one with conventional lecturing, the professor may be a skilful facilitator of questions or question groups which seem to break down the student's sense of being a receptacle in a game of pitch and toss; or he may be, in W. J. McKeachie's delightful phrase, "a hurler of intellectual grenades". Often the class will be seminar size, yet the professor may still deal with his group of adult part-time students as though he were instructing a large group of first year undergraduates. Much more often he will show himself to be an easy and skiful moderator. Although the whole structure and purpose of the course may be his (or hers), within those self-defined boundaries this kind of faculty person will stimulate a great deal of interesting and useful discussion, often promoted by themes known to be of high personal interest to class members. There are now a good many professors, advanced in strategies of instruction, who are able to build the direction of the course partly (in some more spectacular instances, and in certain congenial fields, wholly) in consultation with the group.

Finally, one reaches the extreme position counterbalancing the reactionary instructor who treats a seminar group of adults like an amiable parade ground squad: the teacher who has adopted the curious philosophical position that all adults know their own needs. All the professor is there for is to identify what these needs are, and to stand quietly on the sidelines as the helpful facilitator while his class colleagues press enthusiastically on, reporting to each other and thus constituting the course. If you can adopt this as a total principle for the teaching and leadership of adults, there is no naiveté you will not fail to support. Had we all known our own needs, we would not have spent so many years wandering up and down dead end paths, and passing by celestial fields without seeing them.

The process of having, as the Americans say, to "interact" in and with a group of other adults in a learning situation may be immediately congenial for outgoing, buoyant, articulate people who in any event have been doing much of this for years. The many older adults who have little experience in group discussion and reporting, or who feel, as well they may, that at 65 they are marching to a different drummer from the numerous 30-year-old people in the class, may have feelings of shyness and reticence which reduce them at first to long periods of silence or infrequent and hesitant "footnote" comments. Then in a great majority of cases, something rather wonderful happens. They find that they are readily accepted simply as people by their class colleagues, and *notably* by the delightful types of young adults who enroll in these groups.

Adults who have decided that one of their Ulyssean adventures will be to resume formal studies requiring university or college teaching might do well to try the temperature of the water first by taking a particularly congenial class or seminar on any topic that excites them. In this way, one can try out a few strokes after long disuse in a pleasant pool of discussion and companionship before beginning a long swim in the bracing but often severely testing waters of the world of the Second Chance. Something else may be wise: a personal stocktaking of one's assets and deficits in re-commencing studies. This would include a look at one's speed of reading comprehension; a check and "tuning-up" of one's grasp of vocabulary, using some of the stimulating exercises and re-sources available to expand it; and some analyses of strengths and weaknesses in writing. It is sensible also to take the precaution of examining some of the ways and means to the most productive and efficient study habits. Many adults bring to a resumption of studies rich personal resources in powers of selection, in insights, in capacity for hard work, in stamina, in the repertory of ways to confront discouragement and failure. Nonetheless, in these cir-cumstances a personal inventory is surely at least as necessary as for a lone yachtsman carefully checking his equipment and his physical readiness before he sets out on a transworld odyssey.

As it is, we know all too little about the extremely interesting people in the later 50s and 60s (and older) who recommence studies for professional careers, or to obtain first degrees or diplomas, or simply "to get their feet wet".

In the fall of 1964 just before I resigned as Registrar of Carle-ton University in Ottawa to take on new assignments elsewhere, my staff and I reviewed the distribution of age cohorts among the part-time evening students at Carleton who were enrolled either for a degree or as "special" students. Special students are members of the non-campus community permitted to enroll in regular evening classes at the introductory stages to test whether they wish to continue. (Carleton has been one of the most progressive and enlightened institutions on the continent in its provisions for informal participation by serious and keen adults from off-campus.) The survey showed that the heaviest clustering came in the late 20s and 30s; enrolment continued surprisingly strong into the 40s (two groups contributing to this were career women and women released from family obligations; and a considerable number of retired services officers turning to teaching and other socially related professions). A radical drop came at age 50, although the number enrolled was about 6 per cent of the total; in the late 50s few people registered and none in the 60s. The university did not discourage the enrolment of later adults: the last student I interviewed at Carleton was a vivacious 61-year-old teacher who had been delayed for years in trying to get her Arts degree, and was admitted as a full-time student in what could only be described as an informal little ceremony of joy.

One of the most complete studies ever undertaken of the question: "Who are the part-time students?", a report, financed by the Canada Council, of the number and nature of part-time bachelor degree students in Ontario universities (David A. A. Stager, director) reported a distribution of ages of students remarkably similar to the little Carleton study. In rough percentages the late 20s (age 25-plus) and the 30s together contributed almost 59 per cent of the total; the 40s, over 13 per cent; and the category "50 or over", only 4 per cent. Although the breakdown for age 60 and over is not given, it is fair to assume that it was almost nonexistent.

Why is this so? The fact that later-age enrollees exist proves that the adventure can be begun. In the rather rarefied atmosphere of the graduate courses of the Ontario Institute for Studies in Education, that is, in advanced educational theory, out of an enrolment for degree work of approximately five hundred students, only seven age 55 and older were enrolled in 1973-74 (in addition there was a 66-year-old part-time non-degree student who had received the master's degree at the University of Toronto two years previously). However, three of the seven were age 60 or older and all were seeking the master's degree; four other candidates over 55 were seeking the Ph.D. and there was every reason to believe they would obtain it. It is really useless to say that these academic Ulysseans are "remarkable" and "extraordinary"; they are indeed —but they are not so remarkable or extraordinary that they should be limited to a handful from a potential supply of many thousands of equally bright and vital older adults.

What hinders the many who might come forward? Some reasons seem obvious: the expense of taking courses; the feeling that it may be impractical to study for a late degree; the illusion that at age 60 "one is past all that"; the feeling that there is something eccentric about it, and that there are too many ties and protocols that have to be broken; the apprehension that younger people may condescend or privately deride such an adventure; the conviction that one is out of touch, that one won't fit in. All of these rationales and excuses, except the first two, and in addition the various unnamed *et ceteras* which every one can supply are, although powerful, within the domain of potential control by the older adults themselves. The universities and colleges, however, can not only remove much of the blockage of the expense of tuition, but by devising imaginative programmes for older adults and publicizing them well, they can begin the great liberating process of making study in the later years seem the natural thing it should be.

Some trailbreaker institutions have made splendid beginnings. In 1965 the University of Kentucky began a notable programme, financed with aid from the Donovan Foundation. It provides scholarships for *full-time study* toward a degree by adults age 65 and older. They have to be demonstrably capable of taking on university work, and physically healthy. Often married couples come together. If one visits the Kentucky campus, one can see the Donovan Scholars at work and often in residence on the campus at Lexington, among the thousands of younger students. They are an essentially joyous group: these older people are, after all, doing something with their later years which many of them had long wished to do; they are challenged and stimulated by the adventure itself and the setting in which it takes place.

The origin and dissemination of the Donovan plan is also an interesting example of the transference of ideas. The originator and director of the programme, H. W. Kauffman, was inspired to develop the project at Kentucky by his attendance at the White House Conference on Aging in 1961. In turn, what I said about the general concepts of the Donovan programme in the course of a seminar in 1971 led one of my students, Mrs. Jean Stirling, to persuade the CBC to devote part of a trans-Canada television matinée to the film made at Lexington of the programme in action. When the wife of one of the deans at the University of Prince Edward Island watched the film, her enthusiasm for the Donovan project led her to enlist her husband's support. The result is an innovative scheme at that university, where older adults age 60 and up are invited to enroll without charge in courses of their choice, obviously usually preliminary courses at first.

Long before this, at McMaster University in Hamilton, Ontario, adult people from the community age 65 and over had been quietly invited to "register in many courses without payment of tuition fees." This started out as a non-degree plan: the older adults were invited to audit the courses, although they could write the essays, interim tests, and examinations if they wished. About twenty-five adults took up the initial offer, and this number has since expanded to one hundred. Older adults may now enlist under the plan for regular degree studies, and a group of nine or ten do so. One hundred people over 65 does not seem a large number, but if one hundred can do it, a thousand can do it—where are the Ulysseans to take up these admirable challenges?

It is hard to know which is the more incredible of two situations —the extraordinary lack of publicity which attends these admirable ventures by the institutions imaginative and concerned enough to carry them out; or the insensitivity of the many to whom it never occurs to do likewise, or worse, if they do, rapidly put the thought away.

Surely the most fascinating of developments in terms of its potential for the continuing study of older adults is the Open University in Great Britain, which began operations in January, 1971. Here is a people's university, organized on a home-study basis with a network of various learning channels distributed throughout England, Scotland and Wales, with outlets in Northern Ireland. There are no admission requirements; the assumption being that adults who are serious enough to come forward to register for studies which will occupy them for a minimum of ten hours a week, and which will require in addition attendance at a short annual summer school, are already motivated people with a good deal of life experience behind them. In addition, they are assumed to be readers and in some degree self-directed learners, whatever their field of interest.

An adult enrolling in the Open University for what are called their "foundation courses" is provided with a study guide for each course, a timetable, correspondence study assistance, schedules of the TV and radio broadcast lectures which are another essential component of the scheme, and of course lists of required books. He or she studies much of the time alone, some of the time in groups organized at regional study centres, where the students also meet professors from nearby universities who are assigned to assist them. At the study centres, the students can obtain counselling, and break the monotony of solo study which can be one of the frustrations of correspondence and TV-radio broadcast teaching. Library resources are uneven: lists of necessary books are mailed by the Open University to all public libraries, but these themselves may vary in available funds and in the size of their collections. Fees are required, and the Open University expects to be paid, as its stiff language on the subject makes plain. There are no fee exemptions for older adults. At the same time, there are no restrictions

172 THE ULYSSEAN ADULT

because of age, except, curiously enough, for the young, since
people under 21 are not usually encouraged to enroll.

Aside from the possibly inhibiting effect of cost of tuition, the
Open University plan seems, at least in theory, to present a superb
framework for the encouragement of formal study at the university
level by older adults. The ancient curse of the unyielding matriculation requirements is removed (one must note that throughout
North America many universities now operate a so-called "mature
matriculation" which excuses serious and motivated adults usually
age 23-plus from having to complete university entrance examinations). The problem, which for many older people is a large one, of
having to go to a group of strangers in the unfamiliar setting of a
university classroom, often when fatigued and sometimes after long
car, bus, or city transport trip, is largely solved by the over-all plan
which brings the university to the student.

The solo study arrangements of the course permit the student
a greater option of self-paced learning than is normally the case
in class group situations, and the repertory of study aids is broader
than is often the case in conventional university classes. The
student in the Open University receives slides, tapes, experimental
kits, and other supplements to reading assignments and question-
and-answer responses. The concept of the study centre and the
summer school provides for a cadre of student colleagues embarked
on much the same adventure, many of them with the same problems to deal with in recommencing studies; it virtually guarantees,
also, the stimulus of discussion groups. Each student finds that he
has been specifically assigned an academic counsellor. No doubt
the interest and efficiency of these advisers varies, but at least the
programme moves out to include this arrangement, something
often missing in adult programmes elsewhere. (In Toronto, when
a sudden freeze of finances was imposed by the provincial government in 1971, and the school board began in some agitation and
dismay to lop off supposedly unessential services, the first cancella-
tion was the board's provision for counsellors for adult students in
the evening classes!) Also, very notably, the Open University has
had so much generally favourable publicity throughout the British
Isles that the feeling of somehow being eccentric or foolishly venturesome in enrolling in formal studies in the later years has been
enormously reduced.

How did people respond to the Open University network when it
began operations in January, 1971? When the university opened
its list for applicants in the spring of 1970, more than 40,000 adult
Britons applied; of these, 24,000 students provisionally registered
in January, 1971 for the first three months of the year, and in
April, 1971 some 19,500 students finally registered. By 1974 the
number of people studying for credits under the Open University
system was 42,000, and there was an enormous waiting list.

How many *older* adults have participated, that is, people over 55? This is, for our purpose, a rather crucial question! The percentages supplied by the Open University are: 6 per cent aged 50 to 54; 3 per cent aged 55 to 59; 1 per cent aged 60 to 64; and about 1 per cent 65 or older.

How do the Open University students perform in their course examinations? It must be remembered that many have not studied for years, and that many have no formal qualifications for regular university study. In spite of the insistence of the university on maintaining the equivalent of academic standards elsewhere, no less than 70% of the students throughout the British Isles have passed their courses.

Thus, the British have without fanfare put together an experimental vehicle to help improve human relations and human growth in the midst of what many North Americans persist in believing is an overly-formal and overly-structured society. Because the Open University scheme is obviously exciting, observers from Canada and the United States have visited and studied it, with a view to possibly implementing North American counterparts. There is, of course, a need for caution in simply transferring what might be described as encapsulated educational programmes to other cultural settings. It is not the exact form but the spirit, and the fountain of ideas and of new liberations of attitudes, which can create new domains of learning for older adults.

As everyone knows, a splendid world of *non*-credit education has long been available in thousands of centres in Western society for adult people, including, of course, adults as old as you like. Leaving "skills" courses to one side (public speaking, dancing, cooking, better golf, motor mechanics, and so on) the titles of many of these courses seem inviting to anyone remotely interested in the growth of the mind. For example, "The Universe Around Us" (which was not expected at one university to attract fifteen people, yet enrolled one hundred and seventeen adults on its first night, a dozen or more age 70 to 80-plus); "China Known and Unknown"; "The Undiscovered Self"; "Public Power and Individual Survival"; "The Theory and Practice of Creativity"; "Best-Selling Novels—A Social Phenomenon"; and so on.

Older adults who sign up for and consistently attend the group meetings of a seminar on topics such as these (and hundreds more on every theme under the sun) surely participate in a delightful experience. Whatever tensions are generated in credit courses by the knowledge that one must pass and even "do well" in essay-writing and whatever tests may be required, are absent in these non-credit situations where the objective is to grow and learn in an encounter with a significant topic and other interesting people who are fellow seekers. The encounter is important. There are other delights, of course—reading by oneself, clipping out stimulating material for one's files, watching and personally reacting to some of the occasional programmes on television or radio which really stretch one's mind.

But later adults, like all adults, are "need-bearers"; and among their greatest needs are opportunities to express their individual ideas and to exchange concepts and insights with other adults who also have become enriched by life experience, and who look for a small, intimate, and fraternal forum. When an elderly woman in a "good" nursing home said desperately to a visitor, "If I can't get some good talk otherwise, I'll go down the corridor and knock on every door until I do", she was seeking something much greater than release from loneliness, and much more than "a chat". Bright and equipped with hundreds of ideas, insights, and compassions from the train of the years, she was in search of a place and companionship where her pent-up thoughts could race out in the bracing air of competition with other minds and lives. This is one of the precious values of extension education—and of all informal groups meeting regularly as "enclaves" to encourage and sustain inquiring minds.

There is, certainly, an important advantage to the extra demands of credit study. If we are talking about *learning*, and if it can be best defined, in Birren's words, as an experience which "must be registered, retained, and recalled", then no doubt credit courses often give an extra incentive to active learning. But even in non-credit study high personal interest in a topic and the flashes of illumination that come from the interplay of ideas with those of other interesting adults are their own guarantors that learning even in Birren's cerebral sense is taking place. And then there are other kinds of learning that the whole self achieves which come from man's unrenounceable need to speak with, to argue with, to investigate, to touch, to encounter, to enjoy, to adventure with his or her fellow human beings. Not many Ulysseans begin and maintain their later life voyages, small or great, wholly alone.

Credit study or non-credit, transforming experience though this learning venture in group study in later adulthood can be, it evidently attracts few older adults. One powerful factor not already mentioned may contribute to this. Lifelong habits of non-reading and non-systematic thought cannot easily be reversed in the later years, and few whose life has been lived in that fashion seek to reverse them. Since the repertory of possible Ulyssean exploits is large (as will be seen), it is not surprising that perhaps only a small minority of people who have developed habits of serious analytical reading and thought push off in the direction of degree or diploma work or of non-credit studies that really stretch the mind. In a society like the United States, where the sale of 50,000 copies of a novel is said to raise it to the "best seller" category—and 100,000 copies for a non-fiction book—serious reading is clearly not precisely the pre-eminent national sport (for Canada, as usual, recast the figures as about 10 per cent of the American). The familiar consolation that at least the population is pouring in and out of the thousands of public libraries reading books which do not register on the bookstores' sales lists is rapidly dissipated on looking up the statistics familiar in the library world, of "number of books read per capita in various large and small urban centres".

The objectives, style, reward systems, and tempo of North American life are in general opposed to a life of private contemplation and study, and hence, of course, to anything but a small minority participation in group settings for these (in some places) almost subversive occupations. In addition, many older adults in our society never finished high school; those who did may have been disenchanted with much that they learned, or felt that their diploma was a permanent discharge from formal learning, or were turned off by some aspects of the system and how it affected them.

To the disappointing statistics for formal group learning in the later years, one has, of course, to add the unknown but surely considerable number of people who study fairly systematically as *individuals*—the self-directed or "solo" learners. These are the interesting older adults who enroll in commercial, department of education, or university correspondence courses; who study with private coaches and tutors; who buy do-it-yourself kits, sets, and recordings, or who assiduously pursue through library books or other means some intense personal interest. The "other means" could, of course, include an unusually selective and intelligent use of certain television and radio programmes. In fact, the world of tomorrow is likely to provide a wide selection of what is sometimes called "personalized television", where the viewer and listener, or perhaps more properly the participant, will be able to tune in to obtain what he wants when he wants it. Something akin to this in its theory of individual delivery already exists in the dial-a-diagnosis medical networks for physicians in some areas.

Many other adults study intermittently; their interests are perhaps more likely to be practical than strictly intellectual. Johnstone and Rivera, reporting in 1965 from their huge continent-wide survey of American learning patterns, noted the overwhelming emphasis given to vocational, recreational, and skills courses and systematic self-instruction, compared with the comparatively few topics dealing with current events, Great Books, and religion. They were fascinated by the seemingly enormous number (nearly two million) Americans who tried in a single year to learn something about sewing and cooking. In fact, without benefit of surveys, one can be pretty certain that in most households, rich and poor, there are guitars or other musical instruments, usually discarded, teaching materials on which dust gathers, do-it-yourself kits half-used, wholly used, or never used, painting-by-numbers pictures hung up long ago and almost forgotten. These are not melancholy facts of life: at least not in one very important sense. Man is a creature of "temporary systems", a prober, a tryer-out of things, a curious cat, an experimenter, a dabbler. For him to try and then abandon certain exercises is not a tragedy. Because he is fascinated by the changing kaleidoscope of life, he will often try to match himself somehow to the passing scene. The tragedy will come, however, if the end of his continuing voyage of self-discovery, of personal identity and verification, is "disgust and despair".

The extent to which human adults quietly but continuously engage in forms of learning particularly interests Allen Tough. In the course of some stimulating study reports on the subject, Tough notes how many thousands of unexpected job situations, community involvements, and unexpected but gripping personal demands and needs, all set off what he calls "adult learning projects". Especially intriguing to him are what he calls "high learners", individuals who spend perhaps two thousand hours a year at learning (*not* just operating) and who complete fifteen or twenty different projects in one year. "In their lives," Tough writes, "learning is a central activity; such individuals are marked by extraordinary growth." In fact, Tough's "high learners" have close analogies with Maslow's "self-actualized" people, and with Cyril Houle's "learning-oriented" adults. Tough's description of this attractive group, arrived at from his own data, portrays characteristics common to Carl Rogers' "fully functioning" persons and to much of the profile emerging in the present book of the Ulyssean adult: "efforts to achieve their inherent potential", "curiosity and *joie de vivre*", "understand and accept their own characteristics", "are spurred on rather than blocked by obstacles", "tend in relationship with at least a few people to be compassionate, loving, frank, and effective". Tough has no idea, nor has anyone else, how many of these high learners there are, but he speculates: "as a very low estimate, one adult in a thousand"—this would give as many as 110,000 high learners in the United States, 35,000 in the United Kingdom, or 11,000 in Canada." The estimate is perhaps very low.

Yet the most moving quality about Tough's work so far is not his theories about "high learners", but his obvious delight in seeming to establish that learning projects among adults, so far from being desultory and without much self-stimulation, are a common, almost a universal phenomenon—that in adult life, learning is a natural and continuing function.

This brings us back to a fundamental truth about human beings, well illustrated by an episode involving the great Dr. Samuel Johnson. On Saturday, July 30, 1763, Doctor Johnson and his friend and biographer, James Boswell, set out in a scull down the Thames to Greenwich with a young lad as their sculler. The conversation turned to the advantage, or otherwise, of studying Greek and Latin as part of a good education. (Johnson, of course, thought it essential.)

> *Boswell*: "And yet, people go through the world very well, and carry on the business of life to good advantage, without learning. *Johnson:* "Why, Sir, that may be true in cases where learning cannot possibly be of any use; for instance, this boy rows us as well without learning as if he could sing the song of Orpheus to the Argonauts, who were the first sailors." He then called to the boy, "What would you give, my lad, to know about the Argonauts?" "Sir," (said the boy), "I would give what I have." Johnson was much pleased with his answer, and we gave him a double fare. Dr. Johnson then turning to me, "Sir," (said he), "a desire of knowledge is the natural feeling of mankind; and every human being, whose mind is not debauched, will be willing to give all that he has, to get knowledge."

If this is an overstatement, at least it is a magnificent one. But this still leaves unanswered a great problem: *the apparent abstention in huge numbers of adults in the later years from group-oriented and even self-organized activities which help maintain the growth of the mind and the continuing discovery and actualization of the self.*

To return to Johnstone and Rivera: in their massive study which reported, among many other things, on rates of participation by age of adults who "studied *any* subject by *any* method" (my italics), they noted a precipitous drop in percentage of participation within a group after age 55. Men under 35 participated to the extent of 33 per cent (women 25 per cent). Among men between ages 35 and 54 participation was 21 per cent (women, the same). In men over 55 participation fell to 9 per cent (women, 10 per cent)—and plunged again after age 60. And again, on expressed *interests* in learning, Johnstone and Rivera "also found that these [learning] interests not only fell off continuously in each succeeding decade, but that the rate of decrease was an accelerating one. The extent of decline was particularly precipitous just after the 40s and then again between the 60s and 70s. Up until the 50s, however, there was no appreciable drop-off in learning interests at all; the rates were only 7 per cent higher among persons in their 20s than among those in their 40s."

Johnstone and Rivera are not talking about the supposed decline of intellectual ability to cope—this never enters into their report—but simply about rates of participation "in any subject by any method", and in expressed *interest* in continuing learning in presumably multitudes of ways.

Perhaps what one encounters here is another moment of truth: repetition of experience, however reassuring or delightful it may be, is not usually learning. Taking up the collection and counting it every Sunday at church is commendable, but it is not learning; lawn bowling or curling for thirty years, although pleasurable, is not learning; playing the same piano pieces for twenty years, no matter how charming, is not learning; fishing in the same brooks and bays for the same fish (sorry!) is not learning; chairing committees where one's own attitudes and those of one's colleagues are as predictable as the rising of the sun, is not learning; listening to *The Messiah* as one's inevitable musical treat at Easter for thirty-five years, and eschewing Bach's *The Passion According to St. Matthew* or Leonard Bernstein's *Mass*, is not learning; participating in the same social, fraternal, organizational, academic, or political rituals for half of the life-cycle is not learning; turning to the index of controversial books to confirm your long-held ideas, is not learning; going only to nice movies that never involve one in thoughts of injustice, violence, anguish, and death is not learning, and neither is attending only films that deal with mayhem and sexual cruelty; telling the same stories at age 72 as at age 42, no matter how they may continue to entrance the listeners, is not learning. We must be good to ourselves—that is a major obligation for the growth of the self—but learning is never a wholly comfortable business.

The Ulyssean is a man or woman who makes a step in a new direction at an age when the besotted society expects him or her to continue in well-worn paths (and of course to keep steadily slowing down)—even if the Ulyssean step is at first hesitant, tentative, and very small. Alternatively, an older adult can be Ulyssean while remaining in a trajectory of performance established long ago, but which by its nature continually exposes him or her to new adventures and challenges of mind and spirit.

7. ULYSSEANS IN ACTION

Ulysseans come in every appearance, role, and idiosyncrasy, but their common characteristic is an irresistible desire to "drink life to the lees", as Tennyson's Ulysses puts it; or, in less dramatic language, to continue to grow, to make life a continuous series of explorations. This common and powerful motivation can be expressed, for example, by Ulysseans otherwise so different as an existential philosopher (Gabriel Marcel), a small craft circumnavigator of the globe (Ben Carlin), and a blind teacher of the blind (Susan Miller).

Marcel, who died aged 83 in 1973 and was the founder of a French school of Roman Catholic existentialism, was also a literary critic, playwright, composer, and pianist. To him, life should be a matter of "passionate inquiry and of participation in whatever occurs". Man should not seek detachment from the world but "should consider himself an active participant". To Ben Carlin, "man is not made to go about being safe and comfortable and well fed and amused. Almost any man if you put the thing to him, not in words but in the shape of opportunities, will show that he knows as much. Against his interest, against his happiness, he is constantly being driven to do unreasonable things. Some force not himself impels him and go he must." If this view gives a too idealistic picture of the state of readiness of all men and women in general, at least it well defines a Ulyssean trait. And in the down-to-earth clichés of everyday speech, Susan Miller, born blind 77 years ago, and an Associate in Music of the Royal Conservatory in Toronto whose devoted avocation in late life is weaving, says, "If you own a rocking chair . . . stay away from it. My plans for the future are to keep on going. The rocking chair doesn't fit in there."

Rocking chairs, which have certain charms of their own, and in which it is quite possible that creative ideas might be born, are nevertheless a very negative symbol among Ulysseans. This is because they usually immobilize the productive activity to which the Ulyssean life is devoted—not frenetic, circular activity, mere busyness, like that of the man or woman who cannot join enough committees which yet have no creative function in their lives—not this, but the productivity of growth, whatever the scale. In fact, although the Ulyssean life can of course be developing in the deep self, the "quintessential self", without outer and visible signs, most of the time it is the overt productive or creative act which signals Ulyssean progress. It is true that Ulyssean-like acts may occur which are isolated phenomena in the life of the individual and do not in fact reflect a Ulyssean personality and sustained lifestyle; but we necessarily begin with the discernible performances, and from these establish the good tidings that another Ulyssean personality is at work and at play in our midst.

Of all the arenas where Ulysseans perform in the modern world, none is more appropriate than that of the original Ulysses—the oceans and the seas. Consider, for example, the striking and (in North America) virtually unknown figure of Alain Gerbault who died in 1941 at age 43. He represented in the element of the sea very much what Antoine de Saint-Exupéry did for the saga of men in the air. Gerbault is an exception among the numerous illustrations of Ulysseans in this book, in that he died well before what we have defined as the Ulyssean age begins: but his death was fortuitous, and his lifestyle so well marked and irreversible that it is possible to include him as a superb example of the Ulyssean type in action.

Gerbault was a man who seemed to bear with him something of the drama and tragedy of the time of the Greek gods. He survived the terrible war of 1914–18, in which many of his friends were lost, and after completing studies as a civil engineer went on to become an internationally recognized football player, bridge tournament star, and tennis champion of France. Society and the press sought him out; he had every attribute that attracts the attention, and often the adoration, of the French and European public, and for a time it looked as though he might become one of the enchanted circle of world tennis stars. Instead, at the height of his prospects, in April, 1924, Gerbault began a seventeen-year odyssey in a thirty-nine-foot English cutter, the *Firecrest*, built wholly of teak and oak, which was his only companion in the circumnavigation of the world, and in many other seaborne journeys.

Gerbault's choice was made not so much out of love for the sea, although that was also a powerful motivation, but because he was repelled by most of what he had already seen of modern urban and corporation life and the seeming inhumanity of men. Although he ranged the whole world, he was especially enchanted by the Polynesians and their islands. In Tahiti he met again the same types of French bureaucrats and would-be tycoons who had partly caused him to set out in quest of a new world in the first place. He was appalled at the vulgarization and defilement of Polynesian life by the arrogant imposition of Western commercial and tourist life, especially in Papeete and the more frequented and exploited islands of a once free and still beautiful people. He cared enough about this to abandon to some extent his personal renunciation of the French worlds of power and politics, and to try to use his considerable personal fame and influence to guarantee the preservation of Polynesian culture.

But these interventions could only be episodes in Gerbault's life—his *life* was his testament. He wrote: "Every man needs to find a peak, a mountain top, or a remote island of his own choosing that he reaches under his own power alone in his own good time." In fact, the Ulysseans never do find the ultimate haven, nor did Alain Gerbault: life is the haven—the quest is the fulfilment. Even physically, Gerbault had many adventures analogous to those of Ulysses. Among the Pacific Islands in a powerful gale, he was almost literally left naked on the beach. He and the gallant *Firecrest* were driven separately on the coral shore, and at daybreak he found that the four-ton lead keel of the boat had been torn off and sunk. Gerbault had to spend six weeks waiting among the hospitable Polynesians until help came. Meanwhile, he and his hosts located and dragged the lead keel onto the shore, and then with the arrival of a tramp steamer and a French naval vessel, the *Firecrest* was refloated and Gerbault put out again to sea. He had left Cannes in April, 1924; he returned to Cherbourg in July, 1929, having circumnavigated the world. As usual, he was overwhelmed with praise and publicity. He was named a member of the *Légion d'honneur;* he could have remained a kept hero among the members of café society, but he was indifferent both to acclaim and to the seductions of the so-called smart set.

He continued to rove the world for the next twelve years, during which he wrote two enthralling books, published posthumously, *Flight of the Firecrest* and *In Quest of the Sun.* In the first book he says that he could have settled many times in one of the Polynesian islands, married, and raised a family in a kind of paradise. Like his prototype, Ulysses, who might have remained with Circe and Calypso or at the households of friendly kings, Gerbault was called back to the sea. He writes, "What demon is continually urging me back to the sea?"—and Charles A. Borden, in a brief account of Gerbault, in his fine book *Sea Quest,* says: Sailing [for Gerbault] was part of a need for islands, remote anchorages, solitude, simple people; part of a positive need to wander and *a need for streaming in through the sense of new vistas and experiences.*" (Italics mine.) Although he sought solitude as Ulysses never did—one always thinks of Ulysses surrounded by comrades, in spite of periods of enforced loneliness—Gerbault was in no way alienated from mankind. He was alienated from those he conceived to be the dehumanizers

of the human condition: the getters and go-getters of modern styro-
foam acquisitive society. For the many simple, deeply human people whom he met on his hundred thousand miles of solitary cruising
in the *Firecrest* and in his second boat, the *Alain Gerbault,* he had
a tender communication and love. This revealed itself also in his
passionate crusade on behalf of the preservation of the best of
Polynesian culture.

Gerbault's death was appropriate to the nature of his life. Ill
from malaria and alone on his boat in a far eastern Portuguese
harbour, he was found and cared for until his death on December
16, 1941. He was buried on the lovely island of Bora Bora by the
French Navy.

In terms of the rules of the game of this book, Alain Gerbault
was a younger Ulyssean: he was well into middle age when he died,
but the seventeen years of his wanderings extended from young
adulthood to the early 40s. The same was true of the remarkable
husband-and-wife mariner team of Elinore and Ben Carlin who in
1950 took thirty-one days to navigate the Atlantic from Halifax,
Nova Scotia to the Azores in an amphibious jeep, the *Half-Safe.*
There the astonished islanders proclaimed a *Festa da Jeep.* Seven
years later, Carlin, at first with his wife, then accompanied by
another adventurer, sailed around the world; this, however, was
not the end of the Carlins' odysseys, which have now carried them
into the middle years.

There is something especially moving about the sea exploits
of those veritable Ulysseans, the older navigators of small craft on
the great deeps, at ages when in the homogenized climate of contemporary North America men and women are supposed to be collecting their "golden age" cards, or at the least to be relinquishing
any exploits of physical stamina and intrepidity to the young. A
few examples cited from Borden are illustrative, although Borden
did not write his book especially for or about the type of older adult
whom I have described as Ulyssean.

Consider the remarkable case of Eleanor Wilson, a 59-year-old
missionary and pilot in the Marshall Islands who was suddenly
confronted with the need to become skipper of the schooner *Morning
Star VI*, which helped supply the islands and provided all kinds
of religious services to the islanders. Eleanor Wilson had the training and the skill of a pilot, but to be the captain of a schooner with
an all-male crew was an altogether different and far more demanding challenge. A woman captain in the islands was unheard of.
(How common is it anywhere?) Nonetheless as Borden writes:

> "Sailing the rounds of her 500,000-square-mile parish, Skipper
> Wilson slept on a plank bunk, ate rice and beans with fish
> and an occasional can of bully beef, and ran a taut ship—
> one that 'the Lord wouldn't be ashamed of.' . . . Like most

inter-island schooner skippers, she had her share of heavy weather and a few close calls among the coral atolls and the more than eleven hundred reefs and motus of the low, wind-swept Marshall archipelago. Scores of ships have been lost in the tricky currents, unmarked reefs, and sudden squalls of Micronesia. . . ."

When *Morning Star VI* foundered in the hands of an experienced male captain while Skipper Wilson was on leave, she took over the new *Morning Star VII*, and remained a familiar figure in the South Seas.

The fabulous Joshua Slocum, who completed a forty-six thousand-mile circumnavigation of the world in 1896 and wrote about it in *Sailing Alone Around the World* was seemingly at the end of prospects and resources when, at age 51, he set out from Yarmouth, Nova Scotia. His incredible voyage in his thirty-six-foot sloop, *Spray*, far from exhausting this gaunt and philosophical Nova Scotian, actually rejuvenated him: three years later at the end of his first great odyssey Slocum remarked, "The dial of my life was turned back—my friends all said Slocum is young again." He wrote his book on board, where he had a library of five hundred books, amid the constant interruption of adventures in far places which had seldom or never seen a white-skinned man. It is full of zest, poetry, and humour. Slocum's last photograph, taken at 65, shows a serious weather-worn man with a strong, sombre face, roughly dressed and wearing a large windblown straw hat. Once again he was impoverished on shore, as he had been at the time of his first great voyage, and he had some sad words: "I'm an old man, and I should like once more to feel a deck under my feet before it is too late." The Ulyssean fires still burned. He sailed again, and disappeared from human sight. It was an ending fit for the Ulysses of Dante.

Everyone knows of the exploits of Sir Francis Chichester. Scarcely anyone knows of the exploits of the extraordinary Tom Drake, whom Charles Borden has rescued from oblivion in *Sea Quest*. Drake was brought up on big ships, and from personal choice changed his nautical career from that of captain of large brigs to the solitary sailing of his own schooner, the *Sir Francis*, which he lost in a Caribbean storm and replaced with the thirty-five-foot *Pilgrim*. Drake, an outgoing man who simply loved sea life better than life on land, and enjoyed people everywhere, was 65 and had had a stroke which left him lame in one hip when he sailed *Pilgrim* eastward across the Atlantic from Charleston to London, England, where his attempt to make a temporary docking at one of the more snobbish yacht clubs was rejected.

When at age 66 he lost the *Pilgrim*, this Ulyssean built a new schooner, the thirty-seven-foot *Progress*—the *fourth* schooner which Drake had built for himself—and sailed three thousand miles down

the Pacific coast and over to Hawaii. When in a violent Pacific storm
he broke one arm, Drake steered a long voyage home with his left
hand. He cruised thousands of miles more in the *Progress,* a boat
he had come to love: "She'll never fail me. I don't suppose many
of you can understand this craving of mine for blue water, but you
get mighty close to something big when you're alone at sea. At
times I am lonely all right, but probably no more than an albatross
or the North Star." At age 73, in November, 1936, this joyous and
indomitable voyager left California from the Golden Gate to sail
for the South Seas. Like Joshua Slocum, he was never heard from
again. Such a conclusion of a Ulyssean life is too poetically true
to be tragic.

Slocum and Drake had long lived with the sea before entering
the lonely voyages of their Ulyssean years. On the other hand,
Edward Miles of Memphis, Tennessee, although he spent early years
at sea in his youth, was living the affluent life of a building con-
tractor when, close to age 50, he decided to return to the sea as a
lone sailor to circumnavigate the world. The decision broke up his
marriage; in fact his wife may already have been uneasy about
Miles's obsessive belief that somehow he could reconcile many of
the differences and assuage the prejudices of many peoples. He
took four years to complete his world journey. When he lost his
first schooner, *Sturdy,* in a fire while on the Red Sea, he returned
to the United States to purchase a second, *Sturdy II;* then set out
again for India, Ceylon, the Philippines, and China—at all major
points stopping to speak to any groups of adults and children who
would listen about the need for goodwill and understanding among
men. He sailed into New York harbour in his schooner in June,
1932.

Miles could perhaps have partially recouped his fortunes by
writing and lecturing about his many adventures at sea. His magnificent obsession, however, was the reconciliation of men, and ⁺his
led him to late disasters in his life—episodes, however, which were
in their own way Ulyssean, and which have a poetry as marked as
they are different from the splendid finales of Slocum and Drake.
In the pursuit of his dream of promoting peace and the co-operation
of differing political and religious creeds, Miles sold everything.
He lived in poverty. At one period he slept in the little office which
was the centre of the organization he had founded to promote his
ideals. In 1944, at age 65 he became one of the heterogeneous group
of independents who have run for president of the United States.
Such an act is symbolic only; it can be nothing else; and the strange
assortment of "causes" which find themselves represented among
the virtually anonymous "other" candidates for the presidency include a catalogue of eccentricity. Still, Edward Miles's magnificent
obsession and Ulyssean voyages of his later years were in them-

selves more creative and more self-actualizing than remaining among the rigorous social and political rituals of Memphis society would have been.

Other older adults, however, have been able to pursue conventional careers into the late years, and then—usually to everyone's surprise—become sea-faring Ulysseans. A few instances, briefly described, can complete this description of activities within Ulysses' own arena of the sea: a retired army dentist and his wife, Bill and Gretchen Lee, cruised across the world in a thirty-three-foot sloop, and then with a dental office installed in a new boat, decided to sail to the remote settlements of the Bahamas. In 1966 John Goetzke, at age 72, completed a world circumnavigation during which he was at one time held captive for thirty-nine days by pirates in the South Seas. Goetzcke was a businessman before he joined the fraternity of lone small craft voyagers on the great seas. A former engineer, Frank Casper, occupied his 60s by sailing on a leisurely schedule around the world—a voyage filled with colourful names: Tahiti, Pago Pago, the Cook Islands, Auckland, Timor, and the Indian Ocean.

To launch out into the great seas in a little craft perhaps thirty or forty feet long, perhaps less, and often alone; and to cross and re-cross oceans in one's later years may strike many people as exotic and eccentric—but at least everyone knows that there were ancient mariners and old pilots. On the other hand, the modern motorcycle is wholly identified with youth, (often with brawling, delinquent youth), and it is seen as almost a sexual symbol of youthful adventure and power.

Is there any reason, however, aside from society's deeply grooved prejudices about the incapacity of older adults, why the domain of the motorcycle should be reserved for youth? John Pitt, age 62 in 1973, a resident of North Hatley, Quebec, a real estate appraiser by vocation, and a great-great-grandson of the eighteenth-century British prime minister William Pitt, thought not—and launched himself upon what was perhaps the most remarkable long-distance motorcycle saga in history.

Thirty years earlier, Pitt had been a daredevil rider of motorcycles at rodeos, so that it is true that he was indulging a long-standing passion. In fact, he had kept on riding them from time to time across the years. Yet this takes nothing away from his astounding feat in riding thirty-two thousand miles through nine months to the fabled country of Tierra del Fuego, at the extreme tip of South America, and even brings him closer to his great prototype, Ulysses. Pitt made the decision to do this on a snowbound winter night, after reading a newspaper article about a family living on a sheep farm in Tierra del Fuego. He then wrote to them. As so often happens, in initial Ulyssean adventures, some chance event galvanizes a long-suppressed desire into action almost instantaneously.

John Pitt's itinerary took him down the east coast of the United States to North Carolina, through Texas and into Mexico, to Central America and Panama, where he took a small ship to Colombia. From there he went to Ecuador and Peru, and south on the coastal highway which skirts the lonely and magnificent beaches and dunes of the Pacific, then into the pampas of Argentina, across the Magellan Straits, and at last, after three months, to his hosts in Tierra del Fuego, sixteen thousand miles from his home in Quebec. Pitt's diary, which he kept as carefully as Joshua Slocum kept his, is filled with vivid accounts of the joys, hazards, and exploits of his astonishing journey.

To cross North America on modern transcontinental highways all the way, under settled laws and without a passport, and to do so in one's early 60s, on a motorcycle, the supposed instrument of exuberant youth, would be a superb exploit. But in John Pitt's odyssey, he had to negotiate whole networks of often badly-maintained national highways, encounter successions of puzzled or surly customs guards or police, make dangerous portages or water crossings, and often sleep out night after night in wholly unfamiliar territory. His journal tells of a collision with a "huge white longhorn steer" looming out of the mist in Nicaragua, a collision which forced him to take an hour to reassemble himself and his machine in pouring rain with trucks going by; of nearly disappearing, motorcycle and all, in an oversized canoe struggling to take him and other passengers across stormy waters to a remote jungle village in Colombia. (Pitt's motorcycle helmet saved the day as a bailing instrument); and threading his way, caught by pitch darkness, through the mountain roads of South America, along the edges of precipitous chasms.

Pitt's odyssey even had its episode of romantic love. In the wake of a landslide across a highway in Argentina, he met a lovely Argentinian woman, a professor of history, half his age, to whom he became engaged and who joined him in North Hatley. Pitt's interviewer, a Montreal writer, Don Bell, asked him the inevitable question back beside the blazing fireplace of his home: "Are you ready to settle down?" To which this breaker of stereotypes replied: "Not on your life. I've bought a Ford pick-up truck, and Margarita and I and two Spanish-speaking friends plan to take the whole trip over in 1975, but this time with a movie camera. I'll be driving in front on the motorcycle."

In John Pitt it is possible to see the unconventional man, in spite of the seeming conventionality provided by a distinguished heritage and a comfortable living. Mayra Scarborough, on the other hand, who in 1972 at the age of 57 began a journey on a Honda 450 motorcycle through all of the United States and much of Canada, seems, aside from this astonishing adventure, to be the epitome of the *status quo*. Her mission was to mark the two hundredth anniversary of the American Revolution by presenting special flags to the governors of all fifty states. A professional librarian, Mayra Scarborough first took a degree in science at Duke University, then married. After age 50, she obtained a diploma in librarianship, and a job with a pharmaceutical company. In her spare time she and her husband, a retired communications engineer, enjoy gliding; in addition, she is taking lessons in piloting powered aircraft.

But why the motorcycle? Mrs. Scarborough makes clear that her choice of this most unconventional of all vehicles for adults grew out of a love-hate relationship. She strongly disapproved of her young daughter's buying one; urged her to give it up as much too dangerous; then could not resist trying the machine out herself one day. Her only mishap came at that point—she slipped when standing *beside* the bike and broke her collar bone. But after that she entered a new world—not a new experience for Mayra Scarborough who, with her husband, deliberately seeks new experiences. "We just feel at our time of life we're going to do all the pleasurable things we can," she told the Canadian columnist Lotta Dempsey. By June 1974, she had travelled thirty-four thousand miles of her safari, travelling at speeds of up to eighty miles an hour, and often camping out.

Later-life odysseys of the kind undertaken by the small craft seagoers and by seekers of new worlds like Pitt and Scarborough are testing not only in the possibility of serious crises and dangers, but also in the mere physical stamina and industry required. Earlier we noted what merely changing sail and keeping control of his boat required of Francis Chichester; likewise, in Pitt's case, the care and overhaulage of the motorcycle at hundreds of stopping-places, and the stamina required just to remain alert in the saddle on so long a journey, are all factors which the older adult has to contend with just as a young person does. The powerful will of the Ulysseans— the will to plan and begin the odyssey in the first place, and then to carry it through in spite of put-downs and personal discouragements— this is an asset of these older adult people which may often far exceed that of much younger competitors.

Where the older adult may clearly be handicapped is in loss of efficiency in physical functioning when not aided or extended by the operational power of machines and craft. Our pleasure at the thought that the great airlines have entrusted the piloting of immensely complicated aeroplanes to men in their early 50s must be moderated by the incontestable fact that, of all the roles of man, the physical role is certain to show some decline in the later years. Yet even so, extraordinary people, most of them non-celebrities, make a Ulyssean adventure out of proving that there are potentialities for extended joy and power in the human body which they are determined to explore. Thus, Dr. Jack Wilmore, a physician at the

University of California, who is conducting studies to determine what can be expected as the outer limits of physical fitness for older people, reported in October, 1971, that he had discovered what he termed "a 73-year-old superman—a superman for his age" who has the walk of a teenager and "a heart so strong that he can run the mile in 6½ minutes." The subject of Wilmore's study, Noel Johnson, a retired aerospace executive, had developed his own physical formula for a long life—eat at least twelve times a day and run over one hundred and fifty miles a week!

Much the same achievement has been recorded for an older Canadian athlete, Art Keay, the Toronto ex-policeman, who at 67 continues to be undoubtedly one of the better distance walkers in the world. He also has his trained observers: when in 1972 Keay walked the two hundred and fifty-two miles from Detroit to Toronto for a police games event, he was accompanied by the head trainer for the University of Toronto football and hockey teams, who drove the station wagon back and from time to time gave Keay's legs a light rub to keep him tuned up. Unlike Noel Johnson, Keay eats sparingly most of the time: he does not eat before beginning a day's hike, and walks between twelve and twenty miles before stopping for a breakfast of juice and a sandwich; at the rest stops he drinks water, ginger ale, and stout. Keay enters a number of ten-mile walks each year for men over 60, and often wins. His average distance for each day of the Detroit-to-Toronto walkathon was thirty-five miles.

Meanwhile, in Great Britain, on May 6, 1973 the *Sunday Express* reported the story of surely one of the most remarkable late-life athletes in the world. Douglas MacLean was a first class international sprinter in 1904, when he ran 100 yards in 9.9 seconds. In 1973 MacLean was aged 88 and was still regularly timed as running the 100 yard distance in 14 seconds (and the 100 metres in 14.6 seconds). In Toronto, in August 1975, at the age of 90, MacLean ran the 200-metre dash in 49.2 seconds at the World Masters championships for men over 40. This was 4.5 seconds slower than the gold medal winner, Fritz Schreiber of Sweden. "MacLean was not even perspiring or out of breath minutes after the race," wrote reporter Bob Koen. He wanted to take on Schreiber again! Like many Ulysseans, MacLean had returned to an early love after a long career in a totally different medium. Born in Scotland, and brought up in South Africa where he became the country's champion amateur sprinter, he returned to Britain and became a professional music hall artist for nearly fifty years, at one time understudying Sir Harry Lauder. He and his wife, aged 68, had seven children, all named after islands on the west coast of Scotland, and numerous grandchildren. Since MacLean and his fellow competitors had to pay their own way to the Masters Championships (about £150 each) MacLean raised £100 of the amount by appearing on a television show. And his diet, that endless enigma of the students of creative and zestful old age? MacLean remarked: "The secret of keeping fit is in having the right physical and mental outlook. I don't smoke and I eat very sparingly. I have no special diet, except that I never touch fried food. And I don't mind a drop of liquor now and again." And his future plans? asked the fascinated *Express* reporter. MacLean's reply was Ulyssean: "I plan to run around the track on my 100th birthday. And when I pass on, my ghost will still keep running around it."

Another remarkable older Ulyssean athlete is Herman Smith-Johannsen, honoured in February, 1975, at age 99 as the Dubonnet "skier of the year". Tributes at the New York gathering in his honour named him as "Viking of the century," and in Lowell Thomas's phrase, "the world's most famous skier"—Thomas, still himself a CBS news commentator at 83, is a frequent skiing companion of Smith-Johannsen.

Smith-Johanssen lives in a small bungalow in the Laurentian hills of Quebec at Piedmont, and each morning goes out alone for a five-mile run. In the afternoon, he skis four more miles to pick up his mail. He "works up a good sweat", then settles by the fire with a pipe and a glass of beer. His life has had Ulyssean features before; for example, in his attempt to enlist in the Canadian army ski troops at age 64 in 1940 (he was turned down). In an interview with the Canadian writer Pierre Berton in 1972, Smith-Johannsen showed himself to be joyous and quick-witted. Among his secrets for maintaining his athletic schedule and his trim physique, he cites "the ability to keep from worrying and *a will to live*." (My italics.)

The exploits of women in athletics in the late years are rarely disclosed and are presumably far fewer than men's because of traditional lifestyles. For example, there is no Masters' Tournament for women in track and field. Still, there are enough remarkable examples to remind us that the line that separates the dormant or declining physical life from the Ulyssean one is in many cases a matter of outlook and of will. For example, a grandmother of 67 in Arizona learns to swim and to dance—both of them skills which later adults typically suppose themselves to be past learning, if they have never done them. An 80-year-old great-grandmother, Marg Bailey, has for eight years, including the spring of 1975, cheerfully completed the thirty-mile walkathon of Miles for Millions. She makes one concession to her age: "I plan to walk alone to conserve energy by not yapping too much."

For me the most extraordinary example of the woman Ulyssean in physical achievement is the Toronto centenarian Louise Tandy Murch. A professional teacher of voice and piano, Louise Murch considers her last thirty years "the most productive of her life". After shattering her hip at 75, she rejected a doctor's verdict that she would never walk again; after two years of struggle, she not only walked again without crutches but at age 90 took up yoga. She has since worked out every day in spite of steel pins in both hips inserted there after a second fall and broken hip at age 94. Her astonished interviewer, Bob Pennington, of *The Toronto Star*, noted that Louise Murch could easily do waist bends and put her palms on the floor, do the routine of bicycling with legs raised, and various yoga exercises.

Louise Murch's whole old age is Ulyssean. Her long-sustained good health, other than the accidents, has been a strong source of achievement, but her vitality, love of life and of people, eagerness for new experiences, and openness to the future mean that, in Robert Peck's terms, she has re-invested herself in life and made great age seem almost incidental. She still gives concerts to groups of older people and community college students, accompanying a young singer, Paul Schillaci, whom she coaches, and who says about her, wonderingly, "You have only to meet Louise to change your entire idea about old age." And he adds, significantly, "Many of the older folks we entertain are 20 to 30 years younger than Louise—yet many of them look sad and defeated, reconciled to being old and acting old."

There is no television set in Louise Murch's home. She plays the piano for an hour daily, entertains a great deal, does her own baking, welcomes young people as well as people of all ages who come to see her often when they themselves are depressed or lonely. She periodically flies off to Arizona or other places where her three sons live: "I hope I fly there next in one of those jumbo jets—you could give a recital in one of them." And as a yoga expert and late-life believer in the joy of the body, she takes care to include in her diet a ration of brewer's yeast, cod liver oil, and lecithin, and vitamins B and E—and always whole wheat bread. Thus Louise Tandy Murch at age 100 is really in training, as though she were a continuing competitor in and for a great race—which is exactly what she is.

Investigators like Jack Wilmore and others who make it their special study to try to extend the physical efficiency of the human body into old age, are surely in search of a valuable prize. There continues to be something beautiful and deeply meaningful in the actions and results of the older adult who takes as one form of the Ulyssean adventure the loving care of the body and the faith in it which can help light up his or her own late years, and act as a pilot lamp to so many younger people.

As it is, in spite of the jogging fad, few older men in our society are found in the great company of the YMCA, although they would be welcome. A limited number swim and fish; a number hunt; a substantial group of older executives continue to play golf, often for business contacts rather than self-actualization; a few play tennis. Both men and women continue to curl in Canada, the northern United States, and in Scotland, into the later years, a few into the very late years. A number of men and women lawn bowl, a gentle sport which takes players out into the open air and onto the green grass on a summer evening. Shuffleboard is the game of sea voyagers and of elderly adults—even the name has a geriatric sound.

At all events, here is a great area of study, the human body at play in the later middle and late years, which has been neglected. We should not just stand around, mouth agape, gazing at the Douglas MacLeans, Art Keays, and Noel Johnsons on their rare appearances, but also making this territory of late human life an area for our own Ulyssean experiments, on *whatever scale.*

Often the Ulyssean person at an advanced age astonishes us by the seeming agelessness of his performances—the small craft operator who never ties up in a final harbour, or the old athlete like MacLean who never calls a halt at any point in the life drama. Frequently, such a person will end a late-life odyssey only to leave us wondering what new country his restless mind and spirit will explore next. An interesting case is that of Tom Williams, Canada's "oldest pilot", whose announced retirement at 88 caused modest headlines and notices across the country. Theoretically the air should remain one of the Ulyssean potentialities of our time; in fact, it is not. Yet Williams was not pressed to give up his licence, and before selling his Fleet 21M biplane he made one more lovely flight. Williams has been an idea-maker all his life, in farming and in aviation, and a prolific poet. But is it now to be a fact, as the young reporter wrote in one of the major stories, that "Tom Williams, 88, Canada's oldest pilot, has traded in his airplane for a rocking chair"?

These fascinating Ulysseans share one quality which is an accompaniment of much creative activity in the later years—the quality of deathless childhood: of the child to whom the "incongruous" or the "odd" is simply the intriguing and the delightful. If this trait were not present, it is doubtful whether many or perhaps any of the adventures would take place.

In writing about the adult personality and the innumerable transactions that take place throughout every life, Thomas A. Harris's *I'm OK—You're OK* vividly delineates roles (derived from Eric Berne) which he calls "Child", "Parent" and "Adult", all placed in continuing association. Harris, who devotes only three or four pages of a three-hundred-page book to the subject of creativity, is preoccupied with his description of what he calls the "NOT-OK Child", whose permanently recorded and recurrently playing experiences from childhood rouse (especially in crisis) all the inferiority feelings in the personality, and lead it to seek non-adult and often destructive solutions. But, Harris notes, the part of the grown human being one can call the Child also has a bright side: "In the Child reside creativity, curiosity, the desire to explore and know, the urges to touch and feel and experience, and the recordings of the glorious, pristine feelings of first discoveries." Although Harris insists that the NOT-OK feelings far outweigh the OK elements of childhood, the curiosity and the delight in first discoveries are never lost. To this one might add that a posture of childhood which presumably might be both OK and NOT-OK, namely the resolve to "show them", and while doing so to upset some of the conventions of Mrs. Grundy's world if necessary, seems also to be a trait of the creative adult at all ages.

Picasso, throughout his immensely long and continuously creative life, seems to have always retained something of the outlook and the nature of the entranced and entrancing child. This, in part, accounts for the freshness and virtuosity with which the artist turned in phase after phase to new styles and experiments in painting and sculpture; but it also appeared in continual glimpses of his personality as seen by his friends and mistresses, and by biographers, visiting critics, and writers. When Alexander Liberman visited Picasso for lengthy interviews, the artist was, successively, age 68, 72, and 73. Nonetheless, Liberman's description of their meetings is filled with references to Picasso's childlike qualities or to the way the world of childhood somehow intervened. Thus, Picasso was expecting some Spanish visitors at his two-storeyed yellow villa on the Mediterranean coast at Vallauris: "He decided to get up and dress—in a polka-dotted blue shirt and wide, baggy shorts. With his extremely large head, this short, stocky man seemed like a young boy dressed in his father's clothes. There was a feeling of youth and at the same time of age . . ."

These might seem to be Liberman's subjective impressions, but then the Spanish visitors arrived, and: "The great man walked from one to the other, always with an expression of childish amazement and wonder. He seemed to be surprised at everything— delighted, pleasant, and anxious to put his guests at ease. Time seemed to be of no importance." When the group were ready to go somewhere to eat (no decision had been made),

> "Skira put on a Tyrolean green hat. It amused Picasso so much that Skira gave it to him. He immediately put it on and looked at himself in the mirror delightedly. He has a need, a sort of childish desire, to take and to get inside other people's possessions. . . . He put the hat on and never took it

off until we got to the restaurant. This had made his day. The new toy had made possible a new transformation of himself."

And when later Picasso's son Paolo amused him with a variety of antics, Liberman remarks: "Picasso likes clowns."

Later in a seemingly inexhaustible tour of Picasso's studios and works in painting and sculpture, his perceptive visitor is able to begin the process of bridging these personal qualities with the artist's unquenchable creativity.

Passing through a succession of studios, Picasso opened the door to an immense room crowded with sculpture.

> "A little girl skipping rope was made out of wine baskets. In a corner, a perambulator, made of junk-pile discards, seemed to rock with the weight of a comic-strip baby. This man was playing, trying through play to recapture the innocence of childhood vision, trying through humour to bridge the gulf of years and purge himself of his sophistication. Picasso loves and needs to be near children."

Liberman remarks on the "countless toys" which Picasso made for his own children (he was a father at 64 and again when past 70), such experiences "enriching him and transferring to him some of the energy of youth", and he concludes: "His agile, playful mind needs such amusement. The sense of humor, the sense of theater, the childish delight in play are underlying qualities in many artists. Maybe one dares more under the excuse of play: the creative act becomes less pompous and self-conscious."

Picasso's creative genius included many other components, but the quality of the curious, wondering, and delighted child—furthermore, the child exuberantly showing off, or plunging incautiously into some enchanting project—is essential to an understanding of Picasso and of many other men and women whose creativity continues to burn on through their later years. There is evidence of it in Jean Cocteau's feeling, which he never lost, of magic and delight in the house lights dimming in the theatre, the stage lights going up, and the curtain rising.

The naive pleasure with which the impresario Sol Hurok, whose creativity made possible the careers of many artists and artistic companies, coloured the lives of some of his celebrated performers is another reflection of the delighted child at work. Thus, when Galina Ulanova arrived in New York in 1959 with the Bolshoi Ballet, the news services reported that: "the impresario ushered her into a three-room hotel suite that held a refrigerator stocked with caviar and champagne and other necessities of a ballerina's life." The account might be amended to, "what Hurok conceived to be the necessities of a ballerina's life"—the child was at play, and Hurok at the time was aged 71! In fact, he retained his touch to the end of his long life (March 5, 1974), moving across the world of entertainment in the great arts with (in spite of his tough business sense) much of the "amazement and wonder" with which Picasso strolled delightedly among his guests at Vallauris. There was a large element of the enchanted child in the enormous role which "gut reactions" played in his often instantaneous creative decisions. For example, in 1935, when he first heard the soprano Marian Anderson, then unknown, sing in Paris, Hurok reported that he felt chills dance up and down his spine, and that his hands got wet—he signed her to a contract with a handshake.

In Maurice Goudeket's recollections of his wife, the French novelist Colette, who continued to write powerfully far into her later years, many vignettes of the sensitive and responsive child appear—the creative child whom no number of contacts with the sophisticated and synthetic world of adult protocols nor the sorrows and pain of old age could destroy. Colette's intense and moving empathy with animals was one evidence of this, not only with cats, the most famous example, but with every kind of creature, for example, "addressing animals politely, speaking French to them and not baby-talk," as part of her intimate world. She had almost the same rapport with flowers and vegetables which, with animals and human beings, were all one world to her: "There is only *one* creature."

Colette's spontaneous and always fresh employment of the senses was that of the child to whom the world is new and filled with wonders. Thus, after her third and at last deeply happy marriage, to Maurice Goudeket, in April, 1935, when she was already 62, they lunched at a country inn, and "on our way home, between two sunny intervals, snow began to fall, snow with large flakes of dazzling whiteness. Colette asked me to stop the car and got down to receive this impalpable manna rapturously on her face." Goudeket adds that Colette could never recall the date of her wedding, being usually forgetful of anniversaries, but "she always remembered that springtime snow, to the point of speaking of it eleven years later in *L'Etoile Vesper*."

Colette's reactions to the worlds encountered by her senses were unimprisoned by the usual accumulation of postures and protocols which adults acquire as part of their defensive systems. To illustrate this from a typical episode recounted by Goudeket:

> "Her way of making contact with things was through all her senses. It was not enough for her to look at them, she had to sniff and taste them. When she went into a garden she did not know, I would say to her: 'I suppose you are going to eat it, as usual.' And it was extraordinary to see her setting to work, full of haste and eagerness, as if there were no more urgent task than getting to know this garden. She separated

the sepals of flowers, examined them, smelled them for a long time, crumpled the leaves, chewed them, licked the poisonous berries and the deadly mushrooms, pondering intensely over everything she had smelt and tasted. Insects received almost the same treatment, they were felt and listened to and questioned. She attracted bees and wasps, letting them alight on her hands and scratching their backs. 'They like that,' she would exclaim."

Compare the behaviour of this enchanted child with the restrained and well bred demeanour with which we ordinarily walk about and formally observe and comment when visiting gardens.

Colette was 53 when she first met Goudeket, and he 35; thus, these and hundreds of other episodes he recounts in his memoirs of her written after her death (she died in 1954, at 81) are anecdotes of a woman already in her later middle years—a Ulyssean adult. And one should add the footnote that Colette's fresh and childlike empathy with nature, the residue and re-playing of the wonder of childhood, in no manner alienated her from human nature or blurred her vision. She remains among the small circle of the most penetrating and compassionate observers of human beings to appear in the past century. Both her persistent creativity in her later years and her unclouded vision were in fact partly fed by the child that she never locked out of her adult life.

There is another aspect in which the child appears in the later creative years of Ulyssean adults—in the plunging of one's self into enterprises which delight the mind and warm the heart, without sensibly and cautiously measuring the costs in advance. "A mature person," we say, "would never have got involved like that": but then the "mature person" would never have acted at all. Ulyssean people and exploits can be born, and beautifully so, from among slide rules and balance sheets, but this is not their natural milieu. It would have been more mature for the *chanteuse* Josephine Baker to have adopted only three or four foster children when she was about 50, instead of filling a large villa near Paris with more than two dozen of these lively young human beings from a dozen national and racial cultures as an eloquent symbol to the world of the need for all men to love one another. Because of her impetuous humanity, Baker was for years in difficulty with landlords and creditors and a variety of authorities—still, her action was a great action. Its intrepidity contributed to its splendour, and the element of the child which contributed to it may well also have been one of the sources of the singer's astonishing success in continuing as a fine performer up to her death at 69 in 1975.

Elements of the OK Child are also surely contributory to the qualities of what Maslow defined for his self-actualized adults as a creative attitude not killed by acculturation, or what Carl Rogers defined as an "openness to experience." These also account for the remarkable ability of Ulyssean adults to abandon old rubrics, to take on new roles, to engage in new ventures, large or small, to try to acquire new skills, to branch off from established paths.

Consider a remarkable mother of five sons, a 65-year-old Canadian widow and hospital administrator, Hella Hesse. Exiled as a child and a grown woman by war and revolution, first from Russia and then from Germany—she was able to say recently, "so much has happened to me that there are times when I feel 300 years old"—Hella Hesse found herself an exile in Canada in 1959. She and her young sons took every kind of job to stay alive, Mrs. Hesse working as a hospital kitchen maid and dishwasher, a floor housekeeper in a Bermuda luxury hotel, and, after taking correspondence courses was accepted as the executive housekeeper of a hospital in British Columbia. She was by then 61; her sons had become young men with responsible posts; she had had a life of hardship and poverty ever since the early affluent days of her aristocratic family in Russia. Her husband had been a political prisoner of the Soviets, and had died in Europe before he was able to help his family in Canada. Hella Hesse might well have finished her days in comparative calm and security in the British Columbia hospital job.

Instead, "to the amazement of my sons", she told Bob Pennington of *The Toronto Star*, she applied to a number of international agencies for service abroad. The first to reply was CUSO (Canadian University Service Overseas), and the work offered was health administration in Nigeria. "My sons were startled to see the old lady giving up her job and setting out for another continent, but I'd always wanted to volunteer for an international agency." She thereupon found herself administering one forty-bed district hospital, a rural health centre, and ten dispensaries—work so extensive that during her 1973 furlough in Canada four different people replaced her. In her lengthy interview she showed that the open, ever learning mind and spirit that had sent her on the Ulyssean venture to Nigeria were as active as ever. She did not view herself as a heaven-sent messenger bringing light to a less developed country, although of course she could see the value of her technical skill. On the contrary, for Hella Hesse the Western world had much to learn from the African people: "The cultural wealth and social attitudes of the African people are healthier and more mature than our own. There is much to learn from Nigeria in its refusal to segregate old people and its absolute acceptance and integration of all generations."

On the long flight home on leave in November 1973, Hella Hesse found herself deep in conversation with a man in the next seat who turned out to be a European-born arms peddler attached to no country and busily selling modern missiles to the young African nations. Herself the long-time victim of war and national hatreds, Hella probed at the man's motives and ethics—did he never think of the consequences of such a traffic? "Don't worry," the arms peddler replied, "we are also selling hospital equipment at the same time." Mrs. Hesse confessed herself to be totally at a loss for words: "There was no point in arguing with such a man." She saved her emotions and her energies for the two-month personal campaign on behalf of CUSO she had planned for her vacation—to tell Canadians that through such international projects they were not only giving aid, but were investing in Canada's future and in the future of the world. Thus she has reoriented her whole life in late adulthood, not absorbed in a past full of adventure and certain hardships and sorrows, but looking outward and forward to the possibilities of a more humane world—a Ulyssean exploit.

A celebrated Ulyssean figure who shares the same concepts as Hella Hesse is Paul-Emile Cardinal Léger, the former Archbishop of Montreal, who resigned his archdiocese in 1967 to become a worker first among lepers and then among groups of disadvantaged Africans, and to enlist financial support from North America for these purposes. Léger's Ulyssean adventure is still in progress and its final issue is still unseen. One of the most vivid figures in the supreme hierarchy of the Roman Catholic Church, he has always had strong admirers and sceptical critics. Still, aside from the good work already accomplished in his new role, the Ulyssean symbolism alone of the cardinal's action was magnificent. At age 63, when men and women are popularly expected to settle for comfort and security, perfectly able if he wished to finish his life in a sometimes turbulent but prestigious and ego-satisfying archbishopric, in the midst of a French-speaking culture which must have had deep satisfactions for him, Léger chose to take on a totally new life, almost certainly exposed to certain embarrassments and maladjustments, far removed much of the time from the glamour of great metropolises and their circles of power and success. The action was Ulyssean, not just because Léger was committing himself to the future, but because his voyage was an extension in space and a venture out into the troubled seas of the inhumanity of man to man. Like Hella Hesse he was a swift learner among the Africans. He too spoke movingly of their consideration for family life, and their profound sense of the value of old age. He noted, as one example, how even certain leaders of African nations, perplexed and harassed by problems in international politics, would on their return to their home countries not hesitate to consult old and wise men among their tribal people.

Speaking still of Ulyssean exploits in the modern world that spring from an open and searching human mind and spirit, a striking illustration is the life and work of an extraordinary American woman, Welthy Honsinger Fisher. She also typifies Ulysseanism at work on the international scene. I met her briefly at a symposium in Toronto in October, 1969, when she was on a furlough as president of the World Literacy Movement, centred in India. She was then 89 years of age. She was already celebrated in special circles, for example adult education, for having established Literacy Village near Lucknow, from which thousands of teachers have gone out to provide chances for lifelong learning among enormous numbers of illiterate people. I was one of a group of academic men and women who waited for her to appear at a little afternoon reception and tea; almost no one had met her, and we expected to see a bright but fragile old lady leaning on someone's arm. Instead, a remarkable figure entered the room, alone, erect and poised, handsome and imposing but without pretension, a woman one would turn to look at again. She was dressed gracefully in a sari, and in everything she said her mind was clearly full of India, and of the Third World; yet to speak with her was to feel her intimate interest in people simply as people.

Seven years before she had published a personal memoir, *To Light a Candle*, which had gone into eight printings and which described at least four lives of Welthy Honsinger Fisher: the girl and young woman who might have been a first rate concert singer and perhaps an opera singer; the missionary teacher in China with a host of colourful experiences; the wife and companion across four hundred thousand miles of an American Methodist Bishop, Frederick Bohn Fisher, with whom she worked and travelled throughout India; and then the Ulyssean life, which began about age 60, after the bishop's death.

Because of her love for her husband and her intense companionship with him, Welthy Fisher was extremely lonely. Since she had married late, at age 44, her family consisted of her adopted Chinese daughter with her husband, and a little Chinese grandchild, and these comforted her. She was made a lay preacher of the Methodist Church and a deaconess; she tried to take up the conventional parish work of these roles; but they neither eased her loneliness nor met the demands of what she calls her "undiminished energy." The fact was that something Ulyssean was waiting for her. She felt this instinctively, enough to decide to go around the world, "with no basic reason than to find nothing but myself." When she reached India she fulfilled a vow, and scattered her husband's ashes at sunrise on the great slopes of the Himalayas. That day she made an entry in her journal, one of the refuges from her loneliness: "Oh God, help me to keep my sanity and not to live in the past, for I am sure Bohn is still living in the future, as he always did here." The entry epitomized the openness of spirit of this 60-year-old widow to new experiences, and to the Ulyssean way.

The subsequent years did not yield their special treasure easily. Welthy Fisher found a young American woman as a companion in new enterprises, one of them the renting of a houseboat in Kashmir where she hoped to settle down and write (this proved impossible), and on shopping and travel excursions meant to be joyful. The effort to be carefree was in a way Ulyssean, but it was not enough for Welthy Fisher. For a number of years she continued her "seminars", as she called them, studying educational systems in Mexico, South America, and the whole Middle East—almost parenthetically she recounts how at age 70 she broke her knee, and was on crutches for the whole of her journey through Greece, Lebanon, Syria, Iran, Iraq, Jordan, and Israel. She also learned to speak and read Hindustani, something she had long put off in the busy and exciting years before her husband's death.

The signal for her ultimate Ulyssean adventure was provided in 1948 in a personal interview with Gandhi, six weeks before his death: "As we parted he took my hands and said, 'When you come back to live in India, go to the villages and help them. India is the village.'" It was several years before the message was fully decoded by the steady accumulation of events in Welthy Fisher's life. In 1952 an invitation came from Allahabad to help train teachers in villages to instruct illiterates. This, as it turned out, was the special Ulyssean treasure. Within a few years, she planned and built a ten-acre village, the now celebrated Literacy Village, which opened with the support of American funds, wholly deeded over to Indian ownership at Welthy Fisher's insistence. A new and powerful force had been launched in the world as a result of the energy and zest for tomorrow of this remarkable widow already far into her 70s. Remarkable—still, intensely human, as when she stood shaking at the news that there were cobras in her garden, and when in search of a famous English architect now living in the foothills, she found herself compelled to cross a raging river on a temporary footbridge with a slippery rope railing ("clinging to the improvised railing, I set one foot ahead of the other and prayed").

Openness to experience. The willingness to believe, as a wise European-born Ulyssean friend of mine remarks, that one of the most important phrases in life is, "You never can tell." Life occasionally delivers unexpected reverses and disasters, but one of its enthralling qualities is its frequent delivery of unanticipated achievements and adventures—sometimes, as in the case of the Ulysseans, whole new sectors of life. Thus Welthy Fisher, mourning and lonely for her husband at age 60, in no way anticipated Literacy Village which did not begin to materialize until she was

72. Edith Hamilton, upon retiring to the graceful obscurity of her New England seacoast house in her late 50s, had no conception of the fact that by age 65 she would be internationally known for *The Greek Way*, or that she would continue to write far into her 80s, and would make four European tours in her early 90s. Pablo Casals at his mid-50s could have had no inkling that he would spend the last thirty-seven years of his life in exile from Spain, but that in addition he would become almost a sublime figure of political and human freedom, that he would found the Prades Festival, the school and festival in Puerto Rico, that he would become the deeply beloved and admired maestro every summer of the Marlboro Festival in Vermont, and that at an advanced age he would marry a lovely young woman whose companionship lighted up his last years. Likewise it is inconceivable that Angelo Roncalli, the modest and seemingly half-forgotten Roman Catholic legate to Turkey and Greece at age 60, and the saviour at the time of a shipload of Jewish refugees in an obscure episode, foresaw himself as the pope who at 79 summoned the revolutionary Vatican Council II.

Among the Ulysseans openness to experience means openness to new experiments. This includes the creative life, even where that life has been long productive and successful. Thus two modern performers in the arts who died very recently at advanced ages, Jacques Lipchitz, the sculptor, at age 81, and Edward Steichen, the photographer, at 94, were both described in their lengthy *New York Times* obituaries as being twice-born—but in each case these were Ulyssean adults who continued to create works which showed the perpetual odyssey of their spirits. They were twice-born in the sense that at least once in their careers they made conversions of their artistic lives or their styles so dramatic that they were epoch-making both for them and their admirers. Steichen, a painter, became a photographer of such imagination and perception that he transformed photography into a fine art. Lipchitz, from being a brilliant early avant-garde sculptor, a cubist who never lost what one critic has called "the syntax of cubism", turned his greatest energies to what the same critic has called "the mythological, monumental works . . . that would be capable of sustaining the grandeur and eloquence that haunted him."

Steichen in his old age remained as productive and creative as ever, although he could have stroked himself with the innumerable tributes paid to him as the founder of a modern art form. He could have joined the circle of very old men flattered and consoled by endless honorific citations and testimonials. Instead, when a party was given for him at the Plaza Hotel in New York on his ninetieth birthday in 1969, Steichen took the floor to say: "When I first became interested in photography, I thought it was the whole cheese. My idea was to have it recognized as one of the fine arts. Today I don't give a hoot in hell about that. The mission of photography is to explain man to man and each man to himself. And that is no mean function. Man is the most complicated thing on earth, and also as naive as a tender plant."

The critic Clive Barnes describes this same phenomenon of the artist still creative in the later years and still searching in a review of the recent work of Igor Moiseyev, the 68-year-old Russian choreographer who took the folk dance and built it into the ballet choreography without losing the ethnic roots of the dance itself. Barnes is commenting on Moiseyev's daring attempt to challenge Michel Fokine's classic choreography for Borodin's Polovetsian Dances from *Prince Igor*. Moiseyev's ballet was first presented in Moscow in 1971, to immediate acclaim; this triumph was repeated in Paris a few months later. For Barnes, this attempt by a master choreographer, then in his mid-60s, to match Fokine by integrating classical ballet and folk dance with the continuous use of the dance ensemble rather than individual performers (Fokine had built his ballet around a chief warrior) is a limited success, perhaps a magnificent failure. Still, one can sense throughout Barnes's review the critic's excitement that Moiseyev should be engaged in such an exploit at all, instead of simply sitting back to enjoy the endless applause which greets his great folk dance company; and Barnes ends his review with a passage which discerns with remarkable perception the restless, open, outreaching spirit which makes many creative artists Ulysseans:

> "I notice that a few years ago he started a separate classical troupe, to supplement the ensemble's activities, but this does not seem to have been overwhelmingly successful. Yet I sense that Moiseyev is still searching for something, a search that may be seen in the very aspirations that led him to create in this Prince Igor something more like a genuine ballet than he has given the troupe in previous years."

Perhaps practitioners of the arts, professional or amateur, in their later years are wise (or fortunate) because they have provided the self with an arena of unusual potentiality for maintaining zest of life and creativity. This is sometimes spectacularly seen in noted professional performers: for example, the Lunts on the modern stage, or prolific writers as diverse as Thomas Mann, Agatha Christie, and P. G. Wodehouse, or classical virtuosi like Artur Rubinstein and Robert Casadesus or jazz virtuosi like Eubie Blake and Duke Ellington, or poets like Yeats, Robert Frost, and Boris Pasternak, or dancers and choreographers of the modern dance idiom like Martha Graham.

Graham's life and work, especially in her latest major dances,

performed in New York in May, 1973, are powerful examples of
how the arts fructify the self in the late years, and the self the
arts. What is exciting about Graham is not so much that she
continued to dance with her young company, and dance command-
ingly and beautifully until her retirement at 75—although that
is exciting enough. Rather, it is that in the choreography of her
old age she seeks to find and to express the elusive and divine
synthesis of the creative self and the inner quintessential self, and
their alliance with what might be called the surge of life—it is
really Graham's expression. Her response to the criticism that by
emphasizing pelvic movement in her dancers she created a sexual
emphasis to many of her ballets (she has composed nearly one
hundred and fifty of them) has been to say: "You have to take life
as it surges through you, and sex is part of it."

No wonder it was possible for Graham to tell the newspapers,
"I've just entered a new cycle of energy. I'm going through a
rebirth —with anything artistic, one must die to be reborn." One
of the dances dealt, suitably enough, with the prototypical figure
of Ulysses; the other, *Mendicants of Evening*, interpreted Saint-
John Perse's magnificent poem, "Chronicle". Some conception of
the searching, radiant creativity of its choreographer at seventy-
nine can be seen in the programme notes for the four *pas de deux*:
"In the first *pas de deux*, a couple has an erotic encounter ('Divine
turbulence be ours . . .') in which the flesh meets but the spirits
clash. In the second, the spirits are in harmony, the flesh cool; in
the third, the couple oscillates between tenderness and violence.
Everything is resolved by the last duet('We are herdsmen of the
future'), as spirit and flesh are integrated, the movements marked
by soaring lifts, like birds freed." A Ulyssean achievement— yet
when Martha Graham felt she had to take the decision to retire from
dancing, the crisis was almost more than she could bear; what re-
stored her and maintained the surge of life was her almost equally
deep love for the art of choreography.

What the lively arts do for those who participate in them as
professionals or amateurs in their later years is clearly to permit
the reinvestment of the self in new adventures—where the process
of self-discovery is continuous. Nothing can excel the healing and
generating role of the arts in continuously offering opportunities
for reinvestment of the self in the alternative lives or arenas of life
which Robert Peck outlined in his grid of the later years.

There are some amateur artists, Ulysseans, whose involvement
in painting seems to actualize the self in such a way that not merely
one of Peck's alternative lives is made active, but several at a time.
For an example, I turn to my own personal journal, and an entry
for November 15, 1973, which records an interview with one of the
most interesting Ulyssean adults in Canada. (The entry is necessarily abbreviated.)

In a pelting rainstorm at about the hour of 4:15, I arrive at the home of the noted Canadian classical scholar and writer on Goethe, Barker Fairley.

There is a long pause at the door. The house is one of a series of very pleasant old (1910?) houses set close to the street, which itself is in the old cultural heart of Toronto, near the university campus. Finally one sees the owner coming down the hall as I ring a second time; the door opens, and in the shadows I am invited in with dispatch, then quickly into the living-room and I find myself confronting—or rather confronted by—the Professor Dr. himself who asks me briskly to enlarge on my telephone call of a week ago.

I look with pleased curiosity at this "later adult" (to put it mildly)—he tells me he is 86—and hear with astonishment the accents of Arthur Lismer's Yorkshire. Fairley is marvellously youthful—not only in his alertness (he also hears well, but seemingly has to strain occasionally), but in his whole appearance and walk. He swims every day, he tells me, at the Hart House pool.

Noting my wet state, Fairley invites me to the kitchen to make a choice among the drinks. We return to the living-room, where small oils hang everywhere, sip our brandy, and consider together the important question: from what sources and by what means has Barker Fairley kept himself across eight and one-half decades a productive and creative human being?

Fairley's chief claim to Ulysseanism lies with his painting, which he first took up, he tells me, at 45. He remarks drily, "I was supposed to be able to do nothing in art from the age of 7 on, and so they told me—and I believed them" (we had a short burning digression on the damage done by these pedagogical fiats of God).

At 45 he began to paint because his University of Toronto colleague, Robert Finch, the poet and English scholar, insisted that he should: " 'Why can't you?' Finch asked, and the next Sunday morning brought paints and easel and put them into my hands. I gave breakfast to Finch and his friends, and hoped it would rain." It did not rain, and Fairley at 45 began the career in painting which was to bring him a separate distinction from his main career.

Fairley painted until his mid-50s, then a curious thing happened. He just stopped painting, totally; then, after a number of years, perhaps fifteen, he resumed: "I got pushed back in." Why the hiatus? Fairley thought it was because he had become absorbed in writing books, in university routines, and so on. His study of Goethe came off the presses when Fairley was age 60. "Writing wasn't really my thing. I just try to be a good craftsman—to write well."

In his 60s Fairley resumed painting, which he contends is the especially appropriate medium for the late years: "It's less subjective, brings in the outer world." And he goes on: "Painting has nothing to do with my state of mind. It's not like poetry. I'll write whenever I'm in the mood; on the contrary, I paint every chance I can take."

When he began painting again it was in portraiture. Again a "happy accident" delivered to him in London, England, the English portrait painter, Barbara Niven. To Fairley's protests that he could never hope to do portraits, she responded matter-of-factly, "Try a head," and shoved both the opportunity and the materials at him. "I've painted heads ever since."

The question of why Fairley stopped painting at all still nagged at me. He said, to my surprise, that he needed more encouragement, and again remarked on how filled his life had become with university busyness. Since he had retired late, at age 70, under the old system, I was curious to know what retirement meant to Fairley. "All it meant to me," he said, "was that I had more time to do the things I liked."

By now a younger artist friend of Fairley had come in for tea. As we talked, it struck me that this particular Ulyssean adult seemed to live life very objectively. I tried out on him my anecdote about the Toronto publisher brooding over his "daily" loss of neurons. Fairley frowned slightly,, and said emphatically, "I never think of it. I live as much outside myself as possible, obeying the outside impulses."

It was now 6 p.m., a good time to end the first visit of what might become a friendship. Still, I managed one more question. Fairley obviously was still a reader; new books dotted the livingroom, and there was evidence that he had been into them. But what of music? "There's a stereo around the corner," evidently with quite a few records at hand. It turned out that Fairley's passion is Handel.

My host shook my hand warmly at the door and urged me to return any time I wished. "Besides, I lunch every Tuesday at the Arts and Letters Club, if you can be there."

It is still raining as I go out into the street, but now the rain seems warm and hospitable. I am enchanted.

This remarkable Ulyssean man, by opting for life, not only fills his own path with light but the paths of younger adults to whom his great age is not a barrier but a bridge. In Fairley's case, the painting which is the central motif of his late years is also the force which provides him with a special circle of younger friends who, along with older companions from the campus days and from the Arts and Letters Club, help him to externalize his thoughts and maintain his creative engagement with life.

Another interesting example of the choice of painting as a late second career is the work of Lachlan MacLean Morrison, a former Ontario civil servant who at 70 exhibited a collection of twenty-two oils in a Toronto gallery, all of the paintings done during the previous two years in bars and taverns where Morrison finds the people who fill his canvases. Morrison, who for health reasons cannot drink himself, and who has a hearing impairment which shuts out most of the noise of the bar, makes his sketches there, and then paints his subjects on masonite or board when back at his tiny studio. Kay Kritzwiser's recent account of Morrison and his wife Helen in *The Globe and Mail* brings out strikingly the way in which routine can be allied with Ulyssean adventures. She writes: "The pattern of the Morrisons' days is predictable. 'We watch television until perhaps 10 o'clock,' his wife said. 'Then Lauchie gets into a pair of old paint-stained pajamas and comes into this corner of the kitchenette.' He sets up an ordinary stepladder with a small table nearby. The current painting hangs on hooks on the stepladder. He mixes his oils in old egg cartons, tries out his colours on an age-worn palette, then gets to work. At daylight, he goes to bed. 'And I can't wait to come out into the kitchen to see what he's accomplished in the night,' his wife said."

The late emergence of an artistic talent which then provides the thrust for Ulyssean later years can occur in settings and arenas unbelievably different from the scholarly backgrounds and the glowing tea hours of retired professors. Clementine Hunter is a black painter, age 91, living in her birthplace, Natchitoches, Louisiana. Here is the saga—it is hard to call it anything else—of a Ulyssean adult who did not put brush to canvas until she was over age 60, yet within a few years had the pleasure of seeing Edward Steichen choose one of her paintings "to illustrate an essay he wrote on the meaning of a picture—the inner vision—which sets it apart as a work of art." (The quotation is from a perceptive interview by Mary Gibson, in *Family Circle* magazine, August, 1973.) Clementine Hunter had no formal education; she was for years a farm hand, picking cotton, then a worker at the Melrose Plantation in the Cane River county of Louisiana. One evening, according to the writer and critic Francois Mignon, who was then a guest at the Melrose Plantation, Clementine Hunter simply appeared at his door with several tubes of used oil paints which she had discovered, and announced that she, too, could "mark a picture". Mignon said, "When I told her to keep the paints, I never dreamed of the talent that was about to be released. At dawn the very next day, she returned with her first picture, a vivid primitive scene. Her talent was unmistakable and exciting."

Yet Hunter's talent had been unactualized for sixty years! She has now achieved a certain modest fame, and she is still—thirty years after that summer evening—vigorously producing still lifes, primitives, glowing flower studies, and murals. Mary Gibson's report describes her "standing straight-limbed and proud in a pert blue-flowered dress with big beaded blue earrings, very much a model for her own paintings." She lives in her small house close to the Melrose grounds, chopping her own wood, planting her own garden. Perhaps the earthy simplicity of her life contributes to the vivid humanity which is found all through her painting. It is in the paintings that Hunter's Ulyssean self appears—hardy, independent, life-loving and, even through her portrayals of old days and old customs in the South, expressing the universality of the human condition. In all this one sees much of the "integration" of self which Erik Erikson defined as the redeeming and at least partly victorious way of concluding human life. In Hunter's work, as symbolic of her self and life, we also see the creative choice of the right options in Robert Peck's system of alternatives.

Whether they produce the Ulyssean adult or not, the arts have of course provided a therapy for older adults in times of critical strain or crisis. Thus, Eric McLean, music critic of *The Montreal Star,* tells how the aunt of one of his friends, "a lady in her sixties who had gone through a period of deep depression during which she lost weight, energy, and all interest in social contacts, was persuaded to take up the recorder." McLean goes on to narrate how growing interest in the instrument led to the restoration of her health and morale. Renewal through individual use of the recorder led also to a reawakening of social involvements: 'Now blooming in her early seventies, she is an enthusiastic joiner-in with groups of amateur musicians." In fact, she had achieved a Ulyssean victory.

McLean writes with a sympathy and insight rare among experts and professionals in the musical world on the subject of frustrated would-be learners of instruments who cannot seem to find anything tailor-made for them except music appreciation courses at the conservatories: "We know that the eager but embarrassed forty-year-old is looking for a place to address himself for guidance where he will not find himself, like a doltish Li'l Abner, sitting in the midst of a passle of twelve-year-olds". He cites with enthusiasm the English industrialist W. W. Cobbett as an example of finding oneself in one of the arts (in this case music) in late adulthood. Cobbett was born in 1847 in Blackheath, England, and made a fortune as the founder and chairman of the Scandinavia Belting Company. He retired at 60, and devoted the next thirty years of his life to chamber music, offering prizes for competitions, and scholarships for talented musicians. Cobbett had long been an amateur musician, but dedicating his whole life to it from the ages of 60 to 90 was Ulyssean. Besides, he began the considerable adventure in his 70s of attempting to compile an encyclopedia of chamber music, which in fact he published in two volumes as the *Cyclopedic Survey of Chamber Music,* when he was 82. Cobbett found that taking part in chamber music recitals renewed him, and he put forward an unusual argument for the advantages of playing a musical instrument as against painting or writing:

> "The movements of brush and pen are imperceptible, but to play a violin means constant vibration in every nerve and fibre of the body, and it is this vibration which gives to cham-

ber music practice the therapeutic value of which, I may add, my medical friends are all convinced. . . . I am not exceptionally robust, but the considerable strain involved in three hours' strenuous playing of quartets and sonatas not only leaves me unfatigued, but with a greater sense of buoyancy when the last note is heard than when the first note was sounded."

Whatever else was true of the writer of this statement, *writing in his 80s,* he had achieved something far beyond successful personal therapy from the arts. He had achieved a major Ulyssean adventure in his life at age 60, and enlarged it in his 70s so that by age 90, when Cobbett reached "the Happy Isles", he could look back on a long odyssey which was in effect almost another life.

So varied are the approaches to the Ulyssean life, and so diverse are the personalities of those adults who qualify as Ulyssean, that it is difficult to compose a catalogue of their characteristics as, for example, Abraham Maslow did for his "self-actualized adults." Perhaps this is the way it should be: with all respect and admiration for Maslow, one cannot help feeling that he locked himself into too specified and didactic a description of the self-actualized person. For example, could a person not be highly *self*-actualized at 60 although his life violated half of Maslow's fourteen desired traits reflecting self-actualization, provided that special creative powers and dynamics of the personality flooded him with light and the capacity to grow?

Frank Barron recognized this problem of the all-too-satisfying comprehensive definition when, in the course of his own work as a research psychologist he became fascinated with the question of what made, in his words, "delightful normal people" tick. Barron studied a substantial sample and emerged with a catalogue of characteristics. He also noted that at a conference of psychoanalysts, psychiatrists, and psychologists dealing with "the goals of psychotherapy," there was a considerable consensus on what were the characteristics of a "psychologically healthy human being".

The most commonly mentioned traits were: 1. accuracy of perception of reality; 2. stable body functioning and freedom from psychosomatic disorders; 3. absence of hostility and anxiety; 4. capacity for friendly and co-operative relations; 5. spontaneity and warmth; and 6. social responsibility. Barron listened, he tells us, "in comfort and mild edification" until there drifted across his mind the images of a dozen great creators who not only lacked a number of these qualities or skills, but had some quite opposite characteristics—yet was it possible simply to dismiss them or classify them as psychologically unhealthy? His own list of traits discovered in the delightful young people in his own study seemed too pat to him. Nor did his own studies seem to confirm L. S. Kubie's thesis that neurosis only inhibits, never promotes, creativity. (The reference here to Kubie is my own: readers who care to pursue his point of view, which is not mine, will find it in Kubie's *Neurotic Distortion of the Creative Process.*)

Thus if one were able to invite dozens of Ulyssean adults mentioned in this book, and hundreds of others who could be nominated by readers, to a kind of gala event where the Ulyssean people could take time to observe one another and to exchange experiences, and to be joined by those of us who are fascinated by the Ulysseans, we would surely be struck by the difficulty of devising some well tailored formula for the Ulyssean life and personality. Some would seem "self-actualized", in Maslow's terms; some would seem to have large deficiencies of personality; some would be flooded with success; some confronted with huge reverses of fortune; some would be physically buoyant, some almost immobilized.

Not surprisingly, Ulysseans appear who seem light-years apart in their approaches to self-growth—a fundamental criterion. Thus, Bernard Berenson, the most noted art critic of the twentieth century, was at the very end of his life on earth still engaged in a search for the deeper meanings of the self—this might be called an inland, or inward, odyssey. The journals which he kept from age 88 to 93 are enthralling, and show Berenson in full possession of his powers. He records many impressions of visitors to his villa in Italy, as well as external events, but it is the adventure of his ideas and insights which lends excitement to these late-life entries. Similarly, as mentioned previously, Jung, at age 80, and aided by Aniela Jaffé as transcriber, composed one of the most unusual autobiographies ever recorded, devoted chiefly to Jung's extraordinary experiences in the revelatory world of dreams. Jung's role is that of the mountaineer among the mysterious and awesome ranges and abysses of the inner spirit: part of the domain of the unknown self, the quintessential self. In this function, Jung was not simply reminiscing about old experiences, but reporting new and arresting episodes, and fresh insights which constituted a veritable spiritual or psychodynamic odyssey with its own excitements, dangers, encounters, and rewards.

Seemingly poles apart from these probers of the *inner* self, are the Ulyssean adults who attach themselves to social and political causes heavily involving the persona, the public self, which can be seen to respond and to change in various ways. These active, externalized Ulysseans likewise meet the criteria of sustained creative performance, the acts of will required to accomplish this, and the choice of growth-options in later life. What we cannot have, but can only surmise, is evidence of continuing growth in their inner or quintessential self. However, we do seem to have marvellous examples of all of these forces in action.

Bertrand Russell is perhaps the most notable modern example of an externalized Ulyssean. Russell fulfilled Simone de Beauvoir's exhortation to the very old that they should attach themselves to passionate and burning causes. In the massive autobiography which he completed only a few years before his death at age 97 in 1970, Russell defined the inner flames which had burned undimmed through his life: "Three passions, simple but overwhelmingly strong, have governed my life: the longing for love, the search for knowledge, and unbearable pity for the suffering of mankind." And how did he feel he had fared, as he reviewed his enormously long life? He felt, he said, that only one yearning—the yearning for love —had been fully satisfied, and this only when he was 80 and married his fourth wife, Edith Finch, a 52-year-old American. He felt that he had achieved "a little" of knowledge, "not much"; while as for assuagement of his "unbearable pity" for mankind's suffering, he wrote: "Echoes of cries of pain reverberate in my heart. Children in famine, victims tortured by oppressors, helpless old people (a hated burden for their sons), and a whole world of loneliness, poverty, and pain make a mockery of what human life should be. I long to alleviate this evil but I cannot, and I too suffer."

He suffered, but he also knew joy throughout his life. He had remained open to experience (young people always thronged around him); he had grown continuously; he had been creative as both a thinker and a writer, and as a leader of causes, often intensely unpopular (he organized the highly biased International Peace Court at Stockholm in 1967, and was, of course, accused by his critics of being "senile"). He had lived, not one life, but seven or eight—as mathematician, philosopher, leader of social and political causes, prolific writer, exponent of sexual freedom, educator, conversationalist, and friend of an extraordinary circle of people extending from Alfred Tennyson to Graham Greene and Jean-Paul Sartre. He was only 28 when he engaged in one of the great creative sunbursts of his life: *The Principles of Mathematics*, of which he wrote 200,000 words in three months (Lehman would rejoice at this); yet his long life after age 55 was immensely creative in every sphere. The analysis of his inner self revealed by the autobiography has to be derived from a complex network of actions, positions, ideas, and insights: but at no time have we any doubt at all that we are in the presence of a magnificent Ulyssean.

Russell's life splendidly presented the qualities of creative performance and of growth-of-self as shown in *both* the contemplative and the intensely socially active Ulyssean adult. Vivid examples exist, however, of a type of later-life performer much further removed from the introspective worlds of Berenson, Jung, and Gide, and closer to what Beauvoir meant when she suggested that older adults can be galvanized by passionate causes. A remarkable example is provided by the Canadian public health physician, Gordon Anderson Bates, described with understandable excitement by the columnist Sidney Katz of *The Toronto Star*, in March, 1971, when Bates was 85.

Bates has been a crusader all his life (this is not the same thing as being the kind of person who "goes through life looking for the manager"). Still actively at work in 1975 as director of the Health League of Canada, he gained early attention as a young physician in heading a movement for legislation to control venereal disease. Almost sixty years later, with the VD problem again resurgent in the country, Bates added it to the list of situations which must be reviewed with the objective of developing new strategies and defences. His views are often explosive and extreme, and the logic is not always impeccable (what is one supposed to do with Bates's claim that he has "seen at least 100,000 men with VD, and not a single clergyman among them! . . . We must persuade the young not to act like alley cats.") But the passion of his attachment to his various causes is precisely what Beauvoir was talking about. Thus, when Bates noted that few among the perhaps more than 150,000 victims of Parkinson's Disease in Canada could obtain L-dopa, a new and potent drug to help control the disease, he felt hot indignation and he was not interested in preserving medical niceties and protocols. Katz reports that Bates's blue eyes "blazed with indignation" as he said, "The specialists, like neurologists, are narrow-minded. They think they're the only ones skilled enough to administer L-dopa. And the general practitioners are apparently uninformed, ill-informed, or apathetic." Constant badgering of physicians, hospitals, and government health agencies has led, Bates reports, to one important gain: the University of Toronto medical students are now taught how to use L-dopa in future practice.

Bates has explosive views about the silly custom in present-day society that retirement should come by at least age 65. His response to a question by Katz about his own retirement was heated: "Retire? Never! A person can keep going as long as he wants to. I'll never quit. I'm working 15 hours a day. Look at the things I have to do!" And indeed he is not short of personal projects and professional causes. At 75 Bates flew to Paris, lived with a Parisian family, attended a Sorbonne course, and learned French. He returned to Canada to form the Alliance Canadien, and to join half-a-dozen French language clubs in Toronto. He drives around in a bright yellow Packard touring car, custom-built for the Prince of Wales when the future Edward VIII visited his Alberta ranch in the 1920s.

Needless to say, this veteran of many past health crusades—to fluoridate water, to pasteurize milk, to compel immunization for diphtheria, and in general to support the forces of preventive medicine—is intensely interested in the extension not only of the working life, but of life itself. He studied reports from Russia on the large numbers of enormously long-lived people near the Caspian Sea, and checked further with Paul Dudley White, the noted American heart specialist who visited some of the Georgian communities, and decided that the secret of longevity lay in a simple, abstemious life, non-polluted air, no retirement, and maintenance of an even temper and an optimistic disposition. Bates told Sidney Katz that he himself neither smokes nor drinks, eats lightly with the emphasis on non-fat protein foods, walks a mile a day, and usually goes to bed by 11 p.m. Bates was then able to work out an analogy with the famous Thomas Parr, a 156-year-old wonder still living at the time of Charles I, who (if one can believe it) is alleged to have subsisted throughout his life on cottage cheese, dry bread, and water. Parr, according to Dr. Bates's account, was taken as an exhibit to the King's court in London where he was plentifully supplied with meat, pastries, and wine. "Parr didn't last long after that," Bates told Sidney Katz, presumably with relish.

In 1971 Bates's greater passion was to secure investigations into the neglect of preventive medical agencies by various United Appeals and voluntary health organizations. He makes frequent sorties to Ottawa to apply pressure from his Health League of Canada upon the federal Ministry of Health—Bates was, you will remember, 85 years of age at the time of the interview. His late Ulyssean life is highly externalized. One might interpret his positiveness and his explosiveness as a late-age syndrome of rigidity and intolerance; but the blue eyes probably always "blazed with indignation," and the cutting-edge of his productive life was almost certainly relentless attack. As for openness to experience, perhaps two symbols will do: the French lessons in Paris and the remarkable yellow Packard. Creativity? The foundation of Alliance Canadien, the development of new causes in preventive medicine or new approaches to old causes, the L-dopa campaign, and new studies on longevity. With so highly externalized a personality as that of Gordon Bates, it is impossible to discern what may be going on in the quintessential self—but continuing growth is clearly discernible in the whole man. He is demonstrably a Ulyssean adult.

The sustained, passionate devotion to a cause galvanizes late adults in many political and social arenas, some of them still in positions of power. For example, the astonishing Chou En-lai fascinated Mark Gayn, the Canadian journalist, when he interviewed Chou, then 72, in 1971. Gayn is an able and tough observer of the modern People's Republic of China, and the last person to be taken in by postures and facades. He was enchanted with the premier: "He still looked indestructible—lean, erect, physically fit, intellectually dazzling. The interview ran for more than three hours, but he showed no signs of fatigue." Gayn was struck by the probing curiosity and agility of Chou's mind.

This also was the impression of the Australian-born Harvard professor, Ross Terrill, who met Chou in 1972. Terrill was very much aware that he was meeting one of the three or four major architects of a titanic revolution in which, by the nature of revolutions, millions of people had died in order to achieve the desired rebirth. Terrill did not overlook the tough expression, the steely eyes: "from a side angle, a rather flat nose takes away all his fierceness. The mouth is low in the face and set forward tautly, giving a grim grandeur to the whole appearance." Terrill was clearly impressed by the formidable power of Chou's presence—yet his chief impression was of the premier's youthful resilience in manner and speech: "Recalling his amazing career over half a century, I marvelled at his freshness."

This displayed itself in the lively virtuosity and ease with which Chou engaged Whitlam, the Australian Labour Party leader (with whom Terrill had come to the Great Hall of the People) in a far-flung review of international politics. While he talked, Chou sat back "in a wicker chair, wrists flapping over the chair's arms . . . so relaxed as to be without bones, poured into the chair. Beside this loose-limbed willow of a man, Whitlam, hunched together in concentration, seems stiff as a pine." Without endorsing Chou's ideas, Terrill was struck by the sense of vision that seemed to impregnate his world views. Gayn, who is perhaps equally fascinated by the octogenarian Mao Tse-tung as "a perpetual rebel", sees Chou as the strategist and the stabilizer, able to live through successive and unnerving changes of the revolutionary currents, with immense stamina and the will to fight for convictions to which he is deeply and passionately attached.

Chou, incidentally, has for years broken the pious convention that the proper time for older adults to go to sleep is about 11 p.m. He himself works until 4 or 5 a.m. and then sleeps until mid-morning. Any sleeping arrangement in the later years is good if it accords with the individual body chemistry and the cultural lifestyle of the person: for example, older adults who live in or near great cities and who love classical music can hear hours of splendid recordings hitherto unknown to them played from midnight on through the channels of certain FM stations. An unpleasant illustration of a violation of individual needs is the retirement home or nursing home regulation demanding "lights out" at 11 p.m. or earlier, as though the inhabitants were children and as though they had no individual preferences. (One home considered it an outrage that a vigorous old man wanted to shower at 11 p.m.) These are, of course, the institutions which provide no books, no wine, no facilities for growth. They are matched by the spouse who insists on identical sleeping schedules for his (her) partner in marriage. With the obvious exception of physical emergencies, and with the provision that 11 p.m. sleepers also have rights, the later years in general need not "lights out", but *lights on*, with more music, more conversation, more loving company, more zestful talk about the uncreated things in the great world, many more small personal odysseys. And more working schedules for those who, like Chou En-lai, cherish the hours after midnight, when they take themselves to a high hill from which they do not have to descend until the late morning.

The passionate cause has a way of being associated with "great" leaders and "great" issues, as though the world of human values and achievements were all slide-rules and weighing scales. In fact, a cause involving human rights and the preservation of beauty and civilization is just as splendid when played out in a tiny arena. What might perhaps be called "confrontative democracy" in our time is producing more and more men and women in their later years who lead or take part in movements or demonstrations designed to confront dehumanized bureaucrats or so-called "developers" where there is a need to protect and advance human needs and rights. None of these groups exclude older adults; sometimes the older adults exclude themselves. These groups are usually weak and need support, and adult people in late maturity who are open to experience and able to be lived with, are valuable because their commitment is not confused with having to fight Father at the same time, as is the case with some of the revolutionary young.

There is something about an involvement in good, passionate causes in one's later years that is highly renewing. The noted Canadian lawyer John J. Robinette, commenting in 1973 at age 68 on some of the pleasures of his career, unexpectedly named his participation in the protest against the Toronto Spadina Expressway as a "refreshing experience" which made him feel that he could break away from the perils of being "stodgy" and locked into rigid patterns.

One of the last photographs taken of the crusading American novelist, Upton Sinclair, when he was nearly 90, shows a face marked by age—there is no doubt that he is an old man—but radiant with a youthful smile, so eager and life-loving that one cannot look at it without a lift of the spirit. Here is manifest the ever-renewed self of a man who not only helped right certain terrible national evils with his early novels (which he had to publish himself), but in the years from age 50 also attached himself to certain causes such as EPIC (End Poverty in California), twice running for public office as candidate for governor and senator of the state, and on one occasion at least missing by a hair's breadth.

Nor does attachment to passionate causes usually demand money—just time, a great deal of commitment, and a sense of humour for the rough spots. So it is all the more astonishing that older adults of all classes and conditions have done so little to head up and take part in movements to improve the general lot of older people in our society. Surely this, for older adults, is the cause of causes! The reasons why so few participate seem clear enough: if one is poor, there is an ever-present fear of reprisals—largely illusory: one cannot be deprived of his old age pension; but still, the fear is there, like a cold mist seeping through everything. If one is rich, it's the sort of thing that isn't done. The central problem usually is the conventionality of the lifestyle; we have lived so long with the mask, adjusting our faces to the faces that we meet.

Yet there are many causes worth the passionate attention of older and very old adults which do not demand the added investment of stress and worry about one's image. Of all people, the old have usually the least to lose in expressing their opinions and taking up positions, and some of them show this by a liveliness and forthrightness of attitude and expression rare in their earlier years. And there is also a whole domain of personal "helping" exploits, small-scale creative enterprises which are fine in themselves and which can serve as the introductory country to more political and social involvement.

A case in illustration is a Ulyssean adult, now age 86, living in Vancouver. Yin Lo, a Chinese Canadian, is no less remarkable in his way than Chou En-lai, whose revolution placed Yin Lo where he is. A graduate in naval engineering from Cornell, a former supporter of Sun Yat-sen, a former "guerrilla banker" in South China during World War Two where he had to dodge the Japanese to pay out $1.5 million daily in remittances from overseas relatives of the Chinese, and then a merchant in Hong Kong, Yin Lo has created a whole cluster of enterprises designed to bring new activity and pleasure into the lives of neglected old people, especially of his Chinese group.

Lo obtained a $16,000 New Horizons grant from the federal government to expand the work of his organization, Chinese Elder Citizens (*Kei Hing Wooi*) which he had founded earlier. He has built the group up to about two hundred, with a programme of varied activities. Lo himself lives in a retirement home with forty other old men—the Immaculate Conception Oriental Home—where he volunteered to provide extra care for those among his fellow residents who need it. He did this because "I feel I'm such a fortunate old man. I led a very good life before, and *now it is my time to contribute. Wherever society needs my services, I go.*" (My italics.)

In the retirement home, Lo makes it his concern to see that no one feels abandoned. At the same time, he finds the company of children immensely refreshing and renewing, and he offered his services as a teacher's aide at an elementary school, filling in from time to time for English and Chinese lessons, and for other subjects as well. "I love children. They're very attracted to me, but I don't know why. Every time I see them I feel ten years younger." Lo noted the difference between the older adults necessarily confined at the home where he lives, and the group for whom he is providing a repertoire of new activities: "Once you get them out, a change becomes apparent. . . . They're spirited. They feel young and they act young."

A highly externalized Ulyssean, Yin Lo is light-years removed from the inner Ulyssean voyages into the self of Berenson, Jung, and Gide. Activity is the story of his life: "If I stay in one place and don't work, I get a headache. Sure, my days are pretty busy, but I can still spare time for more activity." And he adds, "Things move so fast . . . you've got to keep hopping"—an unsophisticated definition of the stress placed by the ever-changing macrocosmic society upon the microcosm of the individual life. In fact, for many contemplative older adults, Lo would probably be just too much. Yet he is incontestably a first-rate example of one type of Ulyssean adult: "I'm more or less adventuresome in spirit, and I always liked thrills. I hate to remain in old things."

8. NAKED ON THE SHORE

"And what if the powers above do wreck me out on the wine-dark sea? I have a heart that is inured to suffering and I shall steel it to endure that too. For in my day I have had many bitter and shattering experiences in war and on the stormy seas. So let this new disaster come. It only makes one more."

The speaker is Ulysses; the place, the island of the nymph-goddess Calypso, who has held Ulysses captive for seven years during his adventurous and trouble-filled voyage home; the time, the morning when Calypso, on the orders of Zeus, father of the gods, has told Ulysses that he may go, but that much misery still awaits him before he will see his wife, Penelope.

Helped by the goddess's gifts of working tools and the provision of woodlands, Ulysses cuts down twenty trees, trims them, and within four days has built a splendid boat, well provisioned with water, wine, and appetizing meats. Helped by a warm, gentle breeze springing up at Calypso's command, he sets out on what he hopes will be the last leg of his long homeward journey. For seventeen days, in fact, Ulysses sailed on fair seas under a calm sky, steering by the stars. But on the eighteenth day his implacable enemy, the god Poseidon, raised terrible storms and giant waves—seas so mountainous that, "great heart" though he was, "Ulysses' knees shook and his spirit quailed."

The unrelenting storms destroy his craft. Ulysses finally has to strip, and thrust himself into the monstrous foaming seas, where he swims for two days and nights until finally, partly by his strength and courage, partly by his shrewdness and commonsense, he is able to reach the land which, just before Poseidon's raising of the tempest, he had seen looking "like a shield on the misty sea."

Splendid physical specimen though he yet was, Ulysses seemed for a while more dead than alive: "all his flesh was swollen and streams of brine gushed from his mouth and nostrils. Winded and speechless, he lay there too weak to stir, overwhelmed by his terrible fatigue." He was a king, yet at that moment he owned nothing but his life; he was friendless in a strange country. Naked on the shore, he faced the hard decision whether to sleep overnight beside the wet river bed, chancing chills and illness; or climb the hill, lie down in dense undergrowth, and risk being attacked by beasts of prey. No wonder "he grimly faced his plight."

After reflection, the hungry and naked king decided to crawl into a shelter on the wooded hill, where he fell asleep. In the morning his fortunes turned. The lovely princess Nausicaa with her maidens came to the river to wash, and their shouts of joy wakened Ulysses who, after some understandable hesitation, "crept out from under the bushes, after breaking off with his great hand a leafy bough from the thicket to conceal his naked manhood." At the sight of this salt-encrusted warrior, whom the poet compares to "a mountain lion . . . with fire in his eyes," the maidens scuttled off in every direction, except the young princess, in whom Ulysses soon found that he had a courageous and warm admirer. Nausicaa provided him with olive oil, a cloak and a tunic, and took him to her father Alcinous, ruler of the country. This was the turning-point in Ulysses' fortunes: he was able to reach Ithaca without further peril.

Of all Ulysses' qualities, the one that makes him unforgettable is not so much his capacity for success, as his intense humanity and intrepidity in the face of failure—and Failure was his frequent companion, no less terrifying because so often sent by forces he could not control: the capricious and hostile gods from Olympus. Yet even in the midst of groans and burning tears for comrades lost to the Cyclops, or to Circe's magic, or to Poseidon's storms, Ulysses' fine mind was still at work on how to overcome these disasters, and the strong will, checked for a little while like a naked and battered swimmer resting exhausted on the shore, resumed its Ulyssean journey.

The Ulyssean life—the life of attempting creative and adventurous sorties in the later adult years, when most adults take refuge in the comfort of self-obliterating routines—is bound many times to encounter failure. Its practitioners do not, of course, court failure—courting failure is the domain of the death-wishers, not the life-wishers—but neither do they pretend that it is non-existent. The Ulyssean life is possible in spite of failure, *in the midst of failure*. Furthermore, the Ulysseans have often known enough failure in their earlier lives to recognize it for what it is: sometimes the result of one's own human misjudgments and missteps, but sometimes—many times—the result of circumstances, the result of Fate.

This truth of the human condition is an important corrective to the universal "I'm not OK" guilt feeling of Western man: the terrible (and false) conviction that whenever and however failure occurs, somehow it is all one's own fault. In fact, this is exactly the neurosis to be expected in a culture which adores success and in which credit for whatever the "success" may be is typically and publicly attributed to the individual himself.

Rudyard Kipling, who had certain Ulyssean traits himself, touched unerringly on this point in his famous poem, *If*, which whatever its merits as pure poetry, resonantly strikes the chord of the hazards and inherent heroism in certain Ulyssean adventures in later life:

> "If you can make one heap of all your winnings,
>   And risk them on one turn of pitch and toss,
> And lose, and start again at your beginnings,
>   And never breathe a word about your loss. . . ."

Kipling is certainly talking about men of at least middle age, because he speaks of stooping and building one's life and work again "with worn-out tools."

To live the later years as a Ulyssean may mean never to encounter major failure at all. So invigorating and beautiful can be the hundreds of Ulyssean paths and the principalities of the mind and spirit they lead to, that the inevitable disappointments and setbacks encountered will take little of the radiance away. Still, it is crucial to remember that many ventures in the Ulyssean life may entail the possibility of huge reversals; and especially that Ulyssean people may often be assaulted by uncontrollable forces which dare them to carry on with the high adventure and creativity of their lives.

The Ulyssean answer to great and inexplicable misfortune was furnished by Ulysses himself: to say in effect, "Why has this happened to me? How have I deserved this? Is there no end to such catastrophes?" thus proving that one is a human being; then after this first flood of sorrow and despair, which coincides with one's being naked on the shore, in a strange and lonely country, and bruised and wounded by storms and mysterious forces, to seek new imaginative strategies to recommence the Ulyssean journey.

One Ulyssean exercise is to look upon misfortune as a *learning experience*. Friends of mine have taught me much about the utility of this approach—Helen Ansley of Seattle, Washington, a devoted participant in SAGE, telling me that the rough business of recovering at 75 from a broken hip and having to have a steel pin inserted was "a learning experience"; and Professor Virgil Logan at 68 remarking how intently and with what interest he observed the doctors' arrangements to help him recover from a cerebral hemorrhage. And then there was Percy Wyndham Lewis's wonderful demonstration of this attitude, in his blindness, at 71, writing his *third-last* novel "in silence, hour after hour, dropping each page as it was completed into a deep wooden tray on the floor at his side."*

*Hugh Kenner

Modern times have furnished some striking examples of Ulyssean people whom Fate, in addition to their own decisions and actions, placed naked on the shore, and whose creative imagination as much as their undoubted courage made it possible for them to resume interrupted adventures or launch new ones, or both. Examples will leap to the minds of readers from people they know personally or from some in the pantheon of famous individuals which most of us keep somewhere in our mind. I suggest a few who have intrigued and instructed me.

An interesting case in politics was Harry S. Truman, who began life as the son and grandson of pioneer farmers in Missouri, and spent eleven of his young adult years as a farmer, and a good farmer. Because of a rare malformation of the eyes, Truman had to pass up the conventional sports of boys, and became an omnivorous reader, especially of history, and a competent pianist. Years later, in the Presidency, when he turned to the piano for recreation and escape, he played Chopin, whose music he had always loved. He was later supposed to know only enough of the piano to thump out the Missouri Waltz.

In spite of his bad eyes, he managed to get into World War One, and emerged with a captaincy, and the warm comradeship of hundreds of men attached to his battery. It was chiefly the support of this veterans' group which launched him into politics after the failure of his men's clothing firm, due to the depression. (Truman spent years trying to pay off the creditors.) Truman had the support of the powerful Pendergast organization in Missouri, but the evidence is clear enough that far from being its tool, he was sand in the machine. As a result, he waited for years for the preferments to higher offices which went to more pliable associates. When he was finally nominated and elected, it was because he was of more value to the Pendergasts than they to him. No link has ever been found between Truman and political scandal in Missouri, nor will there be.

When he was chosen by Roosevelt to be his running-mate as Vice-Presidential candidate in 1944, it was not because Truman was a nonentity—although the Vice-Presidency was designed for nonentities—but because he had become a respected member of the Senate. He had completed two years of law school by evening study back in Kansas City and had been a county court judge for ten years; he had kept up his omnivorous reading and homework for senate committees. Although he was a dedicated Democrat, he was very much his own man. On one occasion he sent Roosevelt's press secretary a cryptic message just after supporting a difficult Roosevelt measure: "Tell the President to stop treating me like an office boy."

Roosevelt died in April, 1945, and Truman was catapulted into

the Presidency. After a fumbling start, at which point *Time* maga-
bine with flip omnipotence forecast of him that as he was "a man
of distinct limitations . . . there are likely to be few innovations
and little experimentation", Truman's first administration became
marked by a series of extraordinary events: the Hiroshima attack,
the creation of an Atomic Energy Commission, the magnificent
Marshall Plan to assist in the rebuilding of war-ravaged Europe
(it might as appropriately have been called the Truman Plan),
new Fair Employment Practices legislation, new unemployment
insurance legislation, recognition of the state of Israel (with limitations, however displeasing to some Jewish groups).

In retrospect, and including the problems of a complex network of international chess moves during the continuing period
of the Cold War—NATO, for example, did not formally emerge
until 1949, but was planned for more than a year in advance—Truman's short first Presidency looks rather dazzling, not least in contrast to the comparative somnolence of the subsequent Eisenhower
terms. Still, powerful blocs of the Democratic party were sulking
by the time the nomination months re-appeared in the spring and
early summer of 1948. Ambitious politicians, including notably the
sons of Franklin Roosevelt, (Eleanor, after some hesitation, sided
against her sons) could not believe that the stop-gap President from
Missouri should have another term. For those who chose not to
adjust their blinkers, Truman seemed to lack the dimensions of a
world leader, a "great President": he was, it seemed, too earthy,
too gauche, too stubborn, too party-ridden.

A glamorous candidate appeared from the Republican side:
Thomas Dewey, the governor of New York State, who had once
been the gang-busting district attorney of New York City. The
media, who had never grasped Truman's dimensions, possibly because of his self-destructive tendency to assign heavy credit for new
ideas to legislative and administrative colleagues, had consistently
downplayed his record, and now thought they beheld certain disaster for the Democratic Party in the 1948 elections. (There were,
of course, enlightened exceptions.) Conservative congressmen, both
Republican and Democrat, viewed the "interim" President very
much as conservative members of the Curia must have viewed
John XXIII when they discovered they had an aging (in John's case,
frankly old) tiger on their hands.

Truman was by now 64 years old, no longer a young or even a
younger-middle-aged man. He had been a farmer at 22, a soldier
at 33, a merchant at 36; he had found a career as a publicly elected
administrative official in his 40s, had become a senator at 50, and
an unwilling Vice-President at 60. In a way, nothing had prepared
him for anything else, and yet everything had prepared him for
everything else—notably how to handle failure and the threat of
failure sent by whatever is the modern version of Poseidon.

In the suffocating July heat of the Democratic convention hall in Philadelphia, Truman was indeed renominated, but he rose to accept the nomination in an atmosphere of oppressive gloom. Certain sections of the delegates were unhappy or hostile; the new and prestigious opinion polls week after week rated Truman as being hopelessly behind his younger, seemingly more exciting, and so far unmarked Republican opponent.

In her biography of her father, Margaret Truman would have one believe that from the beginning of this desperate situation in 1948 her father alone exuded quiet confidence. This may indeed have been the outer impression—it is just too much to believe that there were no inward groans. Aside from the odds which seemed to have piled up against him through no fault of his own, Truman must have been terribly wounded by the contemptuous public rejection of himself as leader by sectors of the political party which was very dear to him. Yet at exactly this moment of nakedness on a very barren shore, the bright shrewd mind was at work: not just the courageous nature of the man—courage was not enough, courage alone would take you down like the valiant but misguided captain drowning with his ship—but the imaginative mind, the Ulyssean mind which at 64 was still young with hope and large plans.

The creativity of politics is necessarily a creativity of ideas— that is, ideas are in themselves the material of the art: ideas at their best about ways to improve the lot of the people, and about how to handle people skilfully enough to make the ideas realities. What Truman needed in his acceptance address was not just fighting words, although from his opening sentences in the huge, perspiring, despondent convention far after midnight on the national radio networks, it was evident that his cocky promise that he would defeat the Republicans took the delegates by surprise and galvanized them: "Senator Barkley and I will win this election and make those Republicans like it—don't you forget that." For twenty minutes, in his usual plain language, Truman lambasted the Eightieth Congress which had blocked and excoriated him and which had then had the gall to place the blame for unpassed measures on the President's doorstep. It was an exciting, electrifying performance—but it was not enough. He had saved the best, the imaginative, wholly unexpected idea for the very end of his address:

> "On the 26th day of July, which out in Missouri we call Turnip Day, I am going to call Congress back and ask them to pass laws to halt rising prices, to meet the housing crisis—which they are saying they are for, in their platform.
>
> At the same time, I shall ask them to act upon other vitally needed measures . . .
>
> Now my friends, if there is any reality behind that

Republican platform, we ought to get some action from a
short session of the Eightieth Congress. They can do this job
in fifteen days, if they want to do it. They will still have
time to go out and run for office."

The effect of the statement was not just the pandemonium
which broke loose in the convention hall itself. Across the continent
millions of radio listeners (including great numbers of Canadians,
like myself) felt the electric euphoria of hearing a wholly unexpected stratagem outlined in the crisp Missouri voice of the be-
leaguered President. It was the stratagem of attack, of a supreme
and cool disregard for the odds. In fact, when the dismayed and
angry congressmen assembled for their unheard-of brief pre-
election session later in the summer, little happened. But the
initiative was never lost.

Truman had one other major creative plan, far larger and
equally aggressive, in his fight to retain the kingdom that foes and
sometime friends were trying to take away from him: the whistle-
stop campaign. While Governor Dewey was flying back and forth
across the United States to mass rallies and uttering sonorities
which would not rock the boat, Truman made hundreds of stops
by train to crowds that steadily swelled as the campaign progressed
—warm, friendly crowds that responded to Truman's intimate
speaking style and his relentless attacks on congressional apathy
and the smug self-satisfaction with which he claimed the big
interests were backing his opponent. He was able to make millions
of people feel that somehow his cause was their cause, as to a substantial degree it undoubtedly was.

Even so, Drew Pearson had drawn up in readiness his forecast
of the members of the Dewey cabinet; four days before the election
Life magazine published a photograph of the "next President",
that is, Thomas E. Dewey, travelling by ferry boat across San
Francisco Bay. On election night, the new Univac machine began
forecasting a Truman victory; engineers and announcers anxiously
conferred, and apologized for the machine's malfunction! Even
when at midnight Truman was far more than a million votes
ahead, one of the three or four best-known national commentators
kept insisting that he was sure to lose. A Chicago paper carried
the headline of Dewey's victory in the early morning hours even
as the man who couldn't lose was losing past recall. In fact, Truman got a greater proportion of the total vote than Roosevelt had
got in 1944: he had over three hundred of the votes in the Electoral
College, and he had carried a Democratic majority into Congress
with him.

Truman was 68 when he left the Presidency—still vigorous,
still intensely interested in human affairs. What Ulyssean adventures can ex-Presidents of the United States set out on? Still cele-

brities, although out of power, they drag hordes of curious sightseers wherever they go. Most of them, like all retired chief executives among politicians, become conventionalized persons: directors of large corporations, front names for humane causes. Truman survived his Presidency by twenty years. His deep affection for modest environments and plain people led him back to his old home in Independence where one superb Ulyssean act gave a kind of radiance to the last phase of his life. He was able to obtain the funds to build a library in the centre of the town, to contain millions of public papers which he had the right to take with him from the White House, thousands of private papers, books on history and politics, especially on the Truman era, and colourful murals. History remained his consuming love. His daughter recalls him reading Thucydides to his two young grandsons. And he continued far into his 80s to rise at dawn and to take the 6 a.m. walks which, during his Presidency, had astonished and exasperated the reporters.

Ulyssean women, too, in public careers, especially in the arts or in the humane professions or in hereditary sovereignties, have innumerable times been left naked upon the shore. In private life as well, widowhood and late divorce frequently present the same situation. There is something intensely moving in the sight of older women who begin the process of resuming their personal odyssey through the courage of simply holding on. The great achievement, however, is to begin new enterprises in creativity which are highly personal and idiosyncratic, no matter how small and timid at first.

There are many women from whom one can choose illustrations of the Ulyssean person living creatively in spite of failure, or in the midst of failure. My own examples are put forward simply because they fascinate me, and may intrigue some readers also. One is the Danish novelist, Isak Dinesen, in private life the Baroness Karen Blixen.

Karen Dinesen, as she was known before her marriage, was born in 1885, into a family of wealthy Danish merchants with high-placed political connexions. Her father, who committed suicide when Karen was 10, was a brilliant and versatile man with a marked literary gift which, however, he was reluctant to develop. Because Karen and her father had had a special rapport, his death affected her more than it did the three other children—she was enchanted by the colourful array of creative people, aristocrats, and politicians who had been her father's friends. She herself showed early talents for writing poetry, small plays and stories, and a distinct ability to draw portraits in charcoal. She studied briefly in Paris, and returning to Denmark began to be published in literary magazines. Thus far her life, bounded by a warm family circle (somewhat marred by the hostility which her mother's family felt for the suicide father) and by the pleasant artistic activities of well-to-do Danish people in the early 1900s, could have been replicated thousands of times in the lives of young women her own age across Europe—the Europe that was soon to disappear forever.

In 1913, Karen became engaged to a Danish aristocrat, Baron Bror von Blixen-Finecke, a year younger than herself. The marriage produced two immense and potentially catastrophic changes in her life. One was her husband's decision to emigrate to Africa where he wanted to buy land for a coffee plantation. The couple left for Mombasa in German East Africa in December, 1913, built a house, hunted lions, and in time bought a farm of eight hundred acres chiefly to raise coffee. The other event was that Karen contracted a venereal disease from the marriage which forced her return to Denmark for treatment before she had completed even a year in Africa. By that time the war was on; the progress of the ship was slow; and even when Karen reached Denmark she lost still further precious time in trying to make arrangements for treatment which would conceal the situation from her mother, a kind woman but a typical Victorian. There were no miracle drugs in those days. The best that Karen could do was to halt the advance of the disease; for the rest of her life complications remained to harass her physically. What the episode did to her emotional system can be imagined. She was a glowing, brilliant, warm-hearted girl, none of whose many photographs taken at the time give any inkling of the inner agony she must have known.

She returned to Africa, where in 1921 she and Bror Blixen separated, and for ten years she managed the farm alone as owner of the Karen Coffee Company, helped from time to time by her younger brother, Thomas, who had his sister's charm and zest for life, and had always been particularly close to her. Still, his visits could only be for a few weeks at a time. For ten years Karen Blixen was responsible for the management of this large African plantation. It was a lonely, burdensome role, relieved by her remarkably sensitive and warm understanding of the African people who worked on the farm, and of the neighbouring Masai and the Kikuyu, whose respect for her was shown in the title they gave her: "The Lioness."

Friends and relatives occasionally came out from Denmark to try to break the ring of loneliness. She had need of all the loyalty and company she could command: the coffee market was falling apart in the postwar years; as her markets closed, her debts rose. By the late 1920s it seemed impossible that she could save the farm, or indeed any personal assets. In the midst of this constant atmosphere of gloom and worry, three facets of her world filled her life with a certain beauty. One was her relationships with the native Kenyans and her undoubted simple joy in much of African daily life; another was that she had begun to fill the long, lonely evenings on the plantation by writing again: new stories began to flow from her pen, and she had high hopes of being published again in the Danish magazines. The third was a kind of personal miracle—she met an Englishman, a leader of safaris, whom she rapidly learned to cherish as a close intellectual friend and someone dear to her as a person: Denys Finch-Hatton, son of the Earl of Winchelsea and Nottingham, a radiant, handsome man then in his late 30s who had had a classical education at Eton and Oxford, loved music, and was a first-class athlete and pilot.

In him, Karen Blixen found the companion to whom she could read her stories and test out her ideas. She listened to the new ballet music of Stravinsky on his record player, and heard him sing Handel's songs. Life must have taken on fresh hope for Karen Blixen in the late 1920s. Perhaps the coffee market would right itself, after all; perhaps her manuscripts, now in the mail to Denmark, would give her a new sphere of creative life; perhaps in time her relationship with Denys, who would spend his evenings when he arrived from an air safari teaching her Latin, and Greek verse, and exploring the Bible, would develop into something even deeper and more lasting than dear friendship.

But Poseidon, or some other vindictive god, was watching Karen Blixen's brief journey on fair seas. The Danish journals returned her manuscripts; Denmark was not interested in what she had to write at this stage. The coffee markets collapsed: by late spring, 1931, Karen was certain that she had lost everything; even the sale of the house and plantation could not pacify her creditors. And on May 8, 1931, Denys Finch-Hatton flew his Gypsy Moth from the farm, saying that he would be back the following Thursday. Karen was waiting for him, but the plane never arrived. It had crashed on the flight from Mombasa to Voi, and Denys was killed.

Karen Blixen was now 46. She had lived her life to this point with love and creativity; even in the midst of the conventionalities and protocols of African farming, she had been remarkable for her sense of the needs and, far more, the rights of the native people. At one point she had seriously considered heading a movement to guarantee greater fairness and justice to the native Africans, and would have done so had not financial disaster overtaken her. She could have recouped much of her loss by selling her farm to developers who would carve it up and dispossess the native people who trusted her, but she refused to do so. (In the end this was the fate of her native friends and retainers, anyway.)

Now everything seemed lost. She bore in her body and inner

self the memory and marks, even the residual presence of a terrible disease of which she was the innocent victim. She had lost her plantation, and was in fact destitute. She had failed to regain entry to the literary world of the Danes, and thus to the second career which had seemed to shine ahead of her in the dark months and years of business depression. She had lost Denys Finch-Hatton, opening a wound so deep that thirty years later she was still in symbolic ways in her life remembering him, treasuring him. She was, in truth, naked on the shore.

She could at least go home—that is, to her mother's home—and she had in addition the unswerving support and affection of her brother, Thomas Dinesen. When Karen's ship from Mombasa reached Marseilles on August 19, 1931, Thomas was at the wharf to greet her. Clara Svendsen, in her biography of Karen Blixen, describes how when brother and sister met, Karen was annoyed that her stockings were sagging: in times of catastrophe, details like this often seem to symbolize and underline the disaster. She remarked later that her brother simply suggested going to a shop and buying a new pair of garters, which they did. This easy solution to one of the hundreds of problems that seemed to beset her gave Karen (so she later said) the stirrings of new hope.

Karen Blixen had already lost everything in "one turn of pitch-and-toss"—would she hazard another? Courage was not enough, although it was indispensable. Some imaginative stroke was necessary, some Ulyssean adventure, if this lonely, bankrupt, sorrowing woman was to bring some kind of reviving tide back into her life. Her first act was to look ahead, not back—except for essential books and manuscripts, she unpacked nothing from her African trunks and boxes for thirteen years. She then made an early and heroic decision: she would ask Thomas (who had had his own family for more than five years) to support her for two years while she stayed at her mother's house and wrote in English, for an English market, the stories that throbbed in her mind. She would do this, even although there was no publisher standing by—as indeed throughout the whole period that she wrote there was not.

The book she wrote was *Seven Gothic Tales*, destined to be one of the most famous European books of the century. It was finished within the two-year period. No publisher for it could be found in England. Karen went herself to London to urge the claims of the *Tales*, without success, and she returned, surely close to despair. Then her good angel, her brother, as certain of his sister's creative genius as Vincent Van Gogh's brother was of his, was able to make a contact through the American novelist, Dorothy Canfield, with the American market. The result was publication in the United States. (Its publisher could not resist it, but forecast that it would not sell.) Early in 1934, *Seven Gothic Tales* was chosen as a Book-of-the-Month Club selection, and the author, under the name of Isak Dinesen, was famous in England and America. The following year, when the Danish translation was published, celebrations were held in her honour in Copenhagen. Two years later, with the publication of her account of her life in Africa, *Out of Africa*, Isak Dinesen's fame was secure.

Karen Blixen died in September 1962, at 77. To the end of her long life she continued to produce stories, articles, and taped interviews. In spite of fragile health she travelled much, steadily developed her admirable gifts as a gardener, entertained friends from among the African people who visited her, and encouraged young writers and artists. Her photographs in the later years are filled with warm smiles.

In his foreword to the Clara Svendsen book, Frans Lasson gives a poignant glimpse of Dinesen's inner life. He remarks that Svendsen, who was Karen Blixen's secretary, had for years watched her, each night before going to bed, open the door to the yard, pause, then go to "Ewald's Room," so called because it had once been occupied two centuries earlier by the great Danish poet of that name. Finally, Clara Svendsen asked Karen Blixen what this invariable ritual meant. She explained that the door looked toward Africa, and that she went into Ewald's Room to look at the map of her African plantation. Frans Lasson adds that Blixen did not say that in the same room, always standing on the windowsill by her desk, and never mentioned by her, was the portrait of Denys Finch-Hatton. And Lasson suggests that all this expressed Blixen's longing for wings, her faithfulness to things living now only in the realm of her mind, and the unhealed wounds which enabled her to enrich her writing through the experience of suffering.

Just as forces of circumstance or whatever passes for fate in our time can deal out crushing blows against Ulyssean people, often when their hopes are high and prospects bright and fair, so also powers and events wholly outside their control can rescue them when the situation looks lost beyond recall. The intervention of these beneficent strokes of fortune really takes nothing away from the Ulyssean recovery: the intervention simply creates a new potential to the scene, which it is up to the Ulyssean man or woman to exploit or not.

Examples of this benign interference into Ulyssean dilemmas by outer forces abound, but two illustrations from the eighteenth and nineteenth centuries can make the point vividly. One was the case of George Frideric Handel; the other, a much less well-known episode from the life of Cardinal Newman. In both cases, forces beyond their personal control had halted, and in fact almost immobilized, these high creators, both in their later maturity— Handel was in his mid-50s, Newman well past 60. In both cases good fortune intervened to provide a possibility of recovery and both men seized the occasion to resume their Ulyssean journeys.

Handel was living in London in the early 1700s, where he had achieved an enormous success as a composer of Italian-style operas. Crowds packed the opera theatres to hear his music; he was a great favourite at court; and his creative powers seemed inexhaustible. Handel needed all his genius, because his appearance and manners were unprepossessing. He was grossly stout, awkward, often uncouth, imperious and difficult to deal with. This unattractive outer personality, however, partly concealed a noble inner spirit. He had many enemies in the envious musical world of London in the 1730s, one of them the formidable Prince of Wales; these he could handle, but not the tidal wave of financial failure and debt that came sweeping down upon him when the London audiences abandoned their interest in Italian opera and deserted his theatres. He wrote with his usual abundant creativity —what was said of Saint-Saens many years later could have been said with even greater truth of Handel, that he was throughout his life like a great flowering and ever-fruitful tree—but the market was gone. Simultaneously his health failed—the worst blow was a paralysing stroke from which he slowly recovered after a rest cure in France.

A fine and rarely-seen film about Handel's life, produced in Great Britain in 1947, shows in an especially moving way Handel's bachelor life in those lonely and bankrupt days, shadowed by the menace of the debtors' prison. Except for isolated walks at times when the streets were empty, the composer remained in the house which somehow he had been able to retain, brooding over the dark turn of events—naked on the shore. Then an extraordinary event occurred which was outside of his control. Late one summer morning a delegation of three men arrived from the Duke of Devonshire, to ask Handel to prepare a work for a charitable performance. Almost indifferently, the composer asked, did they have a theme in mind? Rather nervously the leader of the delegation suggested that something involving the New Testament had been discussed. The effect upon the hitherto indifferent, almost somnolent composer was remarkable: "Do you mean," he asked, like someone waking to an unexpected vision or a dear face, "the life of our Lord?"

This was what they did mean, and Handel, accepting the commission, shut himself into his workroom, saw no one but the women who placed his food at the door, and wrote the oratorio, *The Messiah*, in twenty-five days. He was in the grip of a magnificent creative obsession; many times tears flooded his eyes. To his servant he made the famous statement about what was to be the immortal Hallelujah Chorus, "I did think I did see Heaven before me, and the great God himself." He was then age 57, and from the long crisis of terrible financial loss and physical and social desolation, which had lasted many months, he had derived a new masterpiece —to be followed by still others in his late years.

John Henry Newman's experience is a fascinating parallel of seemingly utter failure, intervention by a wholly unexpected event, and creative exploitation of the new circumstance by a Ulyssean adult. Newman was famous before he was 50, as one of the leaders of the new Anglo-Catholic movement in the Church of England. The idea of restoring much of the ancient, beautiful ritual which had been lost in Puritan days in the Church of England, and of restoring some of its Catholic beliefs and practices, had created so great an upheaval in the worlds of thought and belief of the serious, almost too conscientious Victorians, that its leading spokesman became celebrated, hated, and adored. He was the author of a famous hymn; an awesome controversialist and sought-after speaker; a popular and brilliant priest and don.

Then Newman, for reasons that would be irrelevant to enter into here, became a Roman Catholic. At once the whole tenor of his life changed. The huge audience which he had once commanded in the dominant Anglican world now left him; at the same time he found that he had a cold welcome among the Roman Catholics, notably and specifically at Rome itself, where he had expected to receive at least generous respect from Pius IX and the cardinals. All that he gained instead, in these appalling early years after his conversion, was the headship of a group of Oratorian Fathers in the provincial city of Birmingham.

Then came a succession of prospects from outside forces and imaginative ideas of his own which he hoped would advance the cause of Roman Catholicism in Great Britain and restore much of his shattered influence in the prestigious circles of thought. Time and again plans and projects arose which it seemed would surely bring him out from the obscurity and neglect of his Birmingham existence: the offer of a bishopric, mysteriously withdrawn after he had accepted it and had bought the robes; the appointment to the rectorship of a so-called Catholic University of Ireland, which involved him in a period of intense travel and organization in Ireland, only to find a chimera; the prospect of a Catholic hall at Oxford, of which he would be the rector: this was Newman's own plan and dream, a plan defeated by his enemy within the church, Cardinal Manning, also an Anglican convert.

In whatever direction Newman looked he was blocked. With all his great gifts, and in spite of his former fame, he had come, so it seemed, to a complete dead end. It was about this time that Newman wrote in his journal, that he could hardly bear to get up in the morning; the day stretched before him already dreary and defeated. An Anglican clergyman, out for a stroll one day, noticed an elderly man, shabbily dressed and leaning against a garden gate, weeping desolately. The clergyman could not believe his eyes —it was the famous John Henry Newman, who before he took orders as a Roman Catholic priest had been a great force in the curate's own communion. He asked Father Newman whether there was some way he could help. "Oh, no, no," replied Newman. Indeed it seemed there was nothing to be done. He was, in fact, naked on the shore.

Then occurred the mysterious interposition of the gods. Newman, who had been neglected for so long, was suddenly and angrily attacked by Charles Kingsley, one of the most noted Protestant writers of the day, for his desertion to the Roman Catholics, for his insincerity, for his opportunism, for his jesuitry. Kingsley's attack also extended to the church which Newman had espoused. What was Newman to do with these searing and highly personal onslaughts? Turn the other cheek and let them pass? But this would be both masochistic and provocative to further attacks. Write two or three letters to *The Times* and responding letters to the magazine that had published Kingsley's initial paper? But responses in article form to original polemics never carry the weight of the original; and they die with the ephemeral nature of nearly all journalism.

No. What was needed was a book which would give real substance to Newman's defence of himself and his conduct; and which would be read long after he, Kingsley, and the other polemicists were dead. It took Newman seven weeks of intensive work to write a reply to Kingsley which was to become one of the most famous statements in the world of theological debate, yet a book well within the range of the average intelligent person: the *Apologia pro Vita Sua*. Like Handel, Newman often wept as, standing at the wooden lectern on which he wrote most of the *Apologia*, he carried forward his brilliant and eloquent defence of himself and of the Roman Catholic Church. There were days when he slept scarcely more than two or three hours; days also in which as he built one cogent argument upon another with the marvellous use of English for which he had once been famous, Newman must have wondered whether his will power and creative generativity were sufficient for the work. He was, after all, 65 years old—"retirement age," in twentieth century terms.

In fact, Kingsley had been the unwitting rescuer of Newman from utter defeat. The *Apologia*, with its fire and zest and artistry, was a triumph, read and acclaimed everywhere. Without Kingsley, it would never have been written—but then, without Newman, it would only have been another humdrum, jejune treatise ultimately gathering dust on the shelves of pious Victorian homes. Nor did Newman, to the end of his very long life at age 89, lose his ability to think originally and write creatively. The bright, quick mind, with its sensitive humour, mature irony, simplicity of enthusiasm over human projects, and its tender faith, can be said to have remained Ulyssean until the day of Newman's death in 1890.

"But then," says the inevitable cynic of those Ulysseans, "what options had they?" For him, when the desolate hours of disaster and defeat had arrived and they were naked on the shore, the Ulyssean men and women had no choice but to try for the master-strokes or begin the new adventures which would rebuild their fortunes. But if they had no choice, it was because of their essentially life-loving and striving natures, always open to the presence and possibility of creativity. To contradict the cynic, they indeed had other options, important options chosen by innumerable older adults. Because these critical choices are still those of many, one can refer to them in the present tense. One choice is self-pity —"Who has known such woes as I have known?": one can make a career out of this, and many have. Everyone knows of someone who by personal mistakes or, much oftener, the injury and blockage of external fate, has not written the novel, conducted the orchestra, created the business, bought the long-dreamt-of house, visited Scandinavia, painted the portraits as he or she had hoped to do, and whose reaction has been immobilizing self-pity. (Who, on the other hand, had more excuse for self-pity than the remarkable modern Ulyssean Pierre Teilhard de Chardin, whose brilliant books were forbidden publication by his Church up to his death and in the years preceding John XXIII?)

Another option is to live more cautiously; play it safe; move back into the comforting conventions of routine life. There is a basis of good sense and reason here, and of human practice. Even the Ulysseans in terrible misfortune are first saved by the routine: the sane little miracle of going to a shop in Marseilles to buy some garters is a tiny example of the regenerative power of the routine. If you are Thomas Carlyle, and you discover that a housemaid has unwittingly burned the just-completed manuscript of your *History of the French Revolution*, in the writing of which twenty cart-loads of books have been employed, you undoubtedly feel crushed. For the time being it may be the routine that saves you—the cup of tea, the usual walk, the familiar companionship of a dear friend. But because you are Carlyle, and a Ulyssean, you rewrite the history. If you are the painter, Eugène Delacroix, keeping also a journal fine enough to be published years later and read by thousands of people since, and if you leave one complete year of the journal in a Paris cab one night, and never recover it, you can never rewrite the entries: one piece of creative work done over a whole year is permanently missing. The world of small routines will save you, as it saves years of life for lonely and desolate women in their late years—but because you are Delacroix, and a Ulyssean, you do not decide that writing a journal is not worth the risk of another such feeling of hollow loss. You recommence the journal.

The routines of conventional living which get the world up in the morning and keep it on its course can thus heal and save. However, they can and do engulf and enslave. Worse, there are also the demonic conventions which wait for all who have suffered terrible reverses and sorrows: alcoholism, drug addiction, cruelty to other people and oneself, sustained bitterness.

Yes, there are other options in disaster than the heart-broken resumption of the creative life by the Ulyssean adults of the later years.

Sometimes the type of creativity evoked by the depths of disaster is not what Maslow called "special talent creativity," but "self-actualizing creativeness"—how the Ulyssean person responds in his or her personal life to the blows of Fate.

A provocative example of this is the life of the Grand Duchess Olga Alexandrovna, who at her death on November 24, 1960, was the last surviving sister of the Csar Nicholas II, murdered with his entire family at Ekaterinbourg in 1917, ending the three-hundred-year Romanoff dynasty. After the revolution, the Grand Duchess Olga and some other members of the royal family escaped to Western Europe, to Paris and other capitals.

The fleeing grand dukes and grand duchesses, refugee nobility and former ministers had certain critical choices to make. If they had enough money (few had), they could try to maintain the illusion of temporary exile in some villa or resort in Italy or France; if they had not, they could seek some kind of dignified work, or as in many cases, any kind of work. Ideologically, the exiles could continue to live in the vanished world of Imperial Russia. Or they could, while preserving loving contacts and memories, look toward the face of tomorrow—a world from which Imperial Highnesses had vanished.

What was remarkable about the Grand Duchess Olga and her husband, Colonel Nikolai Koulikovsky, was that they made a Ulyssean decision when she was 66 and he was 67 to go to Canada to farm a property of two hundred acres with the aid of their two sons and a couple of elderly servants. The decision was unmistakable in its symbolism. They had chosen for themselves and their sons not the world of yesterday, including the intrigues and jealousies of certain royal and ex-royal circles in Europe, but the world of tomorrow in a wholly new country.

At first the venture seemed successful, but as the years passed Colonel Koulikovsky found it impossible to hire the extra help he needed for his farm; his sons chose new careers; and as his health failed, he and the Grand Duchess moved to a modest house in Cooksville, a small community near Toronto. There was a garden, and Olga made the house charming with many mementos of their former life in Russia and Denmark. Both she and her husband continued to show the maturity with which they handled the cultural shock of a transfer of this dimension. The old servants had died, and Colonel Koulikovsky's health steadily deteriorated until he, too, died in 1957.

The Grand Duchess Olga was left alone in the Cooksville house. What was she to do? Although her health was good, she was 74 years of age. She decided not to move, and by living very simply she was able to carry on. She became a familiar figure in the town, shopping and gardening. There was no Russian Orthodox church in Cooksville, and on frequent Sundays Olga made the trip into Toronto to the Cathedral of Christ the Saviour, where after the service elderly members of the congregation and their families and grandchildren would swarm around her to pay their respects to almost the last living member of the Russian Imperial royal family. "Almost," because there was still one other living grand duchess, her sister in London, England, who as it turned out was to die shortly before Olga's own death in November, 1960.

In his biography (*The Last Grand Duchess*), the Greek journalist Ian Vorres tells that what he had heard of Olga's story so interested him that he drove out to Cooksville from Toronto to see if he could interview her for an article. It was an early autumn day, and after he had found the house, he saw a small, spare woman working in the garden—this was the Grand Duchess Olga. From the beginning Vorres was struck by her ease and graciousness of manner, and by her warm and friendly spirit. He found out that Olga had often been invited to write or permit the writing of her life story, but she had always refused. These refusals all seemed part of the Ulyssean exercise upon which she and her husband had embarked. But the young newspaperman and the elderly grand duchess, then 75, became fast friends; and in the course of subsequent talks Vorres was able to persuade her to let him write her life story—fortunately completed before her death.

It was not only Olga's vitality and courage which drew Vorres's admiration, but her sense of humour and her wise humanity. She had seen much and lost much—in the material sense, almost everything. She was, of course, lonely; she could not blot out the past, and history continued to pursue her. She still received letters and occasional visits from former Russian subjects who cherished her as a symbol, but also tiresome intrusions from impostors. Yet there was a modernity in her matter and her way of thought which reminded people who talked with her that she and her husband had chosen a new country and a new style of life, even though very late in their lives.

In midsummer, 1960, she became ill, and had to enter hospital in Toronto, where the routines tired her and made her unhappy and restless. The medical staff, who had become fond of her, were willing to send her home, but "home" was impossible. There was no one to nurse her in the silent house at Cooksville. Then an elderly Russian couple, Captain and Mrs. Martemianov, an Imperial Russian army officer and his wife, invited her to go with them for "convalescence." They had a small flat above a hairdresser's shop on Gerrard Street East in Toronto. It was there that Olga died on November 24, 1960.

Thirteen years later, also in November, I made a short nostalgic journey across downtown Toronto to visit the site where Olga had last lived and made the following entry in my journal:

> From Gerrard Street East, the sky could be seen slate-blue on the late autumn day above the quiet Sunday traffic, the air frosty and damp. The building housing the apartments one storey above the shops was as photographed in Ian Vorre's life of Olga.
>
> It was only in the last four or five months of her life that the Grand Duchess lived here. Released from hospital, which she hated, she apparently found a certain joy in being at home with an elderly Cossack officer and his wife, who loved her, and in seeing the walls around her bed covered with the beloved icons of her faith.
>
> One can, I think, imagine fairly well the final stage on which Olga played out her days. Her small room, filled with some charming things rescued from the past, but with the simplicity of her poverty; the warmth of being in and being home; the smell of good soup; lamplight; the presence of two or three loving people, and some cards and messages from others; and the visits of the young journalist, a close friend across a difference of forty years of time, who revered and loved her.
>
> Here then, passed from this world that lovely-spirited lady, Olga Alexandrovna, the last grand duchess of the Romanoff dynasty, on a commercial street in Toronto, Canada, among little boys whose bikes turn over and whose jugs of milk are upset, among young couples who dash laughing up the stairs, among schoolgirls carrying books across the parks, among pizza take-outs and cut-rate pharmacies, among amiable truck-drivers and elderly ladies carrying shopping bags, among neon signs and parking lots, among church rummage sales and "ethnic" movie houses and restaurants, among thousands of family groups.

It is not all so incongrous as at first it seems. In a deep human sense, it is not incongruous at all. It has something to do with *"citoyenne du monde"*—something to do with *"noblesse oblige."* And there is something very Ulyssean about it.

Among the disasters that can overtake Ulyssean achievers are crippling illnesses which severely impair or immobilize the body's action. Sometimes, in the case of "special talent" Ulysseans, the disease or disintegrative process attacks exactly the physical instrument provided by the body to carry through the creative performance, although this is rare. A notable example was Auguste Renoir, one of the masters of French impressionism, who was overtaken by severe arthritis in his early 50s. His hands became more and more twisted until, by the time he had reached his late years, the deformation was so complete that he had to have the paints squeezed onto the palette for him, and he moved the brush not by his fingers but by his arm, through an apparatus attached to the rigid fingers and wrist. Nevertheless, he continued to paint great works until his death. Nothing exhausted his great talent— in fact it was inexhaustible, because it was not a bank deposit to be drawn on but an underground river constantly fed by Renoir's own marvellous love of life, sensitivity to colour, and openness to the continuous wonder of human experience. This was true, even although the disease forced him into a wheelchair at so early an age as 60, and he later became bedridden.

Renoir had other harassing afflictions which encroached on his creative domain: for example, the partial atrophy of a nerve in his left eye caused by a severe chill and subsequent cold caught while out landscape painting. For a long time he was in great pain until at last the arthritic fires burned themselves out and left the desolate wreck of the body behind them. When he was 71, the Renoirs actually found a doctor in Paris who was certain that he could make the painter walk again—something that would have been like a gift from heaven. In fact, he did walk again: a few steps around his easel and then back to his wheelchair. But to walk just these few yards was so great an effort that Renoir remarked to the physician that he would use up all his energies just trying to walk; and he needed, he said, all his willpower for his painting. Having to make the choice between walking and painting, he chose painting. In fact, he asked for his paintbox and brushes on the morning of his death, although he was in discomfort from congested lungs, and completed a lovely painting of some anemones brought in for him by the maid. According to his son, Jean, as he completed this painting and had his brush taken away, he said something like, "I think I am beginning to understand something about it"—both the nurse and the cook, Grand' Louise, heard this.

Still, Renoir's condition in late life, cruel though it was, was by no means wholly tragic. He handled the disaster of his physical debacle magnificently: no one can read the account of his performance as man and artist without a surge of something like joy, and without a renewed sense of the wonder of man. Yet he had, after all, a great talent which he realized; he was famous; and although to the very end he disliked death because he had so much to do, to learn, he had accomplished much that he was born to do. But what if one is wholly immobilized at a late age, unknown to the world, and with the feeling that one has never been able to realize whatever gifts one had?

In so dire a situation, one form of the ultimate test of the human spirit can be seen. Is there even creativity in the survival of self over senility? Is it possible that this "I," so encircled by "disgust and despair" that its terrible urge is to take flight into somnolence and extinction of the failed and rejected self, nonetheless creatively maintains its own existence and identity?

An illustrative case of this most calamitous form of being "naked on the shore" is that of Isabelle Buchanan, an aunt of mine, born in the lovely old town of Parkhill, near London, Ontario, in 1870, who died in London in 1963, age 93. Her case seems to be as clear an example of a tragic waste of human talent as the records could disclose. Nor does the achievement of a very long life do much to make up for it.

Belle Buchanan was born into a Highland Scots-Canadian pioneer family, the oldest members of which had helped build the farms and towns in Middlesex County, Ontario. The family had a heritage of great health and vitality. Belle, a beautiful, high-spirited girl, going to the dances, skating parties, sleigh-rides, plays, and church functions of a small Ontario community, had a magnificent obsession: to be a nurse. Nursing was then on its way to becoming a profession, and in those days Detroit was a cultural magnet for people in Western Ontario —that was where you went for training in nursing.

But then Fate intervened. One of Belle's grandmothers in a district ten miles away had a massive stroke. There was no one to nurse her—could Belle do it? It would mean a short postponement of her imminent arrangements to go to a cousin's place in Detroit and then begin her training in a hospital. But the condition of the imperious old lady did not improve. Three years went by; Belle was told that if she nursed her grandmother through the illness, she would be well remembered in the division of property at death, which was the way payment was often made within pioneer families.

The grandmother died; in fact, no provision was made for the girl, who was by now a young woman. The chance to study nursing in Detroit was lost—Belle Buchanan began the life of a spinster in the age of the unliberated woman. Because of her beauty and vivacity, she had a number of offers of marriage, all of which she turned down. In the family, it was said that she was always looking for a Prince Charming who never arrived. She may also simply have been what a later age would call "a career woman." An offer of marriage from a substantial farmer of "good character" came when she was in her late 40s—she refused. Meanwhile, her father died at a great age, then her mother. She and a younger sister were left in the old house, and the two women carried on with the slender funds available from renting land, the sister's skills at dressmaking, and interest from modest investments left by their parents. Keeping up the house with the added chores of orchards and some chickens and cows fell chiefly to Belle because of her sister's arthritis. In spite of this, they entertained many visitors. To have tea with the Miss Buchanans was considered a great pleasure, and it was a pleasure also for two bright, warm-hearted unmarried women to whom the years were bringing increasing privation and loneliness in spite of help given from time to time by a sister and brother, both married and with families, living in Montreal and London.

In 1940, when the incredible had happened and the vivacious girl whose dream had been to be a nurse, was 70, Belle Buchanan had lost something of her radiant health—she had been drenched too often at her work out in the orchards and the grazing land, and something else was working in her to produce the beginnings of arthritis. She was still beautiful: you could see the lovely girl that she had been. In 1941, on a snowy winter night, without warning, her sister died. There was no telephone in the old home. Belle, in the wild panic and sorrow of the crisis, threw on some clothes and went down the tree-lined road and across the street to some neighbours to call for help.

After this, events followed swiftly. The home was sold and its contents auctioned off. Belle's health was irremediably shaken by these personal catastrophes, and the arthritis advanced. At first she found a certain happiness and excitement in staying with relatives in London for a few months; then as a boarded guest in the home of a married nurse whose teen-age daughter filled Belle's days with interest and joy; then, briefly, in a Roman Catholic hospital where the nuns were kind; then finally in a nursing home for old, ill people in London. She entered the nursing home at age 77; here she remained until her death—sixteen years during which she finally arrived naked on the shore.

As nursing homes go, it was a good one, clean and warm. Belle Buchanan was by now wholly immobilized; her weight had gone down to about seventy pounds. Her hands and arms were claws and sticks. Still, if one tried to feed her when the tray arrived for meals, she would push back one's hands and feed herself. She was in a room with seven or eight other elderly women, the majority of whom slept most of the time or were senile. A woman or two, wandering in mind, walked around conversing aimlessly. The staff were good, but there were no stimuli for the mind. Belle was so crippled that it was difficult for her to read. On Sundays, a few members of families appeared to break the monotony of the place; in Belle's life, I came from a busy existence four hundred miles away, three or four times a year, to stay a day or two; and a cousin, Mary Fisher, came in often to talk with her.

As time went on, she had long periods of unbearable loneliness. One calm summer evening, her eyes filling with tears, she hummed for me and half-sang in her still melodious voice the words and tune of "My Ain Folk", the poignant Highland song of exile: "Though I'm far across the sea, It's in Scotland I would be, At Home, in dear old Scotland, with my ain folk." Yet she rarely talked mournfully or resentfully. She was occasionally angry about some episode at the nursing home, for example, the mislaying of some article from her pitifully few belongings, but anger is good therapy, and she had no self-pity. She was always glad to talk about the old family days, but was never morbid. Only very rarely did she seem confused.

Usually her mood was a quiet brightness. I dreaded the day when I might arrive to find her sinking into senility as so many other old women had done in these rooms with the identical beds, the identical bows in the identical hair-do's, the identical routines from the well-organized smiling attendants.

A few years before her death, Belle Buchanan was moved to a front room with two beds. At first she was pleased, assuming that this was the "best room in the house", which in a way was true. But the location increased her isolation and her loneliness. In the other bed in Belle's room was a timid, very fragile, senile (of course) old lady—this was her companionship. Sometimes when this person was especially silly in comments or actions, Belle would draw my attention to her with an ironic smile. Somehow I dimly resented this, as mocking a defenceless old woman and a sister in misfortune. I should have known that it was from this bright ironic humour, still vividly awake, that part of Belle Buchanan's own mysterious defences against senility came.

The last evening, a Saturday, as usual I had supper with her, eating from a tray as she did; giving her the pleasure of feeling that I was her guest, as I was. That October Saturday evening all was at peace. The cool smoke-scented air of a lovely night came through the slightly opened window. We fell into a contented silence, and I drowsed, thinking with pleasure how bright she was. Then to my astonishment she said with great clearness—I am sure that she thought I was asleep—"I should have gone to Detroit."

My aunt was 93. Still, so tenacious was the grip of her girlhood dream that she could mourn after seventy-six years for the great chance lost, for the divide in the road not taken.

The following Wednesday I had word from my cousin in London that Belle Buchanan had died in the early morning—gone in the moment between sleeping and waking.

In what possible sense was such a woman a Ulyssean? Because of her terrible immobilization, she could not have done what Major A. F. Graves of the United Nations Society of Ottawa did at the end of his life when, desperately ill with cancer, he went out in his self-propelled chair into the corridors of the hospital, for weeks comforting other people. Was her creativity, then, self-actualization?

It seems to me now that her defeat of the steady menace of senility in an arena where many others had succumbed was in itself a Ulyssean adventure. She had a whole repertoire of defences and counterattacks against being engulfed. She had learned how to handle loneliness. She was sorrowful and angry at times, and at rare intervals clearly felt that somehow she had been betrayed— but she was then angry and outspoken, not silent and bitter. Incredibly, although she read little and saw few people, she remained open to the rich world of fantasy and dreaming which, in a certain sense, was also one of the deficits of her life. And if at the end she was left veritably naked upon the shore, she eluded self-pity. She retained an unconquerable hope into the late, late years; and when that finally dimmed and perhaps died, she never lost the sense of being the protagonist in a significant drama. Thus, late in the day, I came to attach to her the strong and tender accolade: Ulyssean.

Sometimes the ingenuity and gallantry of the Ulyssean performance outwits death itself. Romain Gary, the French novelist, tells in his memoir, *Promise at Dawn*, of an astonishing adventure which his mother embarked upon during the last two years of her life—during which she expected death.

Refugees after World War One, Gary and his mother had wandered across Europe while she tried to keep them both alive so that he might realize the dreams which she had for him. She felt that her boy should emerge at the top in whatever occupation he chose—from tennis to politics to the army. Her wonderful gutsy sense of life, her *panache*, filled her young son's life with verve and laughter, and robbed his occasional moments of embarrassment of their sting. Naturally, after twenty or more years of such companionship, with the face of poverty and hardship looking in from time to time at the window, mother and son were close in mind and spirit, yet Gary was a real person—he had his own full identity.

In 1940 when Hitler invaded France, Romain Gary joined the Free French air crews flying out of England on sorties over the continent; his mother was left behind with good friends, in what must have been to her a sorrowful separation. Her solution, of course, was to try to bridge the gap by writing to her son wonderful letters, not self-pitying or lugubrious, but designed to keep up his morale until the great days when he could take up one of the careers which she and he had often talked over, and in which, needless to say, he would succeed. Each week brought its letter, adding personal zest and strength to Romain's dangerous life.

When peace came, he rushed home—only to find that his mother had died two years previously.

When she learned that she would probably die before her son's return, she devised a Ulyssean stratagem. She prepared enough letters for every week for a period of more than two years and arranged that the devoted friends with whom she stayed would send them to her pilot son.

The prospect of imminent death may seem too overwhelming for even a Ulyssean to cope with. This all depends upon how powerfully the individuals have learned to internalize their sense of permanent uniqueness or value to life. And, it depends, too, upon their having developed or swiftly grasped toward the end of their lives the undoubted truth that fate is just as capricious one way as the other—that the cause seemingly lost may in time be the cause well won.

The life of the Sicilian prince and author, Giuseppe di Lampedusa, who died in 1959, illustrates this strange working of Fate. Lampedusa at age 60 was a tall, rather heavy, princely-looking man (this is more than can be said for many princes) who had capably fulfilled the demands of his heritage. He was the master of two palaces in Sicily, one of which was obliterated by American bombers toward the end of World War Two. He was also something of an oddity in his aristocratic circle because he was devoted to study and reading; and had for many years talked about writing a novel which no sensible person expected him to write.

He was capable of attempting it. He had already written from time to time, short stories and poetry; at one time, and in his later years, he actually won a prize. But who expects a prince to write a novel that might be published by a commercial publisher and read by all sorts of people? Even in these days when princes have come down in the world, they are embalmed in social protocols, especially if, like Lampedusa, they are administrators of large estates. Administration is the mortal trap of serious activity outside its own sphere.

For many years, Lampedusa's duties as an administrator took

precedence over his urge to write. He had the Ulyssean's open and sensitive reaction to life, and when the war brought the destruction of a great part of his heritage, he was at first obsessed by the loss. To divert his mind, his wife urged him to write. He did so, and we have Alexander Colquhoun's little cameo of the result:

> "From now on, his routine—the café tables he used, the waiters who served him, even the cakes he ate—followed an invariable pattern: breakfast at the Pasticceria del Massimo in Via Masqueda; a call at Flaccorio, the imaginative bookseller and publisher whose shop is a kind of literary club, and who was the first to encourage him to publish; by mid-day he would be settled in his personal version of an ivory tower, the back room of the Café Mazzara under the only skyscraper in town.
>
> The brief case opens. It contains, as well as maybe a few cakes from the last café, books, the addiction which made him as great an object of suspicion to his fellow grandees as his great-grandfather had been with his telescopes and comet-finders. . . . This concentrated reading throughout the day at the Café table (mysterious scribbling) was in a way creative."

What Lampedusa was soon engaged upon was the actual writing of the novel, *The Leopard*, which had been in his thoughts for twenty-five years.

He began it in his mid-60s, and finished it in about three years. Meanwhile he wrote other pieces. He had the novel typed and sent off, encouraged by both his wife and by the bookseller Flaccorio. Now, however, another disaster struck. He was found to have cancer which, as it turned out, ended his life. The publisher, as publishers often will, held the manuscript for weeks. Finally, and just before his death, the letter came—a rejection. Lampedusa received the news with noble composure; still, his inward disappointment must have been intense. A day or two later, while quietly talking with his physician, the prince suddenly died. Within a matter of weeks *The Leopard* had been submitted to another publisher, and accepted. It became an international best-seller and a notable film. It is accepted as one of the distinguished novels of our time.

The performance was splendidly Ulyssean, but who outwitted whom—Death or Lampedusa? Death is a formidable adversary, and platitudes and histrionics do little to assuage his effects. Yet, in this case, Lampedusa had finished his novel, and its effects far outreached his death. Furthermore, the writing of the novel was, *in itself*, a personal fulfilment, a justification and actualization of the self.

This last point is crucial in considering the adventures and attempts of the Ulyssean life. Ulysses' last voyage was a failure, and it was uncompleted—still, this takes nothing away from the splendour and individual creativity of the act. Chichester's last effort to win a trans-ocean race, which he had to abandon because of the pain and immobilizing effect of his last illness, was no less splendid than any of the other Ulyssean adventures of his later years. Surely we do not have to listen more than once to Schubert's *Unfinished Symphony* (which was not only unpublished at his death, but lost for years in a cellar), to understand that creative fragments are beautiful things *in themselves*.

One creative person who thought a lot about this last point was Robert Louis Stevenson, and with reason. Stevenson, who fought a long losing battle with tuberculosis in the late nineteenth century when the medical profession was unable to cure it, dealt superbly with the subject of death and creative achievement in a now almost-forgotten essay, *Aes Triplex*. In that essay, Stevenson notes how wisely and boldly many old people walk among the hazards of possible disablement and death. He takes as one example among many, someone he had long admired, Dr. Samuel Johnson, of whom he writes:

"No one surely could have recoiled with more heartache and terror from the thought of death than our respected lexicographer; and yet we know how little it affected his conduct, how wisely and boldly he walked, and in what a fresh and lively vein he spoke of life. Already an old man, he ventured on his Highland tour; and his heart, bound with triple brass [*aes triplex*], did not recoil before twenty-seven individual cups of tea. . . . Think of the heroism of Johnson, think of that superb indifference to mortal limitation that set him upon his dictionary, and carried him through triumphantly until the end!

Then Stevenson moves to the great question of whether it is worthwhile to begin creative acts which, after all, may turn out to be fragments:

"Who, if he were wisely considerate of things at large, would ever embark upon any work much more considerable than a halfpenny post-card? Who would project a serious novel, after Thackeray and Dickens had each fallen in mid-course? Who would find heart enough to begin to live, if he dallied with the consideration of death?

This is a Ulyssean speaking, even though Stevenson's own life was to end at 44:

"By all means begin your folio; even if the doctor does not give you a year, even if he hesitates about a month, make one brave push and see what can be accomplished in a week. It is not only in finished undertakings that we ought to honour useful labour. A spirit goes out of the man who means execution, which outlives the most untimely ending. All who have meant good work with their whole hearts have done good work, although they may die before they have the time to sign it. Every heart that has beat strong and cheerfully has left a hopeful impulse behind it in the world, and bettered the tradition of mankind.

And even if death catch people, like an open pitfall, and in mid-career, laying out vast projects, and planning monstrous foundations, flushed with hope, and their mouths full of boastful language, they should be at once tripped up and silenced: is there not something brave and spirited in such a termination? and does not life go down with a better grace, foaming in full body over a precipice, than miserably straggling to an end in sandy deltas?

When the Greeks made their fine saying that those whom the gods love die young, I cannot help believing that they had this sort of death also in their eye. For surely, at whatever age it overtake the man, this is to die young. Death has not been suffered to take so much as an illusion from his heart. In the hot-fit of life, a-tiptoe on the highest point of being, he passes at a bound on to the other side. The noise of the mallet and chisel is scarcely quenched, the trumpets are hardly done blowing, when, trailing with him clouds of glory, this happy-starred, full-blooded spirit shoots into the spiritual land."

"By all means begin your folio . . ."

The folio, a natural symbol for a writer, is Stevenson's shorthand for any creative opportunity which appears almost simultaneously with the threat of serious illness. The human tendency, which no one has the right to criticize or patronize, is to abandon everything which seems to interfere with the awesome emergency in one's life presented by a threat which may terminate it. But is this always or even usually the only or the wise action? There remains the possibility of the Ulyssean action, which is what Stevenson is writing about. Two incidents from my own experience may illustrate the point.

About twenty years ago I heard the story of a married couple in their mid-60s. They had planned for years to wander through Europe but had been kept from doing so by family responsibilities and business difficulties. At last they were free to do so. The husband had just been able to retire, and retire comfortably; they were, after many years of marriage, much in love; they had spent some happy months just before his retirement in the early summer planning their itinerary, gathering tourist and guide books, and assembling luggage and clothing. They had their tickets for the passage. Then

each decided to have a medical examination as an extra precaution.
Her returns were clear; her husband's were dismaying—although
the doctors were tactful, their message was specific: the odds were
heavily against the husband's living as long as a year. Shaken and
sorrowful, the couple cancelled their tickets; the husband began
treatment, and in fact lost his fight with his illness in less than a
year.

I learned of this episode sitting at a café table in Montreal from
a close friend of the couple, reporting it to me shortly after the
husband's death. My friend described the wife's poignant double
sorrow: not only the loss of someone dearly loved, but that of the
long planned-for, dreamed-about trip to Europe. When she finished,
there was a few moments' silence between us. Then she said,
"What would you have done?" I said, "I would have gone to Europe."
My friend smiled: "I too. But it's easy for us to say. He was faced,
after all with what turned out to be a fatal illness." "That's true,"
I said, "but there are great physicians in Europe." We watched the
autumn dusk come into the street outside the café, and the lights
come on in lamps and windows. The little candle on our table was
out, and my companion found a match to light it. "They are beautiful people," she said, using the present tense lovingly, as though
the husband was still alive. "I wish that they had strolled in the
sunshine on St. Mark's Square, and sat in a café in Paris. He
wanted so much to see Athens. . . . They could have had a little
odyssey."

In 1967, when travelling by Greyhound bus between Montreal
and Ottawa, I met an extraordinary person. He was a 78-year-old
Australian, spare and heavily tanned, with rather gnarled working
hands, plainly dressed; it was midsummer, and the day and the
bus were intensely hot. It was easy to move into conversation with
this keen-eyed traveller with the quick warm smile. Where was he
going? To my surprise, I learned that he was bound to Calgary for
the Stampede; that he and his wife had arrived in Los Angeles to
cross North America and then Europe by bus, and to find a passage
home from the Near East. He had a daughter and her family in
Montreal, where he and his wife were stopping for a month—
meanwhile the Calgary trip was a personal side expedition to fulfil
a longheld dream. He and his wife would resume their odyssey
when he returned. His wife, he remarked to me, was about his age,
and a "good companion." They both loved travel, and they had long
planned this trip. They liked big buses—you could often stop, stroll,
have the feeling of being close to the land and the people. Sometimes they stopped over; often they travelled through the night,
and in "America" there were usually splendid middle-of-the-night
restaurants and rest stops . . . They had had so much fun seeing
things together.

I asked about fatigue: no, this was not a great problem. If they felt themselves getting too tired, they "stopped over." I did not mention, of course, the inevitable thought held in the back of my mind, placed there by the conventions of our society: suppose one or the other became ill—after all, both were about 78; suppose . . . But it was impossible, talking to this vital, obviously life-loving man to whom I said a warm farewell at the Greyhound station in Ottawa, to keep dwelling on thoughts like these. I knew that I had met another of the Ulysseans.

"By all means begin your folio . . ."

9. ON BECOMING A ULYSSEAN

The Ulyssean life is possible, and the Ulyssean way is accessible and free, because in many ways the conditions required for the creative life are *more available* in the later years of adulthood than earlier in life.

It is essential to make this statement with force, even if it appears to be an overstatement, in order to correct at last the asinine convention in our society that creativity resides chiefly with the young and the "highly-geared." Being in "high gear" is no guarantee that one will be creative— productive, perhaps. Assuming that a constant factor in all creative enterprises is the existence of certain personal gifts, talents, qualities, or self-actualized attributes, there then seem to be conditions or situations which set the stage, or help provide the soil and air—whatever analogy one wishes—for the creative enterprise. And all of them are conspicuously available in the later years.

One is a release of time, not only to think but to rest and not-think. A great forgotten truth about the later adult years is that many older adults, although they undoubtedly feel the constriction of time in the sense of remaining years, also have more time available, either through release from family responsibilities or through retirement or lighter work loads. If many older adults fretted less about the unavailable years and analysed the amount of relaxed time available to them, they would be astonished at the treasure which the years of later and late adulthood have delivered to them. Hundreds of creative ideas of every kind grow in the soil of relaxed time and the relaxed contemplative mind.

Another is the rich store of experiences accumulated throughout life, which are recorded in the apparatus of the mind. In older adulthood not only is the brain operating with abundant power, but the great reservoir of the unconscious is surely more potentially fertile than it was earlier. Many possibilities arise from this—one of them Wordsworth's concept of emotion recollected in tranquility. Older adults have the extended experience, usually together with a greater accessibility to tranquil thought—not confusing "tranquil" with "passive" or "bovine." An example of this possible fusion of experience, perceptive recollection, and tranquility in a creative enterprise is, of course, keeping a journal filled with reflections and ideas. Yet among North Americans the thoughtful personal journal is almost unknown.

Still another advantage exists among older adults. For many of them, at least, the later years mean that they are freer than they have ever been to adopt unorthodox concepts, and unorthodoxy is one of the recognized parents of creativity. Old adults may, of course, choose not to do so; or they may have locked themselves into rigid and arid conventionalities of thought. Nonetheless, freer airs blow for many men and women in their later years: the stakes are less, intimidating jailers are gone, or in the steady process of maturing, new reserves of courage together with wisdom and compassion have brought them to the open fields of change and experiment. One of the loveliest features of the later years is the affinity which many older adults develop for the causes and crusades of the young.

Thus the creative life is not only as possible for men and women in the later years as when they were much younger, but in important respects often *more* possible. Nor does lack of money, nor chronic ill health, nor lack of family and friends remove these advantageous conditions for creativity in many older adult lives. They are still present even when one is naked on the shore.

However, at all ages, notably including the later adult years, the creative life has to be purchased by an effort of the will and by the adoption of a certain lifestyle. Obsolescence of mind and spirit waits for those who think that creativity in the later years descends like manna from the sky. To grow and create, to bring into actuality the unique space-time intersection that is our life, requires *exertion* of the self—exertion undertaken with love, faith, and hope.

Part of this process of self-actualization with a view to creativity in the later years is the sharpening of the senses. At exactly this point we confront another bromide about later life—that the senses fail in efficiency. Indeed to a degree, as we have seen, some of them do. But it is incredible that so little attention is paid to the *deeper* world of the senses. For surely to "see" and to "hear" is a process immensely greater than the physical act. I recall a conversation a few years ago with a group of men at a luncheon where two brothers, both friends of some members of the group, were under discussion. One brother was blind. However, in the rapid exchange of conversation, when one person suggested Bob, the sighted brother, for a committee job, another man cut in quickly, "No. I suggest Jim—he sees things so much more clearly than Bob." At the remark, which nearly everyone at once agreed to, delighted smiles spread among the group. The paradox was true, and the instinctive reference was beautiful.

For purposes of the creative life, there is not much advantage in having 20/20 vision if one really does not "see" very much. In fact, few of us, in the later years or at any time in the life drama, have developed our ability to "see" as we should. The point is developed extensively in a splendid and too-little-known book by Ross Parmenter, *The Awakened Eye*. Parmenter was a journalist and music editor of *The New York Times* until 1964 when he retired in his late 50s to travel and write, and to bring out four years later his book on the awakening of the deeper vision. For Parmenter, the word becomes plural, because he identifies three categories of "seeing" beyond ordinary vision. The first degree above the ordinary he calls *sharpened vision,* and he illustrates this by describing the astonishing array of things in a pack of face cards which ordinary vision never notices, even though one may play bridge for years on end. The next stage he terms *heightened vision*; here he is speaking about more than the greater grasp of detail and greater exactness of sharpened vision, although this is included. In heightened vision the candle on a red-checked café table becomes a symbol of the idealism of man; a wider context appears than simply the candle seen at the moment with the physical eye.

The highest category is *transfigured vision,* and Parmenter illustrates this at length with the description of an episode in 1949 which occurred on the road from California to Colorado when he was driving a 79-year-old retired school teacher, Thyrza Cohen, to her sister's home in Denver. The car was a 1932 four-cylinder Plymouth sedan; and in his inexperience, Parmenter became lost among primitive roads and mountain passes in the area of the Great Divide. He realized bleakly that the car was very old, that his gas supply was giving out, and that they had little food. Fortunately his companion was cheerful and brave. Then suddenly the canyon walls fell away and they could see, beyond upcurving green fields, the town they had sought for the night.

Parmenter describes the euphoria which seized him at the sight. He and Thyrza Cohen had been obsessed with the need of food, of gasoline, of shelter. Now in the ecstasy of relief, Parmenter "saw" what later turned out to be a dingy enough row of houses and filling stations as a Tunisian scene, bathed "in magical light" —the light of the late afternoon sun. The owner of the run-down service station, although "in reality" simply a good-humoured, obliging auto mechanic of considerable skill, seemed far more. In the joy of his rescue from dark prospects, Parmenter saw this supposedly commonplace figure of the service station operator with unusual intensity, not only in his physical self but in his social roles as settler, neighbour, father, helper of strangers—but beyond this, in transfigured vision as the symbol of all men, "millions of such humans who, by pertinacity, mutual kindness, and inventive skill, manage to survive throughout the world, transforming the places where they live into oases where a lost traveler can find security and shelter."

Parmenter asks how it is possible that we can live so close for so long beside human beings to whom we relate and so rarely *see* them with the insights and perspectives of the awakened eye. Not surprisingly, Parmenter sees bridges and links between his three "visions" and the creative process. He gives many instances of the awakening and freshening power, sometimes the wonder-working power, of sharpened, heightened, and transfigured vision. He speaks of a "looking gear" into which one has to shift out of ordinary seeing. Often the day-dreamer can shift into this gear more easily than the no-nonsense man whose mind most of the time is fixed on some non-visual problem—but both must learn to shift into this neglected gear of intenser sight, and a certain amount of self-discipline is involved.

A great deal of joy is involved as well—and Parmenter suggests a host of games which one can play to come alive in employing the marvellous gift of sight. It is clearly one road to the "openness to experience" and "the childlike wonder and curiosity" which help to produce the climate of creativity in the later years.

Closely allied to the zone of new powers of physical vision is the whole domain of creative potentiality made available by the imaginative play of the mind, fantasy, dalliance with the bizarre and the grotesque, the intersection of opposites, the inversion of conventionalities, and "brain-storming". Here we are usually at opposite poles from the staid, carefully sanctified protocols of most conventional living and thinking. This established world of customary process in which we are obliged to spend most— for perhaps a majority of adults, all—the years of our lives, is typified by such adjectives as "normal," "natural," "regular," and "usual"; and by such personalities (among a host of others) as certain socially ambitious and socially self-conscious people whose mighty refuge is their mandated regimen of attitudes and routines, and by certain timid souls frozen into lives of Total Expectedness. But in fact, all adults—not least the older adults—face the problem of keeping alive the imaginative arena in their lives in which transforming creative ideas are born. Into the arena, of course, will come, on their own, exotic and exciting creatures and created things from the mysterious gate labelled "Unconscious"—but others will enter partly because they have been sought out in fantasy, in brain-storming, in a deliberate crossing of opposites and meeting of incongruous concepts.

Thus, Bonnie Cashin tells us that in the early process of opening her mind to daring new ideas in fashion design she will return
to her apartment in Manhattan, take a whole lot of dresses from
the rack in her bedroom, and throw them in wild confusion throughout the room. Sometimes she will hang or wear gowns and coats
upside down, or in bizarre positions, so that from this riotous and
colourful disorder new fashion concepts may leap into her mind.
There is a parallel to this in the comment by one observer of the
creative process, that when a garbage bag bursts on the kitchen
floor, almost invariably we all run hurriedly to clean up the mess
which destroys the valued order of our kitchen—and our lives. Yet
the creative attitude, he suggests, would be at least to pause to
observe the often vivid and idea-provoking patterns, exploding
colours, and unimagined shapes which suddenly appear before us
in this brilliant débris.

The conventional mind, which tends to be at all phases of the
adult life journey the predominant mind, gives all too few occasions
for creative exercises, so much so that many older adults finally
assume that "they are past all that." Their problem is that they
have permitted their minds to follow for many years old familiar
routes, to employ the same tired analogies and associations of ideas
which have served them well, to store their creative ingenuity and
more intrepid ideas and opinions behind a protective screen for
career or social purposes. It is not surprising that when testers of
creativity in adults approach subjects in their 60s to find out how
they react to well-known proverbs, these older people seem to
produce more conventional interpretations than many younger
ones. Our society breeds conformity. Also, one has to set beside
these isolated studies, others which show (as already indicated) an
affinity between elderly and very young rebel adults to a degree not
found between the latter and other age groups. Still, even here, too
many older adults tend to perform as echoes.

This is the general situation; yet "lateral thinking" as Edward
de Bono calls the processes of thought where the mind searches
for creative associations—should be one of the strongholds of later
adulthood. In an effort to stimulate fresher, more original approaches to problems, a Toronto consultant, Savo Bojicic, has
invented a small (3½ pounds) inexpensive "Think Tank" which is
used in a game of putting the imagination to work on new paths.
Manuel Escott in *The Canadian Magazine* for June 8, 1974,
described how this little machine could be used by someone, perhaps an adult in late middle age, to help save his marriage. Suppose
the five words produced by manipulating the knobs of the tank
come up as WOLF, MIMICRY, CONFETTI, VIRGINITY, and
BULLDOZER. Let the mind move, really *move*, imaginatively on
these words (I have space for only two here, the two most seemingly

incongruous perhaps): MIMICRY: Acting, artificiality. Be natural, be human. Distortion, arguments. End this, and abandon pettiness. BULLDOZER: Power. Stop overpowering her. Don't tell her she's stupid. Level up, smooth the edges of our relationship. Demolish, rebuild. Start from the beginning; remember the things that used to give pleasure and repeat them.

In Synectics, a transactional discussion technique which operates best with seven or eight people, and which provides for the gathering-in of *all* the thoughts of the group, no matter how seemingly irrelevant or inconsequential at the time, an exercise occurs which really astonishes people new to the technique. It is in part derived from Charles S. Whiting, and is called the Forced Fit. Suppose the group is struggling with the problem of inventing a more efficient hairdryer, one which will be less noisy than the current models. The manager of the discussion will ask the group members to choose an object as wildly different from the proposed but still uninvented hairdryer as possible. Someone suggests the Taj Mahal! This is accepted, and members of the group strain to find analogies which might confer new attributes upon the proposed dryer, and open up new approaches for a creative invention.

Too fantastic? Too absurd? Yet this technique for stimulating the adult imagination has worked well enough, long enough, in hundreds, perhaps thousands of Synectics groups, to be retained as part of the standard repertoire for this process in the stimulation of an atmosphere for creativity. Synectics also employs the "excursion", which I find indistinguishable from the earlier brain-storming technique: in this, members of a group are invited to release their imaginations freely for ideas and solutions—and notably not to constrain themselves by problems of cost. Two benefits often occur: in the brain-storming or excursion sessions, the air can become electric with ideas—many, perhaps most of them, "far-out", "weird", "bizarre", "grotesque", "absurd"—these are code words, are they not, among the conventional people to describe anything which introduces the strange or fantastic into the even tenor of their lives? These are the lives, alas, of Total Expectedness —safe lives which will never embark on Ulyssean adventures, never teach the sceptical world about the enormous potentialities for creative planning and living among adults of the later years, never risk being left naked on the shore.

"I want to help people to think properly," Savo Bojicic told Manuel Escott, in explaining why he spent over $100,000 developing his little Think Tank; "to widen their potential as human beings, to teach people how to learn again. Thinking skills will become more important as more and more people need to be re-trained." And this searcher for new ways to help adult men and women attain and maintain a creative awareness toward life, concluded with the old proverb: "Give a man a fish and he'll eat for a day. Teach him how to fish and he'll eat for the rest of his life."

The second benefit from the brain-storming sessions is that certain seemingly fantastic ideas developed within their larger-than-life-size dreaming can often be reduced to the small canvas of the problem in such a way as to provide the solution. But why is this technique, rich in its capacity to evoke imaginative responses from people in groups, almost wholly confined to industrial and managerial planning? Why cannot one imagine enclaves of older adults who meet to consider, let us say, how to reshape their communities; how to establish new and imaginative projects to employ the gifts and energies of elderly men and women; how to identify Ulyssean adventures; how not merely to study the future, but actively develop or encourage the stratagems which may provide some solutions for the nation and the world; how to help bring together the lively and humane views of young and older adults in circles, seminars, and meetings freed of tokenism and awkward and isolated overtures?

Such enclaves would employ the techniques of brain-storming and fantasy, where the air is tonic with ideas, good and bad. These need not be merely for the inquiring minds, the high learners, the tiny percentage which Maslow claims for the wholly self-actualized. Since life to its conclusion in this world should be a process of continuing growth, a voyage and not an arrival, older people should be on the way to ever-growing self-actualization—not merely some élite learning and living groups, but all later adults with their immense and unrealized potentials for transforming and actualizing their own lives.

Brain-storming, when practised for highly specific solutions, is a fatiguing technique if carried on for more than a short period. But as an exercise in the adventure in ideas, adapted for use among friends who have decided that there are other delights in life than the round of bridge and the endless mulling-over of the political cavalcade, it can open a new world. Nor should a group be intimidated by the feeling that they lack technical expertise. C. A. Doxiadis of Athens, whose later life is devoted to consultation on creative ideas, has three points to make about creativity which he likes to press home: first, there is a sparkling force of creativity in every human being; second, it must be challenged again and again to survive and develop; third, it must be stimulated, yet not so over-challenged that it is snuffed out.

Important "rules of the game" for idea-arousing sessions organized among older adults are defined by the words "specific" and "delimited." Charles H. Clark reminds us that in brain-storming three types of target questions can be used. One is called the "steam-shovel-type" question: as an example he suggests, "How can we sell more gasoline to retail service stations?" The problem here, he goes on, is that the company sponsoring the session evidently wants to solve in thirty minutes all the problems it has been working on for years. (A perhaps similar question for an enclave might be, "How can we get the United Nations to work better"?) You get answers, but the answers are about as broad and diffused as the original target question. Another type is the "spade-type" question. Using the same area of concern as the first huge question, this one narrows the field to, "How can we better train our dealers to sell more spring change-overs?" (A comparable reduction of the international problem question might be, "How can the United Nations as a working concept be understood and evaluated in our own community?") Then there is the "spade-type" target question of increased focus and specificity: "How can we get more dealers to come to the training session at the Hilton Hotel six weeks from today?" (Similarly the huge original United Nations target question might far more profitably be recast as: "How can an older adult begin to become a 'citizen of the world'?")

It is crucial, of course, that all ideas be accepted and posted; the room should be filled with flip charts and sheets glued to the walls (if funds are scarce, other arrangements will do—*think* about it!) In these sessions, without put-downs, highly workable ideas will emerge and get everybody's recognition. There is no room, however, for the "little killer ideas," as Alex Osborn used to call them: "We tried that last year"; "We are too small for that"; "It isn't worth doing"; "It won't work"; "It costs too much"; or, as recorded at an engineering deans' conference when they were looking at needs and solutions: "Are you serious?"; "You must be joking"; "I've got a better idea"; "It's too early"; "It's too late"; "Nobody would agree to that."

Astonishing and unusual ideas and approaches can ensue from group sessions. Thus, the designer Victor Papanek of the Department of Creative Arts at Purdue University reported in 1969 to a national seminar on creativity that he and his students had been able to originate more than eight hundred ideas which could contribute to the solution of social problems across the world. For example, how to make some gains in communication among the enormous number of illiterate people in India:

> "The Indian villages had no power sources; there were no lights. When the sun set, the people simply went to bed. How could the problem of communication be solved? A radio was designed that works without electricity, has no batteries, and costs less than three cents each to make. This radio is made from whatever used tin cans are available. The inside of the can is half-filled with wax, contains a wick, and has a thermocouple. It also has a folding antenna and a used nail that

serves as a ground wire. (A used nail rather than a new one is utilized because a new nail is worth money in an under-developed country.) When the wax is lit, it generates enough energy to run the one-transistor radio. The conversion is done by the thermocouple. The wax in each radio will last about six months because the single governmental radio station broadcasts only a five-minute, national news bulletin once a day. After the original wax is burned, more wax or anything else that will burn may be added to the can to keep the system going. So far, UNESCO has distributed more than 42 million of these radios.

The radio is ugly. One man in Germany asked, "Why didn't you at least paint the can grey?" There are two reasons. Painting the can grey costs only a fraction of a penny; but when this is multiplied by 42 million radios, it becomes apparent that a rather sizeable sum of money is involved. Also, a foreigner has no right to impose his idea of aesthetics on these people. The natives know their radios are ugly, so they individualize them by glueing bits of colored cloth, broken pieces of mirror, and pebbles or seashells to the can."

Papanek also reported some devices and toys invented by him and student associates in Finland for partly disabled children:

"A 24-square-meter exercising environment for children with cerebral palsy was designed and built in Finland. This environment has built-in toys. It folds up into a two-meter-square cube which, in turn, breaks into two parts to make it transportable through revolving doors or in a microbus. Most clinics in Finland and Sweden do not have the necessary equipment for these children; so this cube is now taken from town to town.

A second cube of this type has just been completed at Purdue University and is designed for use by mongoloids, cretins, and children with other disabilities. In this environment, there are quiet corners in which the children can hide. Other areas are so very, very soft that the children can jump head-first from the top of the six-foot rack and land enveloped by the extra-soft pillows on the floor. These low-cost cubes were designed, built, and completed in 42 hours. They will soon be made available to clinics in the United States.

One of the students working with Papanek in Finland found that when he took a rubber ball, put wooden pegs into it, and then pressed on them, the pegs would spring back. This made an excellent toy for children suffering from paraplegia, quadriplegia, cerebral palsy, and other disabling diseases.*

*The national seminar to which Papanek was reporting was sponsored by the Thomas Alva Edison Foundation, the Institute for Development of Educational Activities, and The Johnson Foundation.

"But these," will perhaps say many readers, "are the products of highly-inventive people with well-developed technical skills." Even if so, is this comment really an escape hatch from the wonderful obligations of the late creative life? *The later years do not inhibit us.* It is our lack of confidence and our lack of will which inhibit us; and our refusal to turn our faces to the winds of change and the wonder and freshness of all the great world.

Papanek's inventions, in addition to their conception, required certain specific workings-out of the products, construction, and packaging, but the original conceptions of radio, cube, and toy were well within the creative range of a group of intelligent older adults. And Papanek himself calls the key to his and his students' success their "wealth of enthusiasm"—exactly the commodity which is so often in short supply among many otherwise well-equipped adults in their later years.

So far the discussion here has concentrated on older adults in idea-arousing groups. The stimulus in joining other men and women in the search for fresh and original approaches to needs and points of view is clear enough, yet there is wide scope in developing one's imaginative gifts as an individual person or, to put it more bluntly, for many older adults who find themselves frequently or constantly alone and lonely.

The same national conference on *Creativity: The State of the Art* brought together a group of about two dozen noted practitioners in the domain of creative potentialities, including Doxiadis, Clark, and Papanek, as well as one of the gurus in the field, J. P. Guilford. The report of the conference invites the reader to try a number of small creative exercises devised to help develop creativity among school children through the magic of words. One of these asks, "Which is bigger, a pain or a pickle?"* The editor of the report remarks:

> Dead silence is exactly how most adults respond, but children in the elementary age group do not hesitate a minute. One says, 'A pain, because you feel it all over.' Another answers, "A pickle, because it is big and long, while a pain is sort of shrimpy." Such questions do not seem nonsensical to them as they do to most adults; youngsters are attuned to questions like this.

Nonsensical? But without some element of the non-sensical in our lives, the drying-up process begins. Fantasy also: the bubbling cataract which can irrigate the drying soil of our imagination. We know very little about how much adult people fantasize in their ordinary lives. How many Walter Mittys are there? And where does simple wishing break off and fantasy begin? The

---

*From *Making It Strange*, by E. Paul Torrance.

Concise Oxford Dictionary has no trouble making the distinction. A "wish" is an "expression of desire or aspiration"; a "fantasy" is an "image-making faculty, especially when extravagant or visionary; mental image; fantastic design"; and the adjective "fantastic" is defined as "extravagantly fanciful, capricious, eccentric, grotesque or quaint in design." Nothing here about "normal," "natural," or "regular." In fact, for older adults who are leading sensible, practical, "well-adjusted" lives (adjusted to what or whom?) there may be something off-putting about the whole thing—the word "eccentric," for example. Everybody knows what that means, old-fashioned though it is: the jolly modern colloquialism just puts it more transactionally, "Say, what are you—some kind of a nut?"

Great, however, are the uses of fantasy, and never more so than in the later years of life. Alan Lekein, the management consultant, suggests that fantasies are good in coping with life and trying to plan one's years productively, but that people tend to censor even their fantasy life, and that in fact "there's nothing wrong with uncensored fantasies." And he goes on, "Don't be afraid to include such far-out wishes as climbing the Matterhorn, going to a group-sex party, eating a whole cheese-cake, taking the year off, building a retirement home in Italy, chartering a yacht, adopting triplets, and losing 40 pounds by jogging an hour a day." The world of fantasy can be the individual adult's "excursion": and in that world, the rules of routine life that inhibit us should be suspended during the game.

The game should be played—because from fantasy can be born great and small adventures of the mind, and performances, also, which set one's feet on the Ulyssean way. From the unleashing of the mind to roam through still embryonic worlds of concepts and people comes most of our prose fiction, our poetry, our plays, our music and ballet, much of our art and architecture; all our utopias, and many of our utopian ideas (children's villages, literacy villages, Pugwash-type conferences); and in addition, many medical breakthroughs, space adventures, astonishing yet seemingly "simple" inventions.

But especially should older people train themselves to turn concepts upside down; intersect opposites; challenge conventionalities; look at the kitchen in one's home or the park around the corner from the retirement home as arenas for the game of "Why and Why Not?" and the game of "How?"

And look at one's self—with love, with understanding, with lively curiosity—but also with imagination—as the still-unfolding being yet capable of Ulyssean adventures, small and great.

In our time, in a society which deluges the TV screens and

living-rooms with canned emotions; in the society of the nuclear family and the insatiable computer, where real death and illness and old age are as deftly hidden as possible, people not only "lose touch" but lose the sense and consolation of physical touch. Hence the appearance of sensitivity groups, T-groups, encounter weekends, Primal Therapy sessions where adults may regain both the ecstasy of actually being touched by others, and the therapy of being able to bring into the open among hopefully sympathetic companions, old traumatic wounds and crippling or inhibiting hangups.

A good side of our age is its willingness to accept the fact that there is a threshold of isolation in the individual life beyond which the estranged or disconsolate self must call out for counsel or comradeship. The result in North America is the continent-wide network of therapy groups, producing finally the scenario so vividly described by Jane Howard in the pages of *Please Touch*. Adults in their 50s and older, potential Ulysseans, who have missed reading that book will find it extremely interesting and rousing. Jane Howard did more than simply visit representative groups practising celebrated techniques and interview their high priests. She often participated in the exercises, and cogently described her personal reactions as an experimental subject.

Those who do read *Please Touch* may, however, be struck by the impression that there is little room for older adults in sensitivity and release sessions. Is it widely supposed that there is a cut-off point on the life journey, say age 60, where it no longer matters whether people are sensitized or not? That perhaps—as it is said in law enforcement circles that elderly criminals are rare and no longer need therapy—so *Please Touch* is for the young, the aggressive careerists not yet past early middle age, and the affluent couples whose marriages are falling apart or who are simply bored to death? Many advertisements of encounter groups across the continent specify age: not over 45, interested people 20 to 40, and so on. What is the rationale here? That older adults lack funds? That they lack the energy? That they are "past all that"?

There is another explanation. Many of the encounter experiences are very abrasive. Organizers of the groups, in addition to fearing that the gap between youngest and oldest may be too great, may also have a conception of later adults as too staid, too conservative, too rigid, too respectable, and so on to be good subjects for the demands (in some cases, actual rigours and grotesqueries) of the encounter situations. At all events, few older adults appear, least of all the ill and the impoverished.

Yet a frequent phenomenon among people from their mid-50s on, and notably in their 70s and older, is that like Gide they *feel themselves* to be far younger than their years. The 80-year-old widow of a famous American judge whom I once met in Vancouver felt herself to be inwardly as young as when she was a girl at college; small and slight, even physically she showed much of the *joie de vivre* of a far younger woman. And a Canadian woman, Olive MacKay Petersen, writing about her reactions to her age in the Toronto *Globe and Mail* states, "I turned 65 last year—and on a good day feel about 25." Thus in spirit and mind many older adults are equipped to respond to the best of the sensitivity groups.

In addition, there are great numbers of men and women in their later years who have carried all their lives secret fears and feelings of sorrow and guilt. Simply because they are now 65 or 75 or older does not mean that the fears, sorrows, and guilt feelings have got up and gone away. Of course in many cases they have been assuaged or compensated for, or in some instances actually outlived—but many in the later years are suffering from personal deficits, anxieties, and open wounds. And what about the large company described by Erikson who end their lives in "disgust and despair"? They are surely as entitled to the consolations and support of touch therapy and transactional empathy as the anxious and disquieted young. It is hard to deny that for many older adults the techniques of some of the encounter groups might indeed be distasteful or ineffective—perhaps injurious. Many, however, would thrive and grow with them.

The later years also offer another exciting potentiality—the possibility of participating on one of the new frontiers of experimentation with the beneficent effect of brain waves—what Maya Pines well calls the "beautiful world" of bio-feedback. Pines documents the advances made in the study of the rhythm of our brain waves: the discoveries that not only mental but also physical states may be transformed by the individual's learning to recognize under guidance the varying waves of the brain—called alpha, beta, theta, and delta—and to employ his or her concentration in such a way as to obtain therapeutic benefits from the alpha states, and to generate from the low-alpha or theta rhythms the kind of reverie which often generates break-throughs and production.

When Pines describes a successful experiment in which she herself took part at the Menninger Foundation under the tutelage of Elmer and Alyce Green—a preliminary exercise in feedback training intended to demonstrate how one could by mental concentration make one's hands get warmer and one's forehead cooler, —she remarks that after emerging with an effort from a highly successful small experiment, she "glanced at my partner, an elderly, retired businessman. He was smiling." Precisely: the elderly retired businessman was in fact a Ulyssean person engaged in helping create new knowledge about the conquest of mind over body.

The extraordinary Swami Rama, a noted yogi from India who

astonished the experimenters at the Foundation by being able in effect to stop his heart (that is, to create a beat so rapid that it could no longer pump blood) for seventeen seconds, was 45, and approaching the Ulyssean gates. Scientists like Neal Miller, Barbara Brown, Joe Kamiya, and the Greens have no inhibitions about the age of their subjects. As is so often the case, it is the *self-image* which older adults have of themselves, and nothing else, which admits or bars them to the new and beautiful worlds of transcendental meditation and bio-feedback.*

There is clearly a need for the development of new kinds of groups and enclaves in which men and women in their later years can talk out their deeper fears and anxieties and find the therapy for remorse which is sometimes provided among sympathetic companions—companions, moreover, whose role in the sessions is that of peers, not gods or high priests. How these newer-style groups might come into being, and what their processes might be, would be excellent target questions in themselves for brain-storming or other idea-arousing meetings among interested older adults. As one suggestion, it is possible that an imaginative revision of E. L. Thorndike's questionnaire on the learning and unlearning of attitudes among adults might provide the initial thrust for a series of valuable therapeutic encounters.

Obviously, Ulyssean voyages can be undertaken not only in the physical world of seas and mountains, of second and third careers in business and the professions, or of exploits in the arts, but in the inner world of the self. Putting aside for the moment the role of the conventional churches, which seems in our time almost as limited among older adults as among younger, a network of cells and groups appears: notably those dealing with transcendental meditation and the study and practice of the occult. Once again, in a number of currently popular cults, the attention is focused on the young. Yet in large cities, at least, many opportunities exist for older adults to further their self-actualization through exploration of mystic lore derived from man's ancient encounters with the mysteries of the universe. What many rather conventional men and women do not seem to understand, who hunger to know more about themselves through these mysteries but never investigate them, is that participation rarely requires abandonment of a long-held faith (a common fear). Two hungers are typical of many older adults who give serious thought to what their whole human life has been about. One hunger is the desire to know more about the supernatural world, or even to establish once and for all whether it exists. Usually they look in vain to the orthodox religions

*The programme of SAGE (Senior Actualization and Growth Explorations) of Berkeley, California, of which Gay Gare Luce is director, is an excellent example of the processes discussed here at work among adults 60 and over.

for illumination or certainty in this field. Many conventional clergy are very quiet or evasive about it, for the excellent reason that they themselves are doubtful or insecure. Some adopt exaggerated social concerns as a substitute for faith in supernatural things.

The second hunger is for the availability of every power which will aid the feeling of integration of one's self: in this case, the sense that one is both a unique being, spiritual as well as physical, and—in spite of the terrible enigmas of seemingly inexplicable evil —part of an essentially harmonious universe. The healing power, therefore, of essentially meditative religions, yoga, and beneficent occult studies can be very great. Orthodox religions have beautiful things to contribute to those willing to make the real effort to grasp them; yet in the meditative and occult groups at their best the seeker can also find a beauty drawn from the universe, its winds, stars, and flowers which can enrich and help integrate the self; the best of the white occult is one example. If older men and women find all these stimuli and consolations in orthodox religions alone, well and good; or in humanism or atheism alone; but if not, why do so few investigate the potentialities of the outer-ring faiths and philosophies? To do so is to engage in a Ulyssean adventure, although one may not move more than ten or fifteen miles from one's home. On the other hand, the search may take one late in life across continents and seas, among strange peoples and to distant cities one never dreamed to see except in fantasy.

There is another way, often neglected, to explore and actualize the unique inner self. This is through the medium of the personal journal. The most typical record book of our society is probably the office calendar—certainly it is the most prestigious. Here are entered the hundreds, finally thousands, of interview engagements, luncheons, committee meetings, and other supports and impediments of the busy executive. "Impediments," because often in his 50s or early 60s he feels the weight upon him of a succession of days already given away to innumerable meetings, however seemingly important; "supports," because so long as the office calendar is filled, he can feel that his existence is justified. It is a testimonial of his identity.

Many women, and some men, keep a diary of events attended, items bought, and other daily happenings, usually recorded in skeleton form. The value of this is obvious—not least for later years when one can check back to revive memories or ascertain when certain personal things occurred. Even so meagre a record helps to break the grey anonymity of days which otherwise stream past, soon lost in limbo. Even if one keeps a personal journal, there is merit in reserving the very top of the page for jotting down succinctly the day's events.

But nothing can equal or replace the personal journal as the sphere of action for a special kind of Ulyssean journey—the continuing quest of the self, seen in the light of events experienced and books and people encountered. The journal is the record of one's reactions to life and to the fascinating thrust and play of the self. As such, it involves both mind and emotions; and it is usually written in the illusion or with the profession that no one is going to read the entries except oneself. For exactly these reasons, the journals of the very young—mid-adolescents, for example—are usually tiresome to read on the rare occasions when they are made available. They are important documents for insight into the writer and, of course, for his or her insight into the self; but the emotions are usually too heavy and melodramatic for older adult readers, and the words are too self-conscious and postured.

These are not usually the faults of personal journals kept by adults in their later years, and again one wonders why the journal as an art form has had so little attention in North America and so much in England and Europe. One obvious answer may be that in older cultures mature men and women have learned to look inwardly into their reactions to life much more than have adults in a largely externalized, volatile society. At all events, it is so—and it is a pity that it is so; and a pity also that, even among the British and the Europeans, only a minority of the people consistently keep a kind of contemplative journal about their lives and thoughts.

In the office calendar, the personal self never enters at all: "At 3 p.m. Mr. Herbert Cloke, National Elevator Company"—what does this tell us later about Mr. Cloke or the person who is going to interview him?

The daily diary of events does better, a good deal better:

May 14, 1974 (Thursday).

Got up at 8 a.m.
Cleaned house, had coffee with Mary.
3 p.m. Paid plumber for fixing drain ($15).
Mary picking up Bobby at school.
I stayed in with the baby and Bobby at night, and read *Silver Chalice* by Thomas Costain. Baby fretful (caught cold Sunday?).
To bed at 11 p.m. Must check on supplementary pension cheque tomorrow.

This clears away the grey anonymity of the days, but it provides little insight into the interesting, and often enchanting, journey of the self. The personal journal is light years in advance of this, and I give a fictional example: (a brief summary of the day's events has already been listed in the upper right hand margin of the journal):

Tuesday, August 27, 1974. A beautiful morning. Sky banked

with dappled clouds, light sweet wind. I went for a stroll in the fields behind the house. Startled a snake which went gliding off down the path and into the deep grass. Also startled me. How can a 60-year-old man and a veteran of forty air missions over Europe still be chilled by a harmless snake? Where did this fear come from? Mother, perhaps: she also feared insects. No—both parents. Can you *unlearn* a fear of snakes? At the campus in the city last week, a notice up inviting "adult subjects" to volunteer for a course on getting rid of fear of water, reptiles, etc.

At suppertime delegation from the town to ask me to run for mayor. I offered coffee and said No. They pressed pretty hard—they are dear people, and hard to refuse. I reminded them that I had twice before run for mayor and been defeated, admittedly by narrow margins. Marge Kelly said, "Mark, everybody loves you but everybody doesn't vote for you," and Doug Ogilvie said, "You're our Adlai Stevenson."

Picked up at random after supper O'Connor's book on the sinking of the Titanic (*Down to Eternity*).Wonderful things turn up: like the bravery of the 50 young bellboys and messengers who spent the last hours "joking with the passengers, with that sparrow-like impudence of the young Cockney." Not one of them tried to get into the lifeboats. Likewise the members of the ship's band. Marvellous *quality* of the so-called "little" people. And the so-called "great"?

Near midnight I turn on the FM. Surprised by a flute concerto by Mozart. The solo flute is about at the bottom of my list, still I listen spellbound. I wonder, is the flute the oldest of wind instruments? shepherd boy on Greek hill, etc.? Feel as always how quiet the house is. It is almost a year. Somehow the flute concerto keeps returning to my mind, and also that group of people from town. A sort of festival?

It is so late. I will look at this in the morning.

This entry has a number of the qualities of the personal journal: insight, reporting to oneself, restrained emotion, the birth of creative ideas. Typical of many journal entries is the switch to the present tense at some point in the entry, sometimes through the whole entry—it has the advantage of bringing an episode back more intensely. Aside from all its other advantages, the personal journal can provide a sustained dialogue for many older adults who feel that they can never seem to find anyone with whom to exchange their many reflections.

One objection to keeping such a journal may be that it takes too much time. "I'm just too busy." But "too busy" doing what? Alan Lekein urges all of us to analyse our use of time—watch ourselves for a week, for example. The journal entry above might take the writer about three-quarters of an hour, far less than a situation comedy programme on TV, and whereas the programme leaves those who watch with a rather flat feeling of temporary risibility, the journal provides an experience in reflection, imagination, and the intimate sense of one's own life. Another objection may be that a journal entry like the foregoing is too close to a literary exercise, although presumably it would be natural enough to many well-read adults. But in any case, the personal journal still functions well on a simpler level:

> *Saturday, June 11, 1972.* Not knowing what else to do today, I cleaned up my room, and went out to the Zoo in the park. It was cloudy but it didn't rain, and afterwards the sun came out. I've been going to the Zoo off and on for years, and then today I had a funny reaction.
>
> I was watching the children looking in at the cages and pits and then running away laughing and shouting, and suddenly it didn't seem to me right that animals should be closed up all the time like that, and everybody else should be free. I actually wondered if it meant anything to the animals that the children could run and jump and be free. I think I would rather go to a safari park such as they write about in the weekend paper where at least the animals can run free. Maybe I know something about being in a cage, when I think of it. Still I can go free in a way they can't.
>
> I loved the children today. I love them anyway. I don't mind their noise—I wouldn't want to be isolated from them. I was thinking this afternoon, my grandmother never seemed to like children. We were always being kept in corners, etc. I wonder why she was like that? Something in her own childhood, perhaps?
>
> At 5 p.m. I found a new little teahouse two blocks over near the subway stop. They have Twinings Tea—Earl Grey tea! And not very expensive, and the service so friendly and nice. I haven't much, but I have enough to be able to go a couple of times a week to that teashop. For the company. *And* the tea. Also, of course, I can buy some Twinings tea bags, when I think of it, and invite in two or three women here who've probably never heard of it.
>
> I have two books here from the library. One I can't read —a story with characters that could never live on land or sea. I don't often pick lemons like that. But the other one I can hardly put down. It's about a woman in her 70s who makes economy trips all over the world. I don't exactly envy her, still I would like to do it. You never can tell. Anyway, I realize today that I've been overlooking the big travel section. One of the girls said to me today, "If you can't go to the world you can bring the world to you." She tells me they have free travel movies every Wednesday night, and why don't I come? Maybe I will.

When we are feeling tired or flat, we may be stimulated in making journal entries by a few questions kept at hand. For example: how did I react to the weather today? Has it been, all in all, a "great" day, "ordinary" day, "dead loss" day—and why? Who was the most interesting person I met today (or this week)? What was the most interesting conversation I had today (or this week)? What was the most interesting, even creative, idea I had? What was my most interesting dream or fantasy? What was the item in the papers or magazines, or on TV or radio, which most widened my horizons? What book, film, or play most intrigued, informed, and moved me? What was my most frustrating experience today (this week)? When did I feel myself to be most real today? (I am indebted to June O'Reilly for adapting these questions from my self-actualization seminars for use in journal-keeping.)

A little book and pens, costing altogether about five dollars a year, does not seem too high a toll to pay for the entrance to what may become across the later years a personal Ulyssean journey, freshening one's mind, reinforcing and illuminating one's identity, helping heal and integrate one's self, and at times stimulating creativity in one's later years.

Another entrance to the Ulyssean way in older adulthood, which helps to actualize one's self not from within but from without, is the devoted, even passionate, commitment to social causes. As already mentioned, even Simone de Beauvoir for whom otherwise old age is shrouded in gloom, sees light pouring from and around such social crusaders as Voltaire, Zola, and Bertrand Russell. Few older adults are placed in the limelight of history as these Ulyssean figures were; but scaling down the dimension of the enterprise does nothing to remove its power for the person whose mind and spirit have been captivated by what they conceive to be a first-rate cause. To adopt the role of confronter of social injustice or watcher against the destruction of beauty or human needs is not an either-or proposition which excludes such internalizing adventures as sensitivity groups or the keeping of personal journals. It may make both more difficult, but it can be done. What is essential for the growth of the self, however, is that the life of passionate causes should not be a facade for mere busy-ness—a flight from the self by the adoption of a feverish routine symbolized by the overloaded office calendar.

What the true exercise does is to enrich the self by experiences in social comradeship, which help to teach it new insights while also testing the strength and variety of its inner resources. To be of any benefit to the man or woman involved in these expeditions into the espousal of causes, provisions for reflection and personal assessment must be built into the operations. A rather interesting example of hidden meditation in action was that of Robert Mac-Namara, the Secretary of Defense for the United States under

Lyndon Johnson during the Vietnam war. MacNamara, while in the full course of an official life loaded with power and jammed with the kind of celebrity excitement which thousands of other bureaucrats adore, suddenly stopped, announced that he sought other styles of service, and found them in world banking and in work with foundations. He had been, he made clear, reflecting, and his reflections obviously were substantially concerned with the damage which his great office was doing to him personally.

At first sight, though, the problem with men and women in older adulthood is less how they can be brought to reflect during the course of a life of passionate devotion to causes, than how they can be got to participate in the first place. The performance record, even the participation record, is meagre, and one asks why it is not better. Where are all the people, especially age 65-plus, well-enough equipped with time, money, and health—where are they in the ranks of the adults in our society who are pitting often slender resources against what they conceive to be the powers of darkness?

Causes come in little packages and big packages; in permanent exercises and temporary exercises. A permanent exercise, for example, is standing watch on the kind of soulless developer who will conduct an endless King Kong expedition through still undestroyed inner city areas unless some one stands up to him; a temporary exercise might be mobilizing public opinion in one of the frequent cases where locked-together groups of management and union disputants callously expose whole populations to the discomforts of stalled transportation systems, immobilized hospitals, reeking jungles of garbage, and stalled mail.

Situations like these call for pressure groups, confrontations, representations through newspapers, radio, and television outlets, and similar techniques. The antagonists have their rights and needs; so has the public; so—very much so—have the older adults. How is it possible for a transit strike, for example, to freeze the public arteries of a great city for a month and, in effect, imprison great numbers of elderly people who have no cars within the tiny orbit of their normal walking range—and for days to pass with no letters of protest, no telegrams, no blocked switchboards at municipal and other government offices or corporation or union headquarters?

"But I keep informed." Many men and women in the later years take a certain pride in the fact that they are well-informed about the issues and crises of the day, including those occurring in their midst—and this is a just pride. It is important for anyone who has some conception of being actualized by outside human events to pick up the newspaper in the morning and evening and read it thoroughly; and especially to evaluate the issues, tune in to press conferences and issues-and-answers programmes, and monitor live telecasts and broadcasts of controversial events. One can also make telephone calls to informed or, even better, uninformed friends about these crises and issues.

It is important—but it is by no means a Ulyssean exercise. The Ulyssean adult is the one who, like the Toronto architect Eric Arthur at the age of 70, sets up a hue and cry about some encroachment on human rights which otherwise will go by unnoticed—in some cases hardly noticed by the encroachers themselves. Arthur organized vigorous opposition to the development plans of a giant merchandising firm which would have destroyed the historic and still beautiful Old City Hall of Toronto as well as other features of the environment which he felt were essential for the preservation of the city's character. In nearly all great cities there are now groups which keep watch over the historical heritage and beauty of the city. Other groups—all of them low in funds and membership—try to keep a city's or county's conscience awake to the need to guard against unnecessary destruction of homes. There is a whole domain of *good* development, but still *ad hoc* groups are needed to protect a lake, a park, a settlement of cottages, a street, or a whole neighbourhood or area.

Few of these active groups seem to include older adults. Incredibly enough, even the desperately needed movement to reform the scandalous conditions in many nursing homes throughout North America has enlisted little active support from the huge population of older adults. Passive support? "I keep informed"? What can passive support accomplish?

The most searing book, and a deeply moving one, about the neglect of the friendless and helpless old in North America, *Nobody Ever Died of Old Age,* was published in 1970 by a young American woman, aged 32. Josephine Lawrence was in her 30s in 1934 when she wrote the powerful and heartbreaking novel, *Years Are So Long*, describing the desolation of an elderly couple who thought they could depend on their family. Jan de Hartog was middle-aged (about 50) when in 1964 he wrote *Hospital*, one of the most chilling documentary accounts ever written, about the terrifying conditions in a huge municipal hospital for blacks and poor whites, many of them old people, in Texas. De Hartog was inspired to write the book by his experience as a volunteer hospital assistant while he and his wife were on a visit to Texas. It was not even their country! And still, millions of older adults listen nightly to vapid remarks passing for humour from television talk show guests about all those oil-rich Texans.

Where is everybody? It is not just Texas—Texas is no worse and no better than anywhere else: it is the human condition, the outcry of the needs of all the world. "My life has been governed," said Bertrand Russell in his 80s, "by . . . an unbearable pity for the sufferings of mankind." Yet, as already indicated, Russell brought joy with him wherever he went. He was a highly self-actualized human being, because he had gone out of himself into great causes, and in losing himself had found himself more and more. Beauvoir tells with obvious delight of the aged and infirm Voltaire, routing himself out of his comfortable chateau where he still enjoyed the varied delights of love, to go great distances by bone-shaking coaches, and insistently pestering the king of France until a terrible wrong to a young man had been righted. Is it a coincidence that everyone speaks of Voltaire's joyousness of spirit in his old age?

Mother Teresa of Calcutta, living as a younger nun for nine years in the protected classrooms and gardens of a convent school far from her native Yugoslavia, was exceedingly well-informed about the unspeakable poverty and lonely death possessing the streets of Calcutta outside the convent walls. Like our newspapers, the situation was waiting for her when she opened the door in the mornings. At length she could stand it no longer, and embarked on a Ulyssean adventure when she was about 40. She obtained permission from the Vatican to go out, aided by two or three companions, to do what she could to relieve the indescribable misery in the streets. From this early enterprise grew a worldwide network of missions. When, in 1972, Malcolm Muggeridge came to interview her on television and write the story of her work, when she was age 68, he described her as filled with peace and joy. She had experienced a process of self-actualization.

The point here is the self-actualizing power of the enterprises, not the exploits themselves. The size of the enterprise is immaterial, so long as the involvement of the person concerned is one of devotion, of losing-one's-self in participation, which in turn enriches and further activates the self and establishes around it the continuing climate of creativity. Almost nothing can hinder older men and women from engaging in some kind of active role in meeting human needs or preserving beauty except actual physical immobilization, and often not even that. One immobilized man, then 76, proved this to me by dictating letters to the newspapers which were published from time to time and were full of good sense, wit, and some creative ideas.

The political game, too, need not be a mere spectator sport for older adults. In Canada, at least, constituency organizations of the different parties often decline in membership between elections until hardly more than a handful of people are maintaining contacts with the party, meeting to review issues at the local level, and sending delegates to regional and provincial area meetings. Many older men and women turn out at election time to help telephone prospective voters, staff campaign office tables, and help at polls.

This is excellent, but it can only be a sporadic exercise. For those who enjoy politics, there is more value to the party organization and immensely more kindling power to the self in being a permanent participant.

To run for political office in the later years can be a big and authentic Ulyssean adventure. Fewer and fewer older adults seem to do it, partly because of the expense, which can be high; and because there is an evident trend in North America for nominating conventions to choose younger candidates. As this process goes on, more and more men and women in their 60s and older will disqualify themselves by silent withdrawal before any nominating meeting has a chance to consider them. As things are, with the exception of small municipal arenas where there occur astounding cases of very old adults nominated to office, the odds still seem good that people in the late 50s can secure nomination rather easily (that is, age is not a barrier); prospective candidates in their 60s are few, and older nominees virtually unknown. Of course, politicians in office often hold on far into the 60s and in some cases into the 70s and even older if their constituents admire them enough. There have been many examples of this in European politics, and in Canada and the United States as well. No one assumes that an American President or a Canadian Prime Minister should retire at 65: Dwight Eisenhower was 63 before he became President, and in fact formally entered political life only the previous year; in Canada, Louis St. Laurent entered Parliament at 59 and became Prime Minister at 66—he had not previously been an active candidate. For most of the twentieth century the chief executives of both countries have been at least in their 50s and have continued in office until advanced in years. Still, the odds against *entering* politics in any major arena after 60 are slim, except in the case of unusual personalities or specially sponsored people like the two mentioned above.

In any case, it is doubtful whether a formal political career does much for the self-actualization and creative life of older adults. Real emotion about deeply held convictions is remarkably inhibited among successful practitioners of the art of politics. In a Canadian general election in 1974, when one of the party leaders kept telling the voters that he was "an angry man" because of the social injustices which he saw in various parts of the country (and seemed to mean it), he did himself no good at the polls.

Yet anger can be a cleansing and self-actualizing emotion. The ill-fated party leader was expressing a big anger; but there are hundreds of justifiable little angers, such as that of Artur Rubinstein when he arrived late and chilled one winter night in Montreal after some abominable mismanagements in plane schedules. The pianist, who was 87 at the time, remarked heatedly to the music critic Jacob Siskind that "the amazing thing is that no one complained. People just accept these things without protesting. I was furious. . . . You can quote me. They are liars! [the airline personnel]. They have no right to treat people in such cavalier fashion!" Siskind reported that Rubinstein's face was slightly flushed by the excitement; but then he had got it off his chest, and "soon we were back to the Old Rubinstein."

No doubt. But the Old Rubinstein of the brilliant and indomitable concert appearances is surely in part a product of the sudden justifiable angers of the Rubinstein who is concerned that people should not be handled like cattle. Anger is therapeutic when used like this; bitterness and frustrating cynicism are not. Passionate involvement is good for the self-actualizing self. It can channel off tensions and self-pity; explode frustrations; bring a certain glow to body and spirit; and promote the zest for life and the active rather than reactive attitude toward the human scene out of which creativity can be born.

Why do older adults *actively* participate so little in hundreds of social causes? For the retired group, at any rate, the answer may be chiefly because they have passively accepted their implicit and often explicit relegation to the sidelines of community and national games. There are creative answers to this, as their sheer numbers and political power grow.*

One answer might be an organization of the retired, consisting of local chapters, devoted to counteracting this exclusion of older adults from the scenes of action. If such a movement begins, it is important that it call itself something less injurious to the image of retired people than a "pensioners" group, a "golden age" fraternity, or a league of "senior citizens."†

The symbol of people creatively involved in social causes in their later years is not that of the woman of whom it was said that "she went through life asking for the manager." On the contrary, it is the happy warrior, whose spirit and thrust the years have not weakened.

To follow the Ulyssean way is to accept the reality of change: not to accept all change passively and reactively, but to negotiate it imaginatively and dynamically for oneself and one's society, *and*

---

*In addition to the bureaus for volunteers in large cities, important national programmes for older adults exist in the United States (e.g., VISTA, RSVP, FPP, and SCRE), in Canada (e.g., CUSO), and also in Great Britain. For executives at a loss to find second careers after forty, a remarkable organization exists in both Canada and the United States: *Forty-Plus*, with offices in Toronto and New York.

†In the United States, the American Association of Retired Persons (AARP), with headquarters in Washington, D.C., accepts members age 55 and up. This association admirably meets some of the needs, but has much necessary development ahead.

to create change. To follow the Ulyssean way is to believe in the growth of the self to the end of life, in the last day of life—and to act on that belief. If to follow the Ulyssean life is to keep oneself open to experience, that does not mean the imitative experience of fads, simply because "everybody's doing it," but it means going to the storeroom of one's ideas and tumbling them out upon the floor. It means venturing out from the safe-and-sound routines of our habits and tastes to make the air of one's life more tonic with the potentialities of creativity and self-actualization. The brilliant pundit of whom it was said that "he could stroke a cliché until it purred like an epigram" was not a Ulyssean. It is impossible to go through life constantly on the balls of one's feet, like an athlete; but to be flatfooted in one's later years, and never to respond to life's infinite variety of untried activities, concepts, and tastes with the zestful response of the athlete, is simply to turn out the lights in the arena.

There are hundreds of ways, small and large, of breaking the cast of routines which otherwise gradually hardens about one until the drying process has desiccated vision, originality, spontaneous responses, and the reflexes of change. Even physical posture and style of dress begin to reflect aridity of old ideas. For example, elderly men who invariably choose drab colours, dispiriting suits and squarely-placed hats to match funereal faces betray their rigidity of response. If, as is usually the case, these physically dried-out and mournful attributes are accompanied by moribund attitudes toward the self and life, then potential creativity dies. Better by far to put on a colourful pullover, buy a beret (cheaper than a hat), pick up an outrageous paperback, and go out to a café to sip the espresso coffee or the cappuccino never tasted in all one's 53 or 73 years. Better to haunt for an hour or two each week the gourmet section of some supermarket and try out Burgundy snails and octopus.

Not many of us follow Colette and turn a dignified procession through a garden into a child's excursion, breaking and smelling petals, tasting and crumbling, stroking the backs of inquisitive insects—but we are the losers. Better, instead of endlessly deploring marijuana from reading about it in the newspapers, and listening to "informed opinions" on the radio and television, to talk with young people who have actually smoked it or, if opportunity offers, smoke a marijuana cigarette oneself. If you have never in your whole abstaining life allowed alcohol to pass your lips, drink a glass or two of wine; if you enjoy wine and for years have castigated abstainers as living drab lives, try going without for two weeks to see if any joy remains in life. Better—to quote one of the most perceptive men I have known in my life, Kenneth Norris— to break the unvarying routine of moderation by doing something too much: "once in a while eat too much, drink too much, love too much, spend too much, play too much. . . ." "Everything in moderation," said Oscar Wilde, "even moderation."

What holds us back from the small creative adventures which, as they multiply, fill life with a certain verve, small exhilarations which build the climate for larger odysseys? The self-image of what we think we ought to be, to match the face of later years and old age which we have seen and been taught to see all our lives—that is what constrains us. It "isn't done," or it "can't be done." Thus an older man will join an exclusive health club for "executives" (an admirable move in itself) rather than joining the YMCA; or, in the YMCA, will take care to join the more expensive businessmen's health club where he will meet the kind of people he has met for thirty years of his life—instead of the general section for men young and old, of all ages and classes, where as time goes on he will absorb a wide variety of points of view from the assortment of people he jogs and swims with. Men and women who would not now hesitate to attend a Billy Graham rally for interest's sake because that has long since become a respectable enterprise, will not set foot within a local Buddhist temple or attend an open and introductory session on yoga or transcendental meditation—not because they are not interested, even fascinated (they have "read a lot about it")—but because it is too heterodox for their idea of what older adults ought to do. Yet each intelligent exploration or participation in a domain new to one's Totally Expected Life (totally expected by oneself as well as by others) brings tonic airs of self-actualization and creative potentiality.

Little evidence exists as to whether adults in their 50s, 60s, and later years can successfully learn to play a musical instrument. What sensible man or woman of these ages, encased in the usual social and family rituals, is likely to announce that he or she has taken up instruction in the violin, the cello, or the clarinet, not to mention the drums or the tenor saxophone? The actor Barry Fitzgerald learned to play the organ at 53, but then organs have some sort of sanctified connection with *The Messiah*, hard-working church choirs, and Easter services. It may be that numbers of adults in the 50-plus years have mastered the guitar and the accordion, but if so we never hear of it. Yet even limited mastery induces growth and generates energy in the whole self. André Gide never mastered Latin, yet he was working happily at it the day he died at 82: the process helped keep him young, and filled part of his days with pleasure.

As we have seen, many people maintain skills far into the later zones of life. To know that Martha Graham was dancing in the theatre at 75 and Fred Astaire for the films at 70 is exciting and extends the boundaries of Ulyssean activity; so does Barker Fairley's devotion to swimming at 85. Arthur Ingham of Niagara Falls in 1971 was still playing golf three times a week at age 91, and supplementing this with a good deal of dancing and swimming. Still, it is the *commencement* of new learning that is particularly renewing in later adulthood: Ingham, for example, took up golf when he was about 75, surely a rather rare phenomenon, and other features of his late life are strong indications of a self-actualizing personality. Thus, Ingham was not only still driving at 91, but the car he chose was a red convertible runabout, a dashing choice for an "old gentleman". When he was 90 he went on a two-month cruise to Fiji, New Zealand, Australia, Manila, Hong Kong, Guam, and Singapore. Jack Marks, who interviewed Ingham, observed that he was "chipper and cheery, walking sprightly and swiftly. He talks and acts the same way."

Ideally, the adult years from the mid-50s on should be excellent for a wide variety of learning adventures. The general capability is there; usually men and women have learned better how to control their time, or simply have more relaxed time than when young, and they have often learned to concentrate their powers. The study of another language and its culture can throw open windows of the mind to a whole flood of new concepts and knowledges. Yet few older adults commence language study, although perhaps the problem here is the lack of a powerful motive.

A preliminary study (1975) of the performance of a large sample of 862 men and women who took the Canadian civil service training programmes in learning French shows the extent to which older adults can learn another language after 40 if they set their minds to it. The study, by Thérèse Sibiga and associates, shows that about 36 per cent of students age 50 and over obtained A or B standing; as against about 33 per cent of those 40 to 49; about 42 per cent for those 30 to 39; and 42 per cent for those 20 to 29. It is a fact that in achievement of A-standing alone the two younger categories markedly outstripped the students 40 and over, but not in the B classification.

The best motivation for studying another language and culture is one which is missed by all but a few Ulysseans—it is that study of a language, undertaken voluntarily and using methods more enlightened than those which Matthew Arnold said led only to the choked vestibule of grammatical rules, can produce many new intersections of thought that enhance the scope of the imagination. One can just conceive a few Ulyssean people also setting out to show that unorthodox and still uncertified new methods of learning a language may be efficient. As volunteers, and with little to lose, these pioneers could, for example, undertake studies under the so-called Lazonov or suggestology technique, based on the theory of suggestion, devised by Georgi Lazonov of the Institute of Suggestology and Parapsychology at Sofia. Lazonov contended in a series of lectures given at universities throughout the United States and Canada in 1971 and 1975 that adults could become proficient in, say, French or English as a second language in a matter of twenty days. Lazonov's interest in the subject came out of his training and practice in psychiatry. The method was born from his own experiences in psychotherapy, and does not employ hypnosis.

Three of Georgi Lazonov's dicta are notably apropos the whole subject of the fears which hold adults back from new adventures in languages, and other fascinating fields of learning. With this technique, he claims, "no longer is a person limited by believing that learning is unpleasant; that what he learns today he will forget tomorrow; that learning deteriorates with age." (Lazonov himself is 47.) And he adds: "The whole of life is learning—not only in school. I believe that developing this high motivation—which comes through the technique—can be of the greatest importance to humanity." For an older adult to volunteer for language learning under this technique would be a small but immensely valuable Ulyssean act. Even more so would be to hazard a second career by becoming a teacher in the technique, trained in the Sofia institute.

The way in which explorations in the direction of a more self-actualized and creative lifestyle frequently lead on to superb Ulyssean adventures is also exciting. For example, a professional man, a 67-year-old widower, "adopts" a young Greek boy under the Foster Parents Plan. His connection with the lad, which will be officially terminated when the boy reaches 16, is maintained by occasional visits to Greece. In the course of their nine-year relationship the foster father becomes deeply interested in modern Greek culture, especially the language and the music: he learns Greek moderately well and develops a deep affection for the bouzouki. He also visits the Greek Islands every other year under the aegis of Swanhellenic Tours from London, England. Finally, as the years pass, he becomes deeply interested in Ulysses and in the modern locations of the voyages, and proficient enough in the subject to be invited to lecture on it in summer courses.

Two women, a nurse and a teacher, both in their late 50s, and friends for several years, decide to give up motoring for cycling, partly as a result of new convictions about the automobile as an environmental pollutant. They take an extension course at a community college in the efficient handling and maintenance of bikes, and in doing so meet two or three people devoted to hostelling as a way of travel life. The two women become keen hostellers—they had always supposed that hostels were only for very young people. In the course of time, their interest in both travel by bike and hostelling takes them through Europe, and to international meetings of hostellers at Stockholm, Paris, Vienna, and Rome. And they become the co-authors of a useful guidebook on hostelling for older adults.

A 61-year-old bachelor taxi driver in Syracuse, New York, living a lonely and seemingly bleak life in a rooming-house, has had a very limited education. Quite late in life, however, he develops two passions: to listen as often as possible to experts on the radio and at library extension meetings talking on all kinds of subjects, who replace the sophisticated reading he has never mastered; and to listen to classical music. One year at the rooming-house a woman from Yugoslavia gets him interested in the folk music she plays on her record player as she practises for a folk dancing group. He also develops a liking for ballet music and for Schubert and Dvorak. Concertos begin to fascinate him, first because the solo players seem to him analogous to the great lonely heroes of certain sports —then their music captivates him. He has saved a good deal of money but he has no special interest in business; he is limited in manners and in the use of English. This has contributed to his loneliness; only a few perceptive people see his quality. He decides to take two months off every summer from the taxi schedules and visit the great music festivals and centres in North America. He begins what develops into a series of annual odysseys driving to many different musical events in Massachusetts, New Orleans, St. Louis, California, and elsewhere. This particular Ulyssean adventure transforms his life. When I meet him, he is developing a package of creative plans to stimulate interest in classical music among elderly people and meet their needs through cheaper and more accessible festivals.

Although small Ulyssean performances lead to great ones, this is simply rhetorical unless we examine still further the ways and means by which the no-longer-creative adult in the later years can regain and retain and increase his or her creativity.

The role of the *will* in later-life creativeness is paramount, but in terms of becoming or becoming again a truly creative person the will does not necessarily produce the way. The word "will" is defined as: "energy of intention"; not merely the intentions which traditionally pave the roads to both heaven and hell, but the *energy* to enforce the intention, to transform it into action. Physical energy is exactly the commodity which seems to be in diminishing supply among many older adults; some commentators on the productivity of creative people attribute their later failure to produce, not to incapacity of mind and talent, but to increasing deficits of will and physical energy. But the greater factor may be loss of *psychic* energy: caused by the ever-deepening and darkening sense that one has become locked into unchangeable ways, or, in the words of Shakespeare's Richard II, "I wasted time, and now doth time waste me." *Lack of confidence*: this is almost the summation of the matter.

How is the older adult to break free from the immobilizing encirclement of these blocking forces: increasing physical inertia, psychic despair, and failure of nerve and confidence? The answers are not easy, because each individual self has its own complex persona and hidden inner domain and unique personal history, often calling for the therapies of love and understanding; for the therapy of individual insight and self-forgiveness; and occasionally for the therapy of extraordinarily sensitive psychoanalysis. Nonetheless, later adults can take important decisions and actions which will help them re-establish or maintain and expand their creative powers.

The first act is one of acceptance—the acceptance of what Alfred North Whitehead called, "the sacred present." This means not to mourn the past fruitlessly, not to sit chilled and immobilized by thoughts of how one is situated on entering the last years of life, but rather to greet the day lovingly, and to live its precious hours as though yesterday's sorrows and tomorrow's hazards were what they mostly are—chimeras luring us from the sweet airs and the beautiful road of the day-by-day actualization of our self.

The second act is one of recognition, the rational acknowledgement that high potentiality remains to human beings in the later phases of life, and that ancient and modern superstitions to the contrary can be examined and rejected. The earlier chapters of this book, and certain other studies from the lengthy bibliography at the end, can help in the process of recognizing the Ulyssean potentialities of men and women.

"But how does one start to live the creative and self-actualized life after years of passiveness, or in the throes of terrible self-doubts about being able to carry through?" The answer, incongruous though it may seem, is not unlike the first actions to restore to its functions a disordered and dust-laden house. (The analogy is strong with the disordered houses of our intellect; our emotions; and our relationships with other people, ourselves, and the cosmic situation.) We must start where we are, in a relaxed mood of friendship with our self and with acceptance of the human comedy of which we are a part, and begin with some simple action of clearing and remaking. It is a holy moment: "the journey of a thousand miles begins with the first step."

When we do this in commencing or seeking to regain the path to creativity in the later years, we find that an enormous and marvellous repertoire of opportunities presents itself. It is not crucial that the first action should turn out exactly right for us—there are

hundreds of alternatives, and the name of the creativity game is
exploration, probing, tuning in and testing, the cat marks of
curiosity.

So simple an action as reaching for a dictionary can be the start
—the dictionary that may have sat neglected for many months,
even years, except for sporadic and hurried uses. Language is the
stimulator of thought, and is an important channel to creativity.
"Language," Peter Abelard insisted, "is generated by the intellect,
and it generates intellect." In the mysterious process known to poets
and other writers, in which thoughts seem to arrive in the ante-
chamber of consciousness, they are many times clearly summoned
by some evocative or nostalgic word, some *image-making* or *image-
summoning* word which the writer recently or long ago made his
own by identifying it, playing with it, and using it at intervals in
his personal and working life.

Nothing speeds the drying-up process of the later years faster
than to be locked into the impoverished vocabulary of early years
or the once interesting but now boringly repetitive words and expressions one used in one's 40s. Keeping up with and using some
of the new jargon of the day is not a betrayal of the language, but
a simple recognition that to communicate easily with younger
people is both a powerful social cohesive and a means for releasing
the creative process. It can be done without abdicating as a guardian
of standard English. Adults who use English well are often repelled,
and with reason, by what vulgar modern usage has done to the
language: a process of uglification. Yet educated, articulate
moderns often throw English vocabulary into new combinations
which are not only delightful but image-making. Older adults,
especially, should be enterprising in trying out new uses of language: turn a traditional adjective into a noun (I did it in this
paragraph with "cohesive"); try an odd variant like Dickens's
"piping cold," from the ecstatic morning of the second chance at
the conclusion of *A Christmas Carol*; and astonish their listeners
from time to time with such a mind-blower as "interdigitate."

As suggested above, to begin learning a new language or re-
gaining a forgotten one is a self-actualizing exercise: in addition, it
aids creativity by throwing open window after window on to new
concepts. But the same is perfectly possible with the pursuit of
one's own language. Vocabulary building is one of the least expensive and most stimulating of sports. Dictionaries provide wonderful
opportunities for detective work on the derivations of words which
we have used without thought all our lives. Also, a considerable
number of delightful paperback books are available such as Max-
well Nurnberg's *Word Play* which uses dozens of games not only
to tease and test the individual reader, but also to delight and
educate him as well—*to make him grow*. A deeper book and not

less entertaining is Nurnberg's and Morris Rosenblum's *All About Words*; and all the paperbacks of Norman Lewis are energizing and growth-producing.

Every so often in stations, libraries, office waiting-rooms, or even on subway trains, one sees the crossword puzzle addict totally absorbed in the latest teaser. This is an admirable exercise, and if somewhere some ancient man or woman has fallen into what is euphemistically known as their "last sleep" while trying to find words to fit blanks, it will have been a very worthy final curtain. In microcosm, provided the exercise is sensibly difficult, it has some important components of the creative process: problem-solving, the mental quest, some limited but real imaginative leaping, some exploration of what one knows and then needs to know. The game should, however, lead on to the deeper and richer personal arena described above: the enchanting search to enliven and enrich one's vocabulary, and through new words to open windows to new concepts.

Hundreds of little odysseys, any one of which may become a larger one, present themselves to the older man or woman who adopts an attitude of curiosity to the great world—who is alert to break the pattern of Total Expectedness. Clipping items of unusual interest from the pages of the newspaper remote from the tiresome cavalcade of front-page events can be a vital exercise, and in time, and with a lively will, some of these items can be collated steadily into new worlds of interest and inquiry, even of expertise. But why do we confine ourselves to one or two local newspapers and perhaps two or three familiar magazines, when new explorations are there for the asking in papers and journals published in very different worlds from ours? Consider a fascinating newspaper like the *Asian Mail* or the *Bangkok Post,* bringing packets of news often exotic to North Americans, and keeping the imagination supple and alive. Older adults also should break the pattern of their walks, of their drives, of their weekend excursions by bus or foot; of course, thousands more should bicycle again, try hostelling even on a small scale, find a way of going by boat along a network of canals, make new coastal steamer trips, climb in the summer and rest on the sides of mountains or hills which have been within easy reach of one's life and limbs for unused years.

What is needed is a new *set*: the "set" which Robert C. Peck described as (in my shorthand) "I-to-life," which demands that one put a quota on the destructive indulgence of sad drifting of thoughts, of nostalgic sorrow for the dear dead days beyond recall, and of resigned passivity and refuge in the routine. To experience recurrent periods of sadness is only proof that one has depth as a human being. It is beautiful to light candles in hospitable churches for people one loves and has loved. But the creative life is not nourished from a lifestyle of sad and stagnant passiveness. A terrifying phrase which has destroyed more creative impulses than any other, is "if only"—"if only I had done (or not done). . . ." To dwell upon missed opportunities is to blaspheme the Sacred Present, and to lose precious chances for entry into the healing and renewing country of creativity.

Why do so few older adults become protectors and friends of desolate and deserted young people and children? Because older men and women have their own grandchildren to think about and fill their lives with? Is this a sufficient rationale for creative and compassionate people? And what of the several million reasonably well-off single adults—well enough off to have some money to spare—single by reason of choice or of death of a life partner: is there no creative exercise by which they can match themselves with the millions of lonely young who also inwardly ache to resolve the enigma of personal isolation and alienation?

There is something intensely moving and renewing in watching a younger middle-aged couple, as I have, who lost their only son, a handsome, laughing, brilliantly talented boy of fourteen, and a year later adopted a little deserted girl of two, naming her, significantly, Dawn; or in observing the transformation of the lifestyle of a dry 60-year-old bachelor lawyer who has had the creative impulse to "adopt" two or three children under the Foster Parents Plan; or in coming to know an impoverished widow or unmarried woman in her 70s whose love of young people takes the form of turning up at free concerts and plays, where attendance is often all too slight, and applauding and encouraging young musical performers and actors. "It's a great function," my own mother used to say, "to clap your hands for somebody else"—and this she did with loving interest and zest until her death at age 84. All of this is what Robert Peck was talking about when he spoke of *ego-transcendence* in the later years: but likewise these are the unrecorded personal odysseys which keep the will and the emotions supple with creative potentiality.

Thus the "set" for creative later adulthood comes in part from looking life in the face: the eye of "I-and-Thou", if one can so term it. But another important approach to the gaining and retaining of creativeness is to re-align much of one's life as problem seeking: not to be the eternal receiver, the droning echoer (which so many older adults become), but the active questioner, the zestful attacker of hundreds of riddles which life delivers to us if we are alive to them, and the joyous redesigner of trite and customary things and shapes.

A "problem", the *Concise Oxford Dictionary* remarks mournfully, is a "doubtful or difficult question"; for example, "how to prevent it is a problem," or "problem child (difficult to control, unruly)." How dour all this is! And how much this point of view is driven home to everyone in Western society by the thousands of solemn panels wrestling, unfortunately often all too fuzzily, with "social problems, family problems, business problems, health problems," and so on and so on. Just at the end of its list of definitions, the *Concise Oxford* discovers the word "challenge": as, for example, "in chess." Then a different air enters, bracing, tonic—the air of creativity. Then one can move off the muddied turf and the circular exercises of the transactional wheelhorses into the amphitheatre of the wonderful games of creativity, where problems become challenges to the applied imagination, and vivid contributors to the creative "set" of older adults.

To be specific: a small enclave of men and women, meeting to stimulate one another's creative zest and skills, as suggested earlier, can find enormous pleasure and motivation from such challenging exercises as these (those asterisked are drawn from Alex Osborn; the rest, except the first, are mine):

1. List all the unusual uses you can think of for empty cardboard boxes. (Resist the temptation to simply keep filling the box!)

*2. Men's canes have gone out of style. What would you do to try to repopularize them?

*3. Make up a parody of a Mother Goose rhyme.

4. Have we exhausted all the creative ideas of cards which we carry with us? Must they always be credit cards, library cards, social insurance cards? What else—opening wholly new arenas of action or new experiences—can you envisage?

*5. Name five practical inventions that the world could use to advantage which have not yet been invented.

6. If you were deeded $150,000 to open a new store or enterprise on the major commercial street nearest your home, on condition that it must present something uniquely creative among all the tired commercial ideas—what three proposals could you make?

*7. List ten unexplored uses for Scotch Tape.

8. Think of three places commonly in use in the routine of one's progress through life which either stifle you with boredom or cause you vague feelings of dread, and describe how you would remove from them the curses of boredom and gloom.

*9. Write down the title of the last moving picture you saw (or book you read, if you are not a movie-goer). Now suggest five other titles you think might well have been chosen instead.

10. Your college-age son, interested in the occult, has persuaded you to provide housing for a few delegates to the witches' convention. How do you explain their presence to

your son's no-nonsense, fabulously wealthy Presbyterian great-aunt who has simultaneously decided to honour you with her presence on the same weekend?

*11. Devise three ways to adapt an old snare drum to other uses.

*12. Describe the most annoying habit of a person close to you in work or in life. Think up six tactics to get that person to change that habit for the better.

13. Take two objects as bizarrely different as possible— for example, a wrench and a brown trout, and see how far you can draw from them analogies, creative ideas, or new concepts filled with productivity for other beings or things.

14. Make a note of every opportunity you have had to use your creative imagination since awakening this morning.

15. Must library shelves retain their present frustrating forms?

16. "Your mind is like a parachute; it's no use unless it's open." To a similar result, complete the following: "Life is like a Bible;——"; "Love is like a flying saucer; ——"; "Love is like Grandma's spectacles;——". (Creative exercise from the London *Spectator*.)

17. Describe an idea for a thoroughly new television show.

18. Suggest your choice of two, three, or four historical people whose meetings beyond time and space would create (a) a bizarre, ludicrous, or comical conversation; (b) a highly creative situation.

19. How do you estimate another person's creativity? Write down your criteria.

20. What uses could be made of a silk hat other than as a head covering?

Exercises like these are particularly successful in group meetings, because members of the group can often hitch a ride on the ideas of others to produce still further ideas, and, of course, a certain creative excitement is generated by a brain-storming group. Individuals, however, working alone can also find immense pleasure and stimulus from these problems. It must be remembered that the best group brain-storming technique calls for individual warmups or initial attacks at the problem before the group meets, which provide for some degree of incubation. In both cases, group or individual, it is essential that the imagination range free, unhindered for the time being by negative objections, put-downs, and so-called practical considerations. In group and private brainstorming, which is the kindler and producer of creativity, we are to be free of all that—in Eric Berne's domain, we have "permission", and we should use it; we have psychological safety to be free, to be absurd, to be outrageous—in a word, to be creative.

Ideas, as Alex Osborn says, are burning embers; judgment is cold water. There is a time and place for judgments, but ideas must first have their day, and in the later years of adulthood, after most of us have spent a lifetime growing grey in the process of issuing and receiving judgments, usually the only hope we have that we can glow again with creativity is that we will think many times of "problems" as challenging games, and then let that beautiful and neglected creature, our mind, roam and play in the wonderful country of the unusual and the absurd.

Inevitably there are objections: good-humoured, courteous, filled with goodwill, but objections. *Objection One*: "Very nice and interesting, no doubt, but I am a practical person. I'm not really interested in hypothetical situations." *Response*: But is there anything more practical, really, than nourishing and extending our creative powers? And do the routines of your practical life provide this? *They do*? Then yours is an exceptional case. The problem of many 60-year-olds, comments a brilliantly creative older adult, the editor, Aron Mathieu, is that they already know from long experience that the thing can't be done. The 30-year-old doesn't know it can't be done; and frequently does it. This, Mathieu, goes on, is what it means to become dated—that the practical man or woman, in later maturity, has stopped looking at the exotic, the off-beat, the simply different.

Objection Two: "But I'm quite an ordinary person who's lived an ordinary life. I haven't travelled much, seen much, read all that much. I'm just out of my depth." *Response*: Provided you are not just being coy, you are in fact stating one of the situations which does seem to affect creative performance. Of course it helps to have filled one's mind with experiences which extend the reservoir of the unconscious: this is perhaps one application of Christ's parable of the talents. Still, the great world is all about us—its seasons, its moods, its people, its creatures, its thousands of human transactions, its triumphs, large or small, its sorrows, the cavalcade of its human events from which none of us is cut off. To be human is to possess the potentiality of creativity, and an expert witness is that extraordinary Ulyssean who has spent most of his life among workers at docks and in casual labour, Eric Hoffer, the writer of *The True Believer*. Calvin Tomkins, in his portrait of Hoffer when he was about age 66, cites Hoffer's continual astonishment at the variety and originality of the many hundreds of men he worked among—men unknown to the world, usually uneducated in any extensive or higher academic sense—yet he said that in their opinions and ideas, their concepts of life and humanity of contact, he would not have exchanged these comrades for any others. It is indeed possible, if one works at it, to become perfectly ordinary, in the sense that one is truly uninteresting to oneself and anybody else; but life only permits so much of it, and it is not a safe or rational escape route from the obligations of the creative life.

Finally, and in complete reverse: *Objection Three*. "I understand and appreciate what you are talking about. However, I have made it a point for years to develop ways and means of keeping creative, and following up any further suggestions in my case would just be overloading the circuits." *Response*: Beautiful. However, perhaps you would take a few minutes to check this list of facilitators of the creative process derived from this book and from other writers and creative people:

The creative life may be heightened by

1. Looking at life with fresh wonderment, as though one were a child—and in fact, whenever possible, staying in the presence of young children and listening uncondescendingly and attentively to the cascades of original reactions and verbal expressions with which they contend with drab reality. Note some of them down: they evaporate like raindrops in the sun!

2. Seeking to generate new ideas by upsetting the neat, tired order of one's thoughts and throwing them in temporary disarray in the room of the intellect, so that new shapes and images may appear from the creative confusion. Taking the trite, stale places, situations, and interactors in one's life and imaginatively reconstructing them: for example, the local park at which one has stood four thousand times waiting for the undeviating bus manned by the automaton driver.

3. Reading, viewing, and reacting with an active learning "set", to break the grey smog of passivity which otherwise stifles new opportunities for learning. Keeping at hand, unobtrusively but invariably, the notebook and the pencil with which to record striking reactions, questions, later brief reflections.

4. Keeping a notebook and pen beside one's bed through the nights, so that one can enter in waking moments fragments of poetry and dreams; the ideas that arise unbidden from the unconscious mind, and which once lost may not re-appear; and concepts and plans hammered out by the restless mind in periods of sleeplessness.

5. Keeping a journal not merely of events concisely noted, but of personal thoughts roused by certain books and films, by contacts with people who have stirred one's curiosity, pity, admiration, amused anger, or whatever; and of reflections on that part of the cosmos which happens to have been reflected in the tiny comprehensive mirror of our own life. Simple or complex, well or not-very-well written, the entries bear the accumulating colours of one's own individuality.

6. Piling up our fresh and strange ideas and points of view, good and bad, so that we may stimulate the practice of the free flow of ideas, and prove what is most certainly true—that continuously advancing years need by no means inhibit the creative potentiality of men and women. Judgments—the choice of the

"best" (for our purpose) and most workable ideas—can come later.

7. Keeping a *changing* list of everyday examples of the ways in which new situations or new products are made out of different elements which are combined, adapted, reversed, substituted, or multiplied, magnified, and minified—to do this as an exercise to keep the mind alert and tuned to change, and to stimulate, for one's own uses, what Alex Osborn calls "applied imagination." It is not the examples noted down—perhaps in a little "idea trap" notebook—which matter, but the watching-out for them and the active "set" of the mind which they produce. Here are a few (an initial exercise might be to add to and improve on these!):

> *Combining products and functions into new relationships:* combining long and short lenses in bifocals; combining three powers of light on a single switch in the tri-lite; combining skis with small motorized vehicles to make snowmobiles; combining kitchen implements in a single tool; packaging cheese in tumblers; placing alphabets in soup; placing stereo on city buses; installing telescopes in parks; switching land-based conferences to shipboard voyages; providing cocktail service on skates; embossing personal initials on licences; providing films on flights; combining a little library with a hotel bar; combining ice-skating with ballet-style choreographies; combining television, tapes, correspondence materials, tutors, seminars, libraries, and summer schools in a single extension service for adults; combining young singers and guitarists with the Catholic mass to form the folk mass.

> *Adapting and substituting uses:* placing arbours and gardens inside otherwise sterile inner-city business skyscrapers; putting the telephone to uses never seen in earlier years—for 24-hour distress centres, for inspirational messages, for long-distance small conference "round-ups", for wake-up services, for widely-separated chess opponents; converting light bulbs to germicidal lamps; substituting fireside tongs as sterilized forceps in childbirth delivery; sending audio and video tapes of seminars on new legal issues to thousands of lawyers throughout the United States; providing a dial-a-diagnosis network for isolated physicians in Saskatchewan; transforming a sleepy town into a Shakespeare festival centre, as Tom Patterson did at Stratford, Ontario; video-taping laboratory demonstrations and making them available *on need* to college students; adapting the water-hose used for cleaning trains into a self-feeding paintbrush; using radar for traffic monitoring and electric beams for supermarket doors.

> *Gaining new uses by magnifying, minifying, or multiplying products and functions:* inventing the jumbo jet (and advertising for staff trained in hotel administration!); multiplying benefits in insurance policies, and doubling compensations, e.g., "double your money back"; producing handy miniatures

of standard products: the tiny portable radio and tape-recorder, the telescoped umbrella, the raincoat to fold in your pocket, the TV dinner package (note that lists like this *cite* applied ideas only, without evaluating them!), the miniature railroad operating on two acres, miniature golf, and the parlour game of hockey; and miniaturing time—e.g. the three-minute sermon, the mini-lecture in universities (the students have the text), and the fascinating little book of sixty one-minute "whodunits."

Seeking ways to re-arrange, to reverse: engaging in role-playing to gain appreciation of other people's feelings and points of view; having visitors to a science centre (Toronto) actually play and do things rather than simply observe; placing shops in the foyer of a bankrupt church, then at length removing the church, building a skyscraper on the site, and giving the church rebirth on the seventeenth floor; placing the eye of the needle of the sewing machine at the point, as Howe did, instead of at the other end; placing animal signs in huge parking lots, thus "animalizing" (i.e., humanizing?) the scene; selling flowers in book stores, books in flower stores, and both in cafés; re-arranging rigid bus schedules to meet dial-a-bus needs; sending meals on wheels to immobilized pensioners; turning zoo animals loose on huge public estates and placing the human spectators behind the glass of car windows; bringing the chef out into the circle of eaters, as the Japanese do, and bringing the eaters into the kitchen to choose, as the Greeks do; producing colourful rugs that double as wall decorations; taking a restaurant into a woods and growing trees in a restaurant; using soil excavated from Montreal's Metro subway in 1966 to build islands in the St. Lawrence for Expo 67.

8. Actually using "the unforgiving minute": creativity has everything to do with making the most of time—not in the sense of frantic pacing, but in the sense of a kind of private peace in which one is quietly making time come alive—rescuing our mind from the long wasteful rambles it too often makes at the expense of enriching, self-actualizing, and creative thinking. Using time to make notes for journal entries or for later reviews is far more possible than most of us realize; so is the drafting of letters. What use can be made of the idle, often (why not admit it?) bored or pointless periods which interpose in almost every day? *Here* is another wasted hour of incoherent mental drifting which is not really incubation but merely more lost time to lower one's life-tone and morale. And *there* is that decaying network of people to be written to, or otherwise contacted—it is a matter of will. What hinders us? The usual excuse is that we have no notepaper handy, no acceptable envelope, no stamp, and of course, no time. Some noted actualizers of friendship circles use the back of small slips or folders, or other

odd pieces of paper, and send off cheerful fragments of messages, or better, *one idea* jotted down, but personal to the receiver. Cheap envelopes are everywhere, and so are stamps.

To perform these small acts of love and will, to do them now, is to maintain the climate of creative "set"—to be more self-actualized indeed, but also to be readier for the creative life. Creativity is not, as some maintain, a matter of choice between living in solitude and living in the world, but a matter of judicious selection of the best of both. We have only to look at the lives of many great "special talent" creators, to say nothing of the great and noble company of the Ulyssean adults.

To gain entry to the country and the company of the Ulyssean people no passport is required. No restrictions exist as to race, class, religion, political ideology, or education—just the reverse. The Ulyssean country is an open commonwealth of older adults of every racial group under the sun; its membership includes every degree of wealth and non-wealth, every level of education, every form of belief and non-belief. Membership has nothing to do with whether one is physically well or dogged by ill-health, whether one is personable or plain, well-travelled or confined to a limited area. It has no special insignia, rings, or medallions; no special hand-shakes or ritualistic greetings; no membership cards or blackballs; no status symbols. No period of years of residence is required for citizenship—citizenship exists, but it is not a static thing, conferred at a ceremony. It is a process, not a state; a process of *becoming*, and great practitioners of the Ulyssean way would certainly describe themselves as voyagers, not inhabitants.

Ulysseans can identify themselves by attitudes verified by actions which, together, constitute a distinctive lifestyle in the years of middle and later adulthood—although of course many enter the process of becoming Ulysseans long before.

These are the attitudes towards life and the later years which are typical of Ulysseans: that life is a process of continuous growth, as much through the later and very late years as in any earlier period; that the capacity to learn is fully operative among human beings across the entire span of life, and that one simply goes ahead and learns, and grows; that human creativity comprises, apart from the splendours of genius, thousands of manifestations of the mind and imagination which transform an individual's own self or his or her environment; that creativity cannot be taught and learned as one can teach and learn a language—but that certain conditions, *all of them potentially available in the later years*, can be fostered so that the creative attitude and powers, on whatever scale, can be liberated. The most important of these conditions are maintenance of a sense of wonder toward life, openness to experience, the sense of search, and scope for the best of the child-self which is present in all of us.

I emphasize that these conditions are *potentially* available, because in our society millions of older adults enter the later decades with such conventional lifestyles and attitudes, their individual identity so diffused or confused, and their powers of creativity so unused and rusted, that only by a gradual process or by the intervention of some revolutionizing event in their lives can new capacities for growth and creativity emerge and begin a transforming process. This is not even a situation of "us" and "them"—few of us are home free. It takes sustained imagination, will, courage, and love to live the later years as Ulyssean adults, to maintain our own identity on our own terms.

We are dealing, after all, with a human journey, not an air-regulated shelter. Everything we know of Ulyssean adults tells us that they are total human beings. They are quite aware that in the important domain of physical powers they no longer possess the prowess they had when young, nor the unbounded energy which among many young adults spills like surging rapids beautifully but uselessly over rocks. The Ulyssean people know that advancing years bring hazards, and they know that either their own misjudgments or external fate, or both, may bring them for a time naked on the shore.

But either because of their nature, or what they have learned, they look into the face of life, not away from it; they cultivate the high art of looking at both the human comedy and the drama of the mysterious universe with intense interest and wonder. They use the remarkable brain-and-mind which is their heritage without fretting about supposed declines and deficits, knowing that there is an abundance of power there, knowing it will serve them well. And day by day they try to foster in themselves the conditions that promote creativity—freshness of outlook, spontaneity of feelings, acceptance of the constructive disorder of change, loving retrospect of the past but with the eye of interpretation and analysis, and the sense of life's adventure, its unexpectedness, its marvellous "you never can tell."

Thus Ulyssean adults maintain and develop their own real identities, quicken the pulses of creative growth in themselves and in the people around them, and help light the windows of the world.

APPENDIX

THE CONTINUING HIGH CREATIVITY OF SCIENTISTS THROUGH THE MIDDLE AND LATER YEARS

In opposition to H. C. Lehman, who asserts that scientists normally attain a peak of creativity in their late twenties and their thirties, and then decline; and advancing beyond Wayne Dennis, who shows the continued productivity of scientists but is not concerned with their creativity as such, *The Ulyssean Adult* contends that scientific creativity should not be evaluated solely by the criterion of productivity, and that to identify a scientist's "peak of creativity" as the occasion when he made his supposedly "most important" discovery is naive.

The creative process is not a simple rising-and-falling curve to and from a supposed single peak; the scientist's whole creative life must be reviewed—and not just "famous" scientists but thousands of distinguished scientists, active in many fields and roles, who have continued to make investigations in enterprises of the first order throughout their 40s, 50s, and 60s, and even in numerous cases into the later years. Ideally, such an investigation should be based on an examination of scientists' whole working lives.

For my own interest, however, although I recognized its serious limitations, I made a study, somewhat Lehman-style, of a large number, chosen at random, of the lengthy abbreviated biographies of scientists no longer living, in the excellent, multi-volume *Dictionary of Scientific Biography*, published by Charles Scribner's Sons commencing in 1970. (The volumes so far published extend to names beginning with the letter R.) Even in this initial exercise, I had no difficulty identifying a large group of scientists who had continuously creative lives. I propose an extended study of this subject, *The Ulyssean Scientist,* for later publication.

Readers interested in the subject of scientific creativity will find it a challenging but rewarding project to do a similar exercise.

CREATIVE SCIENTISTS THROUGHOUT LIFE— A REPRESENTATIVE GROUP

PIETRO D'ABANO, 1257-1315 (medicine, natural history, philosophy); JOHN JACOB ABEL, 1857-1938 (pharmacology, biochemistry); ERIK ACHARIUS, 1757-1819 (botany); FRANK DAWSON ADAMS, 1859-1942 (geology); THOMAS ADDISON, 1793-1860 (medicine); JACOB GEORGE AGARDH, 1813-1901 (botany); ROBERT GRANT AITKEN, 1864-1951 (astronomy); HANS BERGER, 1873-1941 (psychiatry, electro-encephalography); HENRI BERGSON, 1859-1941 (philosophy, encompassing fields of science); JOHANN I. BERNOULLI, 1667-1748 (mathematics); PAUL BERT, 1833-1886 (physiology, comparative anatomy, natural history); ENRICO BETTI, 1823-1892 (mathematics); NIELS HENRIK DAVID BOHR, 1885-1962 (atomic and nuclear physics, epistemology); BERNARD BOLZANO, 1781-1848 (philosophy, mathematics, logic); GIOVANNI ALFONSO BORELLI, 1608-1679 (astronomy, epidemiology, mathematics, physics, physiology); WILLIAM HENRY BRAGG, 1862-1942 (physics); FEDOR ALEKSANDROVICH BREDIKHIN, 1831-1904 (astronomy); ALEXANDRE BRONGNIART, 1770-1847 (geology); ROBERT BROOM, 1866-1951 (palaeontology); FRANZ BOAS, 1858-1942 (anthropology); HENRY CAVENDISH, 1731-1810 (natural philosophy: notably mathematics, optics, magnetism, and geology); AUGUSTIN-LOUIS CAUCHY, 1787-1857 (mathematics, mathematical physics, celestial mechanics); JOHN HENRY COMSTOCK, 1849-1931 (entomology); CHARLES AUGUSTIN COULOMB, 1736-1806 (physics, applied mechanics); PAFNUTY LVOVICH CHEBYSHEV, 1821-1894 (mathematics); FERDINAND JULIUS COHN, 1828-1898 (botany, bacteriology); WILLIAM CROOKES, 1832-1919 (chemistry, physics); PETER JOSEPH WILLIAM DEBYE, 1884-1966 (chemical physics); JULIUS WILHELM DEDEKIND, 1831-1916 (mathematics); LEE DE FOREST, 1873-1961 (electronics); GIRARD DESARGUES, 1591-1661 (geometry, perspective); JAMES DEWAR, 1842-1923 (chemistry, physics); OTTO PAUL HERMANN DIELS, 1876-1954 (organic chemistry); DIETRICH VON FREIBERG, 1250-1610 (optics, natural philosophy); HUGO ALBERT EMIL HERMANN DINGLER, 1881-1954 (philosophy); CORNELIO AUGUST SEVERINUS DOELTER, 1850-1930 (chemical mineralogy); PIERRE-MAURICE-MARIE DUHEM, 1861-1916 (physics, rational mechanics, physical chemistry, history of science, philosophy of science); RENE-JOACHIM-HENRI DUTROCHET, 1776-1847 (animal and plant physiology, embryology, physics, phonetics); ARTHUR STANLEY EDDINGTON, 1882-1944 (astronomy, relativity); LUTHER PFAHLER EISENHART, 1876-1965 (mathematics); JOHANN PHILIPP ELSTER, 1854-1920 (experimental physics); JOSEPH ERLANGER, 1874-1965 (physiology); LEONHARD EULER, 1707-1783 (mathematics, mechanics, astronomy, physics).

GIROLAMO FABRICI, 1533-1619 (anatomy, physiology, embryology, surgery); MICHAEL FARADAY, 1791-1867 (chemistry, physics); ALEXEI YEVGRAFOVITCH FAVORSKY, 1860-1945 (chemistry); GUSTAV THEODOR FECHNER, 1801-1887 (psychology: psychophysics); LEONARDO FIBONACCI, or LEONARDO OF PISA, 1170-1240 (mathematics); ADOLF EUGEN FICK, 1829-1901 (physiology, physical medicine); HOWARD WALTER FLOREY, 1898-1968 (pathology); AUGUST FOPPL, 1854-1924 (engineering, physics); JOHAN GEORG FORCHHAMMER, 1794-1865 (geology, oceanography, chemistry); FERDINAND ANDRE FOUQUE, 1828-1904 (geology, mineralogy); GIROLAMO FRACASTORO, 1478-1553 (medicine, philosophy); JAMES FRANCK, 1882-1964 (physics); BERNARD FRENICLE DE BESSY, 1605-1675 (mathematics, physics, astronomy); GEORGES FRIEDEL, 1865-1933 (crystallography); KARL FRIEDRICH VON GAERTNER, 1772-1850 (botany); GALILEO GALILEI, 1564-1642 (physics, astronomy); FRANZ JOSEPH GALL, 1758-1828 (neuroanatomy, psychology); LUIGI GALVANI, 1737-1798 (anatomy, physiology, physics); GEORGE GAMOW, 1904-1968 (physics); JOHN PETER GASSIOT, 1797-1877 (electricity); ALBERT JEAN GAUDRY, 1827-1908 (palaeontology); JOHN SCOTT HALDANE, 1860-1936 (physiology); GEORGE ELLERY HALE, 1868-1938 (astrophysics); STEPHEN HALES, 1677-1761 (physiology, public health); ASAPH HALL, 1829-1907 (astronomy); MARSHALL HALL, 1790-1857 (physiology, clinical medicine); ARTHUR RUDOLF HANTZSCH, 1857-1935 (chemistry); CHARLES HERMITE, 1822-1901 (mathematics); WILLIAM HERSCHEL, 1738-1822 (astronomy); ALEXANDER VON HUMBOLDT, 1769-1859 (cosmology); JOHN NEWPORT LANGLEY, 1852-1925 (physiology, histology); IRVING LANGMUIR, 1881-1957 (chemistry, physics); ANDREW COOPER LAWSON, 1861-1952 (geology); ANTONI VAN LEEUWENHOCK, 1632-1723 (natural sciences, microscopy); ADRIEN-MARIE LEGENDRE, 1752-1833 (mathematics); GOTTFRIED WILHELM LEIBNITZ, 1646-1716 (mathematics, philosophy, metaphysics); LEONARDO DA VINCI, 1452-1519 (anatomy, technology, mechanics, mathematics, geology); DOMINIQUE-AUGUSTE LEREBOULLET, 1804-1865 (zoology, embryology); FRANZ YULEVICH LEVINSON-LESSING, 1861-1939 (geology, petrography); GILBERT NEWTON LEWIS, 1875-1946 (chemistry); LEONID SAMUILOVICH LEYBENZON, 1879-1951 (mechanical engineering, geophysics); FRANK RATTRAY LILLIE, 1870-1947 (embryology, zoology); OTTO LOEWI, 1873-1961 (pharmacology, physiology); HEINZ LONDON, 1907-1970 (physics); ALEKSANDR MIKHAILOVICH LYAPUNOV, 1857-1918 (mathematics, mechanics); CHARLES LYELL, 1797-1875 (geology, evolutionary biology).

MARCELLO MALPIGHI, 1628-1694 (medicine, microscopic and comparative anatomy, embryology); PATRICK MANSON, 1844-1922 (tropical medicine); ANDREAS SIGISMUND MARGGRAF, 1709-1782 (chemistry); ANDREI ANDREEVICH MARKOV, 1856-1922 (mathematics); GERARDUS MERCATOR, 1512-1594 (geography, cartography); MARIN MERSENNE, 1588-1648 (natural philosophy, acoustics, music, mechanics, optics); JOHN MICHELL, 1724-1793 (astronomy); GUSTAV MIE, 1868-1957 (physics); WILLIAM MILLER, 1817-1870 (chemistry, spectroscopy, astronomy); WILLIAM HOBSON MILLS, 1873-1959 (organic chemistry); CHARLES FRANCOIS BRISSEAU DE MIRBEL, 1776-1854 (botany); AUGUST FERDINAND MOBIUS, 1790-1868 (mathematics, astronomy); ANDRIJA MOHOROVICIC, 1857-1936 (meteorology, seismology); ABRAHAM DE MOIVRE, 1667-1754 (probability theory); GIOVANNI BATTISTA MORGAGNI, 1682-1771 (pathological anatomy); ISAAC NEWTON, 1642-1727 (mathematics, dynamics, celestial mechanics, astronomy, optics, natural philosophy); THOMAS BURR OSBORNE, 1859-1929 (protein chemistry); GUISEPPE PIAZZI, 1746-1826 (astronomy); MUHYI AL-DIN PIRI RAIS, 1470-1554 (geography, cartography); GEORGE NICHOLAS PAPANICOLAOU, 1883-1962 (anatomy); ALPHEUS SPRING PACKARD, JR., 1839-1905 (entomology); LOUIS PASTEUR, 1822-1895 (crystallography, chemistry, microbiology, immunology); KARL PEARSON, 1857-1936 (applied mathematics, biometry, statistics); IVAN PETROVICH PAVLOV, 1849-1936 (physiology, psychology); JAMES PARKINSON, 1755-1824 (medicine, palaeontology); JOSEPH PLATEAU, 1801-1883 (mechanics).

SELECT BIBLIOGRAPHY

Allport, Gordon, *Becoming* (New Haven: Yale University Press, 1954.)
  Pattern and Growth in Personality (New York: Holt, Rinehart, and Winston, 1961.)

Anderson, Harold H., ed., *Creativity and Its Cultivation* (New York: Harper and Row, 1959.)

Anderson, J. R. L., *The Ulysses Factor, the Exploring Instinct in Man* (London: Hodder and Stoughton, 1970.)

Arasteh, A. Reza, *Final Integration in the Adult Personality: a Measure for Health, Social Change and Leadership* (Leyden: E. J. Brill, 1965.)

Barron, Frank, *Creativity and Psychological Health* (New York: Van Nostrand, 1963.)

Barron, Milton C., *The Aging American* (New York: Thomas Crowell, 1961.)

Beauvoir, Simone de, *The Coming of Age* (New York: Putnam, 1972.)

Berdiaev, N. A., *The Meaning of the Creative Act* (New York: Harper, 1955.)

Berenson, Bernard, *Sunset and Twilight* (New York: Harcourt Brace, 1963.)

Berlyne, D. E., *Conflict, Arousal, and Curiosity* (New York: McGraw-Hill, 1960.)

Berne, Eric, *Games People Play* (New York: Bantam Books, 1964.)
  What Do You Say After You Say Hello? (New York: Bantam Books, 1973.)

Birren, James, *The Psychology of Aging* (Englewood Cliffs, N.J.: Prentice-Hall, 1964.)

Bischof, L. J., *Adult Psychology* (New York: Harper and Row, 1969.)

Bode, Carl, ed., *The Selected Journals of Henry David Thoreau* (New York: New American Library, 1967.)

Borden, Charles A., *Sea Quest: Global Blue-Water Adventuring in Small Craft* (Philadelphia: Macrae Smith, 1967.)

Bugelski, B. R., *The Psychology of Learning Applied to Teaching* (Indianapolis: Bobbs-Merrill, 1964.)

Buhler, Charlotte, and Fred Massarik, eds., *The Course of Human Life* (New York: Springer, 1968.)

Burgess, E. W., ed., *Aging in Western Societies* (Chicago: University of Chicago Press, 1960.)

Burns, Hobert W., et al., *Sociological Backgrounds of Adult Education* (Chicago: CSLEA, 1964.)

Burnshaw, Stanley, *The Seamless Web* (New York: Braziller, 1970.)

Butcher, H. J., *Human Intelligence, Its Nature and Assessment* (London: Methuen, 1968.)

Cavan, Ruth, E. W. Burgess, R. J. Havighurst, and H. Goldhamer, *Personal Adjustment in Old Age* (Chicago: Science Research Associates, 1949.)

Chevalier, Maurice, *I Remember It Well* (New York: Macmillan, 1970.)

Clarke, Arthur C., *Profiles of the Future* (New York: Bantam Books, 1964.)

Clements, Robert J., *Michelangelo, a Self Portrait* (New York: Prentice-Hall, 1963.)

Craft, Robert, *Stravinsky: Chronicle of a Friendship, 1948-71* (New York: A. A. Knopf, 1972.)

Creativity: the State of the Art, Report of a National Seminar, undated (Racine, Wisconsin: The Thomas Alva Edison Foundation, the Johnson Foundation, and the Institute for Development of Educational Activities, 1970.)

Cross, Milton, and Robert Ewen, *Encyclopedia of Great Composers* (New York: Doubleday), 2 vols.

Crowther, J. G., *British Scientists of the 19th Century* (London: Penguin Books, 1940), 2 vols.
Famous American Men of Science (London: Secker and Warburg, 1937.)

Cumming, Elaine, and W. E. Henry, *Growing Old: the process of disengagement* (New York: Basic Books, 1961.)

Curtin, Sharon, *Nobody Ever Died of Old Age* (Boston: Atlantic Monthly Press, 1973.)

Cushing, Harvey, *Sir William Osler* (New York: Oxford, 1940.)

Dabrowski, K., *Positive Disintegration* (Boston: Little, Brown, 1964.)

Dante Alighieri, *The Divine Comedy*, trans. Charles S. Singleton (Princeton, N.J.: Princeton University Press, 1970.)

De Grazio, Sebatian, *Of Time, Work, and Leisure* (New York: Twentieth Century Fund, 1962.)

De Ropp, Robert S., *The Master Game* (New York: Delta, 1968.)

Di Lampedusa, Giuseppe, *Two Stories and a Memory*, trans. Alexander Colquhoun (London: Collins and Harwill, 1962.)

Donahue, Wilma, and Clark Willetts, *Aging Around the World* (New York, Columbia University Press, 1962.)

Donahue, Wilma, and Clark Tibbits, *The New Frontiers of Aging* (Ann Arbor: University of Michigan Press, 1957.)

Dorian, Frederick, *The Musical Workshop* (New York: Harper, 1947.)

Drucker, Peter F., *The Age of Discontinuity* (New York: Harper and Row, 1968.)

Dubin, Robert, *The World of Work* (Englewood Cliffs, N.J.: Prentice-Hall, 1958.)

Eckerman, J. P., *Conversations with Goethe* (London: J. M. Dent, 1935.)

ERIC Clearinghouse on Adult Education, *Adult Learning Characteristics*, No. 21, May, 1968.

Erikson, Erik H., *Identity and the Life Cycle* (Psychological Issues, Monograph No. L, 1959.)
Childhood and Society (New York: Norton, 1964.)

Evans, Richard I., *Dialogue with Erik Erikson* (New York: E. P. Dutton, 1969.)

Fair, Charles M., *The Dying Self* (Middleton, Conn.: Wesleyan University Press, 1969.)

Feifel, H., ed., *The Meaning of Death* (New York: McGraw-Hill, 1959.)

Fisher, Welthy Honsinger, *To Light A Candle* (New York: McGraw-Hill, 1962.)

Flesch, R., *The Art of Clear Thinking* (New York: Harper, 1952.)

Foss, J. O., *Ralph Vaughan Williams: A Study* (London: Harrap, 1952.)

Frankl, Victor E., *From Death Camp to Existentialism* (Boston: Beacon Press, 1959.)
The Doctor and the Soul, from Psychotherapy to Logotherapy (London: Penguin Books, 1973.)

Friedmann, E. A., and R. J. Havighurst, *The Meaning of Work and Retirement* (Chicago: University of Chicago Press, 1954.)

Fromm, Erich, *The Art of Loving* (New York: Bantam, 1970.)
The Heart of Man (New York: Harper & Row, 1968.)

Fulton, E., ed., *Death and Identity* (New York: John Wiley, 1965.)

Galton, Lawrence, *Don't Give Up on an Aging Parent* (New York: Crown Publishers, 1975.)

Gardner, John, *Self-Renewal: the Individual and the Innovative* (New York: Harper, 1964.)

Gary, Romain, *Promise at Dawn* (London: Sphere Books Ltd., 1971.)

Gattegno, Caleb, *Towards a Visual Culture* (New York: Dutton, 1969.)

Ghiselin, Brewster, *The Creative Process* (New York: New American Library, 1952.)

Gide, André, *Journals* (New York: Vintage Books, 1956.)

Goble, Frank, *The Third Force: the Psychology of Abraham Maslow* (New York: Simon and Shuster, 1971.)

Goffman, Erving, *The Presentation of Self in Everyday Life* (New York: Doubleday, 1959.)

Goldwater, R., and M. Treves, eds., *Artists on Art* (London: Kegan Paul, 1947.)

Gordon, William J. J., *Synectics, the Development of Creative Capacity* (New York: Harper and Row, 1961.)

Goudeket, Maurice, *The Delights of Growing Old* (New York: Farrar, Straus, and Giroux, 1966.)

Graham, Sheila, *College of One* (New York: Viking Press, 1967.)

Gregory, J. C., *The Nature of Laughter* (London: Kegan Paul, 1924.)

Groch, Judith, *The Right to Create* (Boston: Little, Brown, 1969.)

Gross, Martin L., *The Brain Watchers* (New York: Random House, 1962.)

Hadamard, Jacques, *The Psychology of Invention in the Mathematical Field* (Princeton, N.J.: Princeton University Press, 1945.)

Haefele, J. W., *Creativity and Innovation* (New York: Reinhold, 1962.)

Hall, Edward T., *The Hidden Dimension* (New York: Doubleday, 1966.)

The Silent Language (New York: Fawcett, 1959.)

Halprin, L., *The RSVP Cycles: Creative Processes in the Human Environment* (New York: Braziller, 1970.)

Hanna, Charles B., *The Face of the Deep: The Religious Ideas of C. G. Jung* (Philadelphia: Westminster Press, 1967.)

Hanson, N. R., *Patterns of Discovery* (Cambridge: Cambridge University Press, 1961.)

Harris, Irving D., *Emotional Blocks to Learning* (New York: Free Press of Glencoe, 1961.)

Harris, Thomas A., *I'm OK—You're OK* (New York: Avon, 1973.)

Hartog, Jan de, *Hospital* (New York: Athenaeum, 1964.)

Havelka, Jaroslav, *The Nature of the Creative Process in Art* (The Hague: Nijhoff, 1968.)

Havighurst, Robert J., *Developmental Tasks and Education* (Toronto: Longman's Green, 1960.)

Human Development and Education (New York: David McKay, 1953.)

Hesse, Hermann, *Steppenwolf* (New York: Holt, Rinehart and Winston, 1963.)

Hiestand, Dale L., *Changing Careers after 35* (New York: Columbia University Press, 1971.)

Hoffer, Eric, *The True Believer* (New York: Harper and Row, 1951.)

Hoffman, Banesh, *The Tyranny of Testing* (New York: Collier-Macmillan, 1964.)
 The Temper of Our Time (New York: Harper and Row, 1964.)

Hoopes, Ned E., *Who Am I? Essays on the Alienated* (New York: Dell Paperbacks, 1969.)

Hoopes, Ned E., and Richard Peck, *Edge of Awareness* (New York: Dell, 1969.)

Horney, Karen, *The Neurotic Personality of Our Time* (New York: W. W. Norton, 1937.)

Houle, Cyril, *The Inquiring Mind* (Madison: University of Wisconsin Press, 1961.)

Howard, Jane, *Please Touch* (New York: McGraw-Hill, 1970.)

Ibsen, Henrik, *Peer Gynt*, trans. Michael Meyer (London: Hart-Davis, 1963.)

Jacobs, Jane, *The Death and Life of Great American Cities* (New York: Random House-Knopf, 1961.)

Janov, Arthur, *The Primal Revolution* (New York: Simon and Schuster, 1972.)

Jennings, Eugene E., *An Anatomy of Leadership, Princes, Heroes, and Supermen* (New York: McGraw-Hill, 1960.)

Johnston, William, *Silent Music: the Science of Meditation* (New York: Harper and Row, 1974.)

Johnstone, John W. C., and Ramond Rivera, *Volunteers for Learning* (Chicago: Aldine, 1965.)

Jourard, Sidney M., *The Transparent Self* (New York: Van Nostrand, 1964.)

Jung, C. G., *Memories, Dreams, and Reflections* (New York: Pantheon, 1963.)
 Psychological Reflections, a New Anthology of his Writings 1905-1961, eds., J. Jacobi and R. F. C. Hull (Princeton, N.J.: Princeton University Press, 1970.)
 Aion, Researches into the Phenomenology of the Self (Princeton, N.J.: Princeton University Press, 1959.)

Katz, Robert L., *Empathy* (New York: Free Press of Glencoe, 1963.)

Kazantzakis, Nikos, *Report to Greco* (New York: Bantam Books, 1966.)

Kidd, J. Roby, *How Adults Learn* (New York: Association Press, 1973.)

Kierkegaard, Soren, *Journals, 1834-1854* (London: Collins-Fontana, 1958.)

Kneller, George F., *The Art and Science of Creativity* (New York: Holt, Rinehart, and Winston, 1965.)

Knowles, Malcolm S., *The Modern Practice of Adult Education: Andragogy vs. Pedagogy* (New York: Association Press, 1970.)

Koestler, Arthur, *The Act of Creation* (London: Hutchinson, 1964.)
    The Ghost in the Machine (London: Hutchinson, 1967.)
Koller, Marvin R., *Social Gerontology* (New York: Random House, 1964.)
Kronenberger, Louis, ed., *Atlantic Brief Lives: a Biographical Companion to the Arts* (Boston: Little, Brown, 1965.)
Kubie, L. S., *Neurotic Distortion of the Creative Process* (New York: Noonday Press, 1965.)
Kuhlen, Raymond G., *Psychological Backgrounds of Adult Education* (Chicago: CSLEA, 1963.)
Kutner, B., D. Fanshel, A. M. Togo, and T. S. Langner, *Five Hundred over Sixty* (New York: Russell Sage Foundation, 1956.)
Lasson, Frans, ed., *The Life and Destiny of Isak Dinesen*, text by Clara Svendsen (New York: Random House, 1970.)
Lawrence, Josephine, *Years Are So Long* (New York: Grosset and Dunlap, 1924.)
Lehman, H. C., *Age and Achievement* (Princeton, N.J.: Princeton University Press, 1953.)
Liberman, Alexander, *The Artist in His Studio* (New York: Viking, 1960.)
Liss, Jerome, *Free to Feel: Finding Your Way Through the New Therapies* (New York: Praeger, 1974.)
Lorge, Irving, H. Y. McClusky, G. E. Jensen, and W. C. Hollenbeck, *Adult Education: Theory and Method* (Washington: Adult Education Association of the U.S.A., 1963.)
    Psychology of Adults (Washington: AEA, 1964.)
Losey, Frederick D., *The Kingsway Shakespeare* (London: George G. Harrap, 1927.)
Lowes, J. L., *The Road to Xanadu* (Boston: Houghton Mifflin, 1940.)
MacGregor, Frances Cooke, *Transformation and Identity, The Face and Plastic Surgery* (New York: Quadrangle/The New York Times Book Company, 1974.)
Malraux, André, *La Condition Humaine* (Paris: Editions Gallimard, 1946.)
Mariano, Nicky, *Forty Years with Berenson* (London: Hamish Hamilton, 1966.)
Maritain, Jacques, *Creative Intuition in Art and Poetry* (New York: Pantheon Books, 1953.)
Maslow, Abraham H., *Motivation and Personality* (New York: Harper and Row, 1970.)
    Toward a Psychology of Being (New York: Van Nostrand Reinhold, 1968.)
Mathieu, Aron, ed., *The Creative Writer* (Cincinnati: Writer's Digest, 1961.)

May, Rollo, *Man's Search for Himself* (New York: Signet, 1953.)
   Love and Will (New York: W. W. Norton, 1969.)
McCay, James T., *The Management of Time* (Englewood Cliffs, N.J.: Prentice-Hall, 1959.)
McElwain, Hugh, *Introduction to Teilhard de Chardin* (Chicago: Argus, 1967.)
McKellar, Peter, *Imagination and Thinking, a Psychological Analysis* (London: Cohen and West, 1957.)
McLeish, John A. B., *September Gale, The Life of Arthur Lismer* (Toronto: J. M. Dent, 1973.)
   The Advancement of Professional Education in Canada (Toronto: O.I.S.E., 1973.)
   The Fairfield Journal (Toronto: private printing, 1972.)
McLeish, Minnie Buchanan, *They Also Lived* (Ottawa: Runge Press, 1962.)
Medawar, P. B., *The Uniqueness of the Individual* (London: Methuen and Co., 1957.)
Menninger, Karl, *Love Against Hate* (New York: Harcourt, Brace, 1942.)
Migel, Parmenia, *Titania, the Biography of Isak Dinesen* (New York: Random House, 1967.)
Miles, Matthew, *Innovation in Education* (New York: Teachers' College Press, 1964.)
Monroe, Robert A., *Journeys Out of the Body* (New York: Anchor Books, 1973.)
Mooney, Ross L., *Explorations in Creativity* (New York: Harper and Row, 1967.)
Moustakis, Clark, *Creativity and Conformity* (New York: Van Nostrand, 1967.)
   Loneliness (Englewood Cliffs, N.J.: Prentice-Hall, 1961.)
   The Self (New York: Harper and Row, 1956.)
Muggeridge, Kitty, and Ruth Adam, *Beatrice Webb, a Life, 1858-1943* (London: Secker and Warburg, 1967.)
Muggeridge, Malcolm, *Something Beautiful for God, Mother Teresa of Calcutta* (London: Collins, 1971.)
Neugarten, Bernice L., ed., *Middle Age and Aging* (Chicago: University of Chicago Press, 1968.)
Olney, James, *Metaphors of Self, the meaning of autobiography* (Princeton, N.J.: Princeton University Press, 1972.)
O'Neill, Barbara Powell, *Careers for Women After Marriage and Children* (New York: Macmillan, 1965.)
Ornstein, Jack H., *The Mind and the Brain* (The Hague: Martinus Nijhoff, 1972.)
Osborn, Alex F., *Applied Imagination* (New York: Scribner, 1963.)
   Your Creative Power (New York: Scribner, 1951.)
Otto, Herbert A., *Love Today* (New York: Association Press, 1972.)

Packard, Vance, *The Pyramid Climbers* (New York: David McKay, 1964.)

Parmenter, Ross, *The Awakened Eye* (Middletown: Wesleyan University Press, 1968.)

Parnes, Sidney J., *Creative Behaviour Workbook* (New York: Scribner, 1967.)

Percy, Charles H., *Growing Old in the Country of the Young* (New York: McGraw-Hill, 1974.)

Perry, Bliss, *The Heart of Emerson's Journals* (Boston: Houghton-Mifflin, 1926.)

Piddington, Ralph, *Kinship and Geographical Mobility* (Leyden: E. J. Brill, 1965.)

Pieper, Joseph, *Leisure, the Basis of Culture* (New York: Pantheon, 1954.)

Pines, Maya, *The Brain Changers, Scientists and the New Mind Control* (New York: New American Library, 1975.)

Polanyi, Michael, *Personal Knowledge* (London: Routledge and Kegan Paul, 1958.)

Polya, G., *How To Solve It* (Princeton, N.J.: Princeton University Press, 1945.)

Power, John W., *Issues in Dispute*, especially Whitehorn, John C., "The Development of Mature Individuals" (Washington: AEA, 1960.)

Pressey, Sidney L., and Raymond Kuhlen, *Psychological Developments through the Life Span* (New York: Harper, 1957.)

Price, Lucian, *The Dialogues of Alfred North Whitehead* (New York: Mentor, 1954.)

Prince, Gilbert, *The Practice of Creativity* (New York: Harper and Row, 1970.)

Proceedings: First Ontario Conference on Aging, University of Toronto, May 31-June 30, 1957; and Canadian Conference, Ottawa, January, 1966.)

Quennell, Peter, *Samuel Johnson, his Friends and Enemies* (London: Weidenfeld and Nicolson, 1972.)

Reid, Doris, *Edith Hamilton, an Intimate Portrait* (New York: W. W. Norton, 1967.)

Renoir, Jean, *Renoir, My Father* (Boston: Little, Brown and Company, 1958.)

Rieu, E. V., translator, Homer: *The Odyssey* (London: Penguin Books, 1946.)

Rogers, Carl R., *Freedom to Learn* (Columbus: Bell and Howell, 1969.)

Rosner, Stanley, and Lawrence Abt, eds., *The Creative Experience* (New York: Grossman, 1970.)

Rossman, J., *The Psychology of the Inventor* (Washington, D.C.: Inventor's Publishing, 1931.)

Russell, Bertrand, *Autobiography* (New York: Simon and Shuster, 1969.)

Schutz, William C., *Joy: Expanding Human Awareness* (New York: Grove Press, 1967.)

Selye, Hans, *The Stress of Life* (New York: McGraw-Hill, 1956.) *Stress Without Distress* (Toronto: McClelland and Stewart, 1974.)

Simmons, L. W., *The Role of the Aged in Primitive Society* (New Haven: Yale University Press, 1945.)

Simon, Anne W., *The New Years, a New Middle Age* (New York: Knopf, 1968.)

Skinner, B. F., *Beyond Freedom and Dignity* (New York: Knopf, 1971.)

Smith, Constance Babington, *Rose Macaulay* (London: Collins, 1972.)

Smith, Ethel Sabin, *Passports at Seventy* (New York: W. W. Norton, 1961.)

Spearman, C., *The Creative Mind* (New York: Appleton-Century-Crofts, 1931.)

Stainesby, Charles, ed., *Strip Jack Naked* (London: Marshall Cavendish Publications, 1971.)

Stein, Mauria R., A. J. Vidich, and D. M. White, eds., *Identity and Anxiety* (New York: The Free Press, 1960.)

Stern, E. M., and E. Ross, *You and Your Aging Parents* (New York: Harper and Row, 1968.)

Stern, Karl, *The Pillar of Fire* (New York: Doubleday, 1956.) *The Flight from Woman* (New York: The Noonday Press, 1965.)

Stetson, Damon, *Starting Over* (New York: Macmillan, 1971.)

Stevenson, R. L., *Essays Literary and Critical* (London: Heinemann, 1924.)

Storr, Anthony, *The Dynamics of Creation* (London: Secker and Warburg, 1972.)

Strachey, Lytton, *Eminent Victorians* (New York: Harcourt Brace and Jovanovich, 1969.)

Strindberg, August, *Inferno, Alone* (New York: Doubleday, 1968.)

Taylor, C. W., *Creativity, Progress, and Potential* (New York: McGraw-Hill, 1964.)

Taylor, Gordon Rattray, *The Biological Time Bomb* (New York: Signet, 1968.)

Tettemer, John, *I Was a Monk* (New York: Knopf, 1951.)

Thorndike, Edward L., et al, *Adult Learning* (New York: Macmillan, 1928.)

Toffler, Alven, *Future Shock* (New York: Bantam Books, 1970.)

Tomkins, Calvin, *Eric Hoffer, an American Odyssey* (New York: E. P. Dutton, 1968.)

Tompkins, Peter, and Christopher Bird, *The Secret Life of Plants* (New York: Avon, 1973.)

Torrance, E. P., *Education and the Creative Potential* (Minneapolis: University of Minnesota Press, 1963.)

Tough, Allen, *The Adult's Learning Projects* (Toronto: Ontario Institute for Studies in Education, 1972.)

Townsend, Peter, *The Family Life of Old People* (London: Routledge and Kegan Paul, 1957.)

Truman, Margaret, *Harry S. Truman* (San Diego: Morren Publications, 1973.)

United States President's Council on Aging: *The Older American* (Washington, D.C.: Government Printing Office, 1963.)

Unterecker, John, *Yeats* (Englewood Cliffs, N.J.: Prentice-Hall, 1963.)

Vacca, Roberto, *The Coming Dark Age* (New York: Doubleday, 1973.)

Vedder, Clyde B., *Gerontology, a Book of Readings* (Springfield, Illinois: C. C. Thomas, 1963.)

Vernon, P. E., ed., *Creativity* (London: Penguin Books, 1970.)

von Bertalanffy, L., *Problems of Life* (New York: Harper Torchbooks, 1952.)

Vorres, Ian, *The Last Grand Duchess* (London: Hutchinson, 1964.)

Watson, James D., *The Double Helix* (New York: Atheneum, 1968.)

Watson, Lyall, *Supernature* (New York: Anchor Press/Doubleday, 1973.)

Wechsler, David, *The Measurement and Appraisal of Adult Intelligence* (Baltimore: Williams and Wilkins, 1958.)

Welford, A. T., *Ageing and Human Skill* (Westport, Conn.: Greenwood Press, 1973.)

Whipple, James, *Especially for Adults* (Chicago: CSLEA, 1957.)

White House Conference on Aging, Department of Health, Education, and Welfare, Washington, D.C., April, 1961 (Series No. 7, Religion and Aging. Series No. 2, Education for Aging.)

White, Robert W., *Lives in Progress* (New York: Holt, Rinehart and Winston, 1966.)

  The Study of Lives (New York: Atherton, 1966.)

Widening Horizons in Creativity, Proceedings of the Fifth University Research Conference, University of Utah, C. W. Taylor, Ed. (New York: John Wiley and Sons, 1964.)

Wiener, Philip H., and A. Noland, *Roots of Scientific Thought* (New York: Basic Books, 1957.)

Wiggam, Albert Edward, *The Marks of an Educated Man* (Indianapolis: Bobbs-Merrill, 1930.)

Wilenski, R. H., *Modern French Painters* (New York: Reynal and Hitchcock, 1940.)

Williams, R., and Claudine G. Wirths, *Lives Through the Years* (New York: Atherton Press, 1965.)

Williams, Robin, *American Society* (New York: Knopf, 1970.)

Wolf, A., *A History of Science, Technology, and Philosophy* (London: G. Allen and Unwin, 1950.)

Wolf, Theta Holmes, *Alfred Binet* (Chicago: University of Chicago Press, 1973.)

INDEX

JOHN A. B. McLEISH is a graduate of McGill and Cornell Universities, and a consultant on higher education and adult learning theory whose twenty-five year academic career has included posts at the University of British Columbia, Carleton University, Ottawa, Brandon University (where he was Deputy to the President and Dean of the Faculty of Education), and the Ontario Institute for Studies in Education, where he was Kellogg Professor in the course of a three-year study of improving teaching and learning in professional education. His seminars on the modern adult and creativity in the adult years have been given at the University of Ottawa, Sir George Williams University, and the University of Toronto School of Continuing Studies, as well as at O.I.S.E. and Brandon. He has given papers at the University of Illinois, Urbana, and at Cornell University, and has been a post-doctoral visitor at the Faculty of Graduate Education at Harvard University.

His range of interests is wide, including art, cinema, music, poetry, social causes, and athletics. He wrote the life of the noted Canadian artist, Arthur Lismer (*September Gale*), co-founded the Brandon Film Festival, and was a co-founder of the Vocational Counselling Centre of Ottawa.